Palgrave Macmillan Studies on Human Rights in Asia

Series Editor
Mikyoung Kim, Hiroshima, Japan

This Palgrave Macmillan book series addresses the rising interest in human rights topics in Asia. It focuses on the largely underexplored territory of Asian human rights topics highlighting its empirical manifestations, historical trajectory and theoretical implications. It also goes beyond the problematic dichotomy between "East" and "West" by engaging in rigorous case-specific as well as cross-regional comparisons within South–South context. China's rise in world politics and its emergence as a massive donor, for example, has significant yet troubling implications. The member countries of ASEAN and Northeast Asia, on the other hand, would have different preoccupations and priorities calling for context-sensitive diagnosis and prognosis to promote human right causes.

The series is multidisciplinary in nature and open to submissions focusing on international organization, ethics, criminology, development, freedom of expression, labour rights, environment, human/sex trafficking, democratization, governance studies, disability, reproductive rights, LGBT, post-/colonial as well as post-/authoritarian critiques and social movement, among others.

The series publishes full-length monographs, and edited volumes.

Lara Momesso · Polina Ivanova
Editors

Refugees and Asylum Seekers in East Asia

Perspectives from Japan and Taiwan

palgrave
macmillan

Editors
Lara Momesso
School of Psychology and Humanities
University of Central Lancashire
Preston, UK

Polina Ivanova
Institute of International Relations
and Area Studies
Asia-Japan Research Institute,
Ritsumeikan University
Kyoto, Japan

ISSN 2752-4310 ISSN 2752-4329 (electronic)
Palgrave Macmillan Studies on Human Rights in Asia
ISBN 978-981-97-2866-4 ISBN 978-981-97-2867-1 (eBook)
https://doi.org/10.1007/978-981-97-2867-1

Cover illustration: Bhong-Jin Kim

This Palgrave Macmillan imprint is published by the registered company Springer Nature Singapore Pte Ltd.
The registered company address is: 152 Beach Road, #21-01/04 Gateway East, Singapore 189721, Singapore

Paper in this product is recyclable.

Foreword

Conflict frequently occurs worldwide, which forces numerous people to move out from their places of origin. Thus, the questions of how a country reacts to refugees, and how it *should* react to refugees, are nothing new. However, what about a case in which people try to take refuge in a country that is culturally homogeneous, geographically isolated, and considered to have restrictive policies with regard to inward immigration? This book examines one of the most severe and complex humanitarian challenges currently faced by two island nations, namely, Japan and Taiwan.

In particular, Japan has been attracting media and scholarly attention with the amendment of its Immigration Control and Refugee Recognition Act in 2023, which introduced a complementary protection scheme for refugees. Meanwhile, the amendment has been designed to promote the deportation of asylum seekers despite strong protests. Taiwan, a neighbouring country of Japan, has its own issues regarding displaced people and their protection. The country's increasing interest in humanitarian concerns such as refugee protection may echo its unstable international status.

This book is timely, well grounded, and highly valued as factual material. It elucidates the mechanisms and experiences of refugee acceptance and rejection in Japan and Taiwan, convincingly explaining the commonalities and differences between the two. Towards this end, it addresses three indispensable and interconnected elements relating to the presence of refugees and asylum seekers, namely, legal and policy frameworks, media representation, and lived experiences.

Critical but hopeful, the chapters in this book provide an alternative view, where refugees and asylum seekers are considered as resourceful members in host societies rather than as threats or burdens. Although the mass media often stereotypically frames them as vulnerable entities, this study explores their identities and their manners of action; the vulnerability of refugees and asylum seekers is not the whole story.

This research project has provided a deep understanding of the fact that Japan, Taiwan, and other East Asian countries are, more than ever, in need of innovative and effective policy instruments and civil society-based inclusive support networks to accommodate refugees and asylum seekers.

This book is not just about them. It leads readers to rethink the design of a liberal and democratic society which accommodates increasing numbers of migrants, in particular, refugees and asylum seekers, with diverse backgrounds. I am hopeful that this passionate work will influence our thinking in a manner that prioritises human security among other issues and that East Asia can be transformed into a safer place for those who flee for their survival.

Junichi Akashi
Professor
University of Tsukuba
Tsukuba, Japan

Acknowledgements

First, the editors would like to thank all the contributing authors for their patient and skilful work in revising their manuscripts. The publication of this volume would not have been possible without the expertise and dedicated efforts of our commissioning editor Vishal Daryanomel and all the editorial team of Palgrave Macmillan. We also wish to thank anonymous reviewers for their relevant suggestions.

Our sincere gratitude is extended to the University of Central Lancashire (UCLan) for providing generous funding to finance the Open Access of the entire book. We would also like to thank the Research Centre for Migration, Diaspora and Ethnicity (MIDEX) for offering us both a platform for collaboration and the funding for proofreading, and Dr Simon Green for his efficient and accurate proofreading services. We also wish to thank Dr Moises de Souza (UCLan) for actively contributing to a pre-conception phase of this volume when we co-organised a roundtable on refugee and asylum seekers in East Asia on 24 January 2022 and published a special issue of the policy brief "Refugee protection in East Asia: Taiwan and Japan in comparison" (2022/01) with the Northern England Policy Centre for the Asia Pacific (NEPCAP). A special thank you goes to Professor Niki Alsford (UCLan) for asking "Why don't you put these contributions into an edited volume?"

We owe a debt of gratitude to Professor Kenki Adachi (Ritsumeikan University) and Dr Maja Vodopivec (Leiden University) for taking the time to read our introductory chapter and for providing their insightful comments. Our sincere thanks are due to Professor Junichi Akashi (Tsukuba University) for writing a foreword to this book.

Finally, we must express our deepest gratitude to our families and friends for being supportive and patient with us throughout the creation of this volume.

Lara Momesso
Polina Ivanova

Praise for *Refugees and Asylum Seekers in East Asia*

The impressive array of well-researched case studies on the policies and practices for refugees, asylum seekers and foreign students in Japan and Taiwan amply illuminate the value and relevance of applying the analytical framework of human security that consists of protection and empowerment with the emphasis on human dignity. I hope their findings will contribute to improving policies and conditions for migrant workers.

—Yukio Takasu, *Special Advisor to the UN Secretary General on Human Security, President of NPO "Human Security Forum"*

This edited volume extends the research attention to democratic Asia by offering an in-depth look into the politics of asylum seekers in Japan and Taiwan. Both used to accept refugees on an ad-hoc basis and are now amid the process of liberalising their regulations. As both countries are rapidly ageing with declining fertility rates, migrant workers have made up a substantial source of labour supply—thus contributing to a more liberal attitude toward refugees. This book provides a fine-grained analysis on policy, public, and personal levels of migration politics in Japan and Taiwan.

—Ming-sho Ho, *Professor of Sociology, National Taiwan University*

Thoughtfully curated, showcasing a variety of methods and case studies, and genuinely interdisciplinary, with contributors from fields ranging from sociology, anthropology, legal studies, media studies, as well as activists and professionals, *Refugees and Asylum Seekers in East Asia: Perspectives from Japan and Taiwan* will be indispensable to specialists, students, policymakers and readers interested to know more about migration and refugee issues in Taiwan and Japan

—Isabelle Cheng, *Senior Lecturer in East Asian and International Development Studies, University of Portsmouth,Secretary-General of the European Association of Taiwan Studies (2022–2025)*

Contents

List of Contributors

Sohrab Ahmadian Tokyo University of Foreign Studies, Tokyo, Japan

Firman Budianto National Research and Innovation Agency (BRIN), Jakarta, Indonesia

Min-yen Chiang Flow HK, Taipei, Taiwan

David Green Nagoya University, Nagoya, Japan

Mariko Hayashi Southeast and East Asian Centre (SEEAC), London, UK

Polina Ivanova Ritsumeikan University, Kyoto, Japan

Kristina Kironska Department of Asian Studies, Palacky University Olomouc, Olomouc, Czech Republic

Zdenka P. Kyselova Department of Asian Studies, Palacky University Olomouc, Olomouc, Czech Republic

Christine Lin Center for Gender and Refugee Studies, University of California College of the Law, San Francisco, CA, USA

Shu-Fen Lin National Yang Ming Chiao Tung University, Hsinchu, Taiwan

Bonny Ling Work Better Innovations, Portsmouth, UK; University of Nottingham, Nottingham, UK

Kate Hannah Martin University of Central Lancashire, Preston, UK

Lara Momesso University of Central Lancashire, Preston, UK

Mei-Lin Pan National Yang Ming Chiao Tung University, Hsinchu, Taiwan

Eriko Tomita Nagoya University, Nagoya, Japan

Candia Tong Flow HK, Taipei, Taiwan

Dolma Tsering National Yang Ming Chiao Tung University, Hsinchu, Taiwan

Lisa Unangst Empire State University, Saratoga Springs, NY, USA

Yusy Widarahesty Ritsumeikan University, Kyoto, Japan

Cody Wai Kwok Yau Department of Political Science, Soochow University, Taipei, Taiwan

Yingjiao Zhu Yamaguchi University, Yamaguchi, Japan

List of Figures

List of Tables

CHAPTER 1

Introduction

Lara Momesso and Polina Ivanova

Refugee and Asylum Seeker Acceptance, Protection, and Integration in East Asia

With major ongoing refugee crises in Gaza, Ukraine, Yemen, Afghanistan, Syria, Sudan, Nigeria, the Central African Republic, Iraq, the Democratic Republic of Congo, Venezuela, Ethiopia, and Myanmar, no other issue seems as timely as refugee protection, both in the affected areas and in the host countries involved. Much research has been published on the presence, protection, management, and experiences of refugees in Europe, while the same cannot be said with regard to the other regions of the world. This edited book focuses on the East Asian region.

The literature shows that most Asian states have failed to integrate international refugee laws and regional protection instruments in their national laws, in this way limiting refugees' and asylum seekers' security

L. Momesso
University of Central Lancashire, Preston, UK
e-mail: lmomesso@uclan.ac.uk

P. Ivanova (✉)
Ritsumeikan University, Kyoto, Japan
e-mail: 21v00202@gst.ritsumei.ac.jp

L. Momesso and P. Ivanova (eds.), *Refugees and Asylum Seekers in East Asia*, Palgrave Macmillan Studies on Human Rights in Asia,
https://doi.org/10.1007/978-981-97-2867-1_1

and access to international and regional protection mechanisms (Choi, 2019, pp. 161–162). Indeed, in this region, most states are not signatories of the magna carta of international refugee law, the 1951 Convention Relating to the Status of Refugees (henceforth, the Convention) and the 1967 Protocol Relating to the Status of Refugees (henceforth, the Protocol).

In a culturally and politically diverse region, characterised by a lack of a coherent approach to refugee protection, the literature seems to focus on state security as a crucial feature in refugee and asylum seeker matters (see, for instance, Ali Ashraf, 2021; Chatterjee & Das, 2022; Choi, 2019; Rana & Riaz, 2022). In this collective work, we emphasise how state security is not sufficient to fully understand the complexity behind refugee and asylum seeker acceptance, protection, and integration in Asia. A mix of other factors, including socio-cultural concerns, historical legacies as well as more recent debates about human security, are crucial in shaping current patterns and practices linked to asylum seekers and refugees.

Taiwan and Japan, to some degree, represent the complexity of the Asian region, where geopolitical factors linked to national security and interests intersect with other spheres to shape the acceptance, protection, and integration of refugees and asylum seekers. Taiwan, due to its unsolved sovereignty issue in the context of the "one China" policy, experiences limited international recognition and participation in international organisations. For this reason, Taiwan is among those states that are not signatories of the 1951 Convention and the 1967 Protocol. In this politicised context, not only the presence of certain groups of immigrants, such as citizens from China, Hong Kong, and Macao, is more sensitive than others, but the overall formulation of a domestic refugee law has been hampered due to national security concerns. The result is that the presence of asylum seekers and stateless people has been dealt on a case-by-case basis, on the principle of humanitarian concerns.

Japan holds a different geopolitical position: it enjoys international recognition and participation in international organisations. It signed the Convention in 1981 and the related Protocol in 1982, and for years, the country has been one of the largest donors to the United Nations High Commissioner for Refugees (UNHCR). Though its refugee recognition rates have been remarkably low. In the case of Japan, socio-cultural factors have been crucial in shaping this outcome. Its current ethnocentric identity, which has emerged since the end of the Second World War, has served as a basis for its exclusive citizenship and strict immigration policies. Similar to Taiwan, claims for asylum in Japan are normally considered on an individual basis, with a few exceptions in recent decades.

Exploring beyond the realm of domestic affairs, the two cases reveal intricate connections to broader issues, such as human rights, international law, global governance, international organisations, local and transnational activism, and public opinion. This book questions to what extent refugee and asylum seeker acceptance, protection, and integration can be understood from a narrow perspective of national security interests.

In this collective work we suggest that to understand the complex matrix of interests shaping refugee acceptance, protection, and integration in Taiwan and Japan, and more generally in Asia, it is important to integrate analyses of territorial interests with more nuanced accounts that place the individuals and their security at the centre. With this in mind, we bring into our discussion the notion of human security.

Moving away from state-based, traditional security, human security focuses on people's lives and the protection of their fundamental freedoms, and calls for governments and civil societies to create political, social, environmental, economic, military, and cultural processes that "give people the building blocks of survival, livelihood and dignity" (Commission on Human Security, 2003, p. 4). In other words, emphasising people-centred policymaking, human security calls for a paradigm shift in the way refugee protection is framed, not solely as part of a state's strategy to promote its interests, but also as a sphere that involves and affects a series of other actors.

Along the same line, and framing human security as a two-way process in which state structures interact with social actors and affect one another (Ruggie, 1983), this volume argues that the Japanese and Taiwanese states do not operate in a vacuum but interact with a series of state and non-state actors, including civil society, media outlets, international and regional organisations, local communities, and individual migrants. In light of this argument and by focusing on three different areas, namely legal and policy frameworks, media representation and public opinion, and lived experiences of refugees and asylum seekers, the 14 chapters of this book provide a sophisticated understanding of refugee issues in Asia, where the multiplicity of interests behind the management of refugee security depend on the dissimilar geopolitical context in which the phenomenon occurs, as well as on factors that go beyond a state's interests and intervention.

The chapters of this volume lie at the crossroads of disciplines including sociology, anthropology, legal studies, and media studies, and build on qualitative and quantitative data aiming to demonstrate the constructivist nature of refugee protection, media representation, and experiences in Taiwan and Japan, when national interests forge and are forged by social actors' concerns and actions. Rather than only comparing Japan and Taiwan, the chapters of this volume aspire to offer an in-depth, diverse, and manifold picture of how the two East Asian nations have dealt with the protection, acceptance, and integration of refugees and asylum seekers. More specifically, this volume aims to show how, in these two nations, traditional notions of security operate alongside human security concerns generating complex pictures of interests. Aware that the chapters of this volume cannot be exhaustive, we hope that this work could inspire further research on a much-needed topic.

On a practical level, with this book, we collectively advocate for Japan and Taiwan to embrace a human security agenda in their way of framing and responding to the challenges brought by the presence of non-citizens. Bellamy and McDonald (2002, p. 376) introduce the concept of "sovereignty as responsibility", used to evaluate whether particular states and policies are in accord with the responsibility for humane governance and human security. In line with this, this edited book collectively argues that both Japan and Taiwan should take on the responsibility to protect not only citizens but also non-citizens residing in their territory.

Before moving on to the next section, an explanation of our choice of key terms is crucial. The Convention's definition of the refugee, which is "someone who is unable or unwilling to return to their country of origin owing to a well-founded fear of being persecuted for reasons of race, religion, nationality, membership of a particular social group, or political opinion" continues to be used by the UNHCR (UNHCR, n.d.-d; UNHCR, n.d.-b). The organisation further delineates asylum seekers from recognised refugees in their glossary, stating that an asylum seeker is someone whose claim for refugee status "has not yet been finally decided on by the country in which the claim is submitted" (UNHCR, 2005, p. 441). In its current and continuously updated master glossary of terms, the UNHCR expands its definition of asylum seekers to those who have "not yet submitted an application but may intend to do so, or may be in need of international protection" (UNHCR, n.d.-c).

Despite the revisions in recent years, these definitions have been criticised for their narrow scope, their Eurocentric underpinnings, and their temporal and geographical specificity (Davies, 2008; Ho et al., 2015). Indeed, the integration of the 1967 Protocol aimed to eliminate the temporal and geographical limitations of the Convention but it did not revise the problematic definition of "refugee". A definition that delimits the boundaries of refugee status to a state's persecution of individuals, neglecting a series of other issues specific to the contemporary period, such as terrorism, climate change, or natural disasters (Betts & Collier, 2017; Ho et al., 2015). Furthermore, ratification (or lack thereof) of the 1951 Convention and 1967 Protocol seems to be more of a matter of promoting and protecting national interests rather than protecting the rights of refugees, generating what Betts and Orchard refer to as an "institutionalisation–implementation gap" (Betts & Orchard, 2014, as cited in Choi, 2019, p. 164).

In light of these criticisms, and recognising legal definitions as a useful common basis, this book employs a broader view on refugees and asylum seekers since, in practice, the lines between these two groups of people and other migrant categories, such as economic migrants, undocumented migrants, international students, and marriage migrants may be blurred.

Human Security

Human security is a concept that emerged within the field of international development studies in the 1990s, when the United Nations Development Programme (UNDP) declared "human security" as its primary development goal, stressing the necessity to develop a "people-centred development" for the twenty-first century (Morrissey, 2018, p. 226). It was the first attempt to move away from the framework of traditional security, which was focused on state-based and interest-based approaches and revolved around the territorial state. Instead, the new focus was on people's lives, making an important switch (or at least claiming so) to de-territorialised and values-based approaches (Chandler, 2008, p. 427). More specifically, a human security approach calls for "investing in, and resourcing, interventions of a different kind: in protecting human rights; in insisting upon humanitarian law; in supporting civil society; and in enabling locally attuned rather than top-down security measures" (Morrissey, 2018, p. 227). These considerations are particularly important for migrant populations, whose security is often at risk because they may experience abuse, exploitation, and human rights violations.

Building on the idea that securing people would be the best way to secure states, human security became a fashionable paradigm in international policy circles in the 1990s and early 2000s (Chandler, 2008, p. 428). Human security seemed to offer solutions to global problems that could endanger state security, yet that could not be addressed effectively within a security system based on the Westphalian order, such as poverty, environmental change, global epidemics, natural disasters, gender-based violence, and the transnational mobility of people (Estrada-Tanck, 2016, p. 1). With the aim of addressing these global challenges, after the UNDP declared "human security" as its primary development goal, governments around the world have been asked to take responsibility for, and think cooperatively about, human security in holistic and sustainable ways (Morrissey, 2018, p. 227).

Scholars of different schools and approaches overwhelmingly agree that human security is a practically and academically valuable concept in refugee studies. Indeed, by switching the attention from notions of sovereignty, border control, and citizenship specific to other security paradigms, human security may offer "new ways to think about and to conceptualise protection concerns as well as the perception of non-citizens, may strengthen strategies of protection and empowerment, and in turn reinforce the foundational principles of international human rights law of dignity, quality and justice for all" (p. 5). Within these debates, human security has become a tool for promoting the empowerment of more vulnerable or ignored individuals and communities by addressing a series of intersecting factors beyond that of state sovereignty and non-interference. For instance, Hossain and colleagues (2016, p. 4) argue that a human security framework integrates subjective experiences in the discussion of security and "offers an inclusive framework for an expanded understanding of security that identifies vulnerabilities, self-perceived threats, and ignored risks that affect collective security". Furthermore, it also offers a narrative for civil society and individual actors to challenge existing ways of framing security. Other scholars also believe that human security can complement the earlier notion of human rights (Estrada-Tanck, 2016; Song, 2012). Along this line, Song (2012) views human security as the securitisation of human rights, showing how the former often correlates with the latter: for instance, "personal security is in parallel with freedom from death, violence, exploitation, arbitrary arrest or detention", or community security correlates with "the right to preserve ethnic identity, religious practices or cultural heritage, or not to be discriminated against based on ethnicity, social origin, place of birth, nationality or religion" (Song, 2012, p. 7). Analytically, human security offers scope to explore not only how states and intergovernmental organisations adapt their policies to include broader human security principles in their agenda, but also how society, through the world of non-governmental and non-profit organisations, associations, and networks, shape governmental policies through "bottom-up" initiatives (den Boer & de Wilde, 2008, pp. 9–11). Although the concept of human security has been celebrated for its focus on human safety and the "'added value' of normative people-centred policymaking" (Chandler, 2008, p. 428), it has become a highly contested concept, often criticised for a vagueness that makes it impractical for policymaking (Chandler, 2008, p. 428; de Simone, 2020, p. 169). Also, governments of the Global South have widely criticised the idea of human security for imposing universality and liberal norms and promoting human rights according to values that are not necessarily compatible with non-Western social, cultural, and political realities (Christie, 2018; Takizawa, 2011). Interestingly, however, as Tow (2013, p. 2) argues with regard to the Asia Pacific, a series of major non-traditional security contingencies over the past two decades, as well as the forces of globalisation, have pushed Asian governments to integrate, to a certain extent, human security principles in their domestic and international governance.

An important example is Japan, which has introduced a "broader" interpretation of human security, in opposition to the Canadian "narrow" model. Canada's understanding of human security emphasised "freedom from fear", in the military conflict, and gradually developed into a new concept of "responsibility to protect". In contrast, Japan emphasised "freedom from want" and therefore de-militarised the concept (Adachi, 2023, pp. 205–206). This interpretation of human security brought it closer to the overseas development assistance which led to some criticisms of Japan's version of human security being a mere "rebranding of international development" (Mahmud, 2023) or "social welfare" (Mine et al., 2019). Furthermore, some scholars believe that a "broader" understanding of human security might "inadvertently undermine the international human rights regime" (Howard-Hassmann, 2012, p. 88) for two reasons: firstly, because human rights become reduced to "a subset of human security concerns" (p. 103), and secondly because the individual standing in the human security discourse is less strong compared to the human rights agenda (p. 111). According to Hynek (2012) both interpretations of human security were shaped by domestic factors (in Canada, the liberal model of governance and, in Japan, the bureaucratic authoritarianism) further emphasising how state interests, rather than the security of individuals, could be at the centre of political choices linked to human security.

Due to these critiques and due to a changing world shaped by "rising nationalism" and the resurgence of "traditional security concerns and actors", human security began to lose momentum in the second decade of the twenty-first century (Newman, 2020, p. 33). It is time to revisit and possibly reinvent human security in academic and policy circles to return the focus to individual safety in the face of complex environmental, socioeconomic, and military crises. Reflecting this complexity, this volume will explore the complementarity between human security and traditional security, when state interests intersect with those of civil society groups, local citizens and refugees and asylum seekers.

The literature shows that in the Asian region refugee issues are often treated as a traditional security issue (Ali Ashraf, 2021; Chatterjee & Das, 2022; Choi, 2019; Rana & Riaz, 2022). This does not mean that we should look at refugee protection in Asia solely as a state responsibility or a traditional security matter. The issue of complementarity between human security and the traditional security of the state is an aspect of human security that this book will attempt to address. Sadako Ogata, one of the biggest proponents of human security in the international arena, believed that human security and state security complement each other (Ogata, 2013). Contemporary East Asians express even more nuanced views: most would welcome foreign support during a natural disaster but not political unrest (Mine et al., 2019, p. 15). There is also an emphasis on improved coordination between various state and non-state actors in the region to ensure the security of individuals (Mine et al., 2019, p. 17). In this collective work, we suggest that, to understand refugee experiences in Taiwan and Japan, it is important to integrate analyses of territorial interests with broader considerations linked to human security.

Furthermore, by building on the idea that different countries interpret human security differently due to their dissimilar historical experiences and domestic politics (Lam, 2006, p. 146), and by being endorsed by various actors in a range of contexts (Marhia, 2013, p. 32), this volume suggests that human security should not be seen as a coherent and monolithic project. Instead, a diversity of positionalities and interests, hence interventions, may emerge with regard to human security. This means that the security challenges generated by and for refugees and asylum seekers in Taiwan and Japan vary depending on a series of factors, such as a broader geopolitical context, existing policies in each country, civil society actions, specific refugee/migrant groups' needs, the time the refugee enters the host country, and the locality where they settled.

Finally, this volume suggests that the notion of human security, by stressing a people-centred approach to policymaking, calls for a paradigm shift not only in the way policymakers and states manage security issues, but also in the way they interrogate the very social structures that determine access to protection (Marhia, 2013). Indeed, human security may be distributed unequally, especially for marginalised and systematically discriminated groups. For instance, certain migrants, such as undocumented migrants and refugees who challenge the legal boundaries between citizens and non-citizens, may be neglected in domestic discussions on human security and, even worse, may be seen as a source of insecurity. As Morrissey (2018) argues, refugees are often represented as a threat and a source of insecurities for states, rather than as a consequence of unsafe life conditions elsewhere, serving to reinforce the appropriateness of biopolitical governmental measures to manage such threats. Within this logic, refugees' and asylum seekers' vulnerabilities are neither recognised nor acknowledged, generating, in some cases, human insecurity for these groups. As Newman (2020) argues, refugees "suffering human rights abuse, deprivation and exclusion" are the "embodiment of human insecurity in extremis" (Newman, 2020, p. 36).

In light of these points, Japan and Taiwan constitute two significant cases to discuss the complexity of human security in relation to the problems linked to refugee and asylum seeker protection, integration, and acceptance in the Asian region. Both countries have integrated human security into national and international agenda. However, both governments have failed to extend this principle to the refugees and asylum seekers present in their territory. The next two sections will explore the main issues linked to refugee and asylum seeker presence and protection in Taiwan and Japan, and how these issues intersect with concerns of territorial and human security.

Japan: Chequebook Diplomacy?

Japan signed the Convention in 1981 and the related Protocol in 1982. Among possible reasons behind the country's decision to join both treaties during that time, scholars state pressure from the international community, particularly the United States, to create a legal framework for accepting boat people from Indochina, and Japan's concern about its international reputation (Akashi, 2006; Arakaki, 2004; Hatcher & Murakami, 2020; Tarumoto, 2018).

For years, the country has been one of the largest donors to the UNHCR, ranking second after the United States until 2013 and fourth or fifth from 2014 to 2022 (UNHCR, n.d.-a; UNHCR, 2015). Japan has also been one of the most vigorous promoters of a human security agenda in East Asia (Evans, 2004, p. 271). However, it also seems to use human security mainly as a foreign policy objective to increase its bilateral, regional, and global political and economic influence, rather than as a tool to promote domestic policies (Kim, 2010, p. 94). In contrast to the country's generous financial contribution to the refugee cause, Japan's refugee recognition rates have remained remarkably low: only 915 applicants out of the total 87,892 between 1982 and 2021 received refugee status (MOFA, 2022). Out of a record number of 19,629 applicants in 2017, Japan granted refugee status to only 20 people, namely 0.1% of applicants (Hatcher & Murakami, 2020, p. 71). Due to this contrast of a high financial contribution with an extremely low refugee acceptance, the country has been repeatedly criticised by academics and practitioners for its chequebook diplomacy, both domestically and internationally (Ogata, 2002 as cited in Akashi, 2006, p. 221; Takenaka, 2015; Slater & Barbaran, 2020). In addition, Japan's treatment of asylum seekers has attracted severe criticism with regard to the country's detention practices, including indefinite detention periods, a lack of transparency regarding detention at ports of entry, and human rights violations (GDP, n.d.; Slater & Barbaran, 2020).

Intolerant policies towards refugees are seen as a direct consequence of the country's postwar concept of ethnocentric identity, which served as a basis for its citizenship and immigration policies (Tarumoto, 2018). Similar to other East Asian countries, citizenship in Japan is based on *jus sanguinis* (right of blood), rather than *jus soli* (right of birthplace) which practically denies access to citizenship to non-Japanese, even if they were born in Japan, let alone first-generation immigrants or refugees.

Similar to Taiwan, claims for asylum in Japan are normally considered on an individual basis, with a few notable exceptions being: (1) acceptance of Indochinese refugees in 1978–2005, particularly the first wave, (2) resettlement of Myanmar refugees in 2010–2013, and (3) reception of Ukrainian evacuees during the Russo-Ukrainian War in 2022 (UNHCR, 2010; Yamagata, 2021).

Around the end of the Vietnam War in 1975, communist regimes were established in the three Indochina countries (Vietnam, Laos, and Cambodia), and those who could not fit in with these systems started fleeing abroad. These Vietnamese, Laotian, and Cambodian refugees are collectively called "Indochinese refugees". Being the second largest economy in the world during that time, Japan felt pressure to follow the example of Western liberal democracies who opened their borders to Indochinese refugees (Akashi, 2006). Some went as far as stating that the decision to accept refugees from Indochina was imposed on Japan (Takizawa, 2011, p. 31). Between 1978 and 2005, Japan accepted 11,319 Indochinese refugees, mostly through the Orderly Departure Plan to facilitate family reunion (MOFA, 2022). This did not mean, however, that Japan eased its refugee policies. During the same time, Japan accepted claims from only 376 "Convention refugees", i.e. those from outside Indochina applying within the Convention framework (Akashi, 2006). Moreover, a different screening procedure was applied to the second wave of Indochinese boat people in the 1980s, recognising them as economic migrants and therefore rejecting their claims for asylum (Akashi, 2006).

With regard to Myanmar refugees, Japan was the first Asian country to launch its own resettlement programme, in 2010. The programme, which aimed to resettle Myanmar families from refugee camps in Thailand, was made permanent in 2014 and expanded in 2020 (Akashi, 2021; UNHCR, 2010). Some scholars severely criticised Japan's resettlement programme as highly ineffective (Hatcher & Murakami, 2020). The authors pointed out that the programme was based on restrictive selection criteria, systematically failed to meet its targets, and that "human rights and social conditions of refugees were not prioritised" (Hatcher & Murakami, 2020, p. 71). Substantial weaknesses were identified in the areas of employment, housing, and language support; other hindering factors included social isolation from fellow countrymen, absence of information from the central government, and absence of long-term planning (Yamashita, 2015). In the absence of active support from the government, the effectiveness of the programme largely depended on local non-profit organisations and their ability to act as an intermediary between the state and municipalities (Akashi, 2021).

Overall, acceptance of Indochinese refugees and the third-country resettlement programme for those from Myanmar did not lead to the Japanese government adopting more flexible refugee policies and immigration policies in general (Akashi, 2014). More recently, soon after the outbreak of the Russo-Ukrainian War in February 2022, Japan announced its decision to open its doors to refugees from Ukraine, cautiously referring to them as "evacuees" and providing temporary visas. Similar to previous instances of Japan's refugee acceptance, some experts expressed hope that this initiative could be a turning point for the country's refugee policies (Nagy in McElhinney, 2022), while others remained sceptical (Slater, 2022). Granting access to Ukrainians rather than asylum seekers from Afghanistan or Syria was believed to be a "political decision linked to Japan's foreign policy on Ukraine, rather than a decision based on humanitarian considerations and needs" (Ryall, 2022). Also similar to previous cases, the Japanese government failed to provide adequate socioeconomic integration to newcomers: in December 2022, over 60% of newly accepted Ukrainians remained unemployed despite looking for jobs (Kyodo News, 29 December 2022).

Previous studies on intolerant refugee policies in Japan have highlighted the role of the Ministry of Justice, which, in the absence of constitutional protection for asylum seekers or a strong parliament, became a sole decision-maker on immigration and refugee issues, pursuing restrictive policies and largely ignoring pressures from civil society groups (Tarumoto, 2018). A 2023 amendment to the Immigration Control and Refugee Recognition Act, a domestic law regulating the entry and residence of immigrants and refugees in Japan, made some improvements. However, major issues still remain. Human rights' experts express concern that the bill provides even less protection to asylum seekers as it allows them to be deported after the third unsuccessful asylum claim, thus exposing them to harm and violating the international principle of non-refoulement (Kasai, 2023; UNGA, 2023). As long as the government sees refugees and migrants in general as a threat and continues to endorse the myth of a socio-culturally homogeneous society, it risks prioritising a restrictionist agenda. This agenda, marked by its inconsistencies with contemporary challenges and evolving societal norms, may come at the expense of the human security of vulnerable minorities, conflicting with the country's international agenda supportive of the principles of human security.

Taiwan: National Security and the Refugee Law

According to Kironska (2022), Taiwan receives asylum seekers on a regular basis, both self-identified and already recognised by the UNHCR. For instance, it admitted ethnic Chinese refugees from Indonesia during the ethnic tensions between Indonesian Chinese and indigenous groups in Indonesia in the 1960s (Wang, 2011, p. 171), Vietnamese boat people in the period 1976–1990, and, more recently, Hong Kong political refugees. Also, a community of Tibetans, who arrived in Taiwan in the 1980s and 1990s and overstayed their visa, are presently residing in Taiwan and have either obtained Taiwanese identity cards or are still undocumented (Pan, 2015). Since 2019, Taiwan has also been active in international cooperation related to refugee protection in the Middle Eastern and the Mediterranean region, offering humanitarian assistance with trilateral aid cooperation (Wu & Chien, 2022). In Taiwan, such migrants are not protected by a formal law and their applications are often dealt with on a case-by-case basis, with rather inconsistent outcomes.

Taiwan is not a signatory of the Convention and Protocol and does not have a refugee law. The fact that Taiwan has not ratified the refugee Convention and Protocol is linked to its international status. Since the Republic of China was replaced in the UN China seat by the People's Republic of China in 1971, Taiwan has not officially been able to accede to international conventions and UN treaties, and this also includes the Convention and Protocol. Despite this, there have been a few occasions in which Taiwan has actively integrated international convention principles into its legal system. For instance, in 2007, it joined the Committee on the Elimination of Discrimination Against Women to improve the standard of gender rights in the country and advance gender equality; in 2009, it ratified the International Covenant on Civil and Political Rights (ICCPR) and the International Covenant on Economic, Social, and Cultural Rights (ICESCR). However, there does not seem to be the same degree of openness regarding the integration of the principles included in the 1951 Convention and the 1967 Protocol. Political sensitivity surrounding China–Taiwan relations seems to be the main issue of concern in this regard.

Under the "one China" policy, Beijing sees Taiwan as one of its provinces. Although Taiwan operates as a de facto state, with a democratically elected government, and independent military and monetary systems, it has not yet formally challenged Beijing's "one China" claims. Doing so could lead to a conflict, an option that a majority of Taiwanese people do not seem to want. In light of this, the presence of immigrants from China has often posed challenges to Taiwanese lawmakers, as treating them as international citizens would challenge Beijing's "one China" claims. Migrants from China have been regulated by a separate document, a decision that has generated the much criticised two-tiered citizenship system that discriminates against migrants from China (Friedman, 2010). The presence of refugees from China, especially in the last decade, has raised similar concerns. Indeed, as Kironska (2022) argues, one significant point of contention is to what extent an asylum law should also include people from controversial countries such as China, Hong Kong, and Macau. Legally, a refugee law that includes residents of China, Hong Kong, and Macau, could be problematic as it would challenge the sovereignty claim regarding Beijing's "one China" policy. Indeed, extending the refugee status to citizens from China, Hong Kong, and Macao would mean formalising their international status in Taiwan. There also are matters linked to public opinion. For instance, the Taiwanese public might be concerned that the formalisation of a refugee law that includes citizens from China, Hong Kong, and Macao, could lead to an uncontrollable flow of Chinese people taking advantage of this opportunity to escape their homeland. More importantly, in this politicised context, there is a belief that such an uncontrollable flow of people from the mainland could also bring Chinese spies (Kironska, 2022, pp. 18–19). National sovereignty and security are the main concerns in this legal and public debate. These issues have frozen the development of a refugee law, a much-contested matter in the parliamentary and public debate.

Indeed, a first draft of an asylum law was submitted to the Parliament in 2005, followed by other drafts in 2011, 2012, and 2016 (Kironska, 2022, p. 5). None of these drafts has successfully passed parliamentary review. Independent human rights experts, regularly invited by the government to review the country's progress regarding the ICCPR and the ICESCR, put forward the recommendation to set up refugee protection and political asylum mechanisms in 2013 and 2017; yet, no steps have been taken in addressing these points so far (Kironska, 2022, p. 2). The refugee law in Taiwan remains anchored to national security concerns, as Taiwanese claims of independence could lead to military action from Beijing.

Pressure from civil society has been significant, especially after the protests in Hong Kong. In January 2017, during the national review of the ICCPR and the ICESCR, various NGOs urged the government to move away from its case-by-case approach and protect refugees' and asylum seekers' basic human rights (Choi, 2019, p. 172). The problem became even more pressing after the outbreak of socio-political unrest in mid-2019. The implementation of the National Security Law in mid-2020, in Hong Kong, resulted in an increasing flow of Hong Kong citizens and residents seeking protection in Taiwan. In the first instance, President Tsai Ying-wen showed support towards Hong Kong citizens who fled to Taiwan, though this, as Hung (2021, p. 175) argues, was mainly rhetorical. Article 18 of the Act Governing Relations with Hong Kong and Macau states that, if Hong Kong and Macao residents' freedom and safety are under threat, the government should provide adequate assistance. However, the absence of procedural details in the document does not ensure real protection for the asylum seekers. In other words, most of the responsibilities are transferred to civil society, which, in turn, helps asylum seekers with visas or extensions of residence permits, with accommodation searches, and with other kinds of support. In many cases, Hong Kong residents searching for long-term protection in Taiwan, are advised to enrol in a course of study to obtain a student visa, to invest in a start-up to obtain an entrepreneur's visa, or to work in Taiwanese companies or organisations (Kironska, 2022, p. 8).

As of September 2023, Taiwan still did not have a refugee law, leaving refugees and asylum seekers who landed in its territory unprotected. Clearly, security is an important matter in this conversation. In a context in which Taiwanese claims of independence could lead to Beijing's military action, refugee protection in Taiwan remains anchored to national security concerns. Hence, caution and ambiguity with regard to refugee protection seem to be the answer. This approach, though, does not always assure the protection of refugees' basic human rights and physical security, staining, in this way, Taiwan's image as a democratic, open, and safe country. The debate on human security in Taiwan developed later than in other East Asian societies (Evans, 2004, p. 271). Despite this late evolution, human security has been integrated into governmental debates, seen as a means to promote Taiwan's global image and participation in international organisations. However, the discussion seems to remain focused on the human security of Taiwanese citizens, whereas that of non-Taiwanese migrants, asylum seekers, and refugees does not seem to be a priority in the island (Atkinson, 2018, p. 15).

Organisation of the Book

Japan has been celebrated as "the oldest and most affluent liberal democracy in Asia", "a champion of the global liberal order", and a "prestigious leader in humanitarian support" (Kalicki, 2019, p. 360). Taiwan, after the transition from an authoritarian regime to a democratic political system, has made significant steps in the promotion of the human rights of its citizens. Considered as one of the leading democracies in East Asia, it has created the necessary conditions for the establishment of a rights-based regime (Brysk, 2021). For both governments, human security has been a core principle of their diplomacy, much less of their domestic policies. Despite their great overall political, social, and economic success since the mid-twentieth century, both nations have come under severe domestic and international criticism for failing to offer suitable protection to refugees and asylum seekers, and for their inadequate refugee policies. Clearly, both Japan and Taiwan aspire to stand with their democratic peers with regard to the admission and treatment of refugees and asylum seekers. Yet, both face significant challenges in implementing their aspirations. Regional and domestic geopolitical interests make this goal hard to achieve. Indeed, in a region characterised by a series of territorial disputes and by highly regulated immigration regimes, a defensive concept of sovereignty may also shape the way refugees and asylum seekers are integrated, protected, and perceived. Furthermore, in a region that lacks a degree of consistency with regard to refugee protection, national interests may prevail over the security of non-citizens. The literature suggests that national security is an important matter shaping the approaches used by Japan and Taiwan to manage the presence of refugee and asylum seekers and create related policies.

This volume problematises this view and shows how concerns about national and territorial security intersect with a series of other matters, above all, human security. Human security, however, can entail different meanings and implications. Indeed, dissimilar historical experiences, socio-cultural conditions, and domestic politics may also shape contrasting interpretations and applications of human security. To show this complexity, this volume, through different case studies, explores three main features linked to refugee and asylum seekers, that of legal and policy frameworks, media representation and public opinion, and lived experiences of refugees and asylum seekers.

Part I explores legal and policy-oriented aspects linked to refugee and asylum seeker protection in Taiwan and Japan. International pressures, and domestic debates and concerns often influence how human security is approached with regard to refugee and asylum seeker management and protection. The five chapters of this part will shed light on the intricacies of these debates.

Chapter 2 by Bonny Ling and Mariko Hayashi explores the gaps between international standards in the protection of refugees and asylum seekers, and domestic policies, both in Taiwan and Japan. As previously explained, despite the different legal contexts, both countries have adopted an ad hoc approach to refugee protection resulting in inadequate security for refugees and asylum seekers. Interestingly, this comparison allows readers to understand how a legal framework, a missing feature in Taiwan yet existing in Japan, is not the only condition to promote refugees' and asylum seekers' protection. As the authors argue, unless there is broad acceptance and implementation of the responsibility to protect refugees in society, it will be hard to offer a secure and safe environment to these vulnerable groups.

The following two chapters delve deeper into the legal framework for refugee acceptance and protection. Chapter 3 by Christine Lin stresses the importance of developing a unitary legal framework for refugee and asylum seeker acceptance and protection in Taiwan, rather than using the current model based on separate legislation for different groups. By exploring how the UNHCR has previously operated in non-UN members and non-signatory states around the world, Lin argues that a potential collaboration between Taiwanese institutions and the UNHCR should be sought. Distinguishing this chapter from the others of this section, Lin concludes with policy recommendations for the government of Taiwan and the UNHCR. Chapter 4 by Yingjiao Zhu explores the weaknesses of the Japanese legal framework related to refugees and asylum seekers. By drawing upon legal documents and judicial practices, this chapter argues that the structural problems of the current refugee law include a narrow interpretation of refugee, a heavy burden of proof on asylum seekers, and a lengthy refugee application procedure, which together affect refugees' and asylum seekers' security. Hence, the author calls for a thorough reform of the refugee law.

Chapter 5 by Candia Tong and Min-yen Chiang, building on the events in Taiwan following the political unrest in Hong Kong, sheds light on how the absence of a transparent and accountable legal framework for asylum in Taiwan has led to significant risks for the security of Hong Kong asylum seekers. This chapter offers an overview of Taiwan's ad hoc policy measures and their limitations. It also analyses the contribution that civil society has offered to fill the gaps, which has led to what the authors defined as a quasi-asylum mechanism.

Chapter 6, co-written by David Green, Lisa Unangst, and Eriko Tomita, lies at the intersection of displacement and higher education policies. This chapter draws upon exploratory interviews with Japanese university officials and explores how "student evacuees" have been admitted and supported by Japanese universities since 2017. The authors argue that, despite the positive reception and generous financial support of this new programme, more support and expertise is needed from both local and national government as well as civil society actors to enhance precarious humanitarian protection.

Part II delves into media representation and the public perception of the presence of refugees in Japan and Taiwan, examining how media coverage and public opinion can influence policymaking. Indeed, both Taiwanese and Japanese governments are accountable to the international community and their own nationals, and this is the perspective that Part II brings in.

By building on a text-mining analysis, Chapter 7 by Cody Waikwok Yau explores how the Taiwanese media has portrayed immigrants from Hong Kong, including asylum seekers, in the context of recent political instability. In a bi-partisan political environment shaped by the issue of independence from, and unification with, China, Hong Kong asylum seekers' media coverage has revolved around the issue of security. Whose security, though? According to the author, media outlets have emphasised concerns over both national security and immigrant security, highlighting the complexity of this matter in Taiwanese public debates.

Chapter 8 by Zdenka Kyselova and Kristina Kironska explores public opinion on refugees and asylum seekers in Japan. Drawing from quantitative data collected through a wide-ranging project, the Sinophone Borderlands Indo-Pacific Survey, conducted in 2022, this chapter examines a mixed and diverse range of opinions and attitudes held by the Japanese public towards foreigners, asylum seekers, and refugees. Interestingly, this study's findings contradict the assumption that Japanese people are a priori anti-refugee. Chapter 9 by Kristina Kironska turns the focus to Taiwan. Mirroring the previous chapter, Kironska also draws from quantitative data collected through the Sinophone Borderlands Indo-Pacific Survey and explores Taiwanese opinions with regard to refugees and asylum seekers. The chapter shows that, while there is a lack of discussion about an asylum law in Taiwan, Taiwanese people hold generally positive attitudes towards refugees and support the development of a formal legal framework to regulate their access to Taiwan and protect their rights.

Chapter 10 by Sohrab Ahmadian explores the role of social media in expressing and negotiating Kurdish cultural and political identities in Japan. The fact that Kurdish people, unlike many other displaced communities, do not possess a recognised sovereign territory, intensifies their quest for identity. This distinct feature influences their political actions and motivations. By building up a content analysis of Facebook posts by Kurdish users in Japan, this chapter shows how Kurdish nationalism is at the core of Kurdish refugees' social media activism, helping to foster public awareness, producing and disseminating a coherent and inclusive political discourse on behalf of the Kurdish diaspora, and providing a valuable platform for public diplomacy between Kurdish political elites and Japanese politicians and activists.

Part III brings the perspectives of refugees and asylum seekers into the discussion. Clearly, it is not possible to understand the impact of public opinion or a weak or absent legal framework without taking into consideration the experiences of refugees and asylum seekers. Through their voices, everyday experiences, and collective actions, it is possible to appreciate not only the weaknesses of immigration policies and the impact of a stigmatising media on the public debate, but also how broader social and political changes could eventually be achieved.

Chapter 11 by Mei-lin Pan and Dolma Tsering explores the lived experiences of Tibetan refugees in Taiwan. Drawing on in-depth interviews and government reports, this chapter offers a detailed account of the changing status of Tibetans in Taiwan in light of Taiwan's political transformation over the past few decades. The authors argue that different state interests shaped the status of Tibetan refugees in Taiwan during the periods of authoritarian rule and of democratisation. Chapter 12 by Shu-fen Lin brings attention to the presence of the Vietnamese refugees who arrived in Taiwan after the end of the Vietnam War. Building on the life history of Father Nguyễn Văn Hùng, a Vietnamese refugee who later became a human rights advocate in Taiwan, this chapter explores how the politics of colonisation, civil war, the Cold War, and globalisation have shaped the lives of Vietnamese refugees dispersed around the world, and their transnational activism.

Chapter 13 by Kate Hannah Martin brings into the discussion a timely issue, namely displacement due to climate change. Pacific Islands have been highly impacted by climate change and many of their inhabitants have emigrated. Building on secondary sources on migrant experiences and looking at potential legal protection offered to climate refugees, this chapter explores whether Taiwan and Japan could be a viable option for relocation. This chapter argues that although both Taiwan and Japan have the capacity to accept climate-displaced people from the Pacific Islands, this should be seen as a complex process involving not only financial considerations but also integration patterns, and ensuring that displaced people can become active, valuable members of society.

Chapter 14 by Firman Budianto and Yusy Widarahesty, looks at the presence of Indonesian work seekers who have left their country in hope of gaining a refugee status in Japan. Drawing on ethnographic field notes and in-depth interviews with Indonesian migrants, this chapter highlights the existence of various subjective rationales behind a request for asylum. In the case of Indonesian workers in Japan, it could be motivated by broader structural conditions in the sending and host countries, and it could also be a survival strategy for those who aspire to improve their life and economic opportunities. Chapter 15, co-written by the editors, concludes the volume by summarising its main findings and their implications for research and policy.

References

Adachi, K. (2023). Why did Japan engage in human security diplomacy? In K. Nakatsuji (Ed.), *Japan's security policy* (pp. 198–213). Routledge. https://doi.org/10.4324/9781003231653

Akashi, J. (2006). Challenging Japan's refugee policies. *Asian and Pacific Migration Journal, 15*(2), 219–238. https://doi.org/10.1177/011719680601500203

Akashi, J. (2014). New aspects of Japan's immigration policies: Is population decline opening the doors? *Contemporary Japan, 26*(2), 175–196. https://doi.org/10.1515/cj-2014-0009

Akashi, J. (2021). How a policy network matters for refugee protection: A case study of Japan's refugee resettlement programme. *Refugee Survey Quarterly, 40*(3), 249–270. https://doi.org/10.1093/rsq/hdab001

Arakaki, O. (2004). *Historical aspects of Japan's accession to the Refugee Convention and Protocol*. 11 RPJ/NZACL Yearbook. Retrieved February 25, 2023, from https://www.wgtn.ac.nz/law/research/publications/about-nzacl/publications/nzacl-yearbooks/yearbook-10,-2004/Arakaki2.pdf

Ali Ashraf, A. S. M. (2021). Humanitarianism, national security, and the Rohingya refugee policy of Bangladesh. *Strategic Analysis, 45*(3), 184–206. https://doi.org/10.1080/09700161.2021.1918953

Atkinson, J. (2018). Human security as an instrument of (traditional) comprehensive security in Japan, South Korea and Taiwan. *International Journal of Asia Pacific Studies, 14*(1), 1–25.

Bellamy, A. J., & McDonald, M. (2002). "The utility of human security:" Which humans? What security? A reply to Thomas and Tow. *Security Dialogue, 33*(3), 373–377.

Betts, A., & Collier, P. (2017). *Refuge: Rethinking refugee policy in a changing world*. Oxford University Press.

Brysk, A. (2021). Constructing rights in Taiwan: The feminist factor, democratisation, and the quest for global citizenship. *The Pacific Review, 34*(5), 1–33.

Chandler, D. (2008). Review essay: Human security: The dog that didn't bark. *Security Dialogue, 39*(4), 427–438.

Chatterjee, S., & Das, U. (2022). Refugees in South Asia: Political membership, nation-building projects and securitisation of human flows. In U. Mukhopadhyay (Ed.), *Internal migration within South Asia*. Springer. https://doi.org/10.1007/978-981-16-6144-0_2

Choi, W. G. (2019). Asian civil society and reconfiguration of refugee protection in Asia. *Human Rights Review, 2019*(20), 161–179.

Christie, K. (2018). Introduction: Migration, refugees and human security in the twenty-first century. In M. Boulby & K. Christie (Eds.), *Migration, refugees and human security in the Mediterranean and MENA* (pp. 3–9). Palgrave Macmillan.

Commission on Human Security. (2003). *Human security now: Protecting and empowering people*. Retrieved February 1, 2023, from https://digitallibrary.un.org/record/503749

Davies, S. E. (2008). *Legitimising rejection: International refugee law in Southeast Asia*. Martinus Nijhoff Publishers.

den Boer, M., & de Wilde, J. (2008). Top-down and bottom-up approaches to human security. In M. den Boer & J. de Wilde (Eds.), *The viability of human security* (pp. 9–18). Amsterdam University Press.

De Simone, S. (2020). Beyond normativity and benchmarking: Applying a human security approach to refugee-hosting areas in Africa. *Third World Quarterly, 41*(1), 168–183.

Estrada-Tanck, D. (2016). *Human security and human rights under international law: The protections offered to persons confronting structural vulnerability*. Hart Publishing.

Evans, P. M. (2004). Human security and East Asia: In the beginning. *Journal of East Asian Studies, 4*(2), 263–284.

Friedman, S. (2010). Marital immigration and graduated citizenship: Post-naturalisation restrictions on mainland Chinese spouses in Taiwan. *Pacific Affairs, 83*(1), 73–93.

Global Detention Project (GDP). (n.d.). *Japan*. Retrieved December 3, 2022, from https://www.globaldetentionproject.org/countries/asia-pacific/japan?appsule=106

Hatcher, P., & Murakami, A. (2020). The politics of exclusion: Embedded racism and Japan's pilot Refugee Resettlement Programme. *Race & Class, 62*(1), 60–77. https://doi.org/10.1177/0306396820917068

Ho, E. L., Madokoro, L., & Peterson, G. (2015, April). Refugees, displacement and forced migration in Asia: Charting an inclusive research agenda. Asia Research Institute Working Paper Series No. 236. Retrieved January 15, 2024, from https://ap5.fas.nus.edu.sg/fass/geoehle/eh15%20ari%20wp.pdf

Hossain, K., Roncero Martin, J. M., Petrétei, A., & Holiencin, F. (2016). Introduction: Indigenous peoples of the North and human security. In K. Hossain & A. Petrétei (Eds.), *Understanding the many faces of human security: Perspectives of northern indigenous peoples* (pp. 1–11). Brill.

Howard-Hassmann, R. (2012) Human security: Undermining human rights? *Human Rights Quarterly, 34*(1), 88–112. http://www.jstor.org/stable/41345472

Hung, J. (2021). Why Taiwan should develop exclusive refugee laws for Hong Kong political asylum seekers so as to defy Beijing's interference. *Contemporary Chinese Political Economy and Strategic Relations, 7*(1), 173–185.

Hynek, N. (2012). *Human security as statecraft: Structural conditions, articulations and unintended consequences*. Routledge.

Kalicki, K. (2019). Japan's liberal-democratic paradox of refugee admission. *The Journal of Asian Studies, 78*(2), 355–378.

Kasai, T. (2023, June 14). *Japan immigration law creates new obstacles for asylum seekers: Heightened risk of refugee applicants being returned home to harm*. Human Rights Watch. Retrieved July 28, 2023, from https://www.hrw.org/news/2023/06/15/japan-immigration-law-creates-new-obstacles-asylum-seekers

Kim, S. W. (2010). Human security with an Asian face? *Indiana Journal of Global Legal Studies, 17*(1), 83–103.

Kironska, K. (2022). Taiwan's road to asylum law: Who, when, how, and why not yet? *Human Rights Review, 23*, 241–264. https://doi.org/10.1007/s12142-021-00644-y

Kyodo News (2022, December). *Over 60% of Ukrainian evacuees in Japan unemployed: Survey*. Retrieved February 25, 2023, from https://english.kyodonews.net/news/2022/12/b366ce794860-over-60-of-ukrainian-evacuees-in-japan-unemployed-survey.html

Lam, P. E. (2006). Japan's human security role in Southeast Asia. *Contemporary Southeast Asia, 28*(1), 141–159.

Mahmud, H. (2023, July 13). *Personal troubles, public issues: A sociological approach towards migration studies [Keynote speech]*. NUQ-RU International Workshop "Facing the Challenges of International Coexistence in Asia Today: Welcoming the Migrants, Diasporas, and Refugees of the World". Japan and online. https://en.ritsumei.ac.jp/file.jsp?id=576828

Marhia, N. (2013). Some humans are more *Human* than *Others*: Troubling the "human" in human security from a critical feminist perspective. *Security Dialogue, 44*(1), 19–35.

McElhinney, D. (2022, August 31). *Myanmar, Ukraine war shift Japanese policy on refugees*. Retrieved December 4, 2022, from https://www.aljazeera.com/news/2022/8/31/myanmar-ukraine-war-shift-japanese-policy-on-refugees

Mine, Y., Gomez, O. A., & Muto, A. (2019). Human security in East Asia: Assembling a puzzle. In Y. Mine, O. A. Gomez & A. Muto (Eds.), *Human security norms in East Asia* (pp. 1–22). Security, Development and Human Rights in East Asia. Palgrave Macmillan. https://doi.org/10.1007/978-3-319-97247-3_1

Morrissey, J. (2018). Envisioning human security – commentary to Gill. *Fennia, 196*(2), 225–229. https://doi.org/10.11143/fennia.76029

Newman, E. (2020). Human security. In F.O. Hampson, A. Özerdem, & J. Kent (Eds.), *Routledge handbook of peace, security and development* (pp. 33–44). Routledge. https://doi.org/10.4324/9781351172202

Ogata, S. (2013, June 2). *Development of the concept of human security*. Symposium on human security, Yokohama, Japan. https://www.mofa.go.jp/policy/oda/sector/security/pdfs/sympo1306_ogata.pdf

Pan, M.-L. (2015). Neither compatriots nor refugees: Status discrimination of exiled Tibetans and the contradictory faces of the Republic of China. *International Journal of Asian and Pacific Studies, 11*(2), 41–59.

Rana, Md. S., & Riaz, A. (2022). Securitization of the Rohingya Refugees in Bangladesh. *Journal of Asian and African Studies*. https://doi.org/10.1177/00219096221082265

Ruggie, J. G. (1983). Continuity and transformation in the world polity. *World Politics, 35*(2), 261–285.

Ryall, J. (2022, May 27). *Japan under fire for inconsistent refugee policy*. Deutsche Welle. Retrieved February 19, 2023, from https://www.dw.com/en/japans-ukraine-refugee-policy-criticized-for-putting-politics-over-human-rights/a-61950343

Slater, D., & Barbaran, R. (2020). The whole block goes down: Refugees in Japan's detention centers during the pandemic. *The Asia-Pacific Journal: Japan Focus, 18*(5). https://apjjf.org/2020/18/Slater-Barbaran.html

Slater, D. (2022). *Bait and switch: Japan refugee policy and practice leading to Ukraine, November 18, 2022, David H. Slater*. H-Japan. Retrieved December 4, 2022, from https://networks.h-net.org/node/20904/discussions/11503355/bait-and-switch%E2%80%AF-japan-refugee-policy-and-practice-leading

Song, J. (2012). Introduction. In J. Song & A. D. B. Cook (Eds.), *Irregular migration and human security in East Asia* (pp. 1–20). Routledge.

Takenaka, K. (2015). Japan's tiny refugee community urges Tokyo to open doors wider. *Reuters*. Retrieved December 3, 2022, from https://www.reuters.com/article/us-japan-refugees-idUSKBN0TI00V20151129

Takizawa, S. (2011). Refugees and human security: A research note on the Japanese refugee policy. *Bulletin of Toyo Eiwa Graduate School, 7*, 21–40. https://toyoeiwa.repo.nii.ac.jp/?action=repository_uri&item_id=355.

Tarumoto, H. (2018). Why restrictive refugee policy can be retained? A Japanese Case. *Migration and Development, 8*(1), 7–24. https://doi.org/10.1080/21632324.2018.1482642

The Ministry of Foreign Affairs of Japan (MOFA). (2022, November 9). *Kokunai ni okeru nanmin no ukeire* [Acceptance of refugees in Japan]. Retrieved February 19, 2023, from https://www.mofa.go.jp/mofaj/gaiko/nanmin/main3.html

Tow, W. T. (2013). Introduction. In W. Tow, D. Walton, & R. Kersten (Eds.), *New approaches to human security in the Asia-Pacific. China, Japan and Australia* (pp. 1–11). Routledge.

United Nations General Assembly. (2023, May 29). *Written statement submitted by Human Rights Now, a nongovernmental organization in special consultative status, A/HRC/53/NGO/186*. Retrieved August 19, 2023, from https://hrn.or.jp/eng/wp-content/uploads/2023/05/7243_A_HRC_53_NGO_Sub_En_Japan_Immigration_Law.pdf

United Nations High Commissioner for Refugees (UNHCR). (2010). *Japan: First Myanmar refugees arrive for resettlement*. https://www.unhcr.org/news/briefing/2010/9/4ca1c5899/japan-first-myanmar-refugees-arrive-resettlement.html

United Nations High Commissioner for Refugees (UNHCR). (2015, April 7). *Contributions to UNHCR for budget year 2014 as of 31 December 2014*. Retrieved February 25, 2023, from https://www.unhcr.org/536c960a9.pdf

United Nations High Commissioner for Refugees (UNHCR). (n.d.-a). *Contributions to the UNHCR for budget year 2015 (as of 31 December 2015)*. https://www.unhcr.org/558a639f9.pdf

United Nations High Commissioner for Refugees (UNHCR). (n.d.-b) *Emergency handbook. Version 1.9. Refugee definition*. https://emergency.unhcr.org/entry/55772/refugee-definition

United Nations High Commissioner for Refugees (UNHCR). (n.d.-c). *Master glossary of terms*. https://www.unhcr.org/glossary/

United Nations High Commissioner for Refugees (UNHCR). (n.d.-d). *What is a refugee?* https://www.unhcr.org/what-is-a-refugee.html

United Nations High Commissioner for Refugees (UNHCR). (2005). *UNHCR Global Report 2005: Glossary*. https://www.unhcr.org/449267670.pdf

Wang, H.-Z. (2011). Immigration trends and policy changes in Taiwan. *Asian and Pacific Migration Journal, 20*(2), 169–194.

Wu, Y.-C., & Chien, S.-S. (2022). Northernisation for breaking-through international isolation: Taiwan's trilateral aid cooperation in the Middle East refugee crisis and beyond. *Development Policy Review, 2022*(40), 1–26.

Yamagata, A. (2021). Newspaper discourses on the acceptance of refugees in Japan from the 1970s to the 1980s. *Japanese Studies, 41*(1), 73–92. https://doi.org/10.1080/10371397.2021.1892480

Yamashita, N. (2015). The pilot refugee resettlement program in Japan: What is needed for the successful integration of resettled refugees? *Bulletin of Toyo Eiwa Graduate School, 11*, 67–88. http://id.nii.ac.jp/1093/00000466/

PART I

Legal and Policy Frameworks of the Refugee Regimes in Japan and Taiwan

CHAPTER 2

Refugee Protection in Japan and Taiwan: Common Challenges and Ways Forward for Human Security

Bonny Ling and Mariko Hayashi

Introduction

Contemporary discourse on international migration reflects its status as a volatile political issue. This is the case in various countries and across regions, where metaphors such as "a flood" or "an invasion" of migrants heading to "fortressed" borders have conveniently over-simplified the complex issues of migration (Musolff, 2011; Shariatmadari, 2015). Japan and Taiwan are not exceptions in this political discourse. Concerns of

B. Ling (✉)
Work Better Innovations, Portsmouth, UK
e-mail: bonny.ling@wbi.org.uk

University of Nottingham, Nottingham, UK

M. Hayashi
Southeast and East Asian Centre (SEEAC), London, UK
e-mail: mariko@seeac.org.uk

L. Momesso and P. Ivanova (eds.), *Refugees and Asylum Seekers in East Asia*, Palgrave Macmillan Studies on Human Rights in Asia,
https://doi.org/10.1007/978-981-97-2867-1_2

national security, financial insecurity, and discrimination, in largely ethnically homogeneous populations, make rigorous and objective examination and implementation of migration policies difficult in both Japan and Taiwan. At the same time, an honest and critical examination of refugee protection in both countries is neither a mere academic exercise nor is a topic relating to issues relevant only outside of their borders. For example, in February 2023, reports emerged of local residents of Japan's Okinawa Prefecture, the island groups closest to Taiwan, planning to undergo evacuation drills in case of a Chinese invasion of Taiwan. In such a scenario, official plans indicate that authorities would evacuate around 20,000 local residents to Japan's main southern island of Kyushu each day, by air and sea (United Daily News, 2023). Evacuation would begin from the Sakishima Islands, which include the country's westernmost inhabited island located just over 100 km away from Taiwan. Although the news report does not raise this explicitly, it can be assumed that while local residents of Sakishima are evacuated, Taiwanese refugees would seek safety by sea, potentially trying to reach Sakishima.

The international protection regime for refugees is in many respects accepted in Taiwan and Japan as a diplomatic sign of being a responsible global player. To fully align with the protection regime, this chapter concludes that Japan and Taiwan must go deeper to the foundational aspects of society, offering genuine protection and creating an environment where displaced individuals can thrive. This means creating an environment where individuals are not only free from fear and the political persecution that forms the current definition of a refugee in international law, but also one where the person is free from want and enjoys freedom of speech and belief—the Four Freedoms that conceptually underpin the Universal Declaration of Human Rights (UDHR). On 10 December 1948, member states of the newly formed United Nations (UN) General Assembly met in Paris and adopted the UDHR. The declaration's Article 14(1) sets out that "everyone has the right to seek and to enjoy in other countries asylum from persecution".

The Refugee Convention of 1951 (the "Convention"), as an international treaty, gives legal effect to this right for individuals to seek asylum. It defines, in Article 1(A)(2), a refugee as someone who needs to access this international protection system "owing to well-founded fear of being persecuted for reasons of race, religion, nationality, membership of a particular social group or political opinion, is outside the country of his nationality and is unable or, owing to such fear, is unwilling to avail himself of the protection of that country". A tension is presented in that while an individual has the right to seek asylum, the state is not obliged to grant it (Goodwin-Gill, 1982). This is certainly also true for states that have ratified both the Convention and the 1967 Protocol Relating to the Status of Refugees (the "Protocol") that broadened the Convention's scope of application by removing the geographical and temporal limits that restricted it to post-war Europe. States parties can also, in reality, not accept a significant number of refugees, as in the case of Japan. In this context, the Convention and Protocol, despite their universal applicability, exemplify that ratification "seems to be more of a matter of promoting and protecting national interests rather than protecting the rights of refugees ... in an 'institutionalisation-implementation gap'" (Betts & Orchard, 2014, as in Choi, 2019, p. 164).

Asia–Pacific is not only the world's most populous region, but it also has the largest regional refugee population. In 2019, according to the UN (2020), the Asia–Pacific hosted 7.8 million refugees and people in refugee-like situations, accounting for 38% of the global refugee population. However, the region also has the lowest percentage of countries that have ratified the Convention and Protocol—only 20 out of 48 (Venturi, 2021). Non-ratification countries include Vietnam, Laos, Thailand, Myanmar, Bangladesh, Nepal, India, Pakistan, Brunei, Indonesia, Malaysia, Singapore, North Korea, and Mongolia, whose current governments have not shown any plan towards an eventual ratification. Another common approach in the region is for states to ratify and formally become state parties to the Convention, but then to restrict the domestic implementation of the Convention in such a manner as to offer little protection in reality for those seeking asylum. Japan ratified the Convention and Protocol in October 1981 and January 1982 respectively, and is one of the most important donors to the UN Refugee Agency (UNHCR). Japan, however, has adopted a strict definition of refugees in its asylum process and has granted refugee status to just over 1% of asylum applications during the 40 years from the ratification of the Convention until 2021.[1]

The road forwards for Taiwan in its relationship with the Convention is less clear than either of the options above. Since 1971, Taiwan has existed outside the UN system. It cannot formally become a state party to international treaties, but this doesn't preclude the possibility that Taiwan may hold itself bound to the Convention and commit to the implementation of the treaty domestically, as if it were a state party. Taiwan used a unique procedure for incorporating the two international human rights covenants, the International Covenant on Civil and Political Rights (ICCPR) and the International Covenant on Economic, Social and Cultural Rights (ICESCR), into its domestic law in 2009 (Chen, 2019). Taiwan can do the same for the Convention. In May 2022, the administration of the Democratic Progressive Party (DPP) President Tsai Ing-wen released the country's first National Human Rights Action Plan (NHRAP). Among the eight major human rights priorities identified by the plan was the goal for the government to review Taiwan's refugee protection policies and establish legislative and administrative asylum procedures by 2024 (Executive Yuan, 2022a; Executive Yuan, 2022b; Focus Taiwan, 2022). As it currently stands, the plan does not stipulate if the commitment is to eventually lead to Taiwan legally incorporating the Convention into a national asylum law, or whether it would remain outside the international framework for the protection of refugees.

This chapter examines the current situation of refugee protection in both Japan and Taiwan through an analysis of primary sources (law and policy documents), civil society reports, academic articles, and news reports. For the Taiwanese context, because the island lacks formalised procedures for dealing with asylum seekers, our analysis benefits from detailed discussions with one former member of the Taiwan Association for Human Rights (TAHR) who was engaged in refugee work in Taiwan. For the discussions on Japan's refugee protection regime, a particular

[1] Calculation made by the authors based on official data released by the Immigration Services Agency (ISA, n.d.a) of Japan at https://www.moj.go.jp/isa/content/001393014.pdf on the total number of asylum applications per year from 1982 to 2021 and the number of positive decisions each year. Over the near 40 years, the total number of applicants was 87,892, from which a total of 915 asylum applications resulted in a positive decision. This represented a percentage of 1.04%.

focus is the gap between the international standards in the protection of asylum seekers and refugees and its domestic implementation. These challenges are also present in the Taiwanese context. Since promoting human security is an important aspect of Japan's foreign aid policy and official development assistance (ODA), this chapter uses a human security lens to examine some common challenges in both of these jurisdictions. The chapter concludes with reflections on the potential and the limits of law, if state parties like Japan do not implement the spirit of the Convention domestically, and if countries like Taiwan continue to address refugee protection without an established legislative framework. Implementing a human security lens for refugee protection that promotes equitable and human-centric solutions in Japan, Taiwan, and elsewhere, requires strong public support.

Externalisation of Refugee Protection in Japan

Japan's relationship with the international refugee protection regime is marked by dichotomy. Japan, a state party of the Convention and Protocol, contributed US$167.7 million in 2022 alone, making it the fourth largest government donor to the UNHCR, after the US, Germany, and the European Union (UNHCR, n.d.a, n.d.b). UNHCR (n.d.c) stated that the consistent support of Japan over the years to global initiatives, such as the Sustainable Development Goals, human security, and the humanitarian-development-peace nexus, made the country "unquestionably ... a key supporter of refugees and displaced people". The generosity of the Japanese government in providing funding to the UNHCR, however, stands in sharp contrast to its poor record of granting refugee status to those who seek asylum in Japan. Refugee protection is frequently treated by the government as a distant issue. In his speech at the UN Summit for Refugees and Migrants, held in New York in 2016, then-Prime Minister Shinzo Abe highlighted Japan's efforts in assisting Syrian refugees in Turkey and Jordan through the country's ODA. He announced Japan's commitment, "as an advocate of human security", in providing a humanitarian package of about US$2.8 billion in assistance to refugees, migrants, and host communities in the Middle East (MOFA, 2016). It was notable in these remarks that Abe did not once mention refugees and asylum seekers in Japan. In the following year, the UNHCR criticised Japan for its low asylum acceptance numbers and urged the country to do more for refugee protection (Wilson, 2017).

Refugee Definition "by the letter, if not [the] spirit"

Behind Japan's strict asylum process is a unique definition of refugees. Following a very narrow interpretation of the Convention, the asylum process requires applicants to prove that they are individually targeted and persecuted in order to be recognised as refugees (JAR, 2017). Belonging to a persecuted group or fleeing a war or conflict alone is often not considered as a basis for refugee recognition. Japan's narrow definition of the term refugee means that individuals who would have been recognised as refugees by other countries or the UNHCR might not be granted refugee status in Japan. Providing evidence of individual persecution is extremely difficult or impossible for many people who flee their home countries in crisis situations, resulting in poor success rates of asylum applications (JAR, 2017). Therefore, as Saburo Takizawa, the former representative of UNHCR Tokyo Office, described, most refugees are excluded from Japan's very narrow definition of refugees, underscoring that Japan abides "by the letter, if not [the] spirit" (Chan, 2018) of the Convention.

The strict definition of refugee means that Japan does not recognise individuals fleeing the Russian invasion of Ukraine as refugees. In Japan, Ukrainian people who fled the war are officially referred to as *hinanmin*, literally meaning "evacuees" instead of *nanmin*, the term used for refugees. Compared to individuals fleeing wars and conflicts in other countries such as Syria and Myanmar, the Japanese government showed generous support to Ukrainian *hinanmin*. Just over a month after Russia's invasion began, in February 2022, Japanese Foreign Minister Yoshimasa Hayashi visited Poland and came back to Japan with 20 Ukrainian "evacuees" on a government plane to show Japan's support for the war-torn country (Nikkei Asia, 2022). The government made a number of special arrangements to speedily admit evacuees from Ukraine to Japan and to allow them to switch their visa to ones that permit work and study. Local authorities, businesses, and educational institutions joined the government initiatives to assist Ukrainian evacuees, offering a wide range of support, including help with language learning, employment, and free or subsidised accommodation.

As of March 2023, over 2360 Ukrainians had arrived in Japan, according to official information from the Japanese government (ISA, n.d.b). To place Japan's low asylum acceptance numbers into a comparative perspective, the number of Ukrainian "evacuees" who were accepted in less than one year is more than double the total number of refugee statuses granted by Japan since it ratified the Convention in 1981. Ukrainian evacuees were admitted to Japan without going through the lengthy and complex refugee application process. Conditions for entry of Ukrainian evacuees were relaxed, for example, compared to those for Afghans seeking asylum after the Taliban's takeover in 2021. Naoko Hashimoto, an academic and a refugee examination counsellor for the Ministry of Justice (MOJ), explained that "there are political and geopolitical factors behind this special treatment", with the Prime Minister Fumio Kishida committing to work alongside other Group of Seven (G7) countries on supporting Ukraine (Itakura, 2022).

Similar to the arrangement with Ukrainian evacuees, there was another time when Japan opened its doors to those fleeing a conflict. Following the Vietnam War, in the late 1970s over 11,000 Indochinese refugees from Vietnam, Laos, and Cambodia resettled in Japan (Koike, 2011). With the outbreak of the Indochina refugee crisis, there was increasing international pressure on Japan as the world's then-second richest country, along with domestic public support, to help refugees (Havens, 1990). In response to this pressure, the Japanese Cabinet made an agreement, specifically for accepting Indochinese refugees in 1979, rather than coming up with a comprehensive policy on the treatment of asylum seekers fleeing any wars and conflicts (Flowers, 2008). This experience of accepting Indochinese refugees led Japan to become a state party to the Convention in 1981 and to amend its immigration law to the Immigration Control and Refugee Recognition Act (the "Immigration Control Act") in the following year.

To understand the rationale behind these policy decisions, Flowers (2008) analysed the conflict between the Ministry of Foreign Affairs (MOFA) and the MOJ, the two state departments deeply involved in discussions on the ratification of the Convention. While the MOFA strongly recommended Japan's ratification to promote good relationships with Western governments who were diplomatically important to Japan, the MOJ strongly resisted, based on an objection to abolishing citizenship requirements for social welfare programmes and owing to potential social disruption to the "homogeneous nation" (Flowers, 2008). Ratifying the Convention and amending domestic immigration law, however, did not mean that Japan would continue to open its doors to people who sought asylum, the same way it did for Indochinese refugees. Even after becoming a state party to the Convention in

1981, the MOJ, as the responsible ministry for the asylum determination process, continued to operate with its traditional attitude of control towards foreign nationals, based on its primary responsibility to protect Japan from irregular immigration, rather than embracing the norms and spirit of the Convention.

Control Over Protection

Under the Immigration Control Act, all asylum applications are handled by the Immigration Services Agency (ISA) under the MOJ. Although the agency uses the term "immigration services" in its English name, the original Japanese name *Shutunyukoku Zairyu Kanri-cho* literally translates to "immigration and residence control agency". The names of the law and the competent authority that govern the asylum process imply Japan's predominant focus on the "control" of foreign nationals entering and residing in the country, viewing refugees as subjects to control rather than as rights holders to protect. Some argue that Japan's ratification of the Convention followed the country's strategy to strengthen immigration control and that this strategy has largely succeeded. Koike (2011) contends that Japan, in fact, used the Convention to strengthen its border control by applying the strict interpretation of the Convention to define refugees. This "control over protection" approach is perpetuated in the restrictive asylum process despite a number of amendments to the domestic law and the asylum process.

Since the Immigration Control Act came into force in 1982, and until the first amendments of the asylum process in 2004, the so-called "60-day rule" prevented displaced individuals from applying for asylum 60 days after arriving in Japan or after learning of a change in circumstances in their home countries. This meant that even those who were recognised as refugees would not automatically be granted legal status to reside in Japan, if they did not comply with the rule (Ishikawa, 2021). It was only when the rule was abolished in 2004 that the "permission for provisional stay" was introduced to allow asylum applicants without legal residency in Japan to temporarily remain, so they would not be subject to deportation before their cases concluded. While some improvements were made, Japan's asylum process continued to lack key elements to ensure fairness, such as access to legal support, high-quality and independent interpreters, transparency on decision-making, and an independent appeal process (Flowers, 2008). The Japan Association for Refugees (JAR) (n.d.) has criticised current practices on the grounds that the asylum determination process is highly opaque in comparison to international standards.

From Control to a Rights-Based Policy?

A clear opportunity to further strengthen the control came when the Diet, Japan's national legislature, passed an immigration reform bill to amend the Immigration Control Act in June 2023. The controversial bill was enacted after the Cabinet submitted it to the Diet in March 2023. The amended law allows the government to deport asylum seekers with pending third applications or subsequent appeals if the ISA does not recognise adequate justification. It also makes deportation of first-time asylum applicants possible if they have been sentenced to imprisonment for three or more years or are suspected of being involved in terrorism or similar activities (ISA, n.d.c). The provisions of this amended law mirrors a similar bill debated in the Diet in 2021 which was withdrawn after facing strong criticism from the opposition, civil society, and the international community. This followed the high-profile in-detention death of a Sri Lankan undocumented woman who was denied adequate medical care (Amnesty International, 2023). The UNHCR (2021) had criticised the earlier bill and now the amended Immigration Control Act for contravening both international norms for refugee protection and the principle of non-refoulement, whereby states are prohibited from forcibly returning any individual who would be at risk of irreparable harm upon return.

As the amendment bill made its way through the Diet, several UN human rights experts, including the Special Rapporteur on the human rights of migrants, raised concerns that "the new amendment bill would maintain a system based on a presumption of detention", and that detention is considered to be arbitrary without a maximum period of detention and periodical judicial reviews of continued detention (Morales et al., 2023). Another concern raised by the UN human rights experts, members of the opposition, and civil society organisations is the introduction of "monitoring measures" that would permit asylum seekers who are given detention orders to live outside detention centres but under monitoring and supervision of private actors, such as NGOs, supporters, and family members (Human Rights Now, 2023). These new measures include penalties for those who supervise individuals on release, if they fail to report as required by the ISA, creating and normalising citizen-to-citizen surveillance (Tokyo Shimbun, 2023).

As the debate over the immigration reform bill increasingly attracted public attention in late March 2023, the Japanese government released guidelines on refugee recognition for the first time. The guidelines included gender and sexuality related persecution as terms for consideration and noted that fear of persecution cannot be denied only because the individual is not personally persecuted, while "realistic risks" of persecution must be proved in order for the individual to be considered for refugee recognition (ISA, 2023). While the efforts for improved transparency and what appears to be a possible change in Japan's narrow definition of refugees were welcome, it is notable that the Justice Minister Ken Saito stated in a press conference that the handbook "does not expand the scope of recognition" and is not aimed to "increase the number of people granted refugee status" (MOJ, 2023). Whether the government will re-consider asylum seekers whose applications were rejected prior to the introduction of the guidelines remains unclear.

Taiwan: Civil Society's Longstanding Quest for an Asylum Law

As noted by the editors and other authors in the book, Taiwan currently does not have a national asylum law. Taiwan also operates without an established legislative or administrative framework for refugee protection or for asylum determination. Procedures concerning refugee protection are ad hoc, with official support services rarely provided for those seeking asylum in Taiwan (Former TAHR representative, personal communication, February 2, 2023). Nevertheless, the history of modern Taiwan is not removed from a history of population displacement and resettlement. For example, individuals of Myanmarese origin or descent represent one of Taiwan's largest minority groups, estimated at around 40,000 (Prentice, 2017). After the Chinese Civil War, in the 1950s and 1960s, Chinese Nationalist troops who retreated to Thailand and Myanmar continued to fight against the Chinese Communists by launching periodic border incursions (Chang, 2001; Clymer, 2014; Qin, 2015). While some soldiers and their families were eventually evacuated to Taiwan, others stayed in Southeast Asia and did not enjoy the rights of citizenship of their adopted lands (Cheung, 2019; Qin, 2015). Their descendants, however, could come to Taiwan for language and cultural exchange programmes and, until 1999, could be granted Taiwanese citizenship. When this policy was changed, civil society organisations in Taiwan, including the Thai–Myanmar Chinese Refugee Rights Association, strongly criticised the move. Civil society was subsequently successful in advocating for this stateless population, with its close ties to Taiwan, to be allowed to stay and obtain Taiwanese citizenship after a residency of three years (Cheung, 2019).

Refugees and National Security

In Taiwan, concerns over national security vis-à-vis China, facilitated by a perceived backdoor of espionage through a humanitarian refugee programme—especially as Beijing intensifies its rhetoric of invasion—have long stymied efforts to establish a national asylum system. While these concerns are often raised in contemporary domestic discussions on Taiwan offering some form of protection for individuals fleeing China and Hong Kong, they are not new. Taiwan, owing to its status outside the UN system and under threat of takeover by China, exists under a heightened sensitivity to national security. A significant part of Taiwan's population has vivid family histories of forced migration, with families arriving in Taiwan from mainland China in difficult post-conflict situations brought on by the Chinese Civil War. For Taiwan, the issue of refugee protection, especially for individuals who come from communities that have some link to mainland China, however removed, has a historical background of conflict, mistrust, and questions of political loyalty. This was seen in the treatment of exiled Tibetans decades ago, along with political dissidents from China and the recent arrivals of Hong Kongers.

Exiled Tibetans in Taiwan present a thorny category for the government. Because the Chinese Nationalist leadership that retreated to Taiwan harboured ambitions of retaking China and considered Tibet to be a part of China, many Tibetans viewed the early Taiwanese policies, towards them and towards the Tibetan Government in Exile, with little enthusiasm (Tethong, 2018, p. 64). A small number of exiled Tibetans came to Taiwan and settled during the Cold War, but the vast majority of exiled Tibetans arrived under a state-sponsored programme for vocational and educational training from 1980 to the late 1990s (Pan, 2015, pp. 47–48). This programme provided short-term training for exiled Tibetans aged 16 to 35, with the aim of improving their economic situation, while also showcasing Taiwan as an ally of Tibet (Pan, 2015). During this time, the competent authority for processing the applications of exiled Tibetans for training was moved from the Ministry of the Interior to the Ministry of Foreign Affairs, and Tsering (2022b) noted that treating exiled Tibetans as foreigners or refugees in Taiwan, instead of being overseas Chinese, was a significant policy development. Nevertheless, reflecting their ambiguous status in Taiwanese society, Tibetans in Taiwan are often described as being treated as "neither compatriot nor refugee" (Kironska, 2022; Pan, 2015; Tsering, 2022b).

The cases of the neither-compatriots-nor-refugees Tibetans in Taiwan, the former soldiers of the Chinese Nationalists in Myanmar and Thailand, and their stateless descendants are complex legacies of the Chinese Civil War. Chinese Nationalists lost to the Chinese Communist Party and retreated to Taiwan in 1949, but the ripples of the loss have had a far reach. To fully understand the localised refugee context for Taiwan, one must recognise that the legacy of the Chinese Civil War runs to the present day. Concerns over the national security of Taiwan are not rhetorical but are the ever-present undercurrents that have long stymied efforts to set up a national asylum system. In May 2021, a man from Fujian Province in Southern China sailed through the heavily patrolled Taiwan Strait in his claimed pursuit of freedom and equality in Taiwan. In the immediate aftermath of the crossing, Taiwan's military leaders were quick to doubt the man's intentions and version of events, while assuring the public that the man's successful crossing did not reveal shortcomings in the island's maritime defences (Davidson, 2021). This case exemplifies the challenge of refugee protection for Taiwan, particularly in the way perceived national security breaches took top billing in the news reports of this crossing from China.

It is not unexpected that Taiwan's attention on political asylum, while being framed by national security, is heavily focused on China. National security concerns for the survival of Taiwan have long complicated domestic discussions on granting asylum, whether or not the measures are rational and justifiable. For instance, security concerns and distrust of individuals seeking political asylum from China have remained, despite marriages between Taiwanese and Chinese nationals representing more than 60% of all registered marriages between a Taiwanese national and a foreign spouse from 1987 to 2022.[2] Taiwan started to receive applications of Chinese nationals seeking asylum via irregular migratory routes after 2000, with the first of such asylum cases received by TAHR being that of Tang Yuanjun who was later resettled in the US (Chiu, 2018, p. 157; TAHR, 2002). After Tang, other Chinese dissidents, such as Chen Rongli and Yan Peng, who sought asylum in Taiwan after 2004, were not able to be resettled in a third country and stayed in Taiwan on a succession of three-month visas (Chiu, 2018). During this time, they could not work or enrol for national health insurance. After ten years of waiting, they received their permanent residency and their right to work in Taiwan (Chiu, 2018).

In recent years, Hong Kong residents arriving in Taiwan to escape political crackdowns have brought awareness of the issue of refugee protection to the forefront in Taiwan. While many Hong Kongers may have been attracted by the geographical and cultural proximity of Taiwan to Hong Kong, many were eventually left disappointed by the difficulty of meaningfully integrating into Taiwanese life and society. When individuals fleeing political crackdowns in Hong Kong first arrived in Taiwan in 2019, the Taiwanese government relied on ad hoc measures, such as extending their residency visa on a monthly basis, which severely limited their ability to integrate into Taiwanese life (Nachman & Hioe, 2019). While the situation improved in 2020, the same year that Hong Kong's National Security Law was introduced, Taiwan set up a dedicated Taiwan–Hong Kong Service Exchange Office to assist individuals from Hong Kong and Macau to resettle by making it easier for them to study and work in Taiwan (Hale, 2023).

Serious problems and sensitivities remain. Foremost is the concern over irregular entries into Taiwan, as underscored by separate cases of Hong Kong activists trying to reach Taiwan via boat crossing. While Article 14 of Taiwan's Laws and Regulations Regarding Hong Kong and Macao

[2] Calculation made by the authors based on official data released by the Executive Yuan, Gender Equality Committee of Taiwan and collected by the National Immigration Agency of the Ministry of Interior (Executive Yuan, 2023), and at https://www.gender.ey.gov.tw/GecDB/Stat_Statistics_DetailData.aspx?sn=lJvq%2BGDSYHCFfHU73DDedA%3D%3D, on the number of registered marriages between a Taiwanese and Chinese national, excluding individuals from Hong Kong and Macau (355,124) out of the number of all registered marriages between a Taiwanese national and a foreign spouse (577,900) from January 1987 to December 2022. This represented a percentage of 61.45%.

Affairs requires legal entry into Taiwan or residency of valid duration (i.e. no overstay), this strict prohibition is difficult to maintain in light of the humanitarian imperative and the deteriorating political situation in Hong Kong. The Taiwanese government is walking a tightrope on asylum seekers from Hong Kong, not wanting to escalate tensions with China while seeking to uphold its democratic values. In recent years, more legislative voices have stressed the advantages of a low-key and unofficial system to provide refuge and assistance to political dissidents from China and Hong Kong. Legislator Wang Ting-yu of the DPP in Taiwan stressed in 2020 that Hong Kong activists have already reached Taiwan through "unofficial" channels, without "need[ing] to beat a big drum" and put the government in the spotlight (Jennings, 2020). While discussions on how Hong Kongers can seek asylum in Taiwan remain unresolved—obstructed and complicated by national security concerns that mark all matters—the prolonged unclarity and Taiwan's immigration labyrinth have driven some Hong Kongers to leave, citing the impossibility of integration. Others have stayed in "an imperfect exile" in Taiwan (Lai & Wu, 2022).

National Human Rights Action Plan and Refugee Protection

Reacting to persistent civil society criticism that Taiwan needs a formalised asylum system, Taiwan's Executive Yuan released the country's first NHRAP in May 2022, which identified eight key human rights priorities. Among these priorities was an official commitment on refugee protection. The plan called on Taiwan to codify legal mechanisms for refugees to seek asylum and to clarify related application procedures (Executive Yuan, 2022b). This development was a significant moment for Taiwan civil society's longstanding advocacy for a national asylum law, to better set out the legislative and policy framework for refugee protection. Nevertheless, the NHRAP does not commit Taiwan to legislate an asylum law. It also does not indicate if the official commitment is to eventually lead Taiwan to legally incorporate the Convention and Protocol into a national asylum law, in the same way that both the ICCPR and the ICESCR were incorporated into Taiwan domestic law in 2009 (Chang, 2019). Current advocacy by Taiwanese civil societies for the government to abide by the principle of non-refoulement and the Convention on Torture—without specifically pushing for Taiwan to incorporate the Convention into the domestic legal framework—suggests that the Convention is not regarded as an advocacy priority (Former TAHR representative, personal communication, July 12, 2023). Though important as an international legal instrument, the Convention is seen by some advocating organisations as outdated (Former TAHR representative, personal communication, July 12, 2023).

However Taiwan evolves regarding its relationship with the Convention and the broader issue of addressing the challenge of protection for individuals exercising their fundamental right to seek asylum, the country cannot ignore the urgency for reform. Its current asylum situation is already more complicated than the established landscape of national security and refugee protection that Taiwan is perhaps more attuned to. Beyond cases from China and Hong Kong, Taiwan has already received asylum seekers from Syria, Turkey, Uganda, South Korea, and Egypt, but there are no official statistics released on asylum seekers and applications (Kironska, 2022). For instance, TAHR only finds out about asylum seekers who have arrived in Taiwan from the media or through government contacts. From 2013 to 2017, TAHR counted 40 such cases in Taiwan but this information is not confirmed by the government (Former TAHR representative, personal communication, April 13, 2023). A first draft asylum law was sent for reading in the Taiwanese legislature in 2005. Since then, other versions were also submitted in 2011 and 2012 and were discussed in public hearings but did not proceed further under the previous administration. The latest attempt was in 2016, under the new DPP administration of President Tsai Ing-wen, but that too failed to gain traction within the Parliament past initial readings (Kironska, 2022, p. 246).

Common Challenges for Integration and Human Security

Notwithstanding the fact that Japan and Taiwan are in different situations with respect to the Convention—one is a state party while the other is not and has made no indication that it will consider holding itself bound by the Convention—the most notable point of comparison is the importance of refugee assistance in the foreign policy of both countries. Besides its significant contributions to the UNHCR, Japan's foreign aid assistance to humanitarian projects supporting the protection and integration of displaced populations, refugees, and internally displaced people, is a central prong of its overseas development strategy. This is largely a legacy of Sadako Ogata, the Japanese diplomat and respected academic who served as the UN High Commissioner for Refugees from 1991 to 2000 and continued to be a strong advocate for human security after stepping down from leading the UNHCR. She later served as the Co-Chair of the UN Commission on Human Security and the President of Japan International Cooperation Agency, and supported the use of ODA to help solve the problems of displacement, reconstruction, and reintegration.

Compared to Japan's ODA, Taiwan's overseas development work does not have the same emphasis on human security, with the theme of human security scarcely featuring in Taiwan's annual International Cooperation and Development Reports. In the latest report by Taiwan's Ministry of Foreign Affairs, called the International Cooperation and Development Report of 2020, human security appeared twice and only in the context of material donations to a policy research centre and funds on human security (MOFA Taiwan, 2021). Taiwan's ODA for work with refugees only appeared in Turkey, Jordan, and Thailand (MOFA Taiwan, 2021, pp. 18, 26, 29, 33). Taiwan simply does not prioritise human security to the same degree as Japan in its ODA. This, however, does not mean that refugee protection does not feature in Taiwan's foreign policy or is absent from considerations about how Taiwan wants to be seen domestically and externally. For example, the draft asylum law that was previously read in the Taiwan legislature in 2016 spoke of this desire for Taiwan to be seen as a responsible global player on human rights and refugee protection, citing the asylum procedures and laws of the US, UK, Canada, Japan, and South Korea and other countries to support the case that Taiwan should also have a national asylum law (Legislative Yuan, 2016).

Ad hoc Refugee Protection, with or without the Refugee Convention

Beyond the external layer of diplomacy, however, is a more complicated situation concerning domestic support for refugee protection. Both Japan and Taiwan appear to prefer an ad hoc approach to refugee protection, and the Convention features lightly in both contexts. In the case of Japan, this has allowed it to decide which group can receive preferential treatment, while the asylum determination for others must adhere to a very strict interpretation of a refugee under the Convention. In contrast, Taiwan's process on asylum determination and refugee protection is by default ad hoc and is not established by any law or administrative procedure. While Taiwan's inaugural NHRAP commits the government to codify legal mechanisms for refugees to seek asylum and to clarify related application procedures, it is not clear on whether the government will consider holding itself bound as a state party to the Convention.

The externalisation of the refugee problem by both Japan and Taiwan means that, when refugee protection becomes a domestic issue, policy-setting around this topic, from debates over the ratification of the Convention (as in the case of Japan) or whether to legislate a national asylum law (as in the case of Taiwan), is driven by domestic political considerations and influences. Practically, this means that, like any foreign nationals in most countries, asylum seekers are not part of the electorate at the national level and their rights protection does not dominate press coverage. Politicians are rarely incentivised to speak up on issues of migration, especially during election years. This tension is underscored by the fact that discussions on the protection of refugees, even though the issue is one out of the eight human rights priorities set by Taiwan's inaugural NHRAP that was only released in 2022, hardly featured in the midterm election that took place later in the same year. Likewise, a 2017, 300-page edited volume of academic studies on the Taiwan voter contained not one reference to refugees or asylum seekers (Achen & Wang, 2017). This is not unexpected. Affirming the benefits of migration is often not a popular electoral issue, in Taiwan, Japan, or other countries of destination.

The tension between refugee protection as an external diplomatic tool and domestic implementation of the spirit of the Convention is exemplified by Japan's efforts on refugee resettlement. In 2010, Japan acknowledged the importance of "burden sharing" refugee resettlement worldwide and launched a pilot refugee resettlement programme, the first in Asia to do so (MOFA, n.d.). The programme, however, was only open to a specific preferred group of refugees deemed to be best suited for Japan. As recorded by the Cabinet Secretariat of Japan (2008), the government set a requirement that refugees resettling in Japan must be Karen refugee families in Thailand's Mae La camp, who supposedly "have the ability to adapt to Japanese society and would be able to have a job to earn their own living". The government planned to resettle 90 refugees over three years. In reality, however, only 45 refugees were involved in the three-year pilot programme due to a limited interest from the Karen group in question; some initially considered resettlement in Japan but withdrew as they felt uneasy about their future in Japan (Takizawa, 2015). After the pilot period, the Japanese government later changed the targeted groups to Myanmarese refugees in Malaysia and the relatives of those who had resettled from Thailand in the pilot programme. A total of 250 refugees have resettled in Japan over 13 years, as of April 2023 (MOFA, 2023).

Ager and Strang's (2004) "Indicators of Integration" describe employment, housing, education, and health as markers and means for the achievement of integration. Depending on the groups of refugees (or evacuees) or individual cases, refugees experience these four indicators very differently in both Japan and Taiwan, especially compared to Ager and Strang's ideal scenario of integration. A comprehensive integration support system—informed and co-produced by all stakeholders, including national and local authorities, NGOs, experts in refugee protection, local communities, and refugees themselves—must be provided to asylum seekers. UNHCR's (2002) guideline clearly states that "'integration potential' should not play a determining role in the consideration of protection resettlement cases". The criteria set by the Japanese government for the resettlement programme, which emphasises cultural adaptability and employability, reflects the government's desire to minimise both social and economic costs (Takizawa, 2015) while improving Japan's image in the international community (Koike, 2011). It overlooks the state's responsibility to ensure a comprehensive support system for refugees, regardless of their abilities and qualifications, to integrate into their host society.

Human Security Risks for Asylum Seekers

The integration process is made even more difficult for refugees, in Taiwan, owing to the absence of a national asylum law. Asylum applications and related services are considered on an ad hoc basis and are not framed as a state duty in Taiwan. This can give rise to varying outcomes in the asylum determination process, ranging from receiving some support and temporary residency to deportations that potentially violate the principle of non-refoulement (Kironska, 2022). While the asylum cases are pending and considered on a case-by-case basis, Kironska (2022) noted that the majority of asylum seekers in Taiwan need to rely on civil society groups for assistance, such as for accommodation, medical treatment, and psychological counselling. The same point was made by Pan (2015, pp. 41–42) who noted, in the broader context of the protection of refugees and displaced people worldwide, that they "are also subjected to arbitra[ry] and discriminatory treatment through government policy [or the absence of such policy], even though they are entitled to fundamental human rights under international law".

In contrast to Taiwan, Japan has an established legislative and administrative framework to deal with asylum applications. It, however, focuses more on immigration control than on refugee protection, negatively impacting the human security of individuals seeking asylum. From the point of arrival in Japan, asylum seekers often face financial difficulties and lack of access to daily necessities, such as food, clothing, shelter, or access to health care. Those facing destitution while their asylum cases are being assessed can apply for welfare assistance, which is around two-thirds of the usual welfare benefits available to long-term residents or Japanese citizens, and it is often a time-consuming process (JAR, n.d.). Asylum seekers with legal status can switch their status to be permitted to work temporarily only when their cases are considered to have a "high likelihood" of refugee recognition (MOJ, n.d.). Precarity and uncertainty can continue for many years, since the asylum process, on average, takes up to three years to be determined and, in some instances, ten years (Tamura, 2020). Additionally, welfare assistance for asylum seekers is now limited to only those who are first-time applicants (Ishikawa, 2021).

The situation is much more difficult for those who are seeking asylum as undocumented migrants in Japan, because they are not allowed to work, do not have access to social protection—including national health insurance—and can be subject to detention. Although some are given provisional release from detention depending on their circumstances, without access to work or welfare assistance they must rely on their social network and charitable civil society assistance, as in the case of asylum seekers in Taiwan. The strict and lengthy asylum process, combined with lack of access to work and social welfare, means that many asylum seekers in Japan are highly vulnerable to destitution, poor health, and exploitation. In 2021, a Japanese NGO surveyed 141 individuals, who were given provisional release from detention, on their life conditions (Kitakanto Iryo Sodan Kai (AMIGOS), 2022). Results showed that 65% of those surveyed said they felt it was "very difficult" or "difficult" to afford meals. Health care was also raised as a very serious concern. Survey results indicated that 84% experienced having to give up visiting medical facilities due to financial constraints (AMIGOS, 2022).

Arbitrary and indefinite detention of asylum seekers, and detention conditions, also present significant risks of human rights violations. In

2023, Amnesty International reported that the organisation had interviewed some migrants and asylum seekers in Japan who were held in detention for several years. The detainees reported that they were "treated like animals" and "the only way to get out of the immigration detention centre was to get sick or go on a hunger strike to the point of death" (Amnesty International, 2023). Previously, in August 2020, the Working Group on Arbitrary Detention of the UN's Human Rights Council adopted opinions recognising two cases of asylum seekers from Turkey and Iran who were detained several times—with the longest detention period of three or more years in the examined cases—stating that the detention was arbitrary and in violation of the fundamental human rights of the asylum seekers. One of them experienced physical abuse and both did not receive adequate medical care in detention, resulting in the deterioration of their physical and mental health. The Working Group concluded that the asylum seekers had the right to receive compensation and that Japan had breached its state duty to respect human rights (UN Human Rights Council, 2020).

Dasgupta (2022) highlights that Japan's immigration policy, including its refugee policy, is a typical example of a utilitarian-functional type of policy that looks at foreign nationals through a cost–benefit analysis, treating groups of migrants differently based on their "usefulness" to society, and placing most refugees in the least desirable ranks. The response of Japan to Indochinese refugees, the resettlement programme, or Ukrainian "evacuees" implies that the government prefers to apply ad hoc asylum arrangements to particular groups when it suits the country's political and diplomatic agenda, while continuing to impose strict controls on other asylum seekers. The same criticism can be levied against Taiwan. The situation of Tibetan refugees in Taiwan exemplifies this complexity for Taiwan, which contrasts the government's intent to be seen as a globally progressive, human rights-abiding country, with political concerns of national security. This is combined with the weight of historical baggage from the Chinese Civil War, which resulted in population displacement and distrust amidst groups that once fought. This led one Tibetan scholar in Taiwan to openly ask, "Who are [the Tibetan diaspora in Taiwan] and why they are invisible?" (Tsering, 2022a, 2022b).

Tsering (2022a, 2022b) points to the case of Tibetans who entered Taiwan for vocational and educational training from 1980 to the late 1990s as the most disadvantaged minority group in Taiwan. While Tibetans who arrived in Taiwan under this vocational and educational scheme could be an example of yet another utilitarian-functional type of policy that assesses foreign nationals based on their perceived "usefulness" to the host society, such recognition of their "utility" is not a constant, immune from policy changes, and does not qualify as a fulfilling and safe vocational and employment situation. In 1993, Taiwan's vocational and educational training programme for Tibetans came to an abrupt end as Taiwan formally excluded exiled Tibetans from the status of legal workers under the Employment Services Act (Pan, 2015). Already, before the change in the law that excluded exiled Tibetans from the scope of the Employment Services Act, many of the Tibetan vocational and educational scheme participants in Taiwan absconded from their assigned vocational training due to arduous and unsafe working conditions (Pan, 2015). They became undocumented migrants and faced difficulties in Taiwan that made their lives more precarious than their refugee period in South Asia.

In 1999, a group of undocumented Tibetans petitioned the Taiwanese government and described their lives of insecurity:

> Although we did not have nationality in India or Nepal, we were refugees and at least were admitted as legal foreigners. In Taiwan, however, we still do not have nationality and even worse have become illegal. We cannot go back to our family in India or Nepal because we have no passports. Thus we are trapped and have to live the past decade in fear and with little protection. We can only do odd jobs; we cannot ask for medical help even when we need it; we are afraid of the police in the streets, as we cannot explain to people clearly our absurd situation. We cannot seriously develop a relationship because it is impossible to have a legal marriage under such circumstances. (Pan, 2015, pp. 49–50)

This testimony underscores how immigration policy, including refugee policy, that leans on utilitarian-functionality to assess the usefulness of foreign nationals, can bring about significant human insecurity and rights violations. When government acceptance of their usefulness shifts, or when the label of usefulness is a mere cover for an exploitative labour reality, this can bring economic hardship and human rights abuses for the affected individual. Stating the obvious, human rights abuses can happen even in hosting countries, such as Japan and Taiwan, which are not conflict-affected areas.

Despite the external appearances of both jurisdictions being very different when it comes to refugee protection—one is a party to the

Convention while the other is not (nor considers itself bound to the Convention despite being outside the international intergovernmental system)—there are more similarities than differences. For both countries, refugee assistance serves a diplomatic purpose, by promoting the country's contribution to externalised refugee issues, rather than implementing the international norms and spirit of refugee protection in their own territories. There are, however, differences. Human security features officially and prominently in Japan's ODA in a way that is not seen for Taiwan. Diplomatic concerns in terms of national security are also more pronounced for Taiwan than they are for Japan, since the issue of refugee protection for Taiwan is tied to the thorny question of how to address genuinely those fleeing political unrest from Hong Kong and Mainland China, without being perceived as opening a backdoor to facilitate espionage.

Conclusions

Japan and Taiwan, two countries connected by geography and history, are at an intersection for how they want to engage domestically with refugee protection, beyond it being an issue of humanitarian assistance and foreign aid. In March 2023, Japan released national guidelines on refugee recognition. This is a notable first for Japan, which has consistently faced criticism that it accepts a much lower number of refugees than it should. Similarly, the question of how Taiwan will offer asylum has become ever pressing, with a growing international spotlight on the island's lack of a national asylum law and its acceptance of very few refugees in reality. The deterioration of the political situation in neighbouring Hong Kong, the continuing unrest in Myanmar, and regressions on democracy and human developments in the Asia–Pacific, have highlighted the positive roles that Japan and Taiwan could play to raise awareness and respect for human rights across the region.

The experiences of Japan, both positive and negative, in its domestic engagement with the issues of refugee protection, can provide a useful guide for Taiwan. The current push from civil society for Taiwan to have an asylum law will set normative expectations for the country to abide by international standards, rules, and practices for refugee protection. The Convention, which addresses the specific vulnerability of refugees and people seeking asylum, should be the foundation for refugee protection. Even though Taiwan is outside the UN system, any additional state support for the Convention will be a positive regional development. Despite global challenges of security, and economic downturns that have contributed to population displacement and human insecurity, there are opportunities that lie ahead. Japan and Taiwan do not operate in a vacuum; both can choose to lead the discourse on refugee protection in the Asia–Pacific that historically has seen low support for the Convention.

Looking at the experiences of Japan, ratification of the Convention is not enough. Without a wide base of public awareness and support, there is no meaningful refugee protection that aligns with the spirit of the Convention. Absence of a national law on asylum, as in the case of Taiwan, is detrimental to a transparent, predictable, and consistent channel for asylum determination. However, this too, is not enough. Japan has had the Immigration Control Act since 1982 as the administrative framework for the country's asylum process, but the legislation has not led to meaningful domestic protection of asylum seekers in Japan. The current act focuses on immigration control, and its limitations in protecting refugees are clear, so many human rights and refugee experts have highlighted a need for a separate asylum law focusing on the implementation of a fair asylum process by a specialised institution independent from immigration control (JAR, 2023). The establishment of an independent institution for refugee protection was called for by the opposition in early 2023, but this proposal was not included in the amended Immigration Control Act passed in June 2023 (Kyodo News, 2023).

Without a broad acceptance of the responsibility to take in refugees, refugee protection will continue to be externalised. This calls for a multitude of solutions to build and sustain public support for refugee protection, where gaps in law can be amended and realities can be reimagined to become ones based on respect for human dignity. A glimmer of hope outside of the Convention was when Indonesia released a Presidential Regulation in 2016, setting an operational framework on the treatment of asylum seekers, even though it is not a party to the Convention. With this regulation, asylum seekers in Indonesia are not treated under the immigration act that stipulates the arrest and detention of migrants without documents (Missbach et al., 2018). Limitations, however, are still seen in a lack of resources and political will to implement effective refugee protection under the regulation (Missbach et al., 2018). Jones (2014) examines another alternative for Southeast Asia, a "law of asylum" that guarantees "rights to individuals rather than refugees" by arguing that many of the civil and political rights guarantees in the

Convention are already provided by major international human rights treaties.

While criticisms of both approaches are valid—in that they, for example, present options for states to sidestep the Convention by moving to ad hoc systems—nevertheless, recent developments have illustrated that there is no straightforward path for international refugee protection, as seen in Western countries also backsliding on commitments to protect refugees in search of safety. A practical solution may be to look at soft law instruments, such as the 2018 Global Compact on Refugees and the Global Compact for Safe, Orderly and Regular Migration, to build up broad community support to offer real assistance to individuals seeking sanctuary. The problem, however, is that soft law instruments emphasise the role of state cooperation, without concrete legal commitments. They cannot completely fill the space of the international legal regime for refugee protection. At the same time, the reverse can also be said of the Convention. State ratification alone does not offer effective or meaningful protection if domestic laws render it inapplicable in reality—as in the case of Japan. In the case of Taiwan, it is unclear what the impact of Taiwan holding itself as a state party to the Convention would be if the island continued to operate without an established national mechanism for asylum determination.

There is no one-size-fits-all solution. It calls for us to use all the tools available to foster greater refugee protection, for a region of the world that sees very high displacement risks and no regional human rights treaty. In Japan and Taiwan, civil society has taken the lead in providing refugees with essential lifelines and assistance. In both countries, there is a small but increasingly visible group of migrants and refugees themselves speaking out for their own rights, leading to more meaningful and rights-based debates. Hope lies in this space of active and dedicated civic engagement. The collaborative advocacy of many national and international NGOs, community groups, bar associations, academics, and opposition lawmakers played a pivotal role in bringing significant public attention to the situations of refugees and asylum seekers in Japan during parliamentary debates on the amended Immigration Control Act in 2023. It is the longstanding and constant advocacy by Taiwan's civil society groups that has kept alive the dream for a national asylum law, while the country hopes to balance the duty to protect those fleeing from persecution with measures to ensure its political survival. In both Japan and

Taiwan, as it is in many countries, it is the strength of this civic engagement in democratic societies that sustains our hope for the future, of a more inclusive society where our Four Freedoms meet.

Acknowledgements The authors thank the book editors and the two anonymous reviewers for their constructive feedback on earlier versions of the manuscript. In addition, Bonny Ling is grateful to a former civil society representative who worked with refugees and asylum seekers in Taiwan for very helpful discussions that informed the parts of this chapter that focused on the situation in Taiwan.

References

Achen, C. H., & Wang, T. Y. (Eds.). (2017). *The Taiwan voter*. University of Michigan Press. https://doi.org/10.3998/mpub.9375036

Ager, A., & Strang, A. (2004). *Indicators of integration: Final report*. Queen Margaret University College, Edinburgh for Home Office Research, Development and Statistics Directorate. https://webarchive.nationalarchives.gov.uk/20110218141321/http://rds.homeoffice.gov.uk/rds/pdfs04/dpr28.pdf

Amnesty International. (2023, March 14). *Japan: 'Endless detention': Migrants speak out as government proposes harsh immigration bill*. https://www.amnesty.org/en/latest/news/2023/03/japan-endless-detention-migrants-speak-out-as-government-proposes-harsh-immigration-bill/

Cabinet Secretariat of Japan. (2008, December 16). *Dai Sangoku Teiju ni yoru Nanmin no Ukeire ni kansuru Pairotto Kesu no Jissi ni tsuite* [About the implementation of the pilot cases of refugee acceptance through third country resettlement programme]. https://www.cas.go.jp/jp/seisaku/nanmin/081216ryoukai.html

Chan, T. F. (2018, April 12). *NO ENTRY: How Japan's shockingly low refugee intake is shaped by the paradox of isolation, a demographic time bomb, and the fear of North Korea*. Business Insider. https://www.businessinsider.com/why-japan-accepts-so-few-refugees-2018-4?r=US&IR=T

Chang, W.-C. (2019). Taiwan's human rights implementation acts: A model for successful incorporation? In J. A. Cohen, W. P. Alford & C.-f. Lo (Eds.), *Taiwan and International Human Rights* (Economics, Law, and Institutions in Asia Pacific, pp. 227–247). Springer. https://doi.org/10.1007/978-981-13-0350-0_13

Chang, W.-C. (2001). From war refugees to immigrants: The case of the KMT Yunnanese Chinese in Northern Thailand. *International Migration Review, 35*(4), 1086–1105.

Chen, Y.-J. (2019). Isolated but not oblivious: Taiwan's acceptance of the two major human rights covenants. In J. A. Cohen, W. P. Alford, & C.-f. Lo (Eds.), *Taiwan and International Human Rights* (Economics, Law, and Institutions in Asia Pacific, pp. 207–225). Springer. https://doi.org/10.1007/978-981-13-0350-0_12

Cheung, H. (2019, March 17). Taiwan in time: The lost army's final retreat. *Taipei Times*. https://www.taipeitimes.com/News/feat/archives/2019/03/17/2003711637

Chiu, E.-L. (2018). Wheresoever I am, I am a human being: Refugees in Taiwan—Individuals and institutional policies. *Taiwan Human Rights Journal, 4*(4), 155–164.

Choi, W. G. (2019). Asian civil society and reconfiguration of refugee protection in Asia. *Human Rights Review, 2019*(20), 161–179.

Clymer, K. (2014). The United States and the Guomindang (KMT) forces in Burma, 1949–1954: A diplomatic disaster. *Chinese Historical Review, 21*(1), 24–44. https://doi.org/10.1179/1547402X14Z.00000000027

Dasgupta, A. (2022, April 11). Japan's approach to Ukrainian refugees is what its refugee policy ought to be. *The Diplomat*. https://thediplomat.com/2022/04/japans-approach-to-ukrainian-refugees-is-what-its-refugee-policy-ought-to-be/

Davidson, H. (2021, May 4). Chinese man seeking 'freedom and equality' says he travelled to Taiwan in dinghy. *The Guardian*. https://www.theguardian.com/world/2021/may/04/chinese-man-seeking-freedom-and-equality-says-he-travelled-to-taiwan-in-dinghy

Executive Yuan, Republic of China (Taiwan). (2022a, May 18). *National human rights action plan*. https://english.ey.gov.tw/News3/9E5540D592A5FECD/db879e12-f6bb-46d8-ba80-851185c963dd

Executive Yuan, Republic of China (Taiwan). (2022b, May 5). *Taiwan unveils first national human rights action plan*. https://english.ey.gov.tw/Page/61BF20C3E89B856/d4db0a5a-0a13-47fe-bd4c-bbab6af39405

Executive Yuan, Gender Equality Committee, Republic of China (Taiwan). (2023, May 31). *Waiji peiou yu dalu (han gangao) peiou renshu* [Number of foreign spouses and mainland (including Hong Kong and Macao) spouses]. Retrieved September 4, 2023, from https://www.gender.ey.gov.tw/GecDB/Stat_Statistics_DetailData.aspx?sn=lJvq%2BGDSYHCFfHU73DDedA%3D%3D

Flowers, P. R. (2008). Failure to protect refugees? Domestic institutions, international organizations, and civil society in Japan. *The Journal of Japanese Studies, 34*(2), 333–361.

Focus Taiwan. (2022, May 5). *Taiwan launches national human rights action plan*. https://ocacnews.net/article/309363

Goodwin-Gill, G. S. (1982). Entry and exclusion of refugees: The obligations of states and the protection function of the office of the United Nations High Commissioner for Refugees. *Michigan Journal of International Law, 3*(1), 291–337.

Hale, E. (2023, January 26). *Hong Kong activists unsure of future role in Taiwan*. VOA News. https://www.voanews.com/a/hong-kong-activists-unsure-of-future-role-in-taiwan/6934750.html

Havens, T. R. H. (1990). Japan's response to the Indochinese refugee crisis. *Southeast Asian Journal of Social Science, 18*(1), 166–181.

Human Rights Now (HRN). (2023, May 30). *HRN submits statement to Human Rights Council criticizing Japan's proposed Immigration Reform Bill for not protecting migrants, refugees, and asylum seekers*. https://hrn.or.jp/eng/news/2023/05/30/hrc53_statement_on_immigration_amendment_bill/

Immigration Services Agency of Japan (ISA) (n.d.a). *Waga Kuni ni Okeru Nanmin-higo no Jokyo-to* [Situations of refugee protection in our country]. https://www.moj.go.jp/isa/content/001393014.pdf

Immigration Services Agency of Japan (ISA) (n.d.b). *Ukuraina Hinanmin ni Kansuru Joho* [Information relating to Ukrainian evacuees]. Retrieved March26, 2023, from https://www.moj.go.jp/isa/publications/materials/01_00234.html

Immigration Services Agency of Japan (ISA) (n.d.c). *Nyukanho Kaiseian ni Tsuite* [About the amendment bill to the Immigration Control Act]. Retrieved June 3, 2023, from https://www.moj.go.jp/isa/laws/bill/05_00007.html

Immigration Services Agency of Japan (ISA) (2023, March). *Nanmin Gaitosei Handan no Tebiki* [Handbook on eligibility for refugee status]. https://www.moj.go.jp/isa/content/001393172.pdf

Ishikawa, E. (2021, September). *Nihon no Nanmin-joyaku Kamei kara 40 nen – Tsuminokosaretekita Kadai* [40 years since Japan's ratification of the Refugee Convention – Remaining challenges]. Kokusai Jinken Hiroba (No.156). https://www.hurights.or.jp/archives/newsletter/section4/2021/09/40.html

Itakura, K. (2022, August 26). *Japan's refugee system on trial: Treatment of Ukrainians belies refugee protection principles*. Nippon.com. https://www.nippon.com/en/in-depth/d00823/

Japan Association for Refugees (JAR). (2017, September 10). *Why Japan recognizes only a few refugees? Institutional challenges*. https://www.refugee.or.jp/en/reports/articles/2017/09/japan_recog17_en/

Japan Association for Refugees (JAR). (2023, March 7). *<Nanmin no Sokandehanaku Hogo wo> Nyukanho-Kaisei no Kakugi-Ketttei wo Ukete*. [<Protection

of refugee, not deportation> Response to the Cabinet's decision on amendment bill on immigration control]. https://www.refugee.or.jp/report/refugee/2023/03/imlaw23comment/

Japan Association for Refugees (JAR). (n.d.). *Refugees in Japan*. Retrieved March 15, 2023, from https://www.refugee.or.jp/en/refugee/

Jennings, R. (2020, September 17). *Hong Kong political refugees eye Taiwan, but are speedboats the solution?*. Voice of America. https://www.voanews.com/a/east-asia-pacific_voa-news-china_hong-kong-political-refugees-eye-taiwan-are-speedboats-solution/6195997.html

Jones, M. (2014). Moving beyond protection space: Developing a law of asylum in South–East Asia. In S. Kneebone, D. Stevens, & L. Baldassar (Eds.), *Refugee protection and the role of law: Conflicting identities* (pp. 251–270). Routledge. https://doi.org/10.4324/9780203488010

Kitakanto Iryo Sodan Kai (AMIGOS) (2022, March). *Ikiteikenai – Oitsumerareru Karihomensha, Karihomensha Seikatsu JIttai Chosa Hokoku*. [Unable to survive – Desperate "Karihomensha" on provisional release. Report on life situation survey with those on provisional release]. https://npo-amigos.org/wp/wp-content/uploads/2022/03/c6a8056cb5546ddc67f96ef542378eae.pdf

Kironska, K. (2022). Taiwan's road to an asylum law: Who, when, how, and why not yet? *Human Rights Review, 23*(2), 241–264. https://doi.org/10.1007/s12142-021-00644-y

Koike, K. (2011). *Nihon wa Kawattaka: Daisangoku Teiju Seido ni kansuru Ichi Kosatsu* [Has Japan changed? A consideration of Japan's resettlement programme]. *Nanmin Kenkyu Janaru* [Refugee Research Journal] (No. 1). https://refugeestudies.jp/wp/wp-content/uploads/2020/08/Has-Japan-Changed-A-Consideration-of-Japans-Resettlement-Programme.pdf

Kyodo News. (2023, June 9). *Japan Diet passes controversial bill to revise immigration law*. https://english.kyodonews.net/news/2023/06/2332cd3ad280-japan-diet-passes-controversial-bill-to-revise-immigration-law.html

Lai, J., & Wu, H. (2022, June 24). *Hong Kongers reflect on Taiwan, an imperfect exile*. AP News. https://apnews.com/article/politics-china-hong-kong-immigration-ba64836c313584752c30036dff03cc41

Legislative Yuan, Republic of China (Taiwan). (2016, March 2). *Related documents of Legislative Yuan bills. General council no. 1374; Committee proposal No. 18370*. https://ppg.ly.gov.tw/ppg/download/agenda1/02/pdf/09/01/03/LCEWA01_090103_00037.pdf

Missbach, A., Adiputera, Y., Prabandari, A., Cintika, G., Swastika F. Y., & Raditya Darningtyas, R., (2018). *Stalemate: Refugees in Indonesia—Presidential regulation No 125 of 2016*. Centre for Indonesian Law, Islam and Society. Policy Paper (No.14). https://law.unimelb.edu.au/__data/assets/file/0006/2777667/CILIS-Paper-14_Missbach-et-al_final.pdf

Ministry of Foreign Affairs of Japan (MOFA). (2023, April 3). *Daisangoku Teiju Nanmin Dai-13-jin ni taisuru Teiju Shien Puroguramu no Kaishi* [Start of the resettlement support for the 13th resettlement refugee group]. https://www.mofa.go.jp/mofaj/press/release/press4_009654.html

Ministry of Foreign Affairs of Japan (MOFA). (2016, September 16). *Refugees—Statement by Prime Minister Abe at the United Nations Summit for Refugees and Migrants*. https://www.mofa.go.jp/ic/ha_er/page1e_000101.html

Ministry of Foreign Affairs of Japan (MOFA). (n.d.). *Refugees*. https://www.mofa.go.jp/policy/refugee/japan.html

Ministry of Justice of Japan (MOJ). (2023, March 24). *Homudaijin Kakugigo Kishakaiken no Gaiyo* [Summary of the Justice Minister's press conference after the Cabinet meeting]. https://www.moj.go.jp/hisho/kouhou/hisho08_00399.html

Ministry of Justice of Japan (MOJ). (n.d.). *Application for refugee recognition subject to restriction on employment*. https://www.moj.go.jp/isa/content/930002329.pdf

Ministry of Foreign Affairs of the Republic of China (MOFA Taiwan). (2021). *International cooperation and development report 2020*. https://ws.mofa.gov.tw/Download.ashx?u=LzAwMS9VcGxvYWQvNDAzL3JlbGZpbGUvMjM2LzQxNS9hZTUyYTBkMS1hNjhmLTQzNzQtYmM2Yy0xNDEyNjRkNDVmNmUucGRm&n=MTEwMTAwNS0xMDnlubTluqblnIvlkIjloLHlkYroi7HmlofniYgt57ay6Lev54mILnBkZg%3d%3d

Morales, F. G., Gillett, M., & Ghanea, N. (2023, April 18). *Mandates of the Special Rapporteur on the human rights of migrants; the Working Group on Arbitrary Detention and the Special Rapporteur on freedom of religion or belief. Reference: OL JPN 1/2023*. https://spcommreports.ohchr.org/TMResultsBase/DownLoadPublicCommunicationFile?gId=27995

Musolff, A. (2011). Migration, media and "deliberate" metaphors. *metaphorik.de, 21*, 7–19. http://www.metaphorik.de/21/musolff.pdf

Nachman, L., & Hioe, B. (2019, October 23). Friends from Hong Kong: Taiwan's refugee problem. *The Diplomat*. https://thediplomat.com/2019/10/friends-from-hong-kong-taiwans-refugee-problem

Nikkei Asia. (2022, April 5). *Japan foreign minister brings back 20 Ukraine evacuees*. https://asia.nikkei.com/Politics/Ukraine-war/Japan-foreign-minister-brings-back-20-Ukraine-evacuees

Pan, M.-L. (2015). Neither compatriots nor refugees: Status discrimination of exiled Tibetans and the contradictory faces of the Republic of China (Taiwan). *International Journal of Asia Pacific Studies, 11*(2), 41–59.

Prentice, D. (2017, March 18). Taiwan's 'Little Burma': Huaxin Street in Taipei is home to many of Taiwan's 40,000 Burmese immigrants. *The Diplomat*. https://thediplomat.com/2017/03/taiwans-little-burma/

Qin, A. (2015, January 14). In remote Thai villages, legacy of China's lost army endures. *New York Times*. https://www.nytimes.com/2015/01/15/world/asia/in-remote-thailand-the-lost-soldiers-of-the-kuomintang.html

Shariatmadari, D. (2015, August 10). Swarms, floods and marauders: The toxic metaphors of the migration debate. *The Guardian*. https://www.theguardian.com/commentisfree/2015/aug/10/migration-debate-metaphors-swarms-floods-marauders-migrants

Taiwan Association for Human Rights (TAHR). (2002, October 25). *Urgent appeal by Chinese pro-democracy activists*. https://www.tahr.org.tw/news/117

Takizawa, S. (2015, December). Pilot refugee resettlement program: Japan experience. *FOCUS (Volume 82)*. Asia-Pacific Human Rights Information Centre (Hurights Osaka). https://www.hurights.or.jp/archives/focus/section3/2015/12/pilot-refugee-resettlement-program-japan-experience.html

Tamura, M. (2020, June 27). Asylum seekers in Japan face battle for survival in the time of coronavirus. *The Japan Times*. https://www.japantimes.co.jp/community/2020/06/27/issues/asylum-seekers-coronavirus/

Tethong, T. N. (2018). Tibet and Taiwan: Past history and future prospects. *Bimonthly Newsletter on the Current Situation of Mongolia and Tibet, 15*(4), 59–70. https://mtcc.moc.gov.tw/home/zh-tw/publication2/96757

Tokyo Shimbun. (2023, April 20). *Kyoryoku suru hito wa iruno? Nyukanho Kaiwaian no Shinseido "Kanrisochi" – Zairyushikaku no nai Gaikokujin wo Muhosyude "Kanshi"* [Are there people willing to cooperate? The new system in the amendment bill to the Immigration Control Act "monitoring measures" – "surveillance" of undocumented migrants without remuneration]. https://www.tokyo-np.co.jp/article/245098

Tsering, D. (2022a, November 16). *Tibetan diaspora in Taiwan: Who are they and why they are invisible (1)*. Taiwan Insight. https://taiwaninsight.org/2022/11/16/tibetan-diaspora-in-taiwan-who-are-they-and-why-they-are-invisible-1/

Tsering, D. (2022b, November 17). *Tibetan diaspora in Taiwan: Who are they and why they are invisible (2)*. Taiwan Insight. https://taiwaninsight.org/2022/11/17/tibetan-diaspora-in-taiwan-who-are-they-and-why-they-are-invisible-2/

United Nations. (2020). *Asia-Pacific migration report 2020*. https://www.unescap.org/sites/default/files/APMR2020_FullReport.pdf

UN Human Rights Council. (2020, September 25). *Opinions adopted by the Working Group on Arbitrary Detention at its eighty-eighth session, 24–28 August 2020*. Working Group on Arbitrary Detention. https://www.ohchr.org/sites/default/files/Documents/Issues/Detention/Opinions/Session88/A_HRC_WGAD_2020_58_Advance_Edited_Version.pdf

UN Refugee Agency (UNHCR). (2021, April 9). *UNHCR comments on the Bill for partial amendments to the Immigration Control and Refugee Recognition Act submitted to the 204th Diet session of year 2021 Based on the Recommendations of the Sub-Committee on Detention and Deportation (SCDD), 7th Immigration Control Policy Discussion Panel*. https://www.unhcr.org/jp/wp-content/uploads/sites/34/2021/04/20210409-UNHCR-Full-Comments-on-ICRRA-Bill-English.pdf

UN Refugee Agency (UNHCR). (2002, April 25). *Strengthening and expanding resettlement today: Dilemmas, challenges, and opportunities*. Global Consultations on International Protection 4th Meeting. https://www.unhcr.org/uk/protection/globalconsult/3cd15428a/strengthening-expanding-resettlement-today-dilemmas-challenges-opportunities.html

UN Refugee Agency (UNHCR). (n.d.a). *Donor profiles (Japan)*. Global Focus. Retrieved March 28, 2023, from https://reporting.unhcr.org/donor-profiles?donor=GJPN&year=2022

UN Refugee Agency (UNHCR). (n.d.b). *Donor ranking (2022)*. Global Focus. Retrieved March 28, 2023, from https://reporting.unhcr.org/donor-ranking?year=2022

UN Refugee Agency (UNHCR). (n.d.c). *Japan*. Global Focus. Retrieved March 28, 2023, from https://reporting.unhcr.org/donors-japan

United Daily News (udn.com). (2023, February 18). How to flee in the event of a Taiwan invasion? Okinawan residents will undertake evacuation drills; estimated up to 20,000 people can be evacuated each day. *The United Daily News* (udn.com). https://udn.com/news/story/6809/6979868?from=udn-catelistnews_ch2%201/4

Venturi, E. (2021, July 2). 70 years on, the Refugee Convention Still Struggles to Gain Traction in the Asia-Pacific. *The Diplomat*. https://thediplomat.com/2021/07/70-years-on-the-refugee-convention-still-struggles-to-gain-traction-in-the-asia-pacific/

Wilson, T. (2017, November 20). *UN urges Japan to resettle more refugees after taking just three in first half*. Reuters. https://www.reuters.com/article/us-japan-refugees-idUSKBN1DK0WW

CHAPTER 3

Examining Refugee Protection in Non-Signatories to the Refugee Convention and Protocol: Lessons Learned for the Taiwan Context

Christine Lin

Introduction

Taiwan, also known as the Republic of China (ROC), is not a member of the United Nations (UN) and cannot officially accede to the 1951 Convention on the Status of Refugees ("Convention") and the 1967 Protocol Relating to the Status of Refugees ("Protocol") due to its current status internationally. However, it is widely recognised that the concept of non-refoulement is a principle of customary international law that binds all states (Lauterpacht & Bethlehem, 2003, p. 149). Even though Taiwan is a non-signatory and does not have domestic refugee

C. Lin (✉)
Center for Gender and Refugee Studies, University of California College of the Law, San Francisco, CA, USA
e-mail: linc@uclawsf.edu

L. Momesso and P. Ivanova (eds.), *Refugees and Asylum Seekers in East Asia*, Palgrave Macmillan Studies on Human Rights in Asia,
https://doi.org/10.1007/978-981-97-2867-1_3

legislation, the government has an obligation under customary international law to ensure that non-citizens arriving on the island are not refouled to places where they could face persecution. Additionally, Taiwan has ratified the International Covenant on Civil and Political Rights (ICCPR) and the Convention on the Rights of the Child (CRC). While neither instrument directly refers to non-refoulement, Article 7 of the ICCPR and Article 37 of the CRC have been interpreted to prohibit the return of individuals to a country where they may be subject to torture or cruel, inhuman, or degrading treatment.[1]

Since Taiwan is not a UN member, it is unable to formally participate in the UN treaty body review process. Instead, Taiwan has created its own review process, which involves international experts, the Taiwanese government, and non-governmental organisations (NGOs) (Covenants Watch, n.d.; National Human Rights Commission, n.d.). During both the 2013 and 2017 review processes, the review committee recommended that Taiwan adopt a refugee act that includes the principle of non-refoulement (International Review Committee, 2017, p. 11). Drafts of the refugee act in Taiwan mention cooperation with the United Nations High Commissioner for Refugees (UNHCR) in refugee status determination (RSD) and refugee resettlement (Executive Yuan, 2016, pp. 358, 360; Legislative Yuan, 2016, June 1). While the enactment of a refugee legislation remains stalled, there are individuals seeking protection from persecution on the island who remain in limbo and could benefit from greater cooperation between the Taiwanese government and the UNHCR.

Critics have voiced concern that the UNHCR, which was created in 1950 to respond to the European refugee crisis in the aftermath of the Second World War, and the Convention are Eurocentric and not protective of the needs of individuals displaced from other continents (Hathaway, 1990, p. 132; Janmyr, 2021, pp. 192–193; Madokoro, 2022). For decades, the UNHCR has pushed for comprehensive regional approaches to handle displacement, including in Asia (UNHCR, 1994;

[1] The practice of refugee protection and adherence to non-refoulement principles varies amongst non-signatories to the Refugee Convention and Protocol. Some non-signatories have signed other international treaties with explicit non-refoulement provisions, such as Article 3 of the Convention against Torture and Other Cruel, Inhuman or Degrading Treatment or Punishment (CAT) and Article 16 of the International Convention for the Protection of All Persons from Enforced Disappearance, or complementary protection such as in the ICCPR and CRC.

Watkins, 2022, pp. 663–666). However, regional approaches have had mixed results with regard to responsibility-sharing and protection. In some instances, they have facilitated containment undermining the right of individuals to move freely and seek safety beyond regional borders (Watkins, 2022, p. 667). While regional mechanisms and frameworks have utility and are important, refugee protection remains a global responsibility (UNGA, 2016; United Nations, 2018). As such, the UNHCR, which has over 70 years' experience working in 137 countries, including in non-UN member states and non-signatories to the Refugee Convention and Protocol, is well-placed to work with the government of Taiwan to ensure that asylum seekers and refugees on the island receive protection (UNHCR, n.d.-b; n.d.-e).

This chapter examines the UNHCR's role in non-UN member states, as well as non-signatories in the Asia Pacific region, to draw lessons learned for the Taiwan context. It concludes with recommendations to both the Taiwanese government and the UNHCR to enhance cooperation and establish processes to increase protection for asylum seekers and refugees on the island.

Methodology

To better understand the gaps in protection for asylum seekers, the challenges in adopting a refugee act, and whether the UNHCR could play a role in Taiwan, I spoke with advocates in Taiwan working with asylum seekers and refugees or who have familiarity with the draft legislation. Comparing different drafts of the refugee act over the years provided context for its intended scope and helped highlight points of contention. A literature review of relevant sources also provided additional background.

The UNHCR has coordinated with other non-UN member states: Palestine, Puerto Rico, and Western Sahara. However, these non-member states differ contextually from Taiwan. Puerto Rico's asylum procedures are governed by the United States, which is a signatory to the 1967 Protocol and has a domestic framework for adjudicating asylum claims and refugee resettlement (USDOJ, n.d.; USCIS, n.d.). Whereas Palestine and Western Sahara tend to be refugee-producing, Taiwan is an area where people are seeking protection, and the UNHCR's roles in those contexts make it difficult to draw parallels for Taiwan. In Western Sahara, the UNHCR supports family visits between Sahrawis living in refugee camps in Algeria and individuals in the territory (UNHCR, 2014). With respect to Palestine, the UNHCR's role is limited because, in 1949, prior to the existence of the Refugee Convention, the UN General Assembly established the United Nations Relief and Works Agency for Palestine Refugees in the Near East (UNRWA) to provide humanitarian assistance and protection to refugees and displaced persons fleeing Palestine (UNRWA, n.d.). UNHCR is only mandated to protect Palestinian refugees who are outside of the UNRWA's area operations (UNHCR, 2017).

I also examined the context of Hong Kong. Although Hong Kong does not have its own seat in the UN, it differs from Taiwan and other non-UN members as it is a Special Administration Region of the People's Republic of China (PRC) and enjoys international recognition. Under Article 153 of the Basic Law (1997), the PRC government determines whether to extend its international obligations to Hong Kong; the Hong Kong government cannot decide to become a party to international instruments on its own. This chapter considers Hong Kong to be a non-signatory as the PRC has not extended the Refugee Convention and Protocol to Hong Kong (UNHCR, 2018, July). In Hong Kong, the UNHCR conducted RSD before the adoption of a domestic refugee framework and assisted the Hong Kong government in its transition to a Unified Screening Mechanism (USM) to consider non-refoulement claims under local law. To identify lessons learned for Taiwan, I interviewed academics and practitioners familiar with both the RSD and USM contexts and drew upon my own personal experience representing individuals in RSD claims before the UNHCR while serving as Legal Director of the Hong Kong Refugee Advice Centre[2] in 2009–2011.

Since there are a limited number of non-UN members receiving asylum seekers, I expanded the scope of comparative locales to include UN members who are non-signatories to the Refugee Convention and Protocol in the Asia Pacific where the UNHCR operates, including Bangladesh, India, Indonesia, Malaysia, Pakistan, Sri Lanka, and Thailand. I primarily consulted UN and secondary sources to research these contexts.

[2] In 2014, Hong Kong Refugee Advice Centre relaunched as Justice Centre Hong Kong.

Taiwan's Lack of Official Diplomatic Relationships and the UNHCR Mandate

The ROC, led by the Nationalist Kuomintang (KMT) Party, was one of the founding members of the UN and the Security Council in 1945 when it governed mainland China. During the civil war, the Chinese Communist Party (CCP) defeated the Nationalists and established the People's Republic of China (PRC) on the mainland. In 1949, the Nationalists re-established the ROC on the island of Taiwan and continued to hold the "China" seat in the UN until 1971 when, led by Albania, the UN General Assembly passed Resolution 2758, replacing the ROC with the PRC as the only lawful representative of China to the UN (UNGA, 1971; USDOS, n.d.). Although Taiwan has transitioned from Nationalist rule to a democratic system, the ROC Constitution still governs the island. As a non-UN member state, Taiwan has faced challenges in garnering UN and international support, and only has official diplomatic relationships with 12 UN member states and the Holy See (MOFA, n.d.).

Historically, the majority of UN members have opposed Taiwan's efforts to apply for UN membership because UN General Assembly Resolution 2758 recognises that the PRC is the only lawful representative of China to the UN (Worsnip, 2007). However, in 2021, United States Secretary of State Antony Blinken publicly urged other UN members to support Taiwan's participation, highlighting that "Taiwan's meaningful participation in the UN system is not a political issue, but a pragmatic one" to combat the numerous complex and global issues faced by the international community (Blinken, 2021). For example, although the international community could learn from Taiwan's "world-class" response to the Covid-19 pandemic, Taiwan was not at the World Health Assembly (Blinken, 2021).

The forced displacement of 89.3 million people worldwide, including 27.1 million refugees, 4.6 million asylum seekers, and 53.2 million internally displaced people, is another critical issue (UNHCR, 2022, p. 2). As the number of conflict-affected countries has doubled during the past decade, the cost to human, state, and international security is significant (UNHCR, 2022, p. 5).

While there are no publicly available statistics on refugees and asylum seekers in Taiwan, Hong Kong citizens began fleeing to Taiwan in 2019 in response to the PRC's extradition law; the number leaving increased in 2020 when the PRC imposed a national security law in Hong Kong

(Leong, 2022; Watt, 2020). From 2020 to April 2022, 28,219 Hong Kongers lived in Taiwan (Leong, 2022). However, it is unclear how many Hong Kongers fear return because of their political opinion or another of the Convention's protected grounds, but obtained residency on a different basis. There are also an estimated 1000–2000 Tibetans with residence visas or permanent residence in Taiwan, but there are no accurate statistics how many would have met the Convention definition of a refugee (Hale, 2023; Kironska, 2022). Additionally, individuals from the PRC and Xinjiang, as well as those from Afghanistan, Ukraine, Myanmar, Syria, Thailand, Turkey, Pakistan, and several African countries, have sought protection from persecution in Taiwan (Amnesty International, 2022). According to NGO representatives assisting asylum seekers, the reasons for fleeing their countries of origin generally involved fear of persecution due to political opinion, sexual orientation, or gender identity.

In the absence of a refugee law, Taiwan has provided asylum temporarily on an individualised, case-by-case basis that lacks a clear process. For example, in 2009, Lai Chien-chung, the former ambassador of Taiwan to Honduras, granted temporary political asylum to the daughter of ousted Honduran President Jose Manual Zelaya Rosales on humanitarian grounds and "based on the fact she was not directly involved in politics" (SB, 2009). However, to avoid a political standoff, the Taiwanese government denied asylum to his wife, the current Honduran President Xiomara Castro (SB, 2009).

Drafts of Taiwan's refugee act explicitly include cooperation with the UNHCR, whose mandate is "to lead and coordinate international action for the worldwide protection of refugees and the resolution of refugee problems" (Legislative Yuan, 2016, June 1; UNHCR, n.d.-c). However, the UNHCR has not had a presence in Taiwan even though there are asylum seekers on the island in need of protection. Historically, the UNHCR has supported other non-UN members, such as Palestine and Western Sahara, with refugee or returnee populations (UNHCR, 2002). Additionally, the UNHCR has partnered with other non-signatory governments to the Convention and Protocol to assist in refugee protection.

Disparate Treatment of Different Population Categories in Existing Domestic Legislation

Existing domestic legislation has special provisions for individuals who are from mainland China, Hong Kong, and Macau as well as certain stateless people including Tibetans and non-citizen nationals of the ROC who resided in Thailand, Myanmar, and Indonesia. People from other areas are considered foreigners. This has resulted in the disparate treatment of individuals depending on their place of origin and their ability to remain in Taiwan without being refouled to an area where they may face persecution.

The Ministry of the Interior (MOI) may grant long-term residency to individuals from mainland China on a case-by-case, special project approach out of political, economic, social, educational, science-tech, or cultural considerations (Mainland Relations Act, 2022, art. 17(4)). However, this provision does not apply to mainlanders who enter Taiwan without permission or stay beyond the duration authorised, which has resulted in the repatriation of mainland Chinese in need of protection (Chiu, 2018, p. 158). "Political" considerations include the immediate threat of being persecuted for one's noteworthy role in leading democracy movements, but this case-by-case, special project approach is not equivalent to a pathway or mechanism for seeking asylum or refuge in Taiwan (Mainland Rules, 2021, art. 18(1); Chiu, 2018, p. 158).

Residents of Hong Kong and Macau whose safety and liberty are immediately threatened for political reasons shall be provided necessary assistance (HK & Macau Laws, 2022, art. 18). The term "political reasons" is not defined in the legislation and regulations governing Hong Kongers and Macanese (Lin, 2018, p. 148). Such cases are referred to the Executive Yuan for "special handling" (HK & Macau Enforcement Rules, 2016, art. 25). However, certain categories of individuals may not be granted assistance, including those who enter Taiwan without permission, use a false identity or fraudulent documents, enter with permission, but overstay, or are believed to be involved in criminal acts (HK & Macau Residency Regulations, 2022, art. 22). In June 2020, in response to the CCP imposing a nationality security law in Hong Kong, the Taiwanese government launched the Hong Kong Humanitarian Aid Project to "provide needed assistance to Hong Kong citizens" and "to uphold universal values and support the Hong Kong people's fight for freedom and democracy" (MAC, 2020, p. 1). Due to the absence of a refugee law in Taiwan, certain Hong Kongers may apply for a "special project status" to study and work in Taiwan without a residence permit, but the mechanisms and standard for receiving this type of protection lack clarity (Leong, 2022).

Certain stateless individuals, including exiled Tibetans and descendants of KMT soldiers who were left behind on the Thai-Myanmar border in the 1960s, may apply for residency in Taiwan (Immigration Act, 2022, art. 16). In 2009, Article 16 of the Immigration Act, which governs this population, was amended to allow stateless individuals from India or Nepal, who entered Taiwan between 21 May 1995 and 31 December 2008, to apply for residency and to be issued Alien Resident Certificates—after the Mongolian and Tibetan Affairs Commission has confirmed their Tibetan identities (Loa, 2009). In 2016, this provision was further amended, extending the time period to cover those who entered before 29 June 2016 (Hsiao, 2016; Immigration Act, 2022, art. 16). Such amendments have received criticism for creating exceptions for different groups of people and a refugee act has been proposed as a more "reasonable solution" (Loa, 2009).

Non-citizens who do not fall into the categories above are considered foreigners. Although foreigners who enter Taiwan without permission or overstay their visit or residency could face deportation, the MOI's National Immigration Agency may temporarily suspend deportation on a case-by-case basis under certain conditions (Foreigners' Regulation, 2016, art. 6). However, there is no mention of non-refoulement or suspending deportation for foreigners who fear return to their countries of origin. In 2022, the MOI amended legislation allowing foreigners whose deportation order was suspended to be granted a provisional registration permit (Alien Residency Regulations, 2022, art. 24).

Legislative History of Taiwan's Draft Refugee Act

Since 2002, during the administration of Chen Shui-bian, the first president representing the Democratic Progressive Party, the Taiwanese government has recognised the need for a refugee act. However, over two decades later, Taiwan still has not passed any refugee legislation (Huang, 2010, p. 1). Earlier drafts of the refugee act explicitly included people from mainland China, Hong Kong, and Macau, noting that the mechanisms in Article 17(4) of the Mainland Relations Act, Article 19(3) of the Mainland Rules, Article 18 of the HK & Macau Laws, and Article

16(1)(12) of the Regulations Governing Permits for Hong Kong and Macau Residents Entering the Taiwan Area and Setting up Residence or Registered Permanent Residence do not provide for refugee status determination (Legislative Yuan, 2007, 2008). Recognising that the existing framework treated people from mainland China, Hong Kong, and Macau differently from foreigners and stateless people, these drafts also sought to equalise the periods of time to apply for residency, long-term residency, or citizenship with those of foreigners.

In 2009, the MOI submitted an amended refugee act to the Executive Yuan, who then submitted it to the Legislative Yuan for consideration. The 2009 draft eliminated people from mainland China and residents of Hong Kong or Macau from its applicable scope. Their inclusion was viewed as incompatible with the ROC Constitution and existing legislation, would be unlikely to reach societal consensus, and would potentially cause adverse impacts on cross-straits relations (Huang, 2010, pp. 54–56). Since then, the Executive Yuan has not included these three groups in subsequent versions of proposed legislation, suggesting that existing laws already govern people from those areas. Including these groups as foreigners would likely be controversial and could aggravate cross-strait relations (Huang, 2021).

The March 2016 draft of the refugee act proposed by Hsiao Bi-khim and other members of the Legislative Yuan included people from those areas (Hsiao, 2016). However, the Internal Administration Committee and Foreign and National Defense Committee rejected the inclusion, noting that the applicable laws governing mainland Chinese and residents of Hong Kong and Macau are the Mainland Relations Act and the Hong Kong & Macau Laws, respectively (Legislative Yuan, 2016, February 1, pp. 210–211, 217).

Article 3 of the Executive Yuan's, 2016 draft refugee act adopts the Convention definition of a refugee. This provides that foreigners or stateless people may apply for refugee status in Taiwan if they have left their country of citizenship or residence because of a well-founded fear of being persecuted for reasons of race, religion, nationality, membership of a particular social group, or political opinion, and are unable to avail themselves of protection from that country or are unwilling to return for reasons of such fear. The definition also includes individuals who have been forced to flee their homeland for reasons of war or large-scale natural disaster, and is more expansive than the Convention. Drafts from members of the Legislative Yuan proposed that the definition explicitly include gender, sexual orientation, and gender identity, but the Executive Yuan found it unnecessary to enumerate them as separate protected grounds because they fall under the particular social group ground (Legislative Yuan, 2016, February 1, p. 211). Article 4 of the Executive Yuan's, 2016 draft included provisions allowing foreigners and stateless individuals to apply for asylum from outside of Taiwan, at Taiwan's border, airports, or ports, prior to entering Taiwan, and after entering Taiwan (Executive Yuan, 2016, p. 358). Since 2016, there has been little movement or political will to pass the refugee act.

Based upon publicly available information from the MOI, interviews with NGOs involved with the drafting of the refugee act, and a review of the UNHCR's comments on national legislation on Refworld, it does not appear that the government of Taiwan has worked with the UNHCR during the drafting process (UNHCR, n.d.-a.). Former Deputy Foreign Minister at the Ministry of Foreign Affairs Wu Chih-hung confirmed that the Taiwanese government did not contact the UNHCR from 2008 to 2016, but it is unclear whether the Taiwanese government communicated with the UNHCR before or after that time period (Legislative Yuan, 2016, June 1, p. 197). The MOI report from 2010 mentions that the Taiwanese government would welcome assistance from the UNHCR in conducting RSD and receiving support for refugee resettlement in the event there is a mass influx of refugees in Taiwan (Executive Yuan, 2016, pp. 358, 360; Huang, 2010, pp. 19, 29, 57). All drafts of the refugee legislation in 2016 contemplated cooperation with the UNHCR, including Article 3 of the Executive Yuan's, 2016 draft which called for the MOI to request the UNHCR's assistance in conducting RSD in Taiwan (Executive Yuan, 2016, p. 358; Legislative Yuan, 2016, June 1).

Challenges for Asylum Seekers and Refugees in Taiwan

Taiwan's exclusion from UN membership and its lack of diplomatic relations with other governments is an obstacle to effective refugee protection. As a practical matter, it is challenging for Taiwan to assist individuals in third country resettlement whether they arrive after being recognised as a refugee by the UNHCR elsewhere, or are seeking protection from the Taiwanese government, which lacks a domestic RSD framework.

During joint deliberation meetings of the draft refugee act in 2016, several members of the Legislative Yuan raised the feasibility of requesting the UNHCR's assistance given that Taiwan is not a UN member state (Legislative Yuan, 2016, June 1, p. 187). When asked how the Taiwanese government could handle RSD applications if the UNHCR did not respond to the Taiwanese government's request for assistance, the former Minister of the Interior Yeh Jiunn-rong reaffirmed the necessity of seeking the UNHCR's assistance in processing RSD applications in Taiwan, believing it was possible for Taiwan to receive international assistance as refugee issues are universal human rights concerns (Legislative Yuan, 2016, June 1, p. 191).

In addition to the lack of a formal asylum adjudication process, individuals who find themselves in need of protection in Taiwan face barriers to obtaining work authorisation, accessing health care, and securing stable housing. Since most are not able to work, they rely on NGOs or churches to assist with basic needs. Without a residence permit, asylum seekers are not able to open bank accounts in Taiwan. For example, one Tibetan, who lived in Taiwan for over 20 years before being granted residency, worked without authorisation during that time but could only receive his salary via other people's accounts (Deng, 2016). Additionally, children born to asylum seeking or undocumented women in Taiwan frequently are not registered at birth and become de facto stateless as nationality in Taiwan is based on *jus sanguinis* rather than *jus soli* (Chen, 2022, p. 7). Without household registration, these children have limited access to education and health care. Additionally, according to local NGO representatives, language access is a challenge in Taiwan if the asylum seeker or refugee is unable to communicate in either Mandarin or English.

Observation and Lessons Learned from Hong Kong and Non-Signatory States

For decades, the UNHCR has operated in non-UN member and non-signatory states, often conducting RSD and facilitating refugee resettlement; its mandate allows this with the host's consent. In practice, the UNHCR's role in these areas varies significantly, signing a Memorandum of Understanding (MOU) with some, but not others; moreover, there is no standard approach to the MOUs (Janmyr, 2021, p. 40). Since Hong Kong has a lengthy history with the UNHCR and has developed its own system for non-refoulement protection, there are numerous lessons learned applicable to the Taiwan context. This section also examines the UNHCR's operations in Bangladesh, India, Indonesia, Malaysia,

Pakistan, Sri Lanka, and Thailand. While not an exhaustive review, it draws upon common themes to derive lessons learned for Taiwan.

Expanding the Refugee Act to Include All Populations

To avoid disparate treatment of different populations, a refugee act that is inclusive of mainlanders, Hong Kongers, and Macanese, as proposed in the drafts by the Legislative Yuan before 2009 and by Hsiao Bi-khim in 2016, would enhance protection. NGO representatives in Taiwan have voiced the importance of an inclusive refugee act covering all non-citizens rather than a special project approach. Currently, there are special projects for different populations, such as the Hong Kong Humanitarian Aid Project, but a refugee act that includes all non-citizens would provide greater transparency for accessing fear-based protection and to streamline existing protection mechanisms for all groups.

As including mainland Chinese, Hong Kongers, and Macanese in refugee legislation is controversial and politically sensitive, there may be alternate ways to frame who qualifies for protection. For example, Palestinian refugees have primarily been dealt with outside of the confines of the Convention (Mathew, p. 55). The UNRWA, which operates in Jordan, Lebanon, Syria, the Gaza Strip, and the West Bank, defines Palestinian refugees as "persons whose normal place of residence was Palestine during the period 1 June 1946 to 15 May 1948, and who lost both home and means of livelihood as a result of the 1948 conflict" (UNRWA, n.d.). Pursuant to Article 1(D), the Convention "shall not apply to persons who are at present receiving from organs or agencies of the United Nations other than the [UNHCR] protection or assistance". Therefore, the UNHCR does not have a mandate over Palestinian refugees within UNRWA's area of operations and is involved in conducting RSD in some non-signatory states receiving Palestinian refugees (UNHCR, 2017). However, defining protection needs by specific events would perpetuate the disparate treatment of different populations in Taiwan. It could also result in amending legislation based on political and other events that lead to displacement of these populations and could complicate the processes for protection.

Centralising RSD and Related Non-Refoulement Claims

A centralised and unified process for adjudicating asylum, non-refoulement, and related humanitarian claims results in greater efficiency and fewer disparities in adjudication. Hong Kong and India are two contexts where bifurcated processes have existed, with the UNHCR determining certain types of cases and the government others, showcasing the complexities cause by non-centralised and non-unified processes.

Between 1996 and 2014, the UNHCR conducted RSD in Hong Kong. The UNHCR and the Hong Kong government signed an MOU to allow Hong Kong immigration officials to be seconded to the UNHCR to increase RSD capacity. The Law Society of Hong Kong, Hong Kong Bar Association, and refugee rights advocates criticised the UNHCR's RSD process for numerous deficiencies, including problematic interview procedures, substandard interpretation, insufficient access to evidence or reasoning for negative RSD decisions, lack of an independent appeal mechanism, and limited legal representation (Lee et al., 2012). The Court of Final Appeal's judgements[3] recognising that high standards of fairness apply to torture claims, as well as an independent inquiry on persecution claims prior to removing an individual to their country of origin, prompted the government to adopt the USM (UNHCR Hong Kong, n.d.).

Before Hong Kong established the USM, the government adjudicated torture claims under the Convention Against Torture (CAT) while the UNHCR conducted RSD. The existence of these dual, but parallel paths for protection was "procedurally inefficient, unfair and prone to abuse" (Justice Centre, 2014, p. 7). In many instances, claimants made both refugee and CAT claims in tandem or subsequently lodged a separate claim after the failure of the first claim. This prolonged the processing time of applications, caused significant backlogs, and left claimants in limbo for many years. Since the UNHCR did not share the rationale of a negative RSD claim with the Hong Kong government and there was no process for the government to assess an individual's risk of persecution,

[3] *Sakthevel Prabakar v Secretary for Security* 2004 7 HKCFAR 187; *FB & Ors v Director of Immigration and Secretary for Security* (HCAL 51/2007); *Ubamaka Edward Wilson v Secretary for Security* (FACV 15/2011); and *C & Ors v Director of Immigration* (4HKC 563/2013).

that person could be refouled to a country where they faced persecution. Additionally, this dual system was not trauma-informed, as claimants who experienced past harm were forced to undergo two separate proceedings detailing what happened to different adjudicators. Interpreters were also necessary for both sets of proceedings. Recognising these inefficiencies, Hong Kong launched the USM system. Though the USM has been met with criticism for other reasons, legal professionals and experts in the field had recommended a unified system for considering non-refoulement claims (Daly, 2014).

In India, the government adjudicates refugee claims from neighbouring countries, such as Sri Lanka and Tibet, whereas the UNHCR conducts RSD for individuals from Myanmar and non-neighbouring countries. As the UNHCR is not allowed to set up registration centres in border areas, asylum seekers need to learn about the process and travel to New Delhi, where the only UNHCR office is located, to make a claim (Shanker & Vijayaraghavan, 2020, p. 24). Although the UNHCR provides recognised refugees with identity cards, not all state authorities in India recognise the UNHCR cards, whereas they accept identity documents provided to refugees by the Indian government (Shanker & Vijayaraghavan, 2020, p. 25). This leads to inadequate protection and insufficient access to health care, education, and other basic rights for refugees recognised by the UNHCR.

The contexts of Hong Kong and India demonstrate that using separate processes and laws for people from different areas may lead to disparate treatment amongst groups and can leave more room for protection pitfalls. As such, a cohesive system where one body performs RSD is not only more efficient but enhances refugee protection. It conserves resources, such as interpretation, legal representation, and adjudication, but also helps minimise re-traumatising individuals.

As discussed above, Taiwan has separate legislation for different groups of non-citizens. Although initial drafts of the refugee act included individuals from mainland China, Hong Kong, and Macau, they are omitted from the Executive Yuan's most recent draft in 2016. Excluding these groups could lead to complexities in the future, and the government would be wise to examine other contexts with disparate laws to better understand potential challenges and to contemplate the benefits of centralising RSD for all groups.

Access to Publicly Funded Legal Representation

Lack of access to legal services has been identified as a concerning gap in the implementation of the Hong Kong Humanitarian Aid Project in Taiwan, limiting awareness of the screening criteria and documentation necessary to establish individualised protection (Leong, 2022). Whether an individual is proceeding before the UNHCR or government-mandated RSD, access to publicly funded legal representation is critical to navigate the complexities of the legal processes in a foreign jurisdiction, often in a foreign language. The UNHCR recognises the right to legal representation, acknowledging its importance in establishing fairness and transparency in the RSD process, as well as strengthening decision-making (UNHCR, 2020, p. 64).

In Hong Kong, the Court of Final Appeal in *C & Ors* determined it was unfair and unlawful to: (1) refuse legal representation during screening interviews and oral hearings for torture claims, and (2) fail to provide publicly funded legal representation (Daly, 2014). This case, along with others,[4] clarified what constitutes high standards of fairness in assessing non-refoulement cases and the duties required by the Hong Kong government prior to removing an individual to their country of origin. Under the USM, applicants in theory have access to publicly funded legal assistance, but from 2014 to 2020, only 8% of legal aid applications were approved; the majority of claimants proceeded without counsel (Justice Centre, 2020). Moreover, there are two options for publicly funded legal assistance: (1) the Legal Assistance Scheme for Non-refoulement Claimants independently operated by the Duty Lawyer Service (DLS) or (2) a Pilot Scheme (PS) administered by the Hong Kong government's Security Bureau who selects and pays for lawyers representing applicants (DLS, n.d.; Melwani, 2021, p. e). Under the PS, there is a clear conflict of interest as lawyers are paid for by the same government bureau responsible for removing their clients (Melwani, 2021, p. 2).

The existence of publicly funded legal aid is not enough; it must be accessible and the criteria to receive representation through any such programme should not be so stringent that the majority of applicants end up proceeding without legal counsel. With the enactment of a refugee act in Taiwan, it is paramount that publicly funded legal representation be

[4] *Prabakar*; *FB & Ors*; and *Ubamaka*.

available to assist applicants with navigating the new procedures and to help them understand the types of evidence required to obtain protection in Taiwan.

Establishing an Appeals Process

When the UNHCR conducted RSD in Hong Kong, it did not initially provide written decisions and reasoning for negative RSD determinations, which hindered an applicant's ability to make a meaningful, independent appeal (Hong Kong Human Rights Commission Society, 2006, p. 3). Under the UNHCR's Procedural Standards (2020, p. 270), applicants have the right to appeal a negative RSD decision. The scope of appeal should also take into consideration any new information relevant to the claim, including any changes in the applicant's personal circumstances or in their country of origin. An independent appeal mechanism, which includes meaningful access to legal representation, is necessary to safeguard the protection of individuals who may be returned to persecution in their country of origin.

In Taiwan, any refugee legislation should include a clear process for appealing a case that includes publicly funded legal representation during the appeal. To ensure fairness in the appellate process, the applicant must be provided with a written decision detailing the reasons for the denial.

Designing Trauma-Informed, Context-Specific Training

Although Hong Kong transitioned to the USM, the UNHCR still continues to provide a consultative and supportive role to the Hong Kong government. Before the start of the USM in Hong Kong, the UNHCR conducted trainings for decisions-makers (Security Bureau, 2014, p. 7). The UNHCR has provided technical advice and capacity-building for officers and decision-makers involved in the USM and has given recommendations on screening procedures (UNHCR, 2018, Oct. para. 10). Additionally, the UNHCR has sought durable solutions for refugees.

In Hong Kong, a shortcoming identified was the poor quality of USM decisions, reflecting a low comprehension level of non-refoulement law by decision-makers, including key legal and factual concepts. Some decision-makers also displayed cynicism or hostility towards applicants and lacked gender-sensitivity, reducing sexual and gender-based violence to private matters and dismissing the possibility that they could constitute protected reasons for non-refoulement protection (Justice Centre, 2020). A lesson derived from the Hong Kong context is that regular, ongoing training in both substantive law and the practical considerations in interviewing asylum seekers is necessary for adjudicators, lawyers, and others working on such claims.

In Taiwan, robust, context-specific training regarding the intricacies of the legal requirements and applicable standards for a new domestic legal refugee framework would be critical. Opportunities for additional, issue-specific topics that arise along with ongoing trainings would be important to support a transition to a domestic refugee framework. Training on topics including trauma-informed representation and adjudication, gender-sensitivity, cultural-competency, and working with interpreters would be crucial to communicating with asylum seekers from different backgrounds. Such training should be tailored to the role the attendee is playing in the RSD process, e.g. decision-maker, legal representative, interpreter, social worker, etc. To share lessons learned and enhance collaboration amongst those involved in refugee protection within the Asia Pacific region, refugee advocates in Taiwan have suggested that the UNHCR could also consider convening regional training and invite relevant stakeholders from Taiwan who are involved in the RSD process.

Providing Identity Documents and Registering Births

A common theme emerging from the contexts examined is the importance of providing asylum seekers and refugees with a legal identity document in the country where the RSD process occurs. If the UNHCR issues an identity document to a recognised refugee, a MOU or other agreement with the local government to accept the document as a valid form of legal documentation is critical (Islam et al., 2021, p. 22). For example, the UNHCR in India conducts RSD, facilitates the resettlement of recognised refugees, and has the sole responsibility for granting refugee status certificates (UNHCR India, n.d.). However, the domestic law regarding these certificates and the rights associated with them are subject to the political will of the government and can hold little to no legal authority even though some courts have recognised the legal validity of these certificates (Kaul, 2021). In Malaysia, the government has criticised the UNHCR for independently issuing identity documents to asylum seekers or refugees registered with the agency without their input and approval (Peter, 2022).

Whether the UNHCR or the Taiwanese government conducts RSD in Taiwan, it is critical that any refugee certificate issued be a legally valid form of identity recognised throughout the country. Identity documents, including refugee certificates, are often the primary means to access basic rights, such as housing, health care, and education; they also facilitate the ability to attain banking and other services (Islam et al., 2021, pp. 15–19, 22). As children in Taiwan born to asylum seekers and undocumented mothers face challenges in accessing services, universal birth registration, allowing for the children of non-citizens to be registered, would help prevent issues of statelessness and legal limbo and effectuate access to education, social assistance, and health care (Islam et al., 2021, p. 21).

Allowing Employment Authorisation

In many situations of forced migration, individuals remain in limbo for years before a decision is made on their case. This process may be prolonged in the event of an appeal, a global pandemic, or another circumstance beyond an individual's control. The ability to obtain work authorisation and have meaningful access to employment opportunities in the country where the RSD claim is being processed is critical to achieving self-sufficiency. In the absence of employment authorisation, individuals are often forced to find work in the informal sector and may be more likely to experience exploitative working conditions (Islam et al., 2021, p. 34). Being able to work contributes to personal security, empowers displaced individuals to seek a livelihood, and enables them to contribute to the local economy.

Learning from the experiences described above, although Taiwan has not passed refugee legislation, the Employment Service Act allows for "a refugee who has been permitted to stay" in Taiwan to engage in certain types of work and exempts them from several conditions or requirements imposed on other foreigners (2018, art. 51(1)). Neither the Employment Service Act nor any other laws in Taiwan define or discuss the term "refugee" and there is no formal mechanism for refugees or asylum seekers to obtain employment authorisation (Yang, 2022). However, the Ministry of Labor (2021) has allowed stateless and non-citizen ROC nationals from Thailand or Myanmar who obtained residency under Article 16(3) of the Immigration Act to apply for a work permit with the Central Competent Authority without their employer initiating the process, under this provision. As employment authorisation for a refugee is explicitly contemplated in existing law, the Taiwanese government should clarify who qualifies as a refugee and establish clear processes to obtain such permission.

Accessing Social Services

Access to social services is also critical for asylum seekers. Many individuals have experienced trauma, in their countries of origin, en route to, and inside, the country of reception. Re-traumatisation also may occur during the RSD process. Having access to health care, including mental health services, is an important protection concern.

In addition to conducting RSD in Thailand, the UNHCR provides emergency and life-saving health care, legal and social counselling, and psycho-social support, as well as facilitating access to education, financial and other material support, and seeking durable solutions for vulnerable cases (UNHCR, 2022, December 31). In Sri Lanka, the UNHCR handles all forms of refugee protection in Sri Lanka, including RSD, refugee resettlement, connecting vulnerable refugees with legal resources on housing as well as land and property documents, and assisting with reintegration (UNHCR, n.d.-d).

In Taiwan, asylum seekers have had to rely on NGOs, churches, and others for food, housing, and other basic needs. Looking at the experiences in other countries, in implementing a domestic refugee framework, the Taiwanese government must also consider access to social services, including health care and psych-social support, as a holistic approach to refugee protection. Consulting with the UNHCR regarding its work to connect individuals to such services in Thailand and Sri Lanka could be beneficial.

Re-Thinking Durable Solutions

Asylum seekers and refugees worldwide often remain in limbo for years, without any ability to integrate locally, while waiting a protracted period for third country resettlement. Although host countries are often reluctant for local integration to be a permanent solution, in reality, many individuals are forced to remain in the host country for years and even decades while they await a durable solution. As such, opportunities for local integration, including access to language classes, employment opportunities, and pathways to residency, are important for Taiwan's domestic refugee framework. To combat xenophobia, anti-immigrant rhetoric, concerns about "losing" job opportunities to non-citizens, and perceived misconceptions about national security issues, public education campaigns to allay these fears are strategically necessary in Taiwan for citizens to provide a welcoming environment to asylum seekers and refugees (Amnesty International, n.d.).

Recommendations

After examining the contexts in other non-UN member and select non-signatory states described above and discussing with local refugee advocates in Taiwan what gaps in protection remain, the following recommendations are made to the government of Taiwan and the UNHCR:

To the Government of Taiwan

1. Contact the UNHCR to request consultation on the draft refugee act, determine the UNHCR's capacity to be involved in RSD and resettlement, and explore other potential collaborations to achieve refugee protection in Taiwan.
2. Pass a refugee act that includes an expansive definition of who qualifies for protection, which not only incorporates the Convention definition, but also includes those forced to leave because of war or large-scale natural disaster. Review the refugee definitions included in the Bangkok Principles, Organization of African Unity Convention, and the Cartagena Declaration, which enumerate additional circumstances for extending protection.
3. Include people from the mainland area, Hong Kong, and Macau in the refugee act for inclusive legislation that does not differentiate between different groups of people.
4. Develop clear procedures for RSD rather than an informal ad hoc system decided on a case-by-case basis.
5. Regularly train decision-makers on the correct legal standards and evidentiary considerations for adjudicating asylum claims, to effectuate consistent decisions. Include training on the impact of trauma and working with an interpreter as well as cultural and gender considerations.

6. Establish an independent appeal process for refugee claims.
7. Provide publicly funded legal aid to allow asylum seekers access to representation during first instance and on appeal.
8. Issue identity documents for asylum seekers and refugees to minimise hurdles to accessing housing, health care, and other services.
9. Allow work authorisation for asylum seekers and refugees under Article 51(1) of the Employment Service Act so that they can contribute to the local economy and become self-sufficient. The government has used this provision to allow stateless individuals from Thailand and Myanmar to work, showing that they have employed a broad definition of "refugee" in granting employment authorisation.
10. Extend universal access to health care to asylum seekers and refugees in Taiwan.
11. Increase language access to asylum seekers and refugees by providing interpretation during the asylum process as well as offer opportunities to learn the local language to enhance communication.

To the UNHCR

1. Be open to engaging with the government of Taiwan, local NGOs, and other organisations working with asylum seekers and refugees. This could include connecting the government of Taiwan with other regional and international organisations to provide support. The global protection of human beings who fear for their life transcends the politics of the UN and the "One China Policy".
2. Review, comment, and consult on Taiwan's draft refugee act and encourage its enactment.
3. In the absence of domestic refugee legislation in Taiwan, consider assisting with RSD in Taiwan with the intention to train and build local capacity to conduct RSD.
4. Be available as a resource to provide technical assistance and support, including verifying individuals who have undergone the RSD process in a third country, but find themselves in Taiwan.
5. Assist with resettling recognised refugees to third countries and facilitating connections to other countries that may not have diplomatic

relations with Taiwan to ensure that refugees receive appropriate protection.

6. Provide support for public education campaigns framing refugee narratives, including debunking myths related to national security risks and the displacement of locals from employment opportunities.
7. Convene regional trainings for decision-makers involved in the RSD process in the Asia Pacific region and invite decision-makers from Taiwan to participate.
8. Support Taiwan's transition to a domestic framework if refugee legislation is enacted and engage in capacity-building to train immigration officers and decision-makers.

Conclusion

The UNHCR's involvement in refugee protection in Hong Kong, as well as other non-signatories to the Convention, provides context for informing potential collaboration between the government of Taiwan and the UNHCR. Cooperation between the Taiwanese government and the UNHCR would help increase protection for individuals seeking asylum in Taiwan as well as facilitate resettlement for recognised refugees who find themselves in Taiwan. As proposed in the draft refugee act, the government of Taiwan has contemplated assistance from the UNHCR in RSD and resettlement. A first step for the Taiwanese government is to seek input from the UNHCR on Taiwan's draft refugee act and explore areas for potential coordination in protecting asylum seekers and refugees on the island. If the Taiwanese government approaches the UNHCR for assistance, as the lead refugee agency, the UNHCR would fall short of its mandate if it rejected the request, and asylum seekers and refugees on the island would fail to receive protection and could be refouled to places where they have a well-founded fear of persecution.

Acknowledgements My deep appreciation goes to the refugee rights advocates in Taiwan for taking the time to speak with me and provide critical contextual background: Wang Si, Deputy Secretary-General and Lai Yen-rong, Commissioner on Refugees at the Taiwan Association for Human Rights; Chiu Eeling, Executive Director, Amnesty International Taiwan; Lin Hsinyi, Executive Director, Taiwan Alliance to End the Death Penalty and Huang Yibee, CEO

Covenants Watch, both on the Board of the Human Rights Network for Tibet and Taiwan.

This chapter would not have been possible without the stellar research contributions in English and Mandarin of an individual to whom I am immensely grateful; you know who you are—thank you for all your incredible work. I appreciate Micah Lesch, Giulia Marchi, and Talia Harrow at the University of California, College of the Law, San Francisco, for their research support. I also appreciate everyone who spoke with me about the Hong Kong context.

References

Wān dìqū yǔ dàlù dìqū rénmín guānxì tiáolì [Act governing relations between the people of the Taiwan area and the mainland area (Mainland relations act)]. (2022). https://law.moj.gov.tw/ENG/LawClass/LawAll.aspx?pcode=Q0010001

Amnesty International. (n.d.). *Refugees, asylum seekers and migrants*. https://www.amnesty.org/en/what-we-do/refugees-asylum-seekers-and-migrants/

Amnesty International. (2021). *Taiwan: Submission to the International Review Committee on the domestic implementation of the ICCPR and the ICESCR*. https://www.amnesty.org/en/documents/asa38/3212/2020/en/

Amnesty International Taiwan. (2022, June 20). *Shìjiè nànmín rìjì zhě huì: Zài tái bìhù cùnbùnánxíng, jǐn sù xiūgǎi xiànxíng fǎguī* [World Refugee Day press conference: Asylum seekers are subjected to excessive restrictions in Taiwan, urging the government to amend the existing legislations as soon as possible]. https://www.amnesty.tw/node/12186

Asian-African Legal Consultative Organization. (1966). *Bangkok principles on status and treatment of refugees (Bangkok principles)*. https://www.refworld.org/docid/3de5f2d52.html

The basic law of the Hong Kong Special Administrative Region of the People Republic of China (Basic Law). (1997, July 1). https://www.basiclaw.gov.hk/en/basiclaw/basiclaw.html

Blinken, A. (2021, October 26). *Supporting Taiwan's participation in the UN system*. US Department of State. https://www.state.gov/supporting-taiwans-participation-in-the-un-system/

Cartagena declaration on refugees (Cartagena declaration). (1984, November 22). https://www.refworld.org/docid/3ae6b36ec.html

Chen, S. (2022). *Producing statelessness: How the predicament of migrant workers generates the existence of stateless children in Taiwan*. Humanity Research Consultancy. https://respect.international/wp-content/uploads/2022/11/Producing-Statelessness-How-the-Predicament-of-Migrant-Workers-Generates-the-Existence-of-Stateless-Children-in-Taiwan.pdf

Chiu, E. (2018). *Zuòwéi rénlèi, zài rènhé dìfāng: Táiwān de nànmín gè'àn jí xiāngguān jīzhì* [Wheresoever I am, I am a human being: Refugees in Taiwan—Individuals and institutional policies]. *Taiwan Human Rights Journal, 4*(4), 155–164. https://www.taiwanhrj.org/get/2018122310135178.pdf/3-3.pdf

Clutterbuck, M., Husseing, Y., Mansour, M., & Rispo, M. (2021, July). Alternative protection in Jordan and Lebanon: The role of legal aid. *Forced Migration Review, 67*, 52–56. https://www.fmreview.org/issue67/clutterbuck-hussein-mansour-rispo

Covenants Watch. (n.d.). *Treaty review process*. https://en.covenantswatch.org.tw/treaty-reviews/

Dàlù dìqū rénmín zài táiwān dìqū yī qīn jūliú chángqí jūliú huò dìngjū xǔkě bànfǎ [Rules governing permits for people from mainland China setting up dependent permanent residence]. (Mainland rules). (2021). https://law.moj.gov.tw/LawClass/LawAll.aspx?pcode=Q0060003&kw=大陸地區人民在臺灣地區依親居留長期居留或定居許可辦法

Daly, M. (2014, October). *Refugee and non-refoulement law in Hong Kong: The introduction of the unified screening mechanism*. Hong Kong Lawyer. https://www.hk-lawyer.org/content/refugee-and-non-refoulement-law-hong-kong-introduction-unified-screening-mechanism

Deng, S. (2016). Shénme? Táiwān yěyǒu xīzàng rén [What? there are Tibetans in Taiwan?]. *Humanistic Education Journal, 326*, 84–88.

Duty Lawyer Service (DLS). (n.d.). *Legal assistance scheme for non-refoulement claimants*. http://www.dutylawyer.org.hk/en/torture/torture.asp

Employment service act. (2018). https://law.moj.gov.tw/ENG/LawClass/LawAll.aspx?pcode=N0090001

Enforcement rules of the act governing relations with Hong Kong and Macau (HK & Macau enforcement rules). (2016). https://law.moj.gov.tw/ENG/LawClass/LawAll.aspx?pcode=Q0010004

Executive Yuan. (2016, February 17). *Lìfǎyuàn yì'àn guānxì wénshū yuàn zǒng dì yīsānqīsì hào, zhèngfǔ tí'àn dì yīwǔwǔsānjiǔ hào, zhōnghuá mínguó yī líng wǔ nián èr yuè shíqī rì yìnfā, ànyóu: Xíngzhèng yuàn hán qǐng shěnyì 'nànmín fǎ cǎo'àn'àn* [The draft bill of refugee act submitted to the Legislative Yuan. The Legislative Yuan General No. 1374, Initiative of the Government No. 15539]. https://lis.ly.gov.tw/lgcgi/lgmeetimage?cfc6cfcecfcec8ccc5cccacad2ccc9cd

Hale, E. (2023, January 26). *Hong Kong activists unsure of future role in Taiwan*. VOA. https://www.voanews.com/a/hong-kong-activists-unsure-of-future-role-in-taiwan/6934750.html

Hathaway, J. C. (1990). A reconsideration of the underlying premise of refugee law. *Harvard International Law Journal, 31*(1), 129–184.

Hong Kong Human Rights Commission Society for Community Organization Voices of the Rights of Asylum Seekers and Refugees. (2006, March). *Denial of refugee rights*. LC Paper No. CB(2)1291/05–06(05). https://www.legco.gov.hk/yr05-06/english/panels/ha/papers/ha0310cb2-1291-5e.pdf

Hsiao, A. (2016, November 2). New rules extend residency rights to more Tibetans. *Taipei Times*. https://www.taipeitimes.com/News/taiwan/archives/2016/11/02/2003658407

Hsiao, B. K., Lee, K. T., Chiu, Y. Y., Chen, O. P., Huang, K. S., Chung, K. P., & Lim, F. T. T. (2016, March 9). *The draft bill of refugee act submitted to the Legislative Yuan*. The Legislative Yuan General No. 1374, Initiative of the Government No. 18464. https://lis.ly.gov.tw/lgcgi/lgmeetimage?cfc6cfcecfcbc8cdc5cecec8d2cecdcb

Huang, C. (2010, June). *Nèizhèng bù rù chūguó jí yímín shǔ zìxíng yán jiù bàogào: Wǒguó nànmín fǎzhì dìng xiànkuàng* [Ministry of the Interior research project report: The progress of establishing the refugee rules in Taiwan]. https://www.immigration.gov.tw/media/6020/我國難民法制訂現況自行研究報告.pdf

Huang, J. (2021, December 21). *Taiwan's dilemma in accepting asylum-seekers from Hong Kong*. VOA News. https://projects.voanews.com/china-exodus/english/destination/taiwan.html

Human Rights Watch. (2022). *World report 2021: Jordan*. https://www.hrw.org/world-report/2021/country-chapters/jordan

Immigration act. (2016). https://law.moj.gov.tw/ENG/LawClass/LawAll.aspx?pcode=D0080132

International Review Committee. (2017, January 20). *Concluding observations and recommendations adopted by the International Review Committee*. Review of the second reports of the government of Taiwan on the implementation of the international human rights covenants. https://en.covenantswatch.org.tw/wp-content/uploads/2018/12/2017-ICCPR-ICESCR-CORs_EN.pdf

Islam, S., Hydari, Z., Schupfer, C., & Cole, K. (2021). *Undoing precarity*. Refugee Solidarity Network. https://refugeesolidaritynetwork.org/reports/undoing-precarity-elevating-positive-practices-for-refugee-protection-in-south-and-south-east-asia/

Janmyr, M. (2021, July). Non-signatory states and the international refugee regime. *Forced Migration Review, 67*, 39–42. https://www.fmreview.org/issue67/janmyr

Justice Centre Hong Kong. (2014, May 23). *Meeting the bare minimum: Hong Kong's new screening process for protection*. LC Paper No. CB(2)1621/13–14(07). https://www.legco.gov.hk/yr13-14/english/panels/se/papers/se0603cb2-1621-7-e.pdf

Justice Centre Hong Kong. (2020, November). *Submissions to the legislative council panel on constitutional affairs' meeting*. LC Paper No. CB(2)247/

20–21(01). https://www.legco.gov.hk/yr20-21/chinese/panels/ca/papers/ca20201116cb2-247-1-ec.pdf

Kaul, A. (2021, October 18). *Afghan refugees in India highlight the need for Indian domestic refugee law*. Just Security. https://www.justsecurity.org/78586/afghan-refugees-in-india-highlight-the-need-for-indian-domestic-refugee-law/

Kheshen, N. (2022, December 8). *Lebanon's refugee and asylum legal framework*. The Tahrir Institute for Middle East Policy. https://timep.org/2022/12/08/lebanons-refugee-and-asylum-legal-framework/

Kironska, K. (2022). Taiwan's road to an asylum law: Who, when, how, and why not yet? *Human Rights Review, 23*, 241–251.

Lauterpacht, E., & Bethlehem, D. (2003). The scope and content of the principle of non-refoulement: Opinion. In E. Feller, V. Türk, & F. Nicholson (Eds.), *Refugee protection in international law: Global consultations on international protection* (pp. 87–177). Cambridge University Press. https://doi.org/10.1017/CBO9780511493973.008

Lee, L. I., Nam, N. W., Man, W. N., Wang, Y. C., & Chung, Y. W. (2012). *Studies on protections of non-refoulement claimants in Hong Kong: Should Hong Kong adopt a single, government-lead, unified system to process torture claims, refugee claims, and CIDTP Claims?* LC Paper No. CB(2)1669/12–13(05). https://www.legco.gov.hk/yr12-13/english/panels/se/papers/se0702cb2-1669-5-e.pdf

Legislative Yuan. (2007, February 28). *Lìfǎyuàn yì'àn guānxì wénshū yuàn zǒng dì yīsānqīsì hào, zhèngfǔ tí'àn dì yī líng qībājiǔ hào, zhōnghuá mínguó jiǔshíliù nián èr yuè èrshíbā rì yìnfā, ànyóu: Xíngzhèng yuàn hán qǐng shěnyì 'nànmín fǎ cǎo'àn'àn* [The draft bill of refugee act submitted to the Legislative Yuan. The Legislative Yuan General No. 1374, Initiative of the Government No. 10789]. https://lis.ly.gov.tw/lgcgi/lgmeetimage?cfc9cfcacfcdc8cdc5c7ced2c7c7

Legislative Yuan. (2008, February 27). *Lìfǎyuàn yì'àn guānxì wénshū yuàn zǒng dì yīsānqīsì hào, zhèngfǔ tí'àn dì yīyīyīwǔbā hào, zhōnghuá mínguó jiǔshíqī nián èr yuè èrshíqī rì yìnfā, ànyóu: Xíngzhèng yuàn hán qǐng shěnyì 'nànmín fǎ cǎo'àn'àn* [The draft bill of refugee act submitted to the Legislative Yuan. The Legislative Yuan General No. 1374, Initiative of the Government No. 11158]. https://lis.ly.gov.tw/lgcgi/lgmeetimage?cfc8cfcecfcdc8cac5cecfcacad2cecfc9cb

Legislative Yuan. (2016, February 1). *Lìfǎyuàn yì'àn guānxì wén shū, yuàn zǒng dì 1374 hào zhèngfǔ/wěiyuán tí'àn dì 15539, 18370, 18464 jí 18528 hào* [Legislative Yuan motion brief. Legislative Yuan No. 1374, Executive Yuan/members initiatives No. 15539, 18370, 18464 & 18528. The second session of the ninth Legislative Yuan]. https://lis.ly.gov.tw/lygazettec/mtcdoc?PD090207:LCEWA01_090207_00150

Legislative Yuan. (2016, June 1). *Lìfǎyuàn gōngbào dì yībǎi líng wǔ juǎn dì sìshíwǔ qī wěiyuánhuì jìlù* [Minutes of the first joint deliberation meeting of the draft bill of the refugee act by the committees of Internal Administration and Foreign and National Defense, the first session of the ninth Legislative Yuan]. *The Legislative Yuan Gazette, 105*(45), 173–230.

Leong, K. (2022, June 16). Zài táiwān, chéngwéi yīgè bèi bìhù zhě zhī nán kàn dédào nán ná dào de 'zhuān'àn shēnfèn'—shàng qiān xiānggǎng xúnqiú bìhù zhě tōng bùguò de liǎng dào zhǎi mén [In Taiwan, the difficulty of being an asylee: the hard-to-obtain "special project status"—Two hurdles that obstructed thousands of Hong Kong asylum seekers]. *The Reporter*. https://www.twreporter.org/a/hong-kong-taiwan-asylum

Lin, K. (2018). *Wǒguó nànmín fǎ zhī yánjiū* [A study on the legislation of refugee law in Taiwan]. Master's thesis. National Taiwan University. https://doi.org/10.6342/NTU201804316

Loa, L. (2009, January 9). Tibetans to be granted residency. *Taipei Times*. https://www.taipeitimes.com/News/taiwan/archives/2009/01/09/2003433279

Madokoro, L. (2022). Eurocentrism and the international refugee regime. *Journal of Modern European History, 20*(1), 34–39. https://doi.org/10.1177/16118944221077423

Mainland Affairs Council (MAC). (2020, June 18). *Public information on the Hong Kong humanitarian aid project*. https://ws.mac.gov.tw/001/Upload/297/relfile/8012/75961/2bccf36c-71a9-427c-a66d-e6c0dba51015.pdf

Laws and regulations regarding Hong Kong & Macao affairs (HK & Macau laws). (2022). https://law.moj.gov.tw/ENG/LawClass/LawAll.aspx?pcode=Q0010003

Mathews, P., & Harley, T. (2016). *Refugees, regionalism and responsibility*. Edward Elgar Publishing. https://doi.org/10.4337/9781782547297

Melwani, R. (2021, February 24). *David versus Goliath: Addressing institutional challenges in the implementation of non-refoulement policy in Hong Kong*. LC Paper No. CB(2)823/20–21(01). https://www.legco.gov.hk/yr20-21/english/bc/bc53/papers/bc53cb2-823-1-e.pdf

Ministry of Foreign Affairs Republic of China (Taiwan) (MOFA). (n.d.). *Diplomatic allies*. https://en.mofa.gov.tw/AlliesIndex.aspx?n=1294&sms=1007

Ministry of Labor. (2021, September 30). *Qǔdé rù chūguó jí yímín fǎ dì 16 tiáo dì 3 xiàng guīdìng shēnfèn zhī tài miǎn dìqū qiáomín, dé yī jiùyè fúwù fǎ dì 51 tiáo guīdìng shēnqǐng qǔdé gōngzuò xǔkě*. [For stateless people and non-citizen ROC nationals from Thailand or Myanmar who obtained residency under Article 16(3) of the Immigration Act, they are required to obtain work permit under Article 51 of the Employment Service Act]. https://www.mol.gov.tw/1607/1632/1640/17166/

Missbach, A., Adiputera, Y., Prabandar, A., Cintika, G., Swastika, F. Y., & Darningtyas, R. (2018). *Stalemate: Refugees in Indonesia—Presidential regulation No 125 of 2016*. Centre for Indonesian Law, Islam and Society. https://law.unimelb.edu.au/__data/assets/file/0006/2777667/CILIS-Paper-14_Missbach-et-al_final.pdf

National Human Rights Commission, Taiwan. (n.d.). *The implementation of human rights conventions*. https://nhrc.cy.gov.tw/en-US/monitor/implementation

Organization of African Unity convention governing the specific aspects of refugee problems in Africa (OAU convention). (1974, June 20). http://www.unhcr.org/45dc1a682.html

Peter, S. (2022, November 1). *Malaysia mulls closing UN Refugee Agency Office, sparking refoulement fears*. VOA News. https://www.voanews.com/a/malaysia-mulls-closing-un-refugee-agency-office-sparking-refoulement-fears-/6814184.html

Regulations governing forcible deportation of foreigners. (2016). https://law.moj.gov.tw/ENG/LawClass/LawAll.aspx?pcode=D0080194

Regulations governing permits for Hong Kong and Macao residents entering the Taiwan area and setting up residence or registered permanent residence (HK and Macau residency regulations). (2022, June 13). https://law.moj.gov.tw/LawClass/LawAll.aspx?PCode=Q0020008

Regulations governing visiting, residency, and permanent residency of aliens (Alien residency regulations). (2022). https://law.moj.gov.tw/ENG/LawClass/LawAll.aspx?pcode=D0080129

Rungthong, W., & Stover, C. (2020, January 20). *Thailand's national screening mechanism: Key issues*. OpinioJuris. http://opiniojuris.org/2020/01/28/thailands-national-screening-mechanism-key-issues/

SB. (2009, September 30). Deposed Honduran leader's daughter granted asylum. *Taiwan Today*. https://taiwantoday.tw/news.php?unit=2&post=604

Security Bureau. (2014, May). *Panel on security of the legislative council—Implementation of the unified screening mechanism*. LC Paper No. CB(2)1621/13–14(06). https://www.legco.gov.hk/yr13-14/english/panels/se/papers/se0603cb2-1621-6-e.pdf

Shanker, R., & Vijayaraghavan, H. (2020, November). Refugee recognition challenges in India. *Forced Migration Review, 65*, 24–26. https://www.fmreview.org/recognising-refugees/shanker-vijayaraghavan

Teng, H. (2016). Táiwān yěyǒu xīzàng rén [What? There are Tibetans in Taiwan?]. *Humanistic Education Journal, 326*, 84–88.

United Nations. (2018). *Global compact on refugees*. https://www.unhcr.org/5c658aed4

United Nations General Assembly (UNGA). (1971, October 25). *Resolution 2758, Restoration of the lawful rights of the People's Republic of China in the United Nations*. https://digitallibrary.un.org/record/192054?ln=en

United Nations General Assembly (UNGA). (2016, October 3). *Resolution 71/1, New York declaration for refugees and migrants*. https://www.un.org/en/development/desa/population/migration/generalassembly/docs/globalcompact/A_RES_71_1.pdf

United Nations High Commissioner for Refugees (UNHCR). (n.d.-a). *Comments on national legislation*. Refworld. https://www.refworld.org/cgi-bin/texis/vtx/rwmain?page=type&skip=0&type=NATLEGCOMMENTS

United Nations High Commissioner for Refugees (UNHCR). (n.d.-b). *History of UNHCR*. https://www.unhcr.org/en-us/history-of-unhcr.html

United Nations High Commissioner for Refugees (UNHCR). (n.d.-c). *Mission statement*. https://refugeesolidaritynetwork.org/reports/undoing-precarity-elevating-positive-practices-for-refugee-protection-in-south-and-south-east-asia/

United Nations High Commissioner for Refugees (UNHCR). (n.d.-d). *Sri Lanka*. https://www.unhcr.org/en-us/sri-lanka.html

United Nations High Commissioner for Refugees (UNHCR). (n.d.-e). *Where we work*. https://www.unhcr.org/en-us/where-we-work.html

United Nations High Commissioner for Refugees (UNHCR). (1994, May 3). *Comprehensive and regional approaches to refugee programs*. EC/1994/SCP/CRP.3. https://www.unhcr.org/en-us/excom/scip/3ae68cc80/comprehensive-regional-approaches-refugee-problems.html#:~:text=UNHCR's%20interest%20in%20comprehensive%20regional,in%20promoting%20and%20implementing%20measures

United Nations High Commissioner for Refugees (UNHCR). (2002, September 1). *Country operations plan 2003—Western Sahara*. https://www.refworld.org/docid/3d941f567.html

United Nations High Commissioner for Refugees (UNHCR). (2004). *Country operations plan: Lebanon*. https://www.unhcr.org/3fd9c6a14.pdf

United Nations High Commissioner for Refugees (UNHCR). (2013, March). *Submission by the United Nations High Commissioner for Refugees for the office of the High Commissioner for Human Rights' compilation report—Universal periodic review: Jordan*. https://www.refworld.org/pdfid/513d90172.pdf

United Nations High Commissioner for Refugees (UNHCR). (2014, August). *Western Sahara fact sheet*. https://www.unhcr.org/media/western-sahara-territory-fact-sheet

United Nations High Commissioner for Refugees (UNHCR). (2017, December). *Guidelines on international protection No. 13: Applicability of Article 1D of the 1951 Convention relating to the status of refugees to Palestinian refugees*. https://www.refworld.org/docid/5a1836804.html

United Nations High Commissioner for Refugees (UNHCR). (2018, July). *Submission by the United Nations High Commissioner for Refugees for the office of the High Commissioner for Human Rights' compilation report universal periodic review: People' Republic of China and the Special Administrative Regions of Hong Kong and Macao.* https://www.refworld.org/docid/5b56ffde9.htm

United Nations High Commissioner for Refugees (UNHCR). (2018, October 4). *Submission of United Nations High Commissioner for Refugees.* LC Paper No. CB(2)38/18–19(13). https://www.legco.gov.hk/yr16-17/english/hc/sub_com/hs54/papers/hs5420181018cb2-38-13-e.pdf

United Nations High Commissioner for Refugees (UNHCR). (2020). *Procedural standards for refugee status determination under UNHCR's mandate.* https://www.unhcr.org/4317223c9.pdf

United Nations High Commissioner for Refugees (UNHCR). (2022, June 16). *Global trends: Forced displacement in 2021.* https://www.unhcr.org/62a9d1494/global-trends-report-2021

United Nations High Commissioner for Refugees (UNHCR). (2022, December 21). *Fact sheet: Thailand.* https://www.unhcr.org/th/wp-content/uploads/sites/91/2023/01/MCO-Thailand_31-December-2022.pdf

United Nations High Commissioner for Refugees (UNHCR) Lebanon. (n.d.). *Refugees and asylum-seekers.* https://www.unhcr.org/lb/refugees-and-asylum-seekers

United Nations High Commissioner for Refugees (UNHCR) Hong Kong. (n.d.). *Timeline of HK office.* https://www.unhcr.org/hk/en/596-timeline-2.html

United Nations High Commissioner for Refugees (UNHCR) Malaysia. (n.d.-a). *Goal 2: Legal and policy framework for refugees and stateless people in Malaysia.* https://www.unhcr.org/en-us/goal-2-legal-and-policy-framework-for-refugees-and-stateless-people-in.html

United Nations High Commissioner for Refugees (UNHCR) Malaysia. (n.d.-b). *What we do in Malaysia.* https://www.unhcr.org/en-my/what-we-do-in-malaysia.html

United Nations High Commissioner for Refugees (UNHCR) Pakistan. (n.d.). *UNHCR in Pakistan.* https://www.unhcr.org/pk/unhcr-in-pakistan

United Nations Relief and Works Agency for Palestine Refugees in the Near East (UNRWA). (n.d.). *Palestine Refugees.* https://www.unrwa.org/palestine-refugees

United States Citizenship and Immigration Services (USCIS). (n.d.). *USCIS service and office locator—Puerto Rico.* https://egov.uscis.gov/office-locator/#/asyresults/PR/Puerto%20Rico

United States Department of Justice, Executive Office for Immigration Review (USDOJ). (n.d.). *Guaynabo (San Juan) immigration court.* https://www.justice.gov/eoir/guaynabo-puerto-rico-immigration-court#about

United States Department of State, Office of the Historian (USDOS). (n.d.). *Foreign relations of the United States, 1969–1976, volume XVII, China, 1969–1972*. https://history.state.gov/historicaldocuments/frus1969-76v17/d167

Vidal, M. (2022, July 3). *Jordan's 'other' refugees stuck in limbo with frozen asylum claims*. Middle East Eye. https://www.middleeasteye.net/news/jordan-other-refugees-limbo-frozen-asylum-claims

Wang, Y. (2021, June 23). *Huódòng cèjì] jiǔqiān lǐ lù nànmín jiǎngzuò—nànmín hé tōudù kè de yīxiàn zhī gé*. [Refugee talk—The thin line between refugees and illegal immigrants]. Taiwan Association for Human Rights. https://www.tahr.org.tw/news/2980

Watkins, J. (2022). Regions, containment, and justice in the international refugee regime. *ACME: An International Journal for Critical Geographies, 21*(6), 658–676. https://acme-journal.org/index.php/acme/article/view/2133

Watt, L. (2020, June 24). Hong Kong protesters flee to Taiwan to continue China resistance. *The Guardian*. https://www.theguardian.com/world/2020/jun/25/hong-kong-protesters-flee-to-taiwan-to-continue-china-resistance

Worsnip, P. (2007, September 18). *Ban says Taiwan's U.N. bid legally impossible*. Reuters. https://www.reuters.com/article/us-taiwan-un/ban-says-taiwans-u-n-bid-legally-impossible-idUSN1843007620070918

Yang, C. (2021, May 21). *Wèishéme lái, wǎng nǎlǐ qù —lái tái cáng rén de lísàn zújì yǔ xuǎnzé*. [Why did they come and where should they go: discrete Tibetans]. The Reporter. https://www.twreporter.org/a/exiled-tibetan-in-taiwan

Yang, C. (2022, June 1). *Míntuán zài shìjiè nànmín rì hūyù bǎozhàng zài tái xúnqiú bìhù zhě gōngzuò quán*. [Civil groups call for protection of the right to work for asylum seekers in Taiwan at the World Refugee Day]. CivilMedia@TW. https://www.civilmedia.tw/archives/111965

Zieck, M. (2008, April 30). The legal status of Afghan refugees in Pakistan, a story of eight agreements and two suppressed premises. *International Journal of Refugee Law, 20*(2), 253–272. https://doi.org/10.1093/ijrl/een014

CHAPTER 4

The Legal Framework for Refugee Acceptance and Protection in Japan

Yingjiao Zhu

Introduction

Being one of the biggest donors to the United Nations High Commissioner for Refugees (henceforth, UNHCR) over the years, Japan is considered to have made significant financial contribution to supporting refugees, despite accepting very few refugees to its territory as a host country (Betts & Collier, 2017, p. 208). Nevertheless, the exceptionally low refugee recognition rates in Japan have been criticised for not conforming to international norms of refugee protection (Wolman, 2015), and its restrictive immigration and refugee policies, based on nationalism and ethnic discrimination against foreign nationals, can be linked to many incidents in the immigration administration, such as long-term detention of asylum seekers, hunger strikes, the death of immigration detainees, and the suicide of international students (Onozuka, 2022, pp. 255–256).

Y. Zhu (✉)
Yamaguchi University, Yamaguchi, Japan
e-mail: zhuyinjiao888@icloud.com

L. Momesso and P. Ivanova (eds.), *Refugees and Asylum Seekers in East Asia*, Palgrave Macmillan Studies on Human Rights in Asia,
https://doi.org/10.1007/978-981-97-2867-1_4

Although Japan has acceded to the 1951 Convention Relating to the Status of Refugees and its 1967 Protocol, the Japanese government has not regarded refugee protection as an important human rights issue until recently. The domestic law regulating the entry and residence of immigrants and refugees in Japan, namely the Immigration Control and Refugee Recognition Act (henceforth, ICRRA), provides a strict legal procedure for asylum seekers to obtain refugee status under a narrow interpretation of the definition of refugee. As a result, the law and its implementation have brought about an extremely low refugee acceptance as well as other problems in Japan's refugee recognition process. Additionally, a lack of safeguard for asylum seekers from the judicial system can also be counted as a reason for Japan's inadequate contribution to refugee acceptance and protection within its territory. As the Japanese Supreme Court and inferior courts following the precedent set by the Supreme Court have wrongly ruled on the constitutional guarantees of foreigners' fundamental human rights,[1] the judicial system helps to justify governmental negativism about necessary accommodations for refugees and asylum seekers.

This chapter firstly analyses human rights violations or possible violations in the Japanese refugee recognition procedure, through an examination of ICRRA's existing provisions relating to refugee applications, and explains the legal basis for Japan's negative immigration and refugee policies, especially the judgment and reasoning of the Supreme Court in McLean v. Minister of Justice (henceforth, McLean Case), which should be deemed highly outdated in light of the development of international human rights law. This chapter will then explore recent efforts and progress in Japan's legislation and judicial practice, including two government proposals for revising ICRRA in 2021 and 2023, and a remarkable judicial decision made by Tokyo High Court in September 2021. It can be argued, however, that these recent developments do not drastically improve the situation of refugee acceptance and protection in Japan because some of them are not essentially aimed at providing better safeguard to asylum seekers. Finally, based on the above findings, this chapter will conclude with a brief evaluation of the amendments to

[1] For example, Tokuji Izumi, former justice of the Japanese Supreme Court, has strongly criticised the Court's reasoning in the McLean Case and other lower-court decisions citing this case, for making a huge mistake in the protection of foreigners' rights in compliance with the Japanese Constitution (*See* Izumi, 2021).

ICRRA which were eventually enacted in June 2023, in order to highlight the remaining tasks and challenges for Japan to help it construct a more inclusive immigration and refugee system.

Current Refugee Recognition Procedure and Human Rights Concerns Under ICRRA

After Japan's accession to the Refugee Convention and the related Protocol, the former Immigration Control Order was amended to allow accommodation for refugees and was renamed as ICRRA in 1982 (Buschmann, 2021, p. 81). The current version of ICRRA, which has undergone two main revisions, in 1990 and 2018, stipulates the competence of the Minister of Justice to grant refugee status and the basic structure of the refugee recognition procedure in Chapter 7.2 (from art. 61-2 to art. 61-2-14).[2]

In accordance with the provisions of ICRRA, asylum seekers need to go through a hard and lengthy application for refugee recognition to acquire the refugee status and a long-term resident visa in Japan. Specifically, those who seek refugee recognition must make an application to the Minister of Justice (art. 61-2) and submit documents or materials to prove that they are refugees at the time of application. The Minister of Justice will determine whether or not to grant refugee status based on the facts in the submitted documents and materials. If necessary, an investigation of the facts may be conducted by a refugee investigator at the request of the Minister of Justice (art. 61-2-14). When the applicant is recognised as a refugee, a refugee recognition certificate will be issued (art. 61-2, para. 2) and the various rights and benefits stipulated in the Refugee Convention will be conferred, including a long-term resident visa (art. 61-2-2). When the refugee application is rejected, however, a written statement with the reasons for the inadmissibility will be issued (art. 61-2, para. 2). If the applicant is dissatisfied with the decision, they may request a review by the Minister of Justice (art. 61-2-9, para. 1)

[2] Although the Japanese parliament passed a bill to amend ICRRA on 9 June 2023, the new law has not yet come into effect at the time of writing this paper (the effective date will be prescribed by a subsequent cabinet order within a year) and the specific provisions about refugee application remain largely the same. Therefore, articles mentioned in this chapter are still based on the currently effective version of ICRRA, and certain supplementary information about the new law will be provided if necessary.

within seven days of receiving the statement, which is different from the common provision for the period for requesting a review in the Administrative Complaint Review Act (according to art. 18, para. 1 of this Act, a request for review of a disposition should be filed within three months of the day following the day when the party became aware of the disposition). The applicant can also file an action challenging the final decision of the Minister of Justice afterwards. The waiting time from refugee application to final decision following the review request tends to be several years. For instance, according to the data from the Immigration Services Agency of Japan (henceforth, ISA), it was about three years and eleven months on average in 2022 (ISA, 2023b, p. 6). The time can be even longer if a lawsuit comes after the final decision.

Since ICRRA simply uses the terminology in the Refugee Convention and Protocol without giving any specific definition of refugee (art. 2), the interpretation of refugee in practice becomes an essential part of the refugee recognition process. From a legal and practical perspective, several problems can be observed in the currently adopted interpretation of the word refugee in Japan. Firstly, due to the individual-based examination of the refugee application, asylum seekers have to provide sufficient evidence to show the risk of being persecuted personally, not simply a collective fear of persecution. It is also necessary for them to have a realistic risk of being persecuted rather than an abstract one, though facts of actually being persecuted at the time of application are not required. Whether there is a realistic risk will be determined based on the specific circumstances of each individual applicant (ISA Guide, 2023a, p. 4). Obviously, these requirements narrow down the range of people who can be recognised as refugees to a great extent. Secondly, the meaning of persecution tends to be interpreted in a limited way. In the practice of refugee status determination, the persecution is usually understood as "an infringement or oppression of life or physical liberty by an attack or coercion that causes unbearable suffering to an ordinary person",[3] which means that serious violations of human rights other than

[3] This understanding has been repeatedly affirmed in a number of judicial decisions concerning refugee applications, for example, the Tokyo District Court's decision on 5 July 1989 (Tokyo District Court, 1989), and more recently, its decision on 15 April 2014 (Tokyo District Court, 2014). However, in the recently issued guideline, it is clearly stated that "other serious violations of human rights or discriminatory measures, such as deprivation of livelihood or violence against the mind, may also constitute the 'persecution'",

the threats to life and physical liberty, such as forced labour, denial of religious freedom, and deprivation of education and employment opportunities, may not have been given proper consideration in the judgment about whether a well-founded fear of persecution exists. Thirdly, while there is an alternative measure for granting special permission for residence out of humanitarian considerations to asylum seekers who have failed to obtain the refugee status,[4] the practice of this special permission has possibly obscured the real need of asylum seekers to have the more stable and reliable protection that comes with refugee status. Indeed, those who are granted the special permission for residence under humanitarian protection will be protected from refoulement and will receive certain benefits, such as access to work, health care, and free primary education. However, they are not eligible to receive settlement support, public housing assistance, publicly funded language training, or financial aid for secondary and post-secondary education, nor are they able to bring family members to Japan, in contrast to the benefits and services available for refugee status holders (Obi, 2013, pp. 14–15). The legal status granted is also considered to be too precarious for asylum seekers to live settled and secure lives in Japan, because the residence permit in this situation is a short-term one and needs to be renewed at least annually. In addition, the grants of special permission for residence are highly discretionary in the immigration administration (Arakaki, 2008, p. 101). Even though a guideline released by ISA has listed some positive and negative factors in the determination of the special permission (ISA Guide, 2009), it is not binding on the Minister of Justice. These facts have indicated the necessity of granting refugee status more generously to those who really need it rather than merely offering low-level humanitarian protection, as well as the importance of providing a more comprehensible and effective guide to distinguish humanitarian protection from refugee status when

whereas the common understanding of persecution will continue to be valid (ISA Guide, 2023a, p. 2).

[4] Based on art. 61-2-2, para. 2 of the ICRRA, the Minister of Justice can liberally decide on whether to grant special permission for residence in lieu of refugee status when the refugee application itself has been rejected. But the ICRRA itself does not provide any concrete criteria for granting this special permission until the 2023 revision. The new law will include a provision about considerations in the decision for giving special permission for residence, such as reasons for wishing to stay in Japan, family relationships, behaviours, legal status during the stay, and the necessity for humanitarian protection, to limit the administrative discretion of the Minister of Justice.

applied in practice. It has been argued that legislators should make clear the standards or requirements of special permission for residence in law instead of allowing the administrative power to set its own rules (Kondo, 2023, p. 249).

Furthermore, the burden of proof on asylum seekers in litigations relating to refugee status determination seems to be problematic as well. When a refugee application is rejected, the asylum seeker receiving the disposition of non-recognition may file an action in the court to seek revocation of the disposition, to confirm the invalidity of not granting special permission for residence when refugee status itself is denied, or to confirm the invalidity of the written deportation order by immigration authorities (Kawamura, 2022, p. 66). Nonetheless, it is by no means easy to obtain judicial remedies due to the strict requirements for asylum seekers regarding the burden of proof. There is a general understanding in Japan's practice that, in order to be identified as a person having a well-founded fear of being persecuted, there need to be objective circumstances that would cause an ordinary person in the same position to have a similar fear of persecution, in addition to subjective circumstances that the person is feeling the fear of being persecuted (ISA Guide, 2023a, p. 4). Consequently, even in the court, asylum seekers are expected to submit objective evidence as much as possible, in which both their personal conditions and the situation of their countries of origin are supposed to be included, to fully prove the risk of persecution. In other words, asylum seekers need to prove a realistic risk of persecution as they do in the refugee application, with objective evidence that shows the absence of possible solutions to avoid persecution in the country of origin. The reasons why asylum seekers should take the primary responsibility for proving the risk of being persecuted are often suggested as follows: (1) the legal system requires the asylum seeker to submit documents at the moment of the refugee application; (2) due to the nature of the matter, the asylum seeker who has directly experienced the fear is in the best position to know the circumstances needed for determining refugee status; (3) refugee status is a beneficiary disposition that confers favourable legal status on the asylum seeker, such as the status of long-term resident (Bando, 2018, p. 199).

Certainly, asylum seekers should bear the burden of proof in the refugee application as the UNHCR has already prescribed ("It is a general legal principle that the burden of proof lies on the person submitting a claim" (UNHCR Handbook, 2019, p. 43)). On the other hand, whether this principle can be basically valid in the case of litigation as well is highly questionable. Refugees forced to flee their countries because of persecution often do not have sufficient materials to prove their sufferings. Besides, even if they can prove their personal conditions regarding the risk of persecution, they may not have the ability to collect enough objective evidence showing the situation of their countries of origin, or to present the evidence completely and perfectly in Japanese. In light of these circumstances, it is inappropriate to impose the burden of proof wholly on asylum seekers. For the same reason, the UNHCR has suggested that "in some cases, it may be for the examiner to use all the means at his disposal to produce the necessary evidence in support of the application", and even if such independent research turns out to be unsuccessful, or there are statements that are not susceptible of proof, "if the applicant's account appears credible, he should, unless there are good reasons to the contrary, be given the benefit of the doubt" (UNHCR Handbook, 2019, p. 43). Thus, at the very least, judges in charge of refugee recognition cases should pay attention to the sharing of burden of proof between asylum seekers and the government, acknowledging that the government is liable for investigating and collecting evidence as well, particularly, the evidence concerning the situation of asylum seekers' countries of origin.

Apart from the enormous difficulties in the refugee application procedure, the current legal framework contains other serious human rights concerns that must be dealt with in earnest, such as the lack of public assistance for refugee applicants and insufficient medical assistance for those granted a provisional release from detention (Kan, 2022). One of the most critical issues relating to human rights is the detention of asylum seekers during the refugee application. Asylum seekers who have come to Japan and are in the process of applying for refugee status fall into "refugees unlawfully in the country of refuge" who are conferred certain rights under the Refugee Convention (art. 31 to art. 33), including the freedom of movement. Accordingly, ICRRA has introduced some specific measures, such as special permission for residence (art. 61-2-2, para. 2), permission for provisional stay (art. 61-2-4), and suspension of deportation procedure (art. 61-2-6, para. 2) for the purpose of implementing the Convention. Nevertheless, it is a prevailing rule in Japan that foreign nationals without legal status of residence will, in principle, be detained until the deportation starts or until they obtain a legal status (Kan, 2022, p. 120).

In fact, ICRRA has no provisions on detention specific to refugees. It lists a number of illicit acts that would bring about a deportation order (art. 24) and stipulates that anyone who is suspected of having committed one of the said acts, including unlawful stay or residence, may be detained by a written detention order from the immigration authorities (art. 39). There is a big question about juxtaposing the unlawful stay of asylum seekers with serious crimes in the same provision regarding detention. In August 2020, the UN Working Group on Arbitrary Detention adopted an opinion to express concerns about two asylum seekers' long-term and repeated detention in Higashi-Nihon Immigration Detention Centre (Opinion 58/2020, WGAD). The opinion stated that seeking asylum is not a criminal act but is a universal human right enshrined in art. 14 of the Universal Declaration of Human Rights. Therefore, the deprivation of liberty in the immigration context must be a measure of last resort and alternatives to detention must be sought to meet the requirement of proportionality. In light of this point, the rules of ICRRA allowing for indefinite immigration detention could not be reconciled with the international norms, and the repeated detention of the relevant asylum seekers under ICRRA should be deemed arbitrary. The opinion, as a result, requested the Japanese government to take necessary measures to remedy the situation of the two asylum seekers without any delay, and urged the government to review ICRRA so as to ensure its compatibility with those obligations Japan has undertaken under the international law (Opinion 58/2020, WGAD, pp. 13–16).

Due to the low refugee recognition rate and the unlimited chance of making refugee applications in Japan, there tends to be a large number of repeated applications following previously failed attempts, which consequently result in longer and repeated detention for those lodging several applications. Considering due process of law, however, the issuance of detention orders and the repeated application of detention orders by the immigration authorities should never be conducted without judicial approval or review. It is also pointed out in the aforementioned opinion that, "judicial oversight of any form of detention is a fundamental safeguard of personal liberty and is essential in ensuring that detention has a legal basis", therefore, any asylum seeker undergoing detention must be given the chance to challenge the legality of their detention before a judicial authority (Opinion 58/2020, WGAD, pp. 12–13). The courts should take charge of conducting approvals and reviews of detention, as well as provisional release from detention, based on legal requirements rather than leaving these decisions open to the administrative discretion. This is a requirement of art. 33 of the Japanese Constitution, which intends to prevent abuses of administrative power (Kawamura, 2022, p. 79).

Judicial Precedents Underpinning Japan's Immigration and Refugee Policies

In a liberal democracy, the justice system is expected to play an essential role in protecting human rights, and the courts need to equally safeguard the individual liberty of anyone within its jurisdiction, including both nationals and foreigners. However, the Japanese judicial system has been acting passively for years in safeguarding human rights, especially the rights of foreigners. The leading case on the issue of foreigners' rights in Japan is the infamous McLean Case (Supreme Court, 1978). The ruling of the Supreme Court in this case, which was largely negative about constitutional guarantees towards foreigners, has so far had a long-standing influence on the subsequent judicial decisions concerning rights of foreign nationals. More disastrously, it offers a legal basis for the government to justify and maintain its restrictive immigration and refugee policies, as well as the problematic legal framework for refugee status determination under ICRRA.

In 1970, when an American citizen who was teaching English in Japan lodged an application to renew his visa, the Minister of Justice declined his application on the grounds that he failed to notify the immigration authorities of his change in workplace, and he participated in anti-war demonstrations and other political activities frequently during his stay. Thus, the American citizen, Ronald Alan McLean, brought an action against the Minister of Justice in Tokyo District Court and received a decision in favour of his claims. The decision ruled that the disposition of the Minister of Justice in this case had significantly erred in its evaluation of the substance of McLean's job change and political activities, both of which did not constitute a legal grounding for refusing to renew the period of stay. Therefore, it was considered an illegal disposition that exceeded the scope of discretion granted to the Minister of Justice in view of the constitutional principles of international cooperation and the protection of fundamental human rights. However, when this case came to Tokyo High Court and then to the Supreme Court, the judicial decisions made by those courts, unexpectedly, dismissed McLean's claim to renew his visa.

The Supreme Court's decision on the McLean Case, on 4 October 1978, indicated the following three propositions. Firstly, the Court stated that "under customary international law, a state is not obligated to accept foreigners and can liberally decide whether or not to accept them into its territory, and what kind of conditions to attach to such acceptance, unless there is a special treaty". That is to say, a state has the discretion to decide on the admission and residence of foreigners based on its own judgment (henceforth, Proposition 1). Secondly, "art. 22, para. 1 of the Constitution merely guarantees the freedom of residence and movement inside Japan and does not provide any regulation regarding foreigners entering Japan". Based on this point and Proposition 1, the Court ruled that "under the Constitution, foreigners are not guaranteed the freedom to enter Japan for sure, nor are they guaranteed the right to reside or continue to reside in Japan". In other words, foreign nationals are considered to have no constitutional guarantees of the right to enter Japan as well as the right to reside in Japan according to the Japanese Constitution (henceforth, Proposition 2). Thirdly, "the guarantees of fundamental human rights contained in Chapter 3 of the Constitution should be interpreted as equally applying to foreigners residing in Japan, except for the rights that by their nature must be limited to Japanese nationals". Combined with Proposition 2, however, the third proposition by the Court affirms that "the protection of fundamental human rights for foreign nationals, under the Constitution, is provided only within the framework of the immigration control system, and cannot be interpreted as a safeguard that could bind the discretion of the government to determine whether or not to grant residency, that is, the safeguard to prevent the acts during the stay – which are regarded as fundamental human rights guaranteed by the Constitution – from being taken into account as negative factors at the time of renewing the residency". Therefore, even though the acts of foreigners are constitutional and lawful, the Minister of Justice can still "deem these acts to be unfavourable to Japan from the perspective of appropriateness and inappropriateness and presume that the foreign national is likely to commit acts detrimental to the interests of Japan in the future". In light of this statement, while the fundamental human rights guaranteed by the Japanese Constitution apply equally to foreigners, except in cases where the rights, by their nature, are understood to apply only to Japanese nationals, they are merely protected within the framework of the immigration control system and are subject to administrative discretion (henceforth, Proposition 3) (Kondo, 2021, pp. 1–2).

These propositions, essential to the ruling of the McLean Case, have been broadly criticised by academics and practitioners. It is worth noting that, even though the decision in the McLean Case could possibly be justified at the time it was rendered, there is a huge doubt about its validity in a globalised world in the twenty-first century. With regard to Proposition 1, it should be admitted that there were actually no international laws and norms that could specifically bind Japan on the issue of foreigners' rights when the Supreme Court ruled on the McLean Case. But, soon after this judgment, Japan ratified the International Covenant on Civil and Political Rights as well as the International Covenant on Economic, Social and Cultural Rights in 1979, and has acceded to most of the core international human rights treaties since the 1980s. Certainly, these treaties have imposed considerable international legal obligations on Japan. In this respect, the situation concerning international norms itself has changed significantly since the McLean Case (Sogabe, 2022, p. 13). It is no longer simply the principle of national sovereignty, allowing states to freely determine the acceptance of foreigners, that constitutes the customary international law. Nowadays, the principles of non-refoulement, family reunification, the prohibition on arbitrary detention, and non-discrimination are also considered to be part of the customary international law. That is to say, the customary international law in the contemporary world does not provide unlimited discretion for the state to decide liberally on the entry and residence of foreigners, but rather it asserts a competence of free determination to the extent that it does not violate the basic principles stated above (Kondo, 2021, pp. 2–3). Accordingly, Proposition 1, that asserts an unlimited power of the Japanese government to decide on the admission and residence of foreigners, should be deemed invalid in view of the developments of international human rights law.

Regarding Proposition 2, while art. 22, para. 1 of the Japanese Constitution may be interpreted as a constitutional guarantee of the freedom of residence, limited by the unwritten requirement of being in Japan—thus excluding foreigners newly entering Japan—it is definitely unreasonable to argue that, for those foreigners who have been living in Japan, their right to reside in Japan has no relation to the freedom of residence guaranteed by the Constitution. It seems to be arbitrary to judge that the freedom of residence for foreigners does not require respect, and that the expression of political opinions as an exercise of the freedom of expression guaranteed by the Constitution can be used as a legal basis for restricting another constitutional right, the freedom of residence (Kondo, 2021, pp. 3–4). For this reason, Proposition 2 should also be regarded as manifestly inappropriate and invalid.

As for Proposition 3, there are many more debates due to its ambiguity. With this proposition, the Court simply set aside some fundamental rights under the Constitution that by their nature do not extend to foreigners, but it did not specifically tell what those rights are, leaving the criteria for identifying the "nature" of rights blank (Kondo, 2021, p. 4; Webster, 2006, p. 450). Since there is no specific standard, any interpretation will be possible. In recent judicial practice, with reference to Proposition 1 and Proposition 3, many courts are inclined to assume a logical relation between the state discretion to decide on the acceptance of foreigners and the administrative power to generally control their residence afterwards, which appears to be a plausible explanation for the judgment of the McLean Case to support an immigration control system that can easily exclude constitutional guarantees of human rights when dealing with foreigners. Proposition 3, on this occasion, plays an important role in providing a legal basis for the government to control the residence of foreigners inside Japan within its immigration administration by granting or withholding the Status of Residence. However, legal scholars have argued against this idea, stating that the competence of deciding on admissions does not necessarily lead to the power of unfettered control over the residence of foreign nationals, because there was a common understanding of international law in post-war Japan, even before the tremendous progress in international human rights that has been achieved since, that foreigners were equally granted certain minimum rights and the legal capacity to lead a normal private life. That is to say, the right to life, body, and honour, the right to own and acquire materials necessary for living, and the capacity to make contracts needed for daily life must naturally be granted to foreigners as well as Japanese citizens (Obata, 2021, p. 83). In the meantime, the Status of Residence, namely the qualification enabling foreign nationals to live and carry out certain activities in Japan, is merely supposed to stipulate the conditions of entry in the first place, rather than functioning as a legal concept with which the administrative power is able to regulate every aspect of the foreigners' lives inside Japan. Considering the actual practice that has extended the Status of Residence to generally regulate the lives of foreign nationals, it is necessary to emphasise that residence control over foreigners in the immigration administration should be exercised within the limits derived from the conditions of entry, instead of being exercised arbitrarily due to the existence of these conditions. The judicial practice above, which wrongly backs up an exceedingly powerful immigration control system, is considered to be a serious consequence of the "expansion of Status of Residence", that is, the overusing of Status of Residence, and has further exacerbated this problem at the same time (Obata, 2021).

Additionally, it seems to be a critical mistake to follow the logic of Proposition 3, which has made the immigration control law a higher norm than the Constitution in the legal system. Because of this inversion, the guarantees of fundamental human rights for foreigners are entirely dependent on whether entry and residence are granted (Annen, 1993). In other words, the granting of Status of Residence itself has become the key criteria for protecting human rights. However, a significant question would be raised if the Minister of Justice was allowed to make decisions about the Status of Residence based on his political beliefs under the immigration control system. If the Minister of Justice could, when addressing the admission and residence of foreigners, freely evaluate their acts from the perspective of appropriateness and inappropriateness even though these acts are constitutional and lawful, then all kinds of discrimination against foreigners would probably be constitutional in the immigration administration (Kondo, 2021, p. 4). In terms of this evident error, the logic of Proposition 3 turns out to be highly problematic, making this proposition invalid as a result.

Needless to say, the judgment of the McLean Case can be interpreted in many ways and its reasoning concerning the three propositions may be justified in some particular interpretations. Contrary to the critiques mentioned above, some legal scholars conceive of the reasoning in the McLean Case as an appropriate explanation, at least partly, for the relationship between international obligations and rules of domestic laws. They insist on the predominance of domestic laws and contend that legal obligations in international treaties or customary international law do not have the same binding effect as rules of domestic laws. For example, it is argued by constitutional law scholars that a state that has ratified human rights treaties makes a commitment to the international community to guarantee the human rights enshrined in these treaties—namely the international human rights—of those who are under its jurisdiction. Therefore, the state has an obligation to protect international human rights, but it is an obligation only owed to the international community, not to the people in the state. And, more importantly, this international obligation is understood to be an obligation to create a condition in which the protection of international human rights is realised as an end result, while the process through which the protection is achieved is fundamentally a domestic matter (Takahashi, 2003, p. 74). From this point of view, the international obligations will not be directly applicable in Japan but need to be transformed into specific stipulations in domestic implementing legislation before they become effective. Accordingly, the reasoning of Proposition 3 to prioritise the immigration control system can be supported as long as the distinction between rules of domestic laws and international obligations exists. On the other hand, even scholars holding this view do not agree to interpret the Proposition 3 in a manner that would exclude other legal norms while applying the domestic laws and to provide safeguards for foreigners solely within the framework of immigration control system. Instead, they suggest that judges should embrace a higher level of scrutiny in the judicial review when it comes to issues of international human rights and should offer procedural guarantees equivalent to those of criminal procedure in the case of detention, since it will also cause a serious restriction on physical liberty (Sogabe, 2022, pp. 15–16).

In fact, it is necessary to note that the Supreme Court did not make any ruling about detention in the McLean Case. Some inferior courts, however, have extended the judgment and reasoning of the McLean Case to other cases where the detention of foreigners without legal status of residence is concerned. For instance, the Tokyo District Court, ruling against a Nigerian's request for provisional release from detention, in a decision on 6 October 2020, has affirmed the state's discretion to determine the system of deportation, including detention, with reference to the McLean Case. It stated that the provisional release under ICRRA is an exceptional measure to allow temporary release accompanied by certain conditions to ensure appearance and prevent escape, as an alternative to detention. Since the law does not stipulate any specific requirement for provisional release, it should be understood that the decision on whether or not to grant the provisional release is left to the broad discretion of the directors in the immigration detention centre. Such a decision will be illegal only when it is clear that the decision lacks any basis in fact or is extremely inappropriate in terms of socially accepted viewpoints, which means that the decision deviates from the scope of discretionary power or is an abuse of this power. Thus, the court dismissed the detainee's claim that deprivation of physical liberty must be an exception and the unconditional and indefinite detention based solely on the fact that deportation proceedings are underway falls under the category of arbitrary detention, rashly confirming the legality of the disposition not to grant provisional release in this case.

In summary, as described above, the McLean Case and the subsequent judicial decisions regarding foreigners' rights have raised a number of problems rather than giving sufficient and appropriate safeguards to foreigners in Japan. Meanwhile, the expansion of Status of Residence in the immigration administration, which is legally underpinned and supported by the judicial practice, has problematically blurred the limits of the administrative power to control the entry and residence of foreign nationals, and can partly account for the restrictive immigration and refugee policies under which only foreigners whose activities are deemed useful to Japan will be accepted and granted legal status. However, it must be clearly emphasised that with the development of international human rights, the judgment and reasoning in the McLean Case is significantly out of date and can no longer be maintained in the contemporary world. Instead of supporting an immigration control system with dominant power to exclude other legal norms, the Japanese courts are expected to interpret the domestic laws in conformity with the international norms, including the direct application of these norms, in order to better fulfil the role of protecting human rights under the international obligations (Matsuda, 2022).

Recent Developments in Legislation and Judicial Practice

Whether on a voluntary basis or under international pressure, recent years have witnessed some efforts in Japan's legislation and judicial practice to reform the current immigration control system and offer stronger protection to foreigners. Therefore, changes and new developments are happening indeed in Japanese society, though slowly and gradually.

To solve the broadly criticised problem of long-term detention, an expert group on detention and deportation was established in October 2019, under the 7th Immigration Control Policy Discussion Panel, a private gathering led by the Minister of Justice. The group held ten meetings to discuss issues during 2019–2020, and ultimately compiled a report titled "Recommendations for resolving the issues of deportation evasion and long-term detention" in June 2020. This report has emphasised a shared understanding that the following four points should be taken into consideration as the basic premise for subsequent recommendations in the report. First, in order to identify deportees who need to be deported from Japan, it is necessary that those who should be deported due to the deportation order and those who should be permitted to stay or be granted asylum be properly distinguished and recognised in the preceding deportation proceedings. Thus, improvements in the deportation system and its applications should be made from this perspective. Second, for those who need to be deported, deportation proceedings should be facilitated. Third, the detention period should be as short as possible. Therefore, measures should be taken to eliminate long-term detention and alternatives to detention should also be considered. Fourth, in the event of detention, the treatment of detainees should be carried out in an appropriate manner, with due consideration for human rights and humanity (Expert Group Recommendations, 2020, p. 21). In addition, to prevent prolonged detention, it is suggested that enhancements and improvements to the legal procedure for deciding whether to issue a deportation order should be achieved, in order to appropriately consider the circumstances of each person. Meanwhile, further clarification of factors and criteria for special permission for residence should be considered, in terms of improving the transparency of decisions about granting or denying that permission (Expert Group Recommendations, 2020, pp. 22–24). However, the report has also advocated establishing a new system to increase the effectiveness of deportation proceedings, in which an order would be issued to deportees who refuse to be deported without justifiable reasons, requiring them to apply for a travel document necessary for their deportation or to leave Japan by a certain date, and a penalty would be imposed for violation of such an order. An examination of the appropriateness of the refugee application process, which currently allows repeated applications without limitation, is required as well. The report stated that, in the case of repeated applications, it would be appropriate to consider legal measures to provide exceptions to the suspensive effect on deportation during refugee application procedures (Expert Group Recommendations, 2020, pp. 26–39).

Based on this report, and in response to the aforesaid opinion by the UN Working Group on Arbitrary Detention, the Japanese government submitted a bill to revise ICRRA to the Diet on 19 February 2021.

The bill contained several important amendments to the current legal framework, including instituting an application procedure for the special permission for residence, creating a system of monitoring measures as an alternative to detention, developing procedures and provisions related to the treatment of detainees, introducing a complementary protection system for asylum seekers who are regarded as equivalent to refugees, reviewing provisions with regard to the suspensive effect on deportation during the refugee application procedure, and establishing an expulsion order system that can demand deportation from Japan for those who have evaded deportation.

Part of the proposed amendments will, admittedly, contribute to providing better protection for asylum seekers. For example, a group of provisions concerning the treatment of detainees are going to be newly introduced, ranging from the rights of detainees to perform religious acts and to read books, magazines, newspapers, as well as other publications, to the liabilities of officers in the immigration detention centres and the necessary measures to ensure health and medical care for detainees. Regarding the granting of special permission for residence, it is proposed that considerations formerly presented in the guideline should be included in the new law. That is to say, it will be explicitly stipulated in ICRRA that the Minister of Justice shall, when determining whether or not to grant the special permission for residence, take into consideration the reasons why foreign nationals wish to stay in Japan, their family relationships, their behaviours, the circumstances leading to their entry into Japan, the period of their stays in Japan, their legal status during the period of stay, the facts that result in their deportation, the necessity for humanitarian consideration, as well as the various circumstances in Japan and abroad, and the expected impact on other unlawful residents in Japan. This provision is thought to be of great importance and deserving of a positive reception, since it makes clear the considerations in the law and thus, with its help, judicial review in accordance with the above considerations would be possible (Hasegawa, 2022, pp. 187–188; Sogabe, 2022, p. 15).

Despite these favourable changes, this amendment bill has also introduced many provisions that would put foreigners or asylum seekers at a greater disadvantage. For this very reason, it has received plenty of opposition and critiques ever since it was submitted to the Diet. On the day of its submission, the Japan Association for Refugees (henceforth, JAR) announced an opinion outlining the various problems with the bill with respect to refugee protection (JAR Opinion, 2021). A week later, on 26 February, the Japan Federation of Bar Associations (henceforth, JFBA) also released a statement to express its opposition to the bill, saying that it would reject the bill unless fundamental changes were made to address the issues pointed out in the statement (JFBA Statement, 2021a). Moreover, a joint letter from three Special Rapporteurs of the UN Human Rights Council and the Vice-Chair of the UN Working Group on Arbitrary Detention was sent to the Japanese government on 31 March, indicating the bill's violation of international human rights law (Morales et al., 2021). The UNHCR also expressed concerns about the newly proposed procedures and measures relating to the status and treatment of asylum seekers in its comments on the bill (UNHCR Comments, 2021).

Overall, the bill was mainly criticised for the following reasons. First, it would include new provisions in ICRRA with regard to the lifting of the automatic suspensive effect on deportation in certain cases. Under the currently effective law, deportation is uniformly suspended during the refugee application process, which means that the applicant for refugee status can avoid deportation through repeated applications. Therefore, the amendment bill prescribed that in the case of the third or subsequent application, or applications from persons who have served a prison sentence of three years or more, the suspensive effect on deportation does not apply. It has been contended by several organisations, however, that removing automatic suspensive effect of refugee applications will increase the risk of persons who are in need of international protection being returned, contrary to the principle of non-refoulement (JFBA Opinion, 2021a, pp. 19–20; UNHCR Comments, 2021, p. 10). Second, there would be an expulsion order system, accompanied by penalties, for not complying with such orders, so as to promote the execution of deportation. According to the formal opinion of the JFBA, this system and its penalties are difficult to justify, because they may violate deportees' rights to court access and because there is no need to use criminal penalties to enforce deportation (JFBA Opinion, 2021a, p. 21). Besides, as the UNHCR has noted in the aforementioned comments, for asylum seekers who are normally unable or unwilling to approach the authorities of their countries of origin, the order to apply for a travel document, which forces them to approach the consulates of their countries of nationality, might heighten their risk of being persecuted upon return, or give rise to sur-place refugee claims. For stateless persons or persons of undetermined nationality, in the meantime, there need to be special provisions that grant them an exemption from those orders (UNHCR Comments, 2021, p. 37). Third, the bill intended to introduce a system of monitoring measures as an alternative to detention. Under the current ICRRA, the only way of being released from detention is to obtain a permit for provisional release. However, the measures for managing provisionally released detainees are so insufficient that prevention of their escape becomes impossible, making it a difficult decision to grant the provisional release. In light of this situation, the system of monitoring measures can be regarded as a method to prevent escape as well as to avoid prolonged detention (Hasegawa, 2022, p. 187). Nonetheless, it has been stressed that the proposed monitoring measures in the bill would be no less problematic than detention. While monitors are obliged to notify the supervising immigration inspector of the living conditions of the monitored person, the status of compliance with the conditions attached to the monitoring measures, along with other requested matters, these obligations would be a major detriment in building a trusting relationship between the monitor and the monitored person. Thus, in reality, very few supporters and lawyers would be willing to assume the obligations of notification, making the system largely infeasible (Hasegawa, 2022, p. 187; JFBA Opinion, 2021a, pp. 11–12).

Influenced by the widespread opposition and more crucially, by the death of a Sri Lankan woman at the immigration detention facility in Nagoya, the bill to revise ICRRA was finally discarded in May 2021. Two years later, however, the Japanese government prepared a new bill, similar to the former one to a large extent, and officially submitted it to the Diet again on 7 March 2023. The new bill has made a minor modification to the old one by deleting the controversial provisions for the periodic notification obligations of monitors in the system of monitoring measures, and introducing a new process of reviewing the necessity for detention of those who are being detained every three months and transferring detainees who need not be detained any more to the monitoring measures. On the other hand, the bill still retained numerous provisions relating to the formerly criticised procedures and measures, thus bringing about an opposition movement, with broad participation in Japanese society against its passage. Like its predecessor, the 2023 bill was strongly opposed by JAR and JFBA since it contained few perceived improvements in fact. Furthermore, over four hundred scholars from different areas in Japan signed a joint statement to express their objections to the bill, due to concerns about the human rights violations it contained. A number of civil action groups and student associations joined in the opposition movement by organising protest rallies, holding press conferences, and engaging in information sharing and support seeking via social networking sites, for the purpose of preventing law revision based on the 2023 government bill. In parliament, opposition parties such as the Constitutional Democratic Party of Japan and the Japanese Communist Party spared no effort in opposing the government bill, submitting another amendment bill, joined by several opposition parties, that suggested creating a Refugee Protection Commission as a third-party organisation to grant refugee status in accordance with international norms. Nevertheless, the government pushed its bill through the Diet on 9 June 2023, defying the huge dissatisfaction and massive criticism from opposition parties and the public.[5]

In addition to the latest changes in legislation, there are some new trends in judicial practice that are worth mentioning. As more and more cases related to the human rights of asylum seekers or foreigners come to court, judges are gradually changing their stances and are trying to make improvements in refugee acceptance and protection. Legal scholars have noted that, in recent years, judicial decisions that seem to have taken into account the Handbook by UNHCR are emerging. In reference to the Handbook, judges are more likely to ease the burden of proof on refugee applicants, thus leading to greater inclusion of refugees (Hasegawa, 2022, p. 177).

Among the developments of judicial practice, a remarkable decision rendered by Tokyo High Court on 22 September 2021 must be highlighted (Tokyo High Court, 2021). The court offered recognition of the right to court access in its judgment to two Sri Lankan men, who were deported before they could file an action against the administrative decisions rejecting their applications for refugee status. Considering constitutional guarantees of fundamental human rights, the court specifically ruled that officers in the Immigration Bureau had delayed the notification of the final decision regarding the review request of the

[5] In the legislative process, the government proposed some minor changes to its 2023 amendment bill to include several provisions about due considerations for human rights in refugee status determination and decisions concerning the monitoring measures and the provisional release. The finally enacted amendments to ICRRA included these changes as well. But these provisions are nothing more than abstract ideas, lacking the power to guide actual practice.

disposition of rejecting the grant of refugee status until just before the deportation, on the premise that the parties concerned were subject to mass deportation, and had directly deported them without allowing for contact with any third party after the notification. In light of these facts, it should be deemed that the officers had deprived them of the opportunity to undergo judicial review of their refugee status, thus it is a violation of the right to court access guaranteed by art. 32 of the Constitution, as well as the guarantee of due process provided in art. 31 of the Constitution.

The judgment of Tokyo High Court in this case has marked a stark departure from the McLean Case. By recognising foreigners' right of access to courts under the Japanese Constitution, Tokyo High Court has provided a framework free from the McLean Case which would make it possible to broadly protect the human rights of foreigners, including those without legal status of residence in Japan. In fact, when discussing the constitutional guarantee of due process in art. 31, Tokyo High Court has combined it with art. 13, which contains the right to the pursuit of happiness, a right underlying all other human rights in the Constitution. Therefore, it is reasonable to assume that stronger protection of human rights in the refugee application process will be made available to foreign nationals in the future, especially in the case of detention, the deprivation of physical liberty.

Conclusion

Today, with the development of international human rights law, the predominance of domestic laws that pose a great threat to the human rights of foreigners based on the doctrine of national sovereignty can no longer be justified unconditionally. As discussed in this chapter, the legal framework for refugee acceptance and protection in Japan has structural problems with regard to the narrow interpretation of the word refugee, the heavy burden of proof on asylum seekers, and the lengthy refugee application procedure, which cause not only the low refugee recognition rate, but also various human rights violations. The current refugee law, thus, has been proven to be inadequate and inappropriate in protecting the fundamental rights of asylum seekers, and needs to be thoroughly reformed. Even though the 2023 law revision has tried to deal with some problems, there will probably be no great improvement in the quality of human rights protection in Japan. It is necessary to note that, without fully reviewing the refugee application procedure and the criteria for refugee status determination, the newly enacted amendments to ICRRA, aimed at reducing or eliminating long-term detention, will merely raise new problems of asylum seekers' rights, rather than ameliorating the situation of refugee acceptance and protection.

Therefore, a great number of measures are still needed to reform the legal framework under ICRRA and to construct a more inclusive immigration and refugee system. For example, setting a maximum time limit for detention, introducing judicial review of decisions relating to detention, and reviewing the criteria for granting refugee status. Accordingly, the courts are expected to play a more significant role in the implementation of international norms to further promote human rights. In view of the faithful observance of international treaties (art. 98, para. 2) and the parliamentary approval of these treaties (art. 73) that are explicitly stipulated in the Japanese Constitution, it can be assumed that the rules of international human rights law have direct legal effect in Japan and are directly applicable in judicial practice (Ejima, 2021, pp. 148–149). Judges should take on greater responsibility in judicial review to motivate policymakers to establish an immigration control system in conformity with the international norms.

References

Annen, J. (1993). Rethinking "human rights of foreigners." In Y. Higuchi & K. Takahashi (Eds.), *The development of modern constitutionalism* (Vol. 1, pp. 163–181). Yuhikaku.

Arakaki, O. (2008). *Refugee law and practice in Japan*. Ashgate.

Bando, Y. (2018). Burden of proof for refugee recognition: Through an analysis of two decisions rendered in 2016. *The Economic Review*, *69*(2–3), 183–216. http://hdl.handle.net/10252/00005851

Betts, A., & Collier, P. (2017). *Refuge: Rethinking refugee policy in a changing world*. Oxford University Press.

Buschmann, P. (2021). An evaluation of the Japanese Immigration Control and Refugee Recognition Act's permissibility under the 1951 convention relating to the status of refugees and its 1967 protocol. *Journal of Human Security Studies*, *10*(2), 79–96. https://doi.org/10.34517/jahss.10.2_79

Ejima, A., et al. (2021). International human rights protection system: Towards human rights law. In S. Yokodaido (Ed.), *Constitutional law in the age of globalisation* (pp. 145–163). Koubundou.

Expert Group on Detention and Deportation, 7th Immigration Control Policy Discussion Panel. (2020, June 19). *Recommendations for resolving the issues of deportation evasion and long-term detention*. https://www.moj.go.jp/isa/content/930005829.pdf

Hasegawa, K. (2022). Trends toward inclusion of immigrants and refugees in Japan: Attempts aimed at inclusion observed in the refugee related lawsuits and the bill for amendments to the Immigration Control and Refugee Recognition Act. *St. Paul's Review of Law and Politics, 105*, 172–189. https://doi.org/10.14992/00021645

Immigration Services Agency of Japan (ISA). (2009). *Guidelines on special permission for residence*. https://www.moj.go.jp/isa/content/930002524.pdf

Immigration Services Agency of Japan (ISA). (2023a, March 24). *Guide for determining refugee status*. https://www.moj.go.jp/isa/content/001393172.pdf

Immigration Services Agency of Japan (ISA). (2023b, March 24). *Regarding the number of recognised refugees in 2022*. https://www.moj.go.jp/isa/content/001393012.pdf

Izumi, T. (2021). Mistakes in the judgment of McLean Case. The role of judicial power in the governance structure vol. 2. *Hanreijiho*, 2479 (Special Issue), 185–221.

Japan Association for Refugees (JAR). (2021, February 19). *Opinion on the bill for partial amendments to the Immigration Control and Refugee Recognition Act*. https://www.refugee.or.jp/report/refugee/2021/02/opinion_imlaw21/

Japan Federation of Bar Associations (JFBA). (2021a, February 26). *Statement on the bill for amendments to the Immigration Control and Refugee Recognition Act submitted by the government*. https://www.nichibenren.or.jp/document/statement/year/2021/210226.html

Japan Federation of Bar Associations (JFBA). (2021b, March 18). *Opinion on the bill for amendments to the Immigration Control and Refugee Recognition Act*. https://www.nichibenren.or.jp/library/pdf/document/opinion/2021/210318_7.pdf

Kan, Y. (2022). Living conditions of refugees in Japan. *Journal of International Health, 37*(3), 118–121. https://doi.org/10.11197/jaih.37.113

Kawamura, A. (2022). The research of future reform about Japan's present Immigration Control and Refugee Recognition Act. *Journal of Global Humanities and Social Sciences, 8*, 63–91. http://hdl.handle.net/10069/00041334

Kondo, A. (2021). A fundamental review of the decision in McLean Case: Five principles of customary international law on entry and residence. *Meijo Law Review, 70*(4), 1–22. https://mylib.meijo-u.ac.jp/webopac/TC05264426

Kondo, A. (2023). *International human rights law and constitutional law: Human rights theory in the era of multicultural symbiosis*. Akashishoten.

Matsuda, H. (2022). Interpretation of domestic law in conformity with international law: The detention in immigration control and the International Covenant on Civil and Political Rights. *Horitsu Jiho, 94*(4), 16–21.
McLean v. Minister of Justice, Supreme Court. (1978, October 4). *Minshu, 32*(7), 1223. https://www.courts.go.jp/app/files/hanrei_jp/255/053255_hanrei.pdf
Morales, F. G. et al. (2021, March 31). *Mandates of the Special Rapporteur on the human rights of migrants; the Working Group on Arbitrary Detention; the Special Rapporteur on freedom of religion or belief and the Special Rapporteur on torture and other cruel, inhuman or degrading treatment or punishment*. https://spcommreports.ohchr.org/TMResultsBase/DownLoadPublicCommunicationFile?gId=26325
Obata, K. (2021). The precedent of McLean Case in postwar legal history of foreigners in Japan: A "deadly leap" from unfettered power to refuse entry to unfettered power of residence management. *Horitsu Jiho, 93*(8), 81–85.
Obi, N. (2013). *A review of assistance programs for asylum seekers and refugees in Japan. New issues in refugee research: Research paper no. 259*. UNHCR. https://www.unhcr.org/media/review-assistance-programmes-refugees-and-asylum-seekers-japan-naoko-obi
Onozuka, Y. (2022). National policies and international system for migration and refugees. *The Doshisha University Economic Review, 73*(4), 235–264.
Sogabe, M. (2022). The decision of McLean Case and recent discussions regarding it. *Human Rights International, 33*, 13–18.
Takahashi, K. (2003). The logic of international human rights and the logic of domestic human rights. *Monthly Jurist, 1244*, 69–82.
Tokyo District Court. *Decision on July 5, 1989, Case No. 1987–88 (Gyo-U)*. https://www.courts.go.jp/app/files/hanrei_jp/760/016760_hanrei.pdf
Tokyo District Court. *Decision on April 15, 2014, Case No. 2013–33 (Gyo-U)*. https://www.courts.go.jp/app/files/hanrei_jp/560/084560_hanrei.pdf
Tokyo High Court. *Decision on September 22, 2021, Case No. 2020–1423 (Ne)*. https://www.courts.go.jp/app/files/hanrei_jp/694/090694_hanrei.pdf
United Nations High Commissioner for Refugees (UNHCR). (2019). *Handbook on procedures and criteria for determining refugee status and guidelines on international protection under the 1951 Convention and the 1967 Protocol relating to the status of refugees*. HCR/1P/4/ENG/REV. 4. https://www.refworld.org/docid/5cb474b27.html
United Nations High Commissioner for Refugees (UNHCR). (2021, April 9). *Comments on the bill for partial amendments to the Immigration Control and Refugee Recognition Act submitted to the 204th Diet session of year 2021, Based on the recommendations of the Sub-Committee on Detention and Deportation (SCDD), 7th Immigration Control Policy*

Discussion Panel. https://www.unhcr.org/jp/wp-content/uploads/sites/34/2021/04/20210409-UNHCR-Full-Comments-on-ICRRA-Bill-English.pdf

United Nations Working Group on Arbitrary Detention (WGAD). (2020). *Opinion No. 58/2020 concerning Deniz Yengin and Heydar Safari Diman (Japan)*. A/HRC/WGAD/2020/58. https://www.ohchr.org/en/special-procedures/wg-arbitrary-detention/opinions-adopted-working-group-arbitrary-detention-its-88th-session

Webster, T. (2006). Legal excisions "Omissions are not accidents". *Cornell International Law Journal, 39*(2), 435–455. https://scholarship.law.cornell.edu/cilj/vol39/iss2/7

Wolman, A. (2015). Japan and international refugee protection norms: Explaining non-compliance. *Asian and Pacific Migration Journal, 24*(4), 409–431. https://doi.org/10.1177/0117196815606852

CHAPTER 5

From Non-existence to Unrecognised Existence: The Evolution and Limitations of Taiwan's Hong Kong Asylum Mechanism After 2019

Min-yen Chiang and Candia Tong

Introduction

In 2019, Taiwan implemented a policy of providing humanitarian aid to Hong Kong citizens in response to the Anti-Extradition Law Amendment Bill Movement (Anti-ELAB Movement) generated in Hong Kong. This social resistance movement emerged through combined public support, operating without a centralised leadership structure. Frontline participants, often strangers to one another, relied on ad hoc consensus to resist the armed police, who acted under the authority of the Chinese government (Li, 2021). Violent clashes and bloody suppression were frequently reported on social media and mainstream news outlets. Within protester circles, there occasionally surfaced unverifiable reports of police sexual

M. Chiang (✉) · C. Tong
Flow HK, Taipei, Taiwan
e-mail: mychiang@flowhongkong.net

L. Momesso and P. Ivanova (eds.), *Refugees and Asylum Seekers in East Asia*, Palgrave Macmillan Studies on Human Rights in Asia,
https://doi.org/10.1007/978-981-97-2867-1_5

violence towards movement participants in enclosed spaces, unidentified bodies found floating on the sea or suspected of having fallen from high-rise buildings, and organised workers being stalked and harassed by individuals with Chinese accents. As a result of facing threats of political violence and living under a high-pressure terror rule, many protesters have sought help from civil society organisations (CSOs) and the government in Taiwan.

In addition to the police violence, China, at the time, was in the process of systematically constructing an oppressive regime in Hong Kong (Fong et al., 2020). In early 2020, Covid-19 swept the world and many countries implemented measures such as border closures and restrictions on gatherings, significantly reducing social activities. The pro-democracy camp in Hong Kong, having learned from the painful experience of the SARS outbreak in 2003, self-regulated and initiated anti-pandemic actions, such as organising purchases of masks from foreign countries and reducing gatherings (Tsui, 2023). However, the Chinese government took advantage of the situation and implemented the Hong Kong National Security Law (HKNSL) in response to months-long social protests. This law completely destroyed the remaining space for civic freedom and political autonomy in Hong Kong, rendering the "one country, two systems" framework meaningless. Organisers of the Hong Kong democracy movement faced systematic and comprehensive suppression, and traditional civic organisations, autonomous student groups, and public media were forced to disband (Wu, J., 2022). The effects of the HKNSL have triggered a new wave of emigration from Hong Kong, including many civic organisation workers who have chosen to seek political asylum in Taiwan.

The plight of Hong Kong protesters seeking asylum in Taiwan differs from that of typical refugees, as they continue to face the threat of cross-border oppression by the Chinese regime. Some activists advocating for Hong Kong issues have been subjected to harassment and violent intimidation while in Taiwan, and the heightened cross-border law enforcement by the Chinese police has raised concerns among democratic countries regarding China's authoritarian expansionism (Safeguard Defenders, 2022). The provision of protection to Hong Kong protesters in Taiwan is complicated by Taiwan's diplomatic isolation, which stems from China's suppression of Taiwan's international status.

Taiwan's policy towards China is critical to maintaining peace in East Asia. A conservative and stable policy towards China is in Taiwan's

Western allies' interest, to avoid overstimulating China. However, Hong Kong's young protesters, who grew up after Hong Kong's sovereignty was transferred to China in 1997, have solidified their sense of an independent identity in response to Beijing's violation of the promises made in the Sino-British Joint Declaration, its suppression of Hong Kong's cultural identity, and its blatant police violence (Tsui, 2023). In the eyes of the Chinese government, these protesters, seeking national self-determination, pose a tangible national security threat; any civil action challenging China's territorial claims or the authority of the Chinese Communist Party must therefore be absolutely prohibited. The Taiwanese government, which chooses to provide protesters with protection, is viewed as an outright hostile force. Therefore, a human rights-based aid policy immediately escalates to a national security-sensitive issue.

Due to national security sensitivity and cross-border pressure from China, Taiwan-based Hong Kong protesters often live "unrecognised existences", making it difficult for the public to know anything about the practical implementation of humanitarian aid policies for Hong Kong in Taiwan. One reason for the lack of clear guidance on Taiwan's policy of sheltering Hong Kongers is that Taiwan has never established a complete refugee policy framework. Its refugee law has been stalled in the legislative process for decades, with no political momentum to move it forward. Despite the emergence of a need to provide asylum to Hong Kong protesters in the aftermath of the Anti-ELAB Movement, this political opportunity has not been able to effectively drive the advancement of refugee legislation. Without a clear legal framework, the Taiwanese government bureaucracy could not prepare for the immediate needs of fleeing Hong Kong protesters. The inefficiency of the bureaucratic system and the absence of legal institutionalisation have resulted in the need for CSOs to bear the cost of accommodating and facilitating the social integration of protesters.

This chapter addresses the primary question of how Taiwan can continue to develop a substantive aid policy for Hong Kong while protesters are "unrecognised". From this perspective, what are the limitations of Taiwan's aid policy towards Hong Kong, and what are the prospects for future development?

The authors of this chapter were key participants in the development process of Taiwan's aid policy towards Hong Kong. We previously served in a local non-governmental organisation in Taiwan, the Taiwan Economic Democracy Union (*t'ai wan ching chi min chu lian hê*). We worked with CSOs such as the Taiwan Association for Human Rights (*t'ai wan jên ch'üan ts'u chin hui*) and the Judicial Reform Foundation (*min chien ssu fa kai kê chi chin hui*) to urge and supervise the government in gradually implementing its aid policy towards Hong Kong. Therefore, the essential perspectives of this chapter, and most of the data, come from our first-hand operational experience, as well as our interviews with civil society partners and relevant individuals within the government. We also cite publicly available information from media or government reports to corroborate information that we cannot publicly disclose due to secrecy. This research approach provides an insider's view but, as well as being a positive factor, such a viewpoint can in itself be said to limit the research perspective of this chapter. Nevertheless, our position remains consonant and perspicuous. Hitherto, we have steadfastly advocated for the formulation of a refugee legislation or an equitably structured legal framework by the Taiwanese government, with an ardent commitment to proactively ensuring the protection and well-being of Hong Kong refugees residing in Taiwan. Through our analysis, we hope to provide a more comprehensive public discussion foundation for this policy area.

This chapter reviews the various stages of Taiwan's aid policy towards Hong Kong during its critical turning points and further expands related analysis and discussions through crucial concepts such as national security, public–third sector cooperation, and the institutionalisation of shelter policies.

Three Stages of Taiwan's Aid to Hong Kong

From July 2019 to June 2020: Civilian Guarantees and Case-by-Case Project Review

On the night of 1 July 2019, Hong Kong protesters occupied the Legislative Council chamber for the first time in history, demanding immediate implementation of universal suffrage in both the executive and legislative branches. At midnight, a large number of riot police stormed the Legislative Council and violently cleared the area. Based on past experiences, the Hong Kong government was highly likely to charge the protesters with the "riot" offence, which carries a maximum sentence of up to ten years. Moreover, the judicial system in Hong Kong lacked the spirit of the rule of law. Therefore, many protesters began considering fleeing overseas, with Taiwan being the primary option due to its close geopolitical ties.

On 12 August 2019, President Tsai Ing-wen of Taiwan expressed her willingness to provide humanitarian assistance to Hong Kong protesters through her party spokesperson (Ye, 2019). Tsai's statement motivated many young Hong Kong protesters. During the peak of the movement, we found that many young protesters faced despair due to high-pressure political violence and even experienced family breakdowns due to their differing political views with their family members. The commitment of Taiwanese politicians was like a lifeboat in the ocean, providing a brief hope for survival amidst the stormy seas. However, the then administrative bureaucracy in Taiwan had yet to gain systematic experience in implementing political refugee protection, let alone proposing any policy implementation guidelines. In the absence of any policy and institutional preparation, the government was unable to promptly establish any public ways to receive applications from refugees seeking assistance. Consequently, these political refugees, who had just arrived in Taiwan, had no official channels to seek help from the authorities.

We noticed that, faced with the imminent political crackdown by the Hong Kong government, the first wave of protesters fleeing to Taiwan acted quickly. They initially obtained short-term stay permits through tourist visas and then tried to seek assistance from familiar social networks in Taiwan. Due to the lack of an official coordination mechanism, a plethora of urgent requests for asylum flooded human rights groups, political parties, as well as organisations or individuals who had established personal connections with Hong Kong's social activist circle. As we experienced, in response to this urgent situation, several CSOs came together to organise humanitarian aid for Hong Kong refugees, leveraging their networks of people with similar backgrounds, who were dealing with the same issues, and building on the trust they had developed thanks to past collaboration with social activists.

As we encountered, under the political mandate of President Tsai, the Taiwanese government had maintained a friendly attitude towards Hong Kong refugees. However, officials had become accustomed to relying on the past case-by-case review model for handling foreign refugees. Government agencies could only offer temporary solutions within the limited legal framework, while applicants awaiting official responses had to rely on the assistance of CSOs. The previous legal framework was not easily applicable given the circumstances at that time. This was primarily due to the overwhelming influx of people arriving in Taiwan within a short period, and the tendency of individuals involved to seek assistance discreetly and in secrecy. Despite frequent interactions between Taiwanese CSOs and Hong Kong activists, they still faced difficulties in verifying the identities of a significant number of asylum seekers through their existing networks.

The absence of a structured leadership core in the Hong Kong protests effectively shielded protesters in the short term, as the Hong Kong government was unable to concentrate its efforts on arresting leaders within a specific area. However, this outcome posed an immediate challenge in terms of identifying the participants involved in the protests. Moreover, most young protesters might face economic difficulties, but the Taiwanese government had yet to establish a refugee resettlement institution that provided emergency living assistance. Most significantly, owing to the spectre of Chinese government infiltration into overseas democratic societies, Hong Kong political refugees faced safety risks that prevented them from openly seeking media interviews or making widespread appeals to the community for assistance. Instead, they had to rely on existing social networks and cautiously communicate their difficulties and needs. We learned that these specific contextual factors constrained CSOs from making immediate and extensive efforts to develop feasible operational models.

Based on our findings, initially, the government proposed several short-term measures to address the pressing needs caused by the rapidly evolving situation in Hong Kong. The Taiwanese government expressed a clear willingness to assist the protesters; however, it encountered challenges due to a lack of basic administrative procedures and the necessary human resources to undertake further protection efforts. The initial proposals put forth by the government were also deemed impractical and difficult to implement. In light of the chaotic situation, CSOs had to tentatively establish mechanisms to provide assistance to the substantial number of protesters who arrived in Taiwan in early July. During that period, the civilian shelter mechanism was roughly divided into three steps:

i. Attempting to understand the background of each case from the fragmented network of original information.
ii. Establishing a standard interview procedure to build the necessary information file for each case to apply for residency.
iii. Negotiating with the government to obtain residency status (Chiang, 2020).

Based on our understanding, many civil society workers were fully dedicated to building the mechanism individually and commenced case management, resulting in the formation of a temporary collaboration for civilian refugee resettlement. This was achieved under the highly mobilised configuration of CSOs, overcoming practical difficulties such as identity confirmation, emergency resettlement, and protecting asylum seekers' privacy. The government passively endorsed the civilian mechanism. If applicants were assisted by the specific and reliable alliance of CSOs, there was a high likelihood of receiving administrative assistance from the government, such as extending short-term visas and mitigating administrative obstacles during the residency application process. In our analysis, we have summarised this model as the "civilian guarantees and case-by-case project review" mentioned in the title of this section, which had led to a preliminary consensus on public–third sector cooperation.

During this stage, CSOs were the actual implementers of President Tsai Ing-wen's humane policies towards Hong Kong protesters. In our experience, the civil society-led shelter mechanism often encountered financial and human resource constraints. Additionally, as CSOs lacked official power, individuals seeking help from them could not receive official guarantees through the third-sector procedures. Consequently, we noticed that some individuals were unwilling to trust, and refused to join, the civil shelter mechanism, leaving them in a vulnerable situation where the Taiwanese government could not provide further assistance.

However, we found that Tsai's verbal commitment gave protesters confidence that official assistance would be available, which increased their willingness to flee to Taiwan. This further intensified the burden on CSOs responsible for providing shelter, as they had to raise funds while refining the civil mechanism based on the lessons learned from implementation. After several months of trial and error, CSOs developed a stable intervention mechanism. This mechanism included strengthened case management for refugee placement, provision of emergency accommodation, psychological support, medical services, insurance coverage, legal aid, assistance in applying for residency in Taiwan, and career development planning. Furthermore, regular monitoring of the living conditions of these individuals was conducted by CSOs to help them achieve self-sufficiency. Other civic resources were gradually integrated into the network, such as the "Taiwan Volunteer Lawyers Group Supporting Hong Kong Protesters", which was officially launched during the 29 September "Taiwan with Hong Kong" rally (Lu, 2019). The lawyer's group established a public Telegram (a social media platform widely used by Hong Kong protestors for secret communication during the Anti-ELAB movement) account to help Hong Kong protesters inquiring about the basics of the civil shelter mechanism in Taiwan through social media.

From July 2020 to July 2022: Establishment of a Semi-Official Project Office

After nearly a year of refugee resettlement efforts led by CSOs, the Mainland Affairs Council (MAC) finally announced the "Hong Kong Humanitarian Assistance and Care Action Scheme" (the Scheme) on 18 June 2020, gradually taking over the management of individual cases and related administrative tasks from civil society organisations (Mainland Affairs Council, 2020). This Scheme was established under the "Taiwan–Hong Kong Service and Exchange Office" (*t'ai kang fu wu chiao liu pan kung shih*, Exchange Office) under the Taiwan–Hong Kong Economic and Cultural Cooperation and Promotion Council (*t'ai kang ching chi wên hua hê tso ts'ê chin hui*, ECCPC). This council was initially established with government funding and maintained relationships with Hong Kong's political and civil society sectors in a semi-official capacity, often hosting cultural exchange events. Taiwan's government chose a semi-official, culturally oriented institution to manage the refugee asylum work, demonstrating its desire to downplay the political nature of the Scheme. At the time, as the HKNSL was preparing to be implemented, the Democratic Progressive Party (DPP) government also responded strongly, stating its determination to "provide necessary assistance to the people of Hong Kong, showcasing the government's commitment to upholding universal values and supporting Hong Kong's pursuit of freedom and democracy" (Mainland Affairs Council, 2020).

While Taiwan's support for Hong Kong's position was evident, the wording of official documents was consistently subjected to scrutiny, strictly adhering to soft language to avoid any perception of being overly politicised. This approach involved the use of terms such as universal values, cultural exchange, and caring, which were carefully chosen to convey the message without raising unnecessary political sensitivities. We knew that CSOs who were involved in the previous stage of the shelter work spent several months carefully monitoring whether the Scheme's assistance mechanisms would be fully integrated into the government's internal processes. Due to the CSOs' effort, on the date of the Scheme's announcement, the Exchange Office opened a formal online application window, allowing Hong Kong protesters to seek assistance by phone or email. Most relevant expenses related to the care and resettlement of protesters were borne by the government, and CSOs' resources were redirected to a few financial items that the government was unwilling to bear. This allowed CSOs to focus more on monitoring the effectiveness of the Exchange Office's operations. It is worth noting that the Exchange Office has never publicly disclosed its work details. Even the relevant public information section of the government's financial budget did not show its financial scale. There have been legislators' inquiries regarding the 2021 budget of the ECCPC, questioning officials from the MAC. The official response only mentioned that the ECCPC allocated NT$31.42 million as the total annual expenditure amount (Chen, 2021).

The Taiwanese government chose to keep the operational details of their Scheme undisclosed, citing the need to protect the safety of protesters and other widely accepted reasons. Among these reasons, two stood out: First, publicly disclosing the application process may make it easier for Chinese-affiliated intelligence agents to infiltrate and obtain sensitive information about protesters' identities; second, publicising the details of the Scheme's execution may allow the Chinese government or its local collaborators in Taiwan to gain a complete understanding of the Scheme, which could potentially jeopardise the safety of protesters. In our advocacy experience, we often encountered opposition from some individuals from Hong Kong who, due to these two security concerns, opposed the legislation of the asylum mechanism.

Given the cross-border oppression tactics of the Chinese regime, CSOs did not dispute the importance of protecting the identity of protesters. However, they repeatedly called on the government to examine the rationale for not making the details of the Scheme transparent (TNL, 2020). In the absence of an official mechanism that was transparent and accountable, the potential costs and risks were shifted to the asylum seekers. At this stage, several everyday tensions between the government and applicants had emerged:

i. Applicants were unable to discern the application process and had no clear information on when they would receive notification and feedback from the government.

ii. Applicants were unaware of the criteria for review and were unsure how to prepare their documents to increase their chances of passing the inspection.
iii. Some applicants who had not received official responses faced the issue of their passport expiration. As a result of unclear procedures, they did not have enough information to determine whether they should leave Taiwan early and seek refuge in a third country.

To gain insight into the logic of the official system, civilian actors and public media utilised case interviews and incomplete information to piece together the government's internal review process, while also offering suggestions and criticisms. The following is a model of the review process by officials, pieced together from the information available:

i. Asylum seekers apply for a general stay visa to enter Taiwan (usually holding a tourist visa).
ii. Applicants call or email the Exchange Office and submit preliminary identification information, as well as a description of their involvement in the protests.
iii. Exchange Office staff arrange an interview to clarify and document the applicant's protest participation and the legal risks associated with returning to Hong Kong.
iv. Exchange Office personnel consult with third-sector experts and scholars for evaluation of the individual case.
v. A government review committee composed of officials decides whether to provide the applicant with assistance and care. Once approved, the Exchange Office continues to provide care and assistance in daily living, including most of the support services designed by CSOs in the first stage.
vi. Due to other government regulatory procedures, applicants may be required to undergo further interviews with border or immigration agencies.
vii. Finally, interdepartmental government personnel form a joint review committee to decide whether to grant the applicant "Scheme-based status" (Liu, 2021).

From the perspective of CSOs, one of the criticisms of the process was that even if an applicant successfully obtained the "Scheme-based status", it did not necessarily mean that they were granted refugee status or any other valid residency rights (Liu, 2021). The government did not provide applicants with any official documentation to attest to the receipt of the "Scheme-based status", nor did it offer any other opportunities for residency outside of the usual channels. Therefore, applicants who had completed the screening process typically received only verbal notification from personnel at the Exchange Office that they had obtained the "Scheme-based status". Subsequently, these individuals had to consider whether to pursue higher education, which was the most feasible pathway for young protesters to gain eventual citizenship in Taiwan's existing legal framework.

During this stage, the official application process had not been subjected to a thorough examination due to the curtailment of personnel mobility stemming from the Covid-19 pandemic. At the outset of the pandemic, the Taiwan government promptly implemented quarantine measures for individuals from China, Hong Kong, and Macao and suspended all entry of foreign nationals from 19 March 2020 (Bureau of Consular Affairs, 2020). With the exception of foreign nationals with residency status, individuals with general tourist visas were unable to enter Taiwan. The border ban on Hong Kong nationals persisted until 20 February 2023, for a period of almost three years. Many Hong Kong protesters chose to obtain student status in Hong Kong and enter Taiwan with a student visa (Bureau of Consular Affairs, 2020).

However, these protesters faced a predicament when they reached out to the Exchange Office to express their intention to apply for assistance, as the staff seemed to provide vague reasons for not accepting their cases, leaving them perplexed (Liang, 2022). "Not accepting the case" did not mean rejecting the application. We had several instances where we accompanied the applicants during phone calls to the Exchange Office. These conversations often resulted in a logical impasse, as the perspectives of the applicants and the Exchange Office staff could not align. From the government's viewpoint, successful entry into Taiwan for students meant that they did not necessarily require special assistance since they had already obtained residency status. As a result, the Exchange Office staff indicated their limited ability to offer further legal protection or assistance. Instead, they offered consultation services and encouraged the applicants to seek help if they encountered any future difficulties. However, from the applicants' standpoint, this rhetoric appeared as a disingenuous and tactful refusal. They firmly believed that they needed government assistance, as their involvement in the protests could expose them to harassment or arrest by the Hong Kong government if they were to return. They expected a more straightforward approach from government employees who, operating within an official capacity and wielding the mechanisms of public power, they thought should not employ ambiguous language.

During this stage of Taiwan's aid to Hong Kong, we observed two levels to the role of the Exchange Office:

i. At the level of resettlement and care, it was true that the Exchange Office faced significant challenges in immediately handling all the cases of protesters sent by CSOs, given its recent establishment. This situation was worthy of criticism as the government took nearly a year to establish concrete financial planning and personnel structures to implement President Tsai Ing-wen's promise of providing humanitarian assistance to Hong Kongers. Within the public sector, the Exchange Office gradually developed a systematic workflow, albeit at a slow pace.

ii. At the level of legal protection, the Exchange Office, as a semi-official agency, did not have the power to resolve the long-term residency issues of applicants comprehensively. In other words, while the Exchange Office had replaced CSOs, the ruling party had yet to present a residency application mechanism specifically designed for Hong Kong protesters. The resulting legal and regulatory impasse significantly affected the mental and physical health of applicants, as a lack of legal identity made it challenging for them to feel secure in Taiwan and develop their personal lives (Chen et al., 2019). Therefore, at this level of legal protection, the Taiwanese government had yet to make a clear statement, and the mechanism for sheltering Hong Kong protesters had been stalled.

The non-disclosure of information might, in specific circumstances, be disadvantageous to the ruling party's interests. If the government's assistance was effective, the confidentiality of information might prevent them from promoting their achievements. In February 2022, after approximately a year and a half of operation, a veteran journalist from the Liberty Times, who was well-versed in the business of the MAC, published a report stating that the Scheme had assisted over 130 Hong Kong protesters seeking refuge in Taiwan due to "political reasons" since 2020. The government anticipated that 400–500 Hong Kong residents would continue to seek shelter through this channel in the future. Among these individuals, the youngest protester was not even 18 years old, while the oldest was in their 40s (Chen, 2022a).

The number of 130 was slightly larger than the figures collected by CSOs. Through multiple interviews with limited sources of information, CSOs had learned that as of February 2022, the total number of individuals in the Scheme was approximately 110, with the majority consisting of those directly assisted during the stage one accounting for around 76%. Furthermore, despite the border restrictions imposed during the pandemic, the Taiwanese government still accepted approximately 20–25 individuals to enter with a visa due to exceptional humanitarian grounds, who subsequently became part of the Scheme. It was evident that the telephone and email application window announced by the Exchange Office had only seen around two to three successful applications. Without legal refugee status, most applicants chose to study, with approximately 60–70 applicants holding student visas. These Hong Kong individuals with student visas faced strict restrictions, resulting in many being unable to work full-time legally to earn income. Thus, they fell into financial hardship due to high tuition fees and academic pressure. Through private networks, we learned that some Hong Kong communities in Taiwan had initiated fundraising campaigns to share the burden of tuition fees for these youth protesters, easing the issue to a certain extent. Nevertheless, according to Table 5.1, approximately 16% of protesters who chose to study ultimately failed to adapt to campus life and shifted to employment. However, those who chose employment faced another difficulty. They could only obtain a short-term residency of up to three years, and although the residency could be extended, they could never obtain Taiwanese citizenship, which also prompted some protesters to consider the possibility of leaving Taiwan and moving to the UK. Regarding the Scheme-based status review process, more than 80% of applicants, shown in Table 5.1, successfully completed the final joint review and obtained the Scheme-based status, while the minority were still awaiting processing. Approximately one to three individuals did not pass the review due to unclear legal risks of returning to Hong Kong.

Table 5.1 Implementation status of the Humanitarian Assistance Scheme (as of February 2022)

Category	*Number*	*Description*
Total number of participants in the Scheme	Approximately 110	This refers to the total number of Hong Kong protesters who came to Taiwan and were being cared for by the Exchange Office. Approximately 84 individuals (76%) were those who were directly assisted by CSOs in the stage one. Around 20–25 individuals (18–22%) entered Taiwan during the pandemic through special channels based on humanitarian assistance reasons. Additionally, approximately two to three individuals directly submitted their applications to the Exchange Office and were granted assistance
Career planning		
Employee	40–45	Some protesters chose employment as a means of obtaining residency and striving for self-reliance. This approach could only grant residency rights for up to three years, a time-span which was subject to renewal, but did not lead to citizenship
Student	60–70	Students could not work full-time and relied solely on private resources to support their education, which created a financial burden. Some students lacked the motivation to study but were unable to settle through employment. About ten protesters could not adapt to the school environment and ended up dropping out to pursue employment
Application status		
Successfully passed final joint review	92–99	Individuals who had completed the Scheme procedures and obtained the Scheme-based status
Pending administrative procedures, not yet entered final joint review	10–15	Individuals who had not yet entered the final joint review
Failed to pass final joint review after submission	1–3	Individuals who did not pass the final joint review, likely due to unclear legal risks in their applications

Source Interviews by the authors. The statistics are up to February 2022

After July 2022: The "Quasi-Asylum Mechanism" Not Publicly Disclosed

In July 2022, the Taiwan government internally drafted administrative documents to address the issue of Hong Kong protesters who lacked legal asylum residency status. However, the government did not amend any existing laws or regulations publicly. Instead, all changes were communicated verbally to applicants by personnel from the Exchange Office. The media later summarised the full details of the mechanism from information obtained from Scheme applicants:

i. Applicants who pass the final joint review and obtain the Scheme-based status are eligible to apply for a one year "personal work permit" from the Ministry of Labour.
ii. With this "personal work permit", applicants can apply to the National Immigration Agency (NIA) for a work residency permit, which will be renewed annually along with the personal work permit. The residency permit will also be extended.
iii. From the day of obtaining the Scheme-based status, applicants can apply to become Taiwanese citizens if they have resided in Taiwan for five years and have an average monthly income of 1.5 times the minimum wage in the fifth year.
iv. During the five-year residency period, applicants can participate in the labour market and enjoy national health insurance just like Taiwanese citizens. There are also no restrictions on studying and pursuing further education while working (Chun, 2022b).

At this stage, the general application channels of the Exchange Office were no longer the narrow gateways they used to be, with vague language and difficult access. At the time of writing this chapter, we found that many protesters' applications had been successfully accepted and they had entered into the subsequent interview processes. Under the continuous supervision of CSOs, the Exchange Office had started assigning each protesting applicant a unique case number for tracking the progress of their case review. A responsible government official confirmed this new measure in a phone call with the authors. Although the government has not openly explained whether the aforementioned rule changes have affected the operating standards for case acceptance, it is evident that when the government proposed a superior institutional framework, providing applicants with the opportunity to obtain a dedicated legal residency status through a Scheme-based process, the operational efficiency of the government's front-end execution units functioned seamlessly as anticipated. In terms of the strict refugee legal framework in the international community, Taiwan's humanitarian aid measures for Hong Kong protesters cannot be considered complete. However, in terms of their substantive content, they have already covered the various needs and regulatory support required by asylum seekers in a foreign land (Table 5.2).

Hong Kong protesters now had the right to submit Scheme applications to the Exchange Office, which, after specific review procedures, might offer the opportunity to obtain social rights such as work permits, health insurance, residency rights, and the chance to become a citizen of Taiwan. During the application period, applicants could receive rental subsidies, living allowances, and, when necessary, apply for psychological counselling services or emergency medical care. As such, Taiwan's assistance to Hong Kong protesters could be considered a "quasi-asylum mechanism", but the government was reluctant to openly disclose the content of this mechanism due to its own safety concerns and other national strategic considerations, and was also unwilling to appeal to explicit laws. Under this restriction, long-standing problems persisted:

Table 5.2 Index of names of organisations in Taiwan

English	*Wade–Giles (Pinyin)*	*Traditional Chinese*
Taiwan Economic Democracy Union	t'ai wan ching chi min chu lian hê	台灣經濟民主連合
Taiwan Association for Human Rights	t'ai wan jên ch'üan ts'u chin hui	台灣人權促進會
Judicial Reform Foundation	min chien ssu fa kai kê chi chin hui	民間司法改革基金會
Taiwan–Hong Kong Service and Exchange Office	t'ai kang fu wu chiao liu pan kung shih	臺港服務交流辦公室
Taiwan–Hong Kong Economic and Cultural Cooperation and Promotion Council	t'ai kang ching chi wên hua hê tso ts'ê chin hui	臺港經濟文化合作策進會

i. If there is a change in the ruling party, and Taiwan is governed by a pro-China party, the Kuomintang (KMT) or Taiwan People's Party may be quite likely to suspend the aid mechanism through internal procedures directly. External parties will find it challenging to supervise the amendment without explicit legal provisions as an advocacy lever.
ii. Even if the DPP continues to govern in the coming years, President Tsai Ing-wen's second term will end in 2024. The question remains whether future leaders will still be willing to support this quasi-asylum mechanism.
iii. Applicants must reside in Taiwan for five years before acquiring citizenship, during which any unforeseen circumstances lack legal provisions.

The Legal Challenges of Taiwan's Assistance to Hong Kong

The Use of Regular Immigration to Conceal Political Refugees

At the moment of writing this article, the Taiwanese government has not officially designated its assistance to Hong Kong as "political asylum", and due to the absence of a comprehensive refugee law, protesters seeking refuge in Taiwan are unable to obtain legal refugee status. In the official definition, the assistance provided by the Taiwanese government to Hong Kong protesters seeking help is not heavily politically motivated "asylum", but rather "humanitarian assistance" based on universal values and human rights concerns. Even after the establishment of a "quasi-asylum mechanism" in July 2022, the Taiwanese government had not officially acknowledged any protesters receiving official asylum through proper channels.

Compared to the previous KMT government, the Tsai Ing-wen administration had taken a more definitive stance, refusing and resisting China's intention to annex Taiwan's territory and making significant breakthroughs in foreign relations with democratic countries such as the United States and Japan to elevate Taiwan's actual national sovereignty status. However, President Tsai Ing-wen had consistently shown a tendency not to modify any legal frameworks related to Taiwan's policies towards China, not just concerning Hong Kong but also in issues related to economic security. Despite many international allies' legal adjustments to defend or sanction China in response to its threats, the DPP government had only made minor administrative and regulatory adjustments in a small scope (Chiang, 2022). Regarding policies towards Hong Kong, the Taiwanese government has been unwilling to amend laws, let alone propose legal orders granting administrative agencies the authority to make changes on their own (Chiang, 2022). In the face of China's military threats and diplomatic pressures on Taiwan, President Tsai Ing-wen's cautious and conservative attitude has fundamentally limited the development space for legalising Taiwan's assistance to Hong Kong.

Within the confines of this policy, Taiwan's government formulated a basic strategy during the stage one and two, which aimed to extend humanitarian assistance to protesters for a limited duration, with the expectation that they would opt for the regular immigration channels rather than pursuing the path of asylum or refugee status in Taiwan. One of the quintessential cases illustrating this policy was the predicament of Mr. Lam Wing-kee, the proprietor of Causeway Bay Books, who hailed from Hong Kong. Mr. Lam and his Hong Kong associates operated a specialised bookstore offering publications banned or censored by the Chinese government, many of which divulged accounts of illicit or unethical activities of officials affiliated with the Communist Party. In 2015, Mr. Lam and his fellow shareholders went missing in Hong Kong, and Mr. Lam subsequently confirmed that they had been kidnapped by clandestine Chinese law enforcement personnel and transported to mainland China for trial. This event dealt a severe blow to the confidence of Hong Kong's civil society in the political freedom milieu of their city. Pressured by the increasingly repressive atmosphere for free speech in Hong Kong, Mr. Lam sought refuge in Taiwan in 2019 and founded a new bookstore bearing the same name, "Causeway Bay Books (Taiwan)" (Chen & Chiu, 2022). The Taiwanese government had repeatedly welcomed Mr. Lam's decision to sustain his publishing business in Taiwan, with senior government officials, including the president and the foreign minister, paying visits to the bookstore to unequivocally demonstrate Taiwan's unwavering support for Hong Kong. Bolstered by this strong government endorsement, Mr. Lam undoubtedly satisfied the criteria of being vulnerable to the Chinese government's intimidation and deserved Taiwan's official protection. However, Mr. Lam availed himself of the aid and guidance of government personnel. He first attempted to apply for a start-up visa, but his application failed. Subsequently, he pursued a professional immigration visa, which ultimately culminated in him attaining Taiwanese citizenship (TNL, 2020).

In general, even for those who have fled their homeland or cannot return due to safety concerns, it is not necessary to apply for refugee status. Choosing whether to apply for refugee status or immigration status can be a strategic consideration based on one's own interests. If someone like Lam Wing-kee has sufficient resources and social support, becoming a Taiwanese citizen through the immigration pathway would naturally eliminate the need to go through the arduous process of seeking asylum, which increases their own security risks. However, not every Hong Kong protester who came to Taiwan has had the opportunity to meet the immigration policy standards and successfully obtain residency.

Taiwan's policy towards Hong Kong immigrants has differed from that of other foreigners. Prior to 2019, Taiwan adopted a lenient attitude towards Hong Kong immigrants, with low review thresholds and diverse application channels. The reason for this is that Taiwan was using the Republic of China constitutional framework, whose backbone was created in 1946 in China. Under this constitutional framework, many authoritarian legacies remained, and still remain to this day. Taiwan is unlikely to change this framework until it is able to gain widespread international support and declare de jure independence. Under this framework, the past KMT government stood on the "free and democratic" side of the Cold War binary opposition and hoped that overseas Chinese would choose to come to Taiwan and refuse to join the People's Republic of China. In addition, with the basic policy of ethnic nationalism, the Republic of China government previously identified all people of Chinese descent around the world as its quasi-citizens. Therefore, although Hong Kong Chinese were under British colonial rule, they were viewed by the KMT government as part of a temporary political state. In the long run, the colony of Hong Kong was still to be returned to the Republic of China.

At the time of writing this article, foreigners in Taiwan typically obtain a residency permit before applying for permanent residency. To naturalise as Taiwanese citizens, they must renounce their original nationality. In contrast, the immigration process for Hong Kong residents is fundamentally different. As quasi-citizens of the Republic of China, they can apply for citizenship without naturalisation if they meet specific criteria after obtaining residency. They do not have the option to obtain a non-citizen permanent residency status.[1] There have been various pathways for Hong Kong immigrants to come to Taiwan, including five common categories: "student immigration", "marriage immigration", "investment immigration", "professional immigration", and "entrepreneurial immigration". "Student immigration" was a popular pathway for protesters during the first and second stages of the aid for protestors coming to Taiwan. To become Taiwanese citizens, they were required to study at a Taiwanese college or university, work in Taiwan for at least five years after graduation, earn an average monthly income that was at least twice the minimum wage in the fifth year, and have no gaps in their work history during this period. Additionally, each employer must be willing to apply for a work permit from the Ministry of Labour. In recent years, many economic immigrants from Hong Kong have chosen the "marriage immigration" and "investment immigration" pathways. The former required being married to a Taiwanese citizen for at least three years, while the latter required investing at least NT$6 million in Taiwan for one year. "Professional immigration" and "entrepreneurial immigration" were options that Lam Wing-kee tried. The former required recognition from a competent authority in the professional field and residence in Taiwan for at least one year, while the latter had more complicated criteria, higher thresholds and required residing in Taiwan for at least five years before applying for citizenship.

The Conservative Legislation Strategy

During the Anti-ELAB Movement, Hong Kong youths repeatedly urged the Taiwanese government to confront the unresolved issue of the lack of a formalised asylum mechanism. The ruling party leaders remained conservative and continued to guide protesters through the regular immigration channels. In September 2019, the internationally renowned Hong Kong activist Joshua Wong (2019) wrote a letter of opinion to Taiwanese media, pointing out that a refugee law or other legal mechanisms based on the Act Governing Relations with Hong Kong and Macau would be

[1] At the time of writing this article, the Taiwanese government has attempted to promote amendments to convert the Hong Kong immigration system into a status that is closer to that of ordinary foreigners, but it has not yet become the government's final approved policy (See Chen, 2022b).

an excellent foundation for the DPP's Scheme legislation. Wong added that without solving this issue, many practical difficulties would arise for protesters coming to Taiwan. At that time, Premier Su Tseng-chang immediately denied the legitimacy of Wong's questioning, affirming that Taiwan's then mechanisms were complete and that there was no need to revise the refugee law (Chiao, 2019). In December 2019, violent clashes broke out as the police forcibly entered the campuses of several universities in Hong Kong, causing many injuries and turning the tide of the Anti-ELAB Movement towards a more pessimistic state of affairs (BBC News, 2019). The then president of the Hong Kong Baptist University Students' Union commented on the DPP government's failure to establish a legal basis for an asylum mechanism, which was then spun by Taiwan's pro-China media as the DPP's exploitation of Hong Kong protesters to gain votes. The negative effects of this incident continued to ferment in Taiwan's media, and the Taiwanese government proved unwilling to address the core problem, resulting in a decline in the quality of public discourse. Eventually, the former president of the Students' Union publicly apologised, putting an end to the chaotic situation (Huang, 2019).

Premier Su's notion of a "comprehensive legal system" referred to Article 18 of the Act Governing Relations with Hong Kong and Macau and Article 25 of the Enforcement Rules of the Act Governing Relations with Hong Kong and Macau, which provided a legal basis for the government to assist Hong Kong protesters facing political emergencies (Mainland Affairs Council, 2017). However, these two provisions contained only one sentence each, without regulating any procedures, working frameworks, or the legal rights of applicants. In June 2020, CSOs proposed a civilian version of the Enforcement Rules of Article 18 of the Hong Kong and Macao Relations Act, based on previous advocacy experiences, with the aim of improving the then weak and ineffective legal framework design (Taiwan Association for Human Rights, 2020). This version emphasised the supervision and participation of civilian experts and scholars. Former chairman of the MAC, Chen Ming-tong, accepted the group's opinion and proposed amending the enforcement regulation in the Legislative Yuan, prepared to institutionalise the existing shelter work system. Despite Premier Su's public opposition, the MAC persisted on its opinion, and the implication at that time was that the MAC would further strengthen the legal system of shelter in response to the HKNSL (Chen, 2020). However, after the establishment of the Exchange Office,

Premier Su again publicly opposed the regulative amendment, citing the "completeness of existing laws and regulations" (Liu, 2020). He did not proactively explain how the government would operate a project without a legal basis, nor did he explain how previous practical difficulties would be solved in the new model of the Exchange Office. Premier Su's tough stance also suppressed public discussion of the issue within government departments, and even the DPP-dominated Legislative Yuan adopted a consistent stance, blocking all possibilities for amendment. However, the suppression of public discussion did not mean that social conflicts and practical difficulties no longer existed (Chiang, 2020).

Due to the practical difficulties encountered in its work, the MAC had to seek temporary solutions within the existing legal framework. In the second stage, in collaboration with the Ministry of Labour, the MAC invoked Article 51 of the Employment Service Act to exempt protesters who had obtained the Scheme-based status from work restrictions. This new administrative measure was not officially announced or implemented, but its implementation was verified through interviews with the protesters and direct contact with employers hiring these protesting individuals. The Employment Service Act has been the primary regulation relating to the employment of foreigners in Taiwan since it was enacted in 1992. Article 51 clearly stipulates that refugees with residency permits can join the job market under the same conditions as ordinary citizens. The concept of "refugee" was already included in the law when the Employment Service Act was enacted in response to the trend at the time of various countries enacting refugee laws. However, a Taiwanese version of a refugee law has never been enacted, being consistently delayed in the Legislative Yuan. Ironically, the existence of Article 51 served as evidence supporting the claim made by Su Tseng-chang regarding the "completeness of existing laws and regulations". While it was difficult to ascertain Su's thoughts, from our perspective, this evidence actually highlighted the necessity of having a legal basis for asylum work. If there had been no Article 51, the influx of a large number of asylum seekers could have led to adverse consequences. The case-by-case processing approach failed to provide protesters with legal rights to participate in the labour market, instead placing a significant burden on public resources to cover their various living expenses, rather than facilitating their self-reliance. Taiwan's reluctance to amend its legal system to enhance its Hong Kong policy might have achieved geopolitical stability, but it also intensified the administrative burden on government agencies and CSOs. Moreover, the question remained as to whether the geopolitical consideration holds logical and substantial significance.

Troubling National Security Considerations

The Taiwanese government has consistently avoided public discussion of its support for Hong Kong and has refrained from making legislative changes, often citing the need for discretion. This approach is grounded in three analytical perspectives. Firstly, the government seeks to protect the safety of Hong Kong protesters by avoiding public disclosure of details regarding the aid projects. Secondly, the government aims to avoid the complex geopolitical issues that may arise from enacting asylum policies. Lastly, since existing legislation has been deemed sufficient, the government sees no need for further action. These perspectives seemed to be widely accepted in Taiwanese society, as evidenced by Lam Wing-kee's affirmation of the official position that "actions are more important than words" when evaluating Taiwan's aid to Hong Kong (Chung, 2020).

However, the term "Taiwanese government" does not denote a homogeneous entity with identical interests. Even the disagreement between the MAC and the premier exposed the fragility of the "actions are more important than words" approach. The modalities of executing the Scheme have remained contentious, revealing considerable debate within government agencies. Consequently, President Tsai Ing-wen's circumspection on the topic of legalising such initiatives for national security purposes might result in inconsistencies due to divergent interpretations and definitions of "national security" across various government and societal domains.

In August 2020, the MAC issued a regulatory order to amend existing laws in order to enhance national security screening. Under the new regulations, all Hong Kong residents applying for residency or citizenship in Taiwan were required to declare whether they were born in China, whether they had ever worked for a Chinese-funded institution, and whether they had any connections to the Communist Party or the Chinese government. The government did not explicitly state what direct effects would result if the answer to the aforementioned question were "yes". At the time of its announcement, the amendment did not attract opposition, but rather was seen as a necessary response to China's continued military intimidation of Taiwan. However, when the first batch of immigration applications was processed under the new regulations, many Hong Kong investment immigrants found their applications rejected due to reasons such as "harmful to national interests" and "likely to engage in terrorist activities" (Lin, 2022). One widely publicised case involved an applicant who had worked at the Chinese University of Hong Kong (CHHK), which was deemed by the Taiwanese government to be a government-funded institution, and was therefore deemed to have connections to the Hong Kong government (Executive Yuan, 2022). This decision was difficult to understand, as staff at CUHK were not government officials, and many of them were even supporters of the pro-democracy movement. Some applicants who were dissatisfied with the government's screening opinions, questioned the NIA about the national security considerations underlying its decision-making. However, according to what applicants told us, the NIA's response admitted that due to the overwhelming volume of applications, the execution of its operations was not always adequate, and that there had been misunderstandings caused by the imprecision of details in the administrative documents. From the end of 2021 to the beginning of 2022, many media outlets reported on these failed immigration cases, exposing the chaos of the government's national security screening (Chun, 2022a; Kuo & Chen, 2022; Lee, 2023). The MAC clarified that the government rarely rejected applications based solely on the applicant's Hong Kong identity background, and that the majority of rejections were due to the applicant's failure to meet the investment immigration requirements (Shen, 2022).

In a parallel timeline, in April 2022, the MAC unveiled a plan to establish a new immigration route aimed at tackling the residency predicament faced by Hong Kong protesters residing in Taiwan. This initiative provided a plausible chance for these individuals to gain citizenship following their employment in Taiwan. Despite the apparent disconnect with political asylum, this move by the Taiwan government was consistent with their long-standing approach of sidestepping sensitive terminologies such as "political asylum" by embedding humanitarian aid within broader immigration frameworks (Shen & Chen, 2022). Surprisingly, members of the same political party opposed this bill. The DPP legislators castigated the MAC's officials for their lack of adherence to national security duties, citing China's total control over Hong Kong. Thus, they argued that to ward off Chinese infiltration, Taiwan must eschew the creation of new immigration channels for Hong Kong residents and instead restrain them. The ruling party's "national security" discourse was confounding, as the head of the Executive Yuan claimed the extant legal framework for the humanitarian Scheme was comprehensive, thus rejecting the MAC's initial amendment proposal in mid-2020. Concurrently, DPP legislators cooperated in circumventing any policy discourse in the Legislative Yuan while abiding by the national security concerns of their superiors. However, the MAC twice proposed amendments that enfolded political refugees within immigration policies while taking into account national security considerations, only to be criticised by DPP legislators for their alleged lack of national security awareness (Wu, J., 2022). The convoluted discourse on national security emanating from the ruling party left many protesters feeling uneasy, according to our observation. The national security concerns have not brought about a sense of security; instead, they have led to troubling consequences. After several months of political negotiations and manoeuvring within the DPP, the Taiwanese government ultimately decided to transform the proposed legislative amendments into internal documents that would not explicitly alter existing laws, thus commencing the third stage of its Hong Kong aid policy.

Conclusion

Returning to the initial question of how Taiwan can continue to develop substantial assistance policies towards Hong Kong activists without being formally recognised, the lack of legal recognition of these activists is due to Taiwan's national strategic considerations. However, the operational definition of national security is riddled with flaws, resulting in many internal contradictions within the government system and the DPP. In other words, the government, even if it aims to prioritise national security concerns, lacks a consistent operational method to fully conceal the legal existence of activists and to convincingly demonstrate the effective upholding of national security. Therefore, under these circumstances, the government has difficulty completely denying the existence of political asylum for Hong Kong activists. By avoiding the root of the problem, the government misses the opportunity to foster good public discourse within a democratic society.

On the other hand, the critical factor for the existence of Taiwan's assistance policy towards Hong Kong lies in the substantial presence of Hong Kong exiles on Taiwanese land. The real presence of the exiled community inevitably brings urgent livelihood needs that require the government to use legal tools to intervene and protect their social rights, as well as to plan long-term citizenship pathways. The actual need for asylum makes the government have to consider how to create an effective mechanism within the system. In this process, advocacy actions initiated by CSOs and participation in assistance networks have played a significant role. It is precisely because of the flexibility and initiative of civil society that the government opened up to assistance work early on and created the foundation for subsequent public–third sector cooperation. At least within the scope of resettlement and care services, the government considers civil society opinions highly. Moreover, this foundation of public–third sector cooperation has led the MAC to propose further policy proposals for legalising asylum.

The result of the interaction of various factors has led Taiwan's assistance policy towards Hong Kong to be divided into three development stages since 2019. The common background that runs through the three stages is the consideration of national security and the real need for asylum. However, different actors in the process of developing humanitarian assistance continued to negotiate and to push for solutions, ultimately resulting in Taiwan developing its quasi-asylum mechanisms. This has successfully given hundreds of Hong Kong activists the opportunity to pursue a free life with government assistance, starting a new stage of their lives in Taiwan.

References

BBC News. (2019, November 17). *Hong Kong: Protesters and police in fiery stand-off at university.* https://www.bbc.com/news/world-asia-china-50452277

Bureau of Consular Affairs. (2020, March 18). *In response to the continued global expansion of the Covid-19 pandemic, Taiwan will restrict entry for non-Taiwanese nationals.* Bureau of Consular Affairs, Ministry of Foreign Affairs. https://www.boca.gov.tw/cp-56-5392-49f27-1.html

Chen, H.-Y., Huang, S., & Huang, J. (2019, December 16). Fighting for Hong Kong but unable to return—Rootless "travelers" under the anti-extradition movement. *The Reporter*. https://www.twreporter.org/a/hong-kong-extradition-law-protests-escape-to-taiwan

Chen, J.-X. (2020, May 29). Institutionalizing support for Hong Kong: Mainland Affairs Council to revise regulations for implementing Hong Kong and Macau laws. *ET Today*. https://www.ettoday.net/news/20200529/1725415.htm

Chen, P.-B., & Chiu, Z.-Y. (2022, November 6). Lam Wing-kee applies for settlement in Taiwan: Defending Taiwan's democracy and freedom, I won't leave even if there is a war. *Central News Agency*. https://www.cna.com.tw/news/acn/202211060097.aspx

Chen, Y.-F. (2021, September 18). Kuomintang questions budget for supporting Hong Kong, Mainland Affairs Council: Not a pretext. *Liberty Times Net*. https://news.ltn.com.tw/news/politics/breakingnews/3665599

Chen, Y.-F. (2022a, February 14). Over 130 Hong Kong people seek political asylum in Taiwan, mainly young people with the youngest being under 18. *Liberty Times Net*. https://news.ltn.com.tw/news/politics/paper/1500483

Chen, Y.-F. (2022b, August 2). Relaxing entry for Hong Kong people to Taiwan, considering long-term residency. *Liberty Times Net*. https://news.ltn.com.tw/news/politics/paper/1532116

Chiang, M.-Y. (2020). The failure of the legalization of Taiwan's asylum mechanism for Hong Kong protestors. *Taiwan Human Rights Journal*, *5*(4), 159–170.

Chiang, M.-Y. (2022, October 13). Why has Taiwan become a battleground for the semiconductor industry? *Up Media*. https://www.upmedia.mg/news_info.php?Type=2&SerialNo=156300

Chiao, W.-G. (2019, September 1). Joshua Wong urges Taiwan to expedite "refugee law", Premier Su: Current mechanism is well-equipped and operational. *Up Media*. https://www.upmedia.mg/news_info.php?Type=24&SerialNo=70503

Chun, Y. (2022a, January 18). [Hong Kong People's immigration to Taiwan] originated from mainland China as "original sin"? At least 40 cases blocked from approval—Mainland Affairs Council: Extremely low disapproval rate. *Radio Free Asia*. https://www.rfa.org/cantonese/features/hottopic/feature-taiwan-01182022045010.html

Chun, Y. (2022b, August 18). The prospect of resettlement for Hong Kong protesters in Taiwan after working for as little as five years—Dawn of hope? *Radio Free Asia*. https://www.rfa.org/cantonese/features/hottopic/twvisa-08182022093915.html

Chung, L.-H. (2020, June 4). Taiwanese government provides aid to Hong Kong "Actions speak louder than words," Lam Wing-kee: I agree. *Liberty Times Net*. https://news.ltn.com.tw/news/politics/breakingnews/3186821

Executive Yuan (Taiwan). (2022). Administrative appeal decision (Case no. 1110174743).

Fong, B. C. H., Wu, J., & Nathan, A. J. (Eds.). (2020). *China's influence and the center-periphery tug of war in Hong Kong, Taiwan, and Indo-Pacific* (1st ed.). Routledge.

Huang, S.-X. (2019, December 10). DPP accused of "human blood dumplings" for supporting Hong Kong Protesters? President of Baptist University Student

Union, Fong Chung-yin, clarifies and apologizes. *Newtalk*. https://newtalk.tw/news/view/2019-12-10/338417

Kuo, L., & Chen, A. (2022, May 31). Taiwan offered hope after they fled Hong Kong. Now, they're leaving again. *The Washington Post*. https://www.washingtonpost.com/world/2022/05/31/taiwan-hong-kong-immigration-china/

Lee, J. (2023, January 20). Hong Kong immigration wave: Hong Kong people in Taiwan caught in legal and national security dilemma. Will the "second immigration wave" continue? *BBC News*. https://www.bbc.com/zhongwen/trad/chinese-news-64316121

Li, L. F. (2021). *Actors of the era: The group portrait of the Anti-Extradition Law Amendment Bill Movement*. Oxford University Press.

Liang, J.-H. (2022, June 17). The "special status" that is hard to obtain but can be seen—The two narrow doors that thousands of Hong Kong asylum seekers cannot pass. *The Reporter*. https://www.twreporter.org/a/hong-kong-taiwan-asylum

Lin, Z.-W. (2022, January 11). Hong Kong immigration wave: Taiwan tightens approval, emphasizing "national security concerns", mainland students and Hong Kong immigrants face setbacks. *BBC News*. https://www.bbc.com/zhongwen/trad/chinese-news-59919729

Liu, P.-H. (2020, July 5). Mainland Affairs Council reverses decision not to revise Hong Kong and Macau Laws, Premier Su: Sufficient legal basis does not require amendment. *Radio Taiwan International*. https://www.rti.org.tw/news/view/id/2070815

Liu, Y.-T. (2021, June 28). Taiwan's humanitarian aid to Hongkongers faces new questions amid geopolitical uncertainties. *The Reporter*. https://www.twreporter.org/a/hong-kong-extradition-law-second-anniversary-taiwan-english

Lu, I.-H. (2019, September 29). Taiwan lawyers call for assistance in helping Hong Kong people safeguard their rights. *Liberty Times Net*. https://news.ltn.com.tw/news/politics/breakingnews/2930949

Mainland Affairs Council. (2017). *Laws and regulations regarding Hong Kong and Macao affairs*. https://www.mac.gov.tw/en/News.aspx?n=2EA6ADFC159E7A0D&sms=8675D7361543DE23

Mainland Affairs Council. (2020, June 18). *MAC announces Hong Kong humanitarian aid project and establishes the Taiwan–Hong Kong Office for Exchanges and Services to provide necessary assistance to Hong Kong citizens*. https://www.mac.gov.tw/en/News_Content.aspx?n=A921DFB2651FF92F&sms=37838322A6DA5E79&s=5BEB9EE8F2AF92AB

Safeguard Defenders. (2022, September 12). *110 overseas Chinese transnational policing gone wild*. https://safeguarddefenders.com/sites/default/files/pdf/110%20Overseas%20%28v5%29.pdf

Shen, P.-D., & Chen, P.-B. (2022, April 20). Government plans to relax employment and settlement for Hong Kong residents, benefiting exiled protesters.

Central News Agency. https://www.cna.com.tw/news/acn/202204200134.aspx

Shen, P.-D. (2022, June 9). Foreign media claim Hong Kong residents have difficulty settling in Taiwan, Mainland Affairs Council: Denials may be due to false investments. *Central News Agency*. https://www.cna.com.tw/news/acn/202206090196.aspx

Taiwan Association for Human Rights. (2020, June 9). *[Press release] One year anniversary of Anti-ELAB Movement: "The struggle continues, Taiwan and Hong Kong stand together"*. https://www.tahr.org.tw/news/2692

TNL. (2020, August 31). Lower capital requirements for Hong Kong people immigrating to Taiwan for entrepreneurship, Lin Rongji also chooses this path. *The News Lens*. https://www.thenewslens.com/article/139902

Tsui, E. S.-Y. (2023). *Neverland never more: The intellectual history of Hong Kong's "democratic reunion" generation*. Rive Gauche.

Wong, J. (2019, September 1). *"Emergency law" will bring Hong Kong to its end. Aboluowang Net*. https://tw.aboluowang.com/2019/0901/1337054.html (The original webpage has disappeared after Apple Daily was forced to shut down by the Hong Kong government).

Wu, J. (2022). The Hong Kong–Taiwan nexus in the shadow of China. *The Asia-Pacific Journal*, *20*(16).

Wu, S.-W. (2022, April 28). Hong Kong and Macau "environmental activists" become Taiwanese citizens in five years—Legislators: Does Taiwan lack these talents? *Liberty Times Net*. https://news.ltn.com.tw/news/politics/breakingnews/3908858

Ye, S.-P. (2019, August 12). Democratic Progressive Party: Hong Kong police brutality is a bloody crackdown that has not yet deployed tanks. *Central News Agency*. https://www.cna.com.tw/news/aipl/201908120191.aspx

CHAPTER 6

Refugees by Another Name: Displaced Learners in Japanese Higher Education

David Green, Lisa Unangst, and Eriko Tomita

Introduction

Genocide, environmental crises, and armed struggles during the last ten years have resulted in the highest ever recorded number of displaced people worldwide: over 100 million (UN News, 2022). Waves of displaced learners—this intentionally broad grouping including those with refugee, asylee, and a variety of temporary protected statuses—have catalysed a suite of relevant services at Higher Education Institutions (HEIs). Those initiatives include credential/prior learning evaluation, bridging or pathway programmes providing language training, mentorship programmes, legal clinics, and so forth (e.g., Hartley et al., 2018; Sontag, 2019). Moreover, regional compacts have been established which are relevant to higher education access (e.g., Sarmiento, 2014).

D. Green (✉) · E. Tomita
Nagoya University, Nagoya, Japan
e-mail: david.green@law.nagoya-u.ac.jp

L. Unangst
Empire State University, Saratoga Springs, NY, USA
e-mail: lisa.unangst@esc.edu

L. Momesso and P. Ivanova (eds.), *Refugees and Asylum Seekers in East Asia*, Palgrave Macmillan Studies on Human Rights in Asia,
https://doi.org/10.1007/978-981-97-2867-1_6

Japan is a country known for being largely closed to immigration and notorious for admitting very few refugees (Horiuchi & Ono, 2022). The admission of displaced learners is a new phenomenon in Japan, beginning with only a handful of institutions in 2017 and expanding considerably with the onset of the Russian invasion of Ukraine in February 2022.

As of 2022, Japan's foreign population stood at just 2.4% of its overall population, and the country admitted only 44 out of 10,375 asylum applicants in 2019 (ISA,). However, more Japanese HEIs have begun to host displaced learners, reflecting a possible moderation of refugee policy. Specifically, HEIs appear to be admitting learners who would otherwise qualify as refugees outside of Japan, providing a place for them to live, complete their studies, and potentially to find a job.

This chapter considers HEI supports for displaced learners in Japan, a topic on which there is a dearth of scholarship and a lack of comprehensive data. We analyse how international officers at Japanese HEIs describe the enrolment of and support for displaced learners. To our knowledge, this work is the first of its kind to consider the intersection of migration policy, higher education administration, and the internationalisation of higher education. Drawing from a thematic analysis (Saldaña, 2021) our findings show a willingness on the part of Japanese HEIs to host displaced learners and provide generous financial packages to them, as well as the prevalence of short-term and precarious legal statuses in Japanese humanitarian protection. Furthermore, we identify differential treatment of displaced learners based on nationality. We conclude that local and national government can do more to assist displaced learners and the HEIs hosting them; we recommend harnessing the momentum of support given to Ukrainian evacuees any applying it to other nationalities, and we probe the implications, on Japanese refugee policy, of admitting displaced learners. This conclusion is connected to an expansive understanding of security as discussed by Rothschild (1995) among others, moving beyond a construction of security as relevant to nation states and considering the security of people, itself involving economic, social, and political security.

We begin by examining extant refugee policy in Japan before turning to the internationalisation of higher education in comparative and Japanese contexts. A discussion of research methodology follows, along with a presentation of our findings. We conclude the chapter noting the implications of our project for future research and for migration policy in Japan.

Refugee Resettlement in Japan

While Japan, alongside other comparatively wealthy countries, serve as primary funders of the supranational architecture supporting refugees, refugee resettlement in Japan by number of displaced persons lags far behind most other countries. Japan was the fourth highest governmental donor to the United Nations High Commissioner for Refugees in 2022 (UNHCR Global Focus, 2022), yet the country remains strongly against admitting refugees. To illustrate this, in 2020 the Ministry of Justice received 3936 asylum applications, yet only recognised 47 applicants as refugees (Human Rights Watch, 2022). Japan's refugee recognition rate was just over 1% for 2020, a rate that was in fact higher than previous years.

In comparison, three fellow Organisation for Economic Co-operation and Development (OECD) member states hosted more than one million refugees in 2019: Colombia, Germany, and Turkey (Amnesty International, 2022). Given this state of play, it is useful to briefly parse the legal and policy framework limiting refugee resettlement in the Japanese context, identifying ways in which displaced people experience policy liminality (Unangst & de Wit, 2021). By policy liminality, we refer to learners being "positioned between [policy] discourses rather than being centered within a cohesive suite of federal, state, and institutional-level policy initiatives" (Unangst et al., 2022a, 2022b, p. 44), a circumstance with import for future policy iteration. Policy liminality may be perceived (reported) by learners, and, we argue here, it may also be identified by policy actors such as university administrators closely connected to the development and implementation of relevant policy levers.

Dean and Nagashima (2007) argue that Japan "did not become a party to the 1951 Convention Relating to the Status of Refugees (the Convention) and its 1967 Protocol (the Protocol) until 1981 ... [and it was] not until the mid-1970s, when Indo-Chinese refugees began to arrive on its shores, [that Japan had] to face the issue of refugees within its national boundaries" when absent legal and social welfare frameworks became clear (p. 482). In comparison with other OECD states where civil society has played an active role in supporting refugee resettlement, Flowers (2008) observes that "there was a noticeable absence of Japanese NGOs until 1989" and that those emergent NGOs have, broadly, had relatively positive relations with the Ministry of Foreign Affairs and antagonistic relations with the Ministry of Justice, a circumstance that again has inhibited the further development of policy at the nexus of migration and protection, perpetuating "Japan's pattern of low compliance with the Refugee Convention's norm of protection" (pp. 335, 339). This resulted in refugee status being granted in 330 cases from 3544 overall applications for asylum between 1982 and 2004 and "although it became possible to grant a form of humanitarian status after 1991, this has happened in only 284 cases" (Dean & Nagashima, 2007, p. 482). Akashi (2021) notes that through 2019, Japan's national yearly quota for resettled refugees was 30.

Tarumoto (2019), among others, has connected constrictive policy around displacement to an exclusionary, ethnonationalist construction of Japanese identity:

> A myth is that Japan is (and/or should be) a racially homogeneous country without having immigrants ... The myth is based on, and is enforced by, Japanese essentialist ethnonational identity: Japanese must share the same origin of race along blood lineage. As a result, Japan holds fewer foreigners and immigrants within for a highly industrialized country. As of the end of 2016, foreign residents comprised only 1.9 per cent to the whole population, that is 2,382,822. (Ministry of Justice [MOJ], 2017, p. 8)

Public perception of immigration also remains largely negative (e.g., Green, 2017). Indeed, "in Japan, the definition of 'immigration' or 'immigrants' is highly elusive. There is no public consensus or official definition of the terms" (Endoh, 2019, p. 326). Immigration as an umbrella concept tied to displacement illuminates possibilities and limitations around humanitarian protection specific to the national context.

What does the process of obtaining protection in Japan look like from the perspective of the applicant? As summarised by the Japan Association for Refugees (JAR) in 2017, key challenges include that the interpretation of "persecution" is extremely narrow and typically limited to threats on a person's life or personal freedom. Additionally, asylum seekers must provide objective proof that they cannot return to their home country, which is very difficult for displaced individuals to provide. In terms of the process itself, all relevant documents are available in Japanese only, neutral interpreters may not be available for interviews, and rejected applicants are not given an explanation as to the grounds for rejection (JAR, 2017).

In all, Japan has one of the lowest concentrations of immigrants in the developed world and admits very few refugees. Yet despite these low numbers, the government has been slowly opening the door to increased immigration and the foreign population has been gradually increasing, largely due to concerns over the rapidly aging population. These efforts to increase the foreign population have been made quietly and largely away from the public eye (Green, 2021). The admission of displaced learners could represent a similar attempt on the part of the government to quietly admit refugees through a different means. Rather than having to directly change the very strict refugee admissions criteria, admitting refugees as "displaced learners" or "evacuees" may work to achieve similar humanitarian goals while being more palatable to the public. At the same time, admitting individuals as displaced learners rather than refugees places the burden of teaching Japanese, providing housing, and basic necessities on the host institutions rather than the government. Before we delve further into the Japanese higher education system we will first look to the comparative context.

Higher Education Access: A Comparative View

How, in a comparative, trans-national context, may higher education access and support structures for displaced learners be categorised? As a first step, it is important to emphasise that more economically developed contexts host a minority of the world's displaced people (e.g., Ergin, 2020), while countries that account for just 1.3% of the global GDP hosted 40% of all refugees in 2021 (International Rescue Committee, 2021). Higher education systems and institutions in those settings respond in distinct ways informed by national specificities and a range of resource streams. In the Turkish setting, for example, federal-level policy, developed as millions of Syrians entered the country, facilitated new Arabic-language degree programmes on the Syrian border, with a tuition-free status and scholarships available to Syrian learners. This policy, offered in a higher education system with limited student places allocated through exam scores, generated a backlash (Ergin et al., 2019). In Ethiopia, as described by Woldegiyorgis (2020), refugee-background students from neighbouring countries account for the largest proportion of degree-seeking international students in the country. Tamrat and Habtemariam (2020) outline that Ethiopia's Out-of-Camp Scheme has, since 2010, enabled "self-sponsored refugees among the 20,000 Eritreans who live in Addis Ababa to attend local private higher education institutions on a fee-paying basis" with many of those fees being funded through remittances from the Ethiopian diaspora.

A variety of more and less supportive policy approaches are in evidence across OECD member states. A recent Eurydice report concluded that 22 national systems analysed reflected "top-level steering documents covering higher education [that] mention asylum seekers and refugees, while an almost equal number (19 systems) say nothing" (European Commission et al., 2019, p. 13). The most comprehensive policy approach was identified in Germany where "a number of actions addressing recognition of qualifications and prior learning, bridging programmes, guidance and counselling services and financial support" were in place alongside a "clear budget allocation" (European Commission et al., 2019, p. 13).

Across national settings, there is often a gap between policy supports for approved refugees and asylees and those with pending status or temporary status. In the United States, even states with the highest concentration of refugees infrequently offer in-state tuition to asylees with pending cases (Unangst & de Wit, 2021). There are no established federal sources of funding for higher education among displaced learners, though eligible learners might eventually be able to access sources of funding aimed at lower-income learners, individuals leaving the foster care system, or other pools of money supporting established student equity groups. In Australia, asylum seekers "are treated as international students and are ineligible for Federal Government financial assistance programmes" (Hartley et al., 2018; Webb et al., 2019)", leaving 23 of 43 Australian HEIs to offer stopgap institutional scholarships (Dunwoodie et al., 2020, p. 248). Thus, a range of policy responses is evident across more economically developed systems, though the most coordinated efforts have supported the degree-course enrolment of tens of thousands of recently arrived refugees.

Displacement Alongside Internationalisation

How can we understand the alignment of Japanese internationalisation policy with refugee policy? Internationalisation here refers to—as defined by Knight (2003)—"the process of integrating international, intercultural or global dimensions into the purpose, functions, or delivery of postsecondary education" (p. 2). A specific avenue for internationalisation has been proposed by Leask (2010, 2015): "internationalisation at home" refers to internationalisation activities that centre on the experiences of institutional students, staff, and faculty present on the home campus, and on engaging with international elements via (formal and informal) curriculum, professional development, and all other institutional activities. As argued by Unangst and Barone (2019), internationalisation at home frequently engages community actors, who "add capacity and direction to ... college internationalization efforts" (p. 191). Indeed, there is an entrenched history of coordinated internationalisation activities across the Japanese higher education sphere, with clear government directives promoting internationalisation in education since the 1980s (Burgess et al., 2010). Billions of yen have been invested in degree courses offered in English; international student support services are well-funded; the Japan Exchange and Teaching Programme welcomes international teachers; and various excellence schemes including the 2014 Top Global University Project (Nonaka & Phillips, 2017) have been implemented. Support for international students varies by university type: major public universities as well as some larger private institutions have courted international students since the 1980s (Burgess et al., 2010). However, in spite of increased efforts to recruit international students, Yonezawa (2019) notes that "there is no specific 'internationalization expert' category among the university staff in Japanese universities... [as] departments allocate different types of staff members from both academic and administrative groups" to engage with specific initiatives (p. 378).

In sum, nationally coordinated internationalisation policy is well established in Japan but generally decentralised at the institutional level. Furthermore, as Nonaka and Phillips (2017) have argued, internationalisation or *kokusaika* policies "may be largely driven by the economic or political desire to compete globally (Ishikawa, 2009; Kariya, 2014), rather than by the desire to respond to changing economic and population realities such as Japan's rapidly aging and diversifying society" (p. 15). Here, it seems clear that internationalisation conditions contribute to what we term policy liminality on the part of displaced learners: existing national and institutional structures do not engage with expansive definitions of internationalisation policy or practice that might problematise or interrogate what internationalisation means in the context of a global displacement crisis equivalent to the 14th most populous country in the world (UN News, 2022).

Recent Innovations Across Japanese HEIs

As noted by Kuroda (2020), Japanese HEIs are free to develop tailored admissions policies and procedures, although all universities require students to take and pass an entrance examination as a prerequisite for admission. Japanese HEIs comprise, as asserted by Yonezawa (2019), "777 universities divided into national (86), local public (91), and private (600) institutions" (p. 376). University size and focus can vary considerably in Japan. The former "imperial" universities, founded by the Japanese Empire starting in the late 1800s, represent the major public institutions typically hosting the largest numbers of international students. There is likewise a large range of private universities, with some HEIs, such as Waseda and Keio universities, representing the elite of Japanese institutions and similarly admitting a relatively larger number of international students, while others can be quite a bit smaller and more parochial.

Broadly, limited engagement with displaced learners is evidenced across the Japanese higher education system. Some of that engagement is taking place under the auspices of initiatives spearheaded by various non-profit groups. For example, the Syrian Scholars Initiative was a scholarship programme developed by a foundation associated with International Christian University to support Syrian students impacted by the conflict in that country, this work being done in collaboration with the Japan Association for Refugees (JAR). This effort has been relatively small scale in terms of students enrolled. Six students were admitted to Japan in 2016, and per a 2017 JAR report, the second iteration of the programme garnered 1091 applicants with the goal of admitting eight (JAR, 2017). Kalicki (2019) has described how JAR, during the first year of this initiative, framed it as partly inspired by the success of private refugee sponsorship in the Canadian setting, where private donors, religious groups, and businesses sponsored Syrians fleeing conflict. The six Syrians initially selected were exempt from tuition fees and benefitted from private sponsorship of travel costs and language training. Students paid for living expenses via part-time jobs and were made aware that working visas would be available to them upon graduation.

Similarly, the Japanese Initiative for the future of Syrian Refugees (JISR) operated by the Japanese International Cooperative Agency announced that up to 150 master's level Syrian students would be accepted over five years, with this programme developed in collaboration with the UNHCR. Participants were living in Lebanon and/or Jordan at the time of application, were required to be 22–39 years of age, and attended one of seven participating universities in Japan.

Most recently, the Japanese government began admitting Ukrainian nationals in response to the Russian invasion of Ukraine in February 2022. Where the Syrian Scholars Initiative and JISR have been small-scale precedents in admitting displaced learners to Japan, the Ukraine crisis represents a clear expansion of these initiatives. As of March 2023, Japan has admitted a total of 2211 Ukrainian nationals since the onset of the conflict (MOJ, 2023). Data on the exact numbers of displaced learners among Ukrainian evacuees are not readily available, but listings published by the Japan Student Services Organization, under the jurisdiction of the Ministry of Education, Culture, Sports, Science and Technology (MEXT), show 52 Japanese universities hosting approximately 200 displaced Ukrainian students, and another 66 Japanese language schools hosting approximately 250 Ukrainians as of March 2023 (JASSO, 2023).

Given the expansion of academic institutions in Japan sponsoring and supporting displaced learners with the onset of the Ukraine crisis, it is necessary to understand in more detail the activities of Japanese host institutions, the kinds of services and financial support they provide to displaced learners, how these institutions interact with government and other non-governmental organisations, and the types of challenges they face.

Methodology

To understand how Japanese HEIs have been supporting displaced learners, the authors conducted in-depth interviews with individuals charged with assisting international students at both public and private institutions. Given the focus on HEIs, we have excluded Japanese language schools although, as noted above, Japanese language schools host a reasonably large number of displaced learners and are important sites for future inquiry. The authors contacted most of the 18 universities participating in the Japan Educational Pathways Network (JEPN), a network of private universities, and the Pathways Japan non-governmental organisation. Eight of the former imperial public universities, including Tokyo, Kyoto, Osaka, Nagoya, Hiroshima, Kyushu, Tohoku, and Hokkaido universities were additionally contacted for interviews.

There were eight interviewees in total, including staffers based at four private universities, three public universities, and the Pathways Japan NGO. Owing to the sensitive nature of the topic and the sometimes rigid rules in place for administrators when discussing university activities, interview subjects and their university affiliations are kept confidential in order to allow administrators to freely express their opinions. Pathways Japan had no objections to being named directly. Interviews were conducted both in-person and online, between 1 December 2022 and 16 January 2023. Interviews were semi-structured, with a number of common questions and also the ability to transition onto other topics or issues as necessary. Discussions were conducted in either English or Japanese, at the discretion of the interview subject. Japanese language interviews were translated into English and checked for accuracy. Interviews lasted 45 minutes to one hour on average.

To organise and analyse the interviews, transcripts were subjected to a thematic analysis (Saldaña, 2021, p. 175). Each of the authors independently reviewed the interview transcripts, coding for recurrent topics and issues, grouping interview details into several broad themes and then noting the subcomponents for each theme. The authors' thematic notes were then compared and compiled, leading to the establishment of our categories and subtopics of discussion.

Given the study's small sample size, broad generalisations about displaced learners and relevant administrative coordination are not possible. However, despite these limitations, some general trends in the reception of displaced learners are apparent. Japanese HEIs, according to our data, confront similar challenges as they admit and seek to support displaced learners and likewise anticipate similar issues going forward, particularly regarding the long-term residence of displaced learners and the procurement of resources to support them.

Results

Displaced Learner Support

In discussing university support, we narrow our terminology, referring specifically to "student evacuees" as this is the term used by HEI-based interview participants. Student evacuees are students admitted to Japanese HEIs who could make a credible case for status as an asylum seeker or refugee. Furthermore, this term refers to students entering Japan to escape conflict or persecution, rather than students in Japan at the time a crisis unfolded. It is worth noting that while a small number of student evacuees from Syria and Afghanistan came to Japan before the Ukraine crisis, the vast majority of student evacuees to Japan are now from Ukraine. The discussion around admissions, visa status, and benefits is therefore oriented around Ukrainian evacuees except where noted.

Our data indicate, with respect to international student support, that many departments in national universities have specifically appointed faculty members to assist international students with daily-life issues, and that many offer degree programmes in English. Private universities are more variable: the relevant HEIs in our sample ranged from the highly internationalised with classes and administration entirely in English, to those having a very small international student population with classes and administration almost completely in Japanese.

Differences between public and private universities also extend to how they support student evacuees. All of the private universities represented in our study are members of JEPN, a group of 18 universities operating in tandem with the Pathways Japan NGO, to receive and support Ukrainian evacuees. All of the public universities sampled were acting independently of any organisation or network. That is, the public universities exhibited very little pooling of information or resources. Even within public universities, our participants note that there can be very little cooperation across institutional units (or silos). At least some of this independent streak can be attributed to strict rules and operating procedures in Japanese public universities, where budgetary and administrative hurdles impede collaboration and coordination.

Apart from an outlier HEI, the Ukraine invasion was the first instance of student evacuee enrolment at all universities sampled. However, there is precedent for universities to receive displaced students as all of the public universities included in this study enrolled a small number of students from Myanmar, those students becoming displaced with the 2021 coup d'état. However, these Myanmarese nationals were admitted as regular students and only "became" displaced after arriving in Japan. Several Japanese universities likewise hosted Afghan civil servants and university teachers from 2011 to 2019 as a part of a government programme, but these individuals were admitted as regular, short-term students and required to return to Afghanistan on the completion of their studies (Japan International Cooperation Center, 2021).

Of the universities analysed, overall international student population size ranged from about 1.5% to over 50% of the total student population, or from a low of 36 international students to a high of approximately 2500 students. Each university had admitted a relatively small number of Ukrainian evacuees, between one and nine, and it was most common for the universities to admit no more than three evacuees. Similar rates of evacuee admissions are confirmed by the available statistics (see, e.g., Pathways Japan, 2022).

Our interviews reflect that university admissions processes highly prioritised some connection to Japan, particularly familiarity with the Japanese language. If Japanese proficiency was low, a high level of English was required, and all universities had the expectation that student evacuees would work hard to improve their Japanese abilities during the initial period of admission. Across the universities we studied, all evacuees who gained admission were female and of typical college age; one university administrator noted that college-age males are most likely involved in the fighting in Ukraine. University administrators uniformly reported positive feelings toward hosting student evacuees, such as “I am happy to be able to provide these opportunities to them. They are all very good students” (Public-4), and “I’ve told them I’ve worked with thousands of students, but I think this has been the most meaningful and impactful project that I’ve worked on in my career. I’m happy that I’ve been able to help them” (Private-1). We will address a number of points concerning student evacuees below: admissions, visa status, public and private funding, and challenges with student evacuee hosting efforts.

Admissions

All universities sampled initially admitted Ukrainian evacuees as non-matriculated auditing students for up to one year. One significant difference between public and private universities was the possibility of extending students’ stay. One public university, for example, only admitted Ukrainian evacuees coming from home universities having an exchange agreement with the Japanese institution. Much like a typical study abroad programme, the Ukrainian students could receive course credit for their classes in Japan and would be expected to leave the country after their one year stay. Private universities, by contrast, demonstrated more willingness for extension: after an initial six month–to one year period, student evacuees seeking to continue study could, upon passing an entrance exam, be admitted as matriculated degree-seeking students and continue to receive identical financial benefits for the duration of their studies.

The short initial period of student evacuee enrolment is partly attributed to the timing of the Ukraine crisis. Ukrainian evacuees began to enter Japan in May 2022. The Japanese academic year usually starts in April, with entrance exams several months earlier, typically in January or February. All universities accepted Ukrainian students in an expedited manner due to the emergency situation, opting to evacuate the students as quickly as possible rather than waiting until the start of the next semester. As such, the universities were not able to admit the evacuees as a part of the regular admissions cycle.

The other justification behind the short initial period of enrolment related to language study. In that first period of admission, language learning is vital for evacuees, a good understanding of Japanese being required for university entrance exams, themselves a prerequisite for study in programmes offered exclusively in Japanese. These entrance examinations are notoriously difficult to pass, with admissions to many universities being highly competitive even for Japanese nationals (Kuramoto & Koizumi, 2018). University administrators in our study made no mention as to whether any special allowances would be given to evacuees taking the examinations; admitting any such special allowances could be controversial. Moreover, very strict admissions rules at most institutions indicate that any special considerations for student evacuees will be minimal.

Should the evacuee be unable to pass the entrance examination, a distinct possibility given the difficulty of obtaining strong Japanese proficiency in such a short period of time, according to our interview participants their fate would be unclear. One option for the host university would be to extend the duration of the evacuee's stay under the same status, giving them the opportunity to re-take the entrance exam again the following year. Alternately, facilitating the evacuee's transfer to another institution might be another option. In a worst-case scenario, the evacuee might forego an academic path and instead try to find work in Japan. Having intensively studied the Japanese language, the idea, according to Pathways Japan, is that the evacuee should be better placed to obtain a position. Among private university staffers, the assumption is that the evacuees will not be returning home in the near future, and that universities will potentially be supporting them for several years. In the case of the public staffers interviewed, we learned that evacuees were only admitted on a short-term basis with no clear possibility of entering a degree programme. Discussions regarding the continuation of student evacuees' status were ongoing at public universities, but no decisions had been made at the time of the interviews.

Visa Status

All student evacuees were admitted to Japan on short-term visas without recognition of refugee status by the Japanese government. In the official parlance, these students are referred to as "evacuees" (*hinanmin*), rather than "refugees" (*nanmin*) (Takahara, 2022). This is an important distinction, where "refugee" implies long-term, potential permanent residence in Japan, while "evacuee" denotes a short-term stay. There is also an important distinction between evacuees and refugees in terms of the benefits available. Officially recognised refugees are entitled to permanent residency in Japan, are able to bring their immediate families with them, can participate in a government-sponsored resettlement programme with Japanese language and cultural instruction, and can obtain vocational support at no cost (Akashi, 2021). Student evacuees are entitled to none of these benefits, are not permitted to bring their families, and are the responsibility of their sponsoring institutions rather than the government.

After entering Japan on a short-term visa, according to study participants, almost all evacuees changed their status to a "designated activities" visa, rather than a student visa. "Designated activities" is a broad designation that has been used in several different contexts, including as a work visa for highly skilled professionals (MOFA, 2015a), a stopgap measure for university graduates engaged in paid internships, and for individuals on a working holiday in Japan with financial reserves of at least 30 million yen (MOFA, 2015b). The designated activities visa is usually given for a period of six to twelve months, with the possibility of renewal before the visa expires.

According to the interview participants, designated activities status carries with it both advantages and disadvantages. The main advantage is that it provides more flexibility than a student visa. Under designated activities, a student is not required to maintain a full-time courseload. Unlike a student visa, should a displaced learner on a designated activities visa drop below full-time status they are not required to leave Japan. This can be especially helpful for learners adjusting to life in Japan or experiencing mental health problems stemming from their earlier experiences in conflict zones. By the same token, if academic life proves too challenging for any reason, evacuees can easily transition to work without having to immediately change their visa status.

Although the designated activities visa affords a reasonable degree of flexibility to students, the main disadvantage is its short period of validity and the accompanying instability. Student evacuees must renew their visas annually, with the criteria necessary for renewal being unclear and subject to the discretion of immigration agency officials. Evacuees' residency is not guaranteed unless they are able to switch to a more secure, longer-term visa such as a student or working visa. Considering its advantages and disadvantages, most university administrators had a favourable assessment of the designated activities visa, commending its flexibility over instability concerns; we note that student-focused research might well produce different results. Only one university helped change Ukrainian evacuees to student visas, although another university was planning on having evacuees change to student visas if they were admitted to a degree programme.

Discussion of the designated activities visa also indicates the differences between Ukrainian, Syrian, and Afghan evacuees. All three groups of evacuees have used the designated activities visa, but it has been applied differently to Syrians and Afghans. According to the Pathways Japan representative we spoke with and one of the university officials, Ukrainians are encouraged by the immigration agency to maintain the designated activities visa, while Syrians and Afghans are discouraged from using it. Syrians and Afghans are asked to maintain either a student or working visa and are only permitted to obtain a designated activities visa as a stopgap measure, for example, if they graduate from a Japanese university and are trying to find a job. If Syrians or Afghans apply for a designated activities visa, the processing time is reportedly around six months, with a heavy burden of proof to justify the application. Ukrainians, on the other hand, are reportedly able to obtain the designated activities visa in a matter of hours with little apparent difficulty. University administrators are also confident that Ukrainians' designated activities visas will be renewed without much trouble from immigration officials, at least for the foreseeable future.

One administrator (Private-1) believes the differential treatment of Ukrainians is a conscious government decision: Ukrainians are the victims of international aggression, which is a breach of international law. This is fundamentally different from the civil wars or internal instability that

Syrians and Afghans have encountered, and, as such, Ukrainians are entitled to favourable treatment. Another administrator was much more direct (Private-2), attributing favourable Ukrainian treatment to racial preferences on the part of the Japanese public. In this view the Japanese government exhibits a distinct racial bias, likely because of ingrained racist tendencies in Japanese society, which has resulted in more positive media coverage of Ukrainian evacuees and more favourable treatment by government. As the international literature has reflected on the racist migration and education policies to which displaced learners are subjected (e.g., Villegas & Aberman, 2019), Japan seems to be implicated alongside other more economically developed countries and this issue must be interrogated further.

Public and Private Funding

Past refugee support in Japan has exclusively been in the public sphere, with national and local government responsible for refugees' expenses and integration until they are able to work and sustain themselves in Japanese society. Student evacuees are different in that the HEI, either public or private, is responsible for evacuees' wellbeing. Evacuee support often blends the public and the private, where a public university might use taxpayer money to finance an evacuee's stay but could also solicit private donations. Likewise, private universities have in some cases utilised local government funds to underwrite the cost of supporting evacuees. In both scenarios, however, government has little direct involvement in evacuee support.

According to our respondents, there is not much variation in funding packages for student evacuees across public and private universities, where all universities sampled provide free tuition and housing, as well as a monthly stipend of 60,000–80,000 yen per month for Ukrainian evacuees. Travel expenses to Japan are usually covered as well. All universities bear some amount of the burden in housing and educating student evacuees, although there are some differences in how funds are obtained. One of the private universities we studied exclusively utilised its own internal budget (Private-3), one underwrote evacuees' costs with its own budget and donations from its alumni association (Private-2), and another had a more layered approach, securing additional funding from the local government, a corporate sponsorship, and through the Nippon Foundation (Private-1), a philanthropic organisation that has been donating funds to universities hosting Ukrainian evacuees as well as to evacuees directly (Kageyama, 2023).

Public university staffers, by contrast, indicated a much higher level of instability in funding and were more likely to utilise donations to underwrite the cost of hosting student evacuees. Three of the public universities created specific "Ukrainian disaster relief funds" to solicit donations—aimed at supporting Ukrainian evacuees alone—but all relevant staffers observed that long-term financial support for evacuees is an ongoing challenge. One public university official was explicit that, despite donations, evacuees' funding packages could be guaranteed for only one year (Public-4). Moreover, just one of these HEIs received additional support from their local government and none received financial support from other organisations.

While public and private universities generally appear to eschew major collaborations with outside organisations, Pathways Japan is much more collaborative. Funding is secured through donations and crowdfunding, various domestic philanthropic foundations, religious organisations, and corporate sponsors. In December 2022, Pathways implemented its own scholarship for student evacuees, looking to support four to five evacuees annually, regardless of nationality, admitted to undergraduate or graduate degree programmes in Japan for up to four years. In addition, Pathways maintains direct communication with various government officials, including contacts in the immigration agency, MEXT and the Ministry of Foreign Affairs. Reportedly, MEXT officials have been participating in JEPN meetings regarding Ukrainian evacuees. None of the universities, by contrast, report any direct collaboration with national government agencies or ministries. Private universities affiliated with the JEPN and Pathways Japan may be able to indirectly access government officials through links with Pathways Japan, although this does not appear to be the case with public universities.

Challenges

University officials outline a number of challenges in supporting student evacuees. One of the primary issues is the instability students face in admission and funding. Private universities are able to at least offer the possibility of a longer-term stay, but residency beyond one year is not guaranteed at any of the institutions interviewed. Programme admission remains a problem for student evacuees, where there are significant hurdles to passing university entrance examinations in Japanese after only one year of study. Student evacuees may have a comparatively easier time gaining admission to English-language programmes, which are offered for a limited range of degrees at major public and private institutions, but the problem of limited space and highly competitive admissions remains. If evacuees are unable to pass entrance examinations, what is the next step available for them? Will they be able to acquire enough language skill to transition into working in Japan instead? Will they be able to stay in Japan under a different type of visa? The universities sampled did not have any answers to these questions.

Insecure funding appears to go hand-in-hand with the short initial period of enrolment at public universities, where despite soliciting donations and occasionally collaborating with local government, public universities simply lack the financial ability to make long-term commitments to student evacuees. Along the same lines, with limited funds, limited expertise, and little prior experience hosting evacuees, public and private universities lack the capacity to address some of the problems evacuees face, particularly Post-Traumatic Stress Disorder (PTSD) and other mental health issues. According to one subject, "These students are struggling, and yet there are very few resources for them to seek help … There aren't very many therapists or counsellors who can help them in English, much less Arabic or Ukrainian" (Private-2). The lack of resources across multiple sectors thus remains an ongoing challenge for university officials.

One respondent pointed to minimal government involvement with student evacuees as exacerbating the problem of limited resources. Although the national government has not prohibited universities from sponsoring evacuees, it has not been actively helping them. Pathways Japan similarly criticises government response to evacuees as being decentralised and lacking integration across departments. According to this perspective, there is a need for better communication across government, as well as for government to collaborate more closely with the private sector. With universities playing the central role in receiving student evacuees, a significant question is to what extent national and local government should be involved in supporting evacuees. For the most part, university officials would like to see additional government support.

In discussing the challenges of supporting student evacuees, several HEI officials mentioned the differential treatment of Ukrainians. Though the conflict galvanised support for some evacuees, acknowledgement of and support for displaced learners of other nationalities has been less forthcoming. The number of admitted Ukrainian evacuees is much larger than all other categories of displaced learners, in spite of the fact that Ukrainians only started being admitted to Japan in 2022. Media attention, donations, visa flexibility, and general support have skewed disproportionately in favour of Ukrainian evacuees. Pathways Japan notes, for example, that their crowdfunding efforts for Syrian and Afghan evacuees brought in 3.5 million yen in 2021, while similar efforts for Ukrainian evacuees reached a total of 8 million yen in 2022.

Discussion

Overall, we find a positive attitude toward admitting and hosting student evacuees among Japanese HEI constituents. University administrators almost unanimously report that students, faculty, and staff have a positive impression of hosting student evacuees. However, while evacuee hosting efforts have increased, student evacuees still make up a very small portion of most universities' student bodies, with usually no more than three evacuees at any given institution. The student evacuee experiment has gradually grown in scale and appears likely to continue expanding given the positive assessments so far, but limited financial resources, relevant training for staff and minimal government support could impede the stability of HEI support going forward.

Support for student evacuees is generally the same across public and private universities studied, although both appear to be much more likely to support Ukrainian evacuees than other nationalities. Neither type of institution is able to guarantee long-term residence, but private universities are at least able to offer the possibility of an extended stay. Public universities, by contrast, appear only able to accommodate Ukrainian evacuees for one year, after which their situation is unclear. Public universities may have good intentions, but instability after evacuees' initial period of residence could be potentially harmful as they try to navigate their next move without any certainty. Overall, Japanese universities appear to have successfully evacuated some, mostly Ukrainian, students out of conflict zones and have been generous in their initial funding but need to consider the longer-term implications of hosting evacuees. Greater involvement with, or collaboration from, local and national government could potentially help universities in securing more long-term accommodation for evacuees and overcoming some of the limitations in expertise and resources HEIs are grappling with. This relates to de facto and de jure migration and education policy.

Incongruities in the treatment of evacuees of different nationalities at national and local government levels should also be given attention. There is a perception on the part of some university administrators that racial biases play a factor in the favourable treatment of Ukrainian evacuees. Racial bias is frequently covert, and public approval of Ukrainian evacuees compared to displaced learners or refugees of other nationalities likely plays an important role in the favourable treatment Ukrainian evacuees receive. This comparative privilege may be the result of positive media coverage, broader systems of racism/racialisation in Japan, or some combination of these factors. One challenge for government and university administrators is to extend the momentum and positive sentiment for Ukrainian evacuees to other nationalities, admitting and serving comparable numbers of displaced learners and thereby contesting exclusionary policies. This would serve to further internationalisation at Japanese HEIs and would offer an opportunity for those HEIs to (re)consider their raison d'être.

The Ukraine conflict and the subsequent expansion of student evacuee reception represents a subtle but significant shift in Japanese immigration and refugee policy. The student evacuee pathway is a new avenue for the Japanese government to evacuate refugees from conflict zones to a safer environment. For a country like Japan that admits very few refugees, the evacuee route appears to be more palatable to both the public and government. Indeed, the number of admitted evacuees in 2022 alone was already far greater than the number of all refugees admitted between 2000 and 2022. However, these evacuees are not given an acknowledged refugee status and are unable to receive a similar level of benefits. Their stay is inherently short-term and precarious, likely with consequences for individual wellbeing. The reception of student evacuees thus represents a shift toward a perhaps greater level of openness to refugees, but Japan still lags far behind other countries, and questions over the longevity of displaced learners' residency in Japan remain.

Limitations to this study should additionally be noted. Our sample size was small and was not necessarily representative of Japanese HEIs as a whole, but the depth of the interviews does raise some interesting points regarding the reception and treatment of student evacuees. More research is needed on this topic, especially as evacuees settle in Japan for longer periods of time. While this project focuses mainly on university outreach to student evacuees, interviews with evacuees themselves regarding their experiences in Japan will provide important data and will help identify areas for improving evacuee policy/programmes. In focusing exclusively on Japanese HEIs, we did not address language schools; as there are a reasonably large number of student evacuees and displaced learners at those institutions, future work might examine how they have been received and compare levels of support between HEIs. Additionally, research on displaced students residing in Japan at the time of a crisis in their home country is called for as those individuals will likely have some Japanese proficiency and already be enrolled in a degree programme.

Conclusion

Japan has one of the lowest rates of refugee admissions in the world, typically approving less than 1% of asylum applications in a given year. However, its higher education sector has been gradually internationalising. Located at the intersection of these phenomena, a side door to students displaced from conflict areas appears to be slowly opening in Japan, starting in a limited capacity in 2017 and expanding considerably with the onset of the Russian invasion of Ukraine in 2022. Although these displaced learners are not given official refugee status, hundreds were admitted in 2022 alone. This chapter has looked to this new category of displaced learners or "refugees by another name" coming to Japan to study, asking how and to what extent Japanese Higher Education Institutions are able to support this newly-defined and dynamic group.

Based on exploratory interviews with university administrators, we find that a small number of student evacuees have received a positive reception and generous financial support. However, admissions decisions were in most cases made on a short-term time horizon, with student evacuees only being guaranteed residency for a maximum of one year. More support and expertise from local and national government as well as civil society actors could go a long way in stabilising the situation of displaced learners and alleviating some of the burden faced by HEIs at present, which are grappling with policy liminality as institutions, just as learners grapple with liminality at the individual level. In addition, that investment of resources would bolster human security in Japan and beyond.

There are two major challenges going forward. On the research side, more information about government plans and priorities regarding displaced learners is needed, as is a comprehensive understanding of how HEIs address displacement. This chapter has attempted to take an initial step in this direction by interviewing university officials, discussing their activities, and identifying the problems they face, but quite a bit more work is needed. On the policy side, the Japanese government and public must contend with the question of what exactly humanitarian protection entails. Should displaced learners in Japan be considered refugees? Should they be admitted on a short-term basis under the responsibility of universities and language schools, which is not the predominant model in economically developed settings? Are the displaced learners coming to Japan refugees by another name, or do they reflect a new category of temporary, precarious humanitarian protection?

References

Akashi, J. (2021). How a policy network matters for refugee protection: A case study of Japan's refugee resettlement programme. *Refugee Survey Quarterly, 40*(3), 249–270. https://doi.org/10.1093/rsq/hdab001

Amnesty International. (2022). *The world's refugees in numbers*. https://www.amnesty.org/en/what-we-do/refugees-asylum-seekers-and-migrants/global-refugee-crisis-statistics-and-facts/

Burgess, C., Gibson, I., Klaphake, J., & Selzer, M. (2010). The "Global 30" project and Japanese higher education reform: An example of a "closing in" or an "opening up"? *Globalisation, Societies and Education, 8*(4), 461–475.

Dean, M., & Nagashima, M. (2007). Sharing the burden: The role of government and NGOs in protecting and providing for asylum seekers and refugees in Japan. *Journal of Refugee Studies, 20*(3), 481–508.

Dunwoodie, K., Kaukko, M., Wilkinson, J., Reimer, K., & Webb, S. (2020). Widening university access for students of asylum-seeking backgrounds: (Mis)recognition in an Australian context. *Higher Education Policy, 33*, 243–264.

Endoh, F. (2019). The politics of Japan's immigration and alien residence control. *Asian and Pacific Migration Journal, 28*(3), 324–352.

Ergin, H. (2020). Questioning the ethics and rationale of refugee research. In L. Unangst, H. Ergin, A. Khajarian, T. Delaquil, & H. de Wit (Eds.), *Refugees and higher education: Transnational perspectives on access, equity, and internationalization* (pp. 20–31). Brill Sense.

Ergin, H., de Wit, H., & Leask, B. (2019). Forced internationalization of higher education: An emerging phenomenon. *International Higher Education, 97*, 9–10. https://doi.org/10.6017/ihe.2019.97.10939

European Commission, EACEA, & Eurydice. (2019, February 7). Integrating asylum seekers and refugees into higher education in Europe: National policies and measures, Eurydice report. *Publications Office of the European Union*. https://ec.europa.eu/migrant-integration/library-document/integrating-asylum-seekers-and-refugees-higher-education-europe_en

Flowers, P. R. (2008). Failure to protect refugees?: Domestic institutions, international organizations, and civil society in Japan. *The Journal of Japanese Studies, 34*(2), 333–361.

Green, D. (2021). Charting *Tabunka Kyōsei*: An assessment of municipal-level "multicultural coexistence" and immigrant integration efforts in Japan. *Journal of Asian Sociology, 50*(2), 401–429.

Green, D. (2017). Immigrant perception in Japan: A multilevel analysis of public opinion. *Asian Survey, 57*(2), 368–394.

Hartley, L., Fleay, C., Baker, S., Burke, R., & Field, R. (2018). *People seeking asylum in Australia: access & support in higher education*. National Centre for Student Equity in Higher Education, Curtain University. https://www.ncsehe.edu.au/publications/people-seeking-asylum-in-australia-access-and-support-in-higher-education/

Horiuchi, Y., & Ono, Y. (2022). Susceptibility to threatening information and attitudes toward refugee resettlement: The case of Japan. *Journal of Peace Research, 60*(3). https://doi.org/10.1177/00223433221079455

Human Rights Watch. (2022). *Japan: Events of 2021*. https://www.hrw.org/world-report/2022/country-chapters/japan

Immigration Services Agency of Japan (ISA). (2020). *Reiwa gan'nen ni okeru nanmin ninteishasū-tō ni tsuite* [The number of recognized refugees in 2019]. https://www.moj.go.jp/isa/publications/press/nyuukokukanri03_00004.html

Immigration Services Agency of Japan (ISA). (2023). *Zairyū gaikokujin tōkei* [Foreign resident statistics]. https://www.moj.go.jp/isa/policies/statistics/toukei_ichiran_touroku.html

International Rescue Committee. (2021, July 28). *Which countries host the most refugees?* https://www.rescue.org/article/which-countries-host-most-refugees

Ishikawa, M. (2009). University rankings, global models, and emerging Hegemony: Critical analysis from Japan. *Journal of Studies in International Education, 13*(2), 159–173.

Japan Association for Refugees (JAR). (2017). *Acceptance of Syrian refugee students second round selection in Turkey completed, Japanese language school in Okinawa to accept students to go to International Christian University*. https://www.refugee.or.jp/report/activity/2017/11/post_452/

Japan International Cooperation Center (JICE). (2021). *International student service*. https://www.jice.org/en/activities/student.html

Japan Student Services Organization (JASSO). (2023). *Support measures for Ukrainian students by Japanese Universities and Japanese Language Institutes.* https://www.studyinjapan.go.jp/en/other/news/000165.html
Kageyama, Y. (2023, February 26). Refugee-averse Japan welcomes Ukrainians after Russia war. *Japan Today.* https://japantoday.com/category/national/refugee-averse-japan-welcomes-ukrainians-after-russia-war
Kalicki, K. (2019). Japan's liberal-democratic paradox of refugee admission. *The Journal of Asian Studies, 78*(2), 355–378.
Kariya, T. (2014). Japanese university reforms and the illusion of international competitiveness. *Nippon.com.* https://www.nippon.com/en/in-depth/a02803/
Knight, J. (2003). Updating the definition of internationalization. *International Higher Education, 33*, 2–3.
Kuramoto, N., & Koizumi, R. (2018). Current issues in large-scale educational assessment in Japan: Focus on national assessment of academic ability and university entrance examinations. *Assessment in Education: Principles, Policy & Practice, 25*(4), 415–433.
Kuroda, C. (2020). Higher Education Systems and Institutions, Japan. In P. Nuno Teixeira & J. C. Shin (Eds.), *The international encyclopedia of higher education systems and institutions* (Vol. 2, pp. 1179–1190). Springer.
Leask, B. (2010). "Beside me is an empty chair": The student experience of internationalisation. In E. Jones (Ed.), *Internationalisation and the student voice: Higher education perspectives* (pp. 3–17). Taylor & Francis.
Leask, B. (2015). *Internationalizing the curriculum.* Routledge.
Ministry of Foreign Affairs (MOFA). (2015a). *Highly skilled professional visa.* https://www.mofa.go.jp/j_info/visit/visa/long/visa16.html
Ministry of Foreign Affairs (MOFA). (2015b). *Specified visa: Designated activities (long stay for sightseeing and recreation).* https://www.mofa.go.jp/ca/fna/page22e_000738.html
Ministry of Justice (MOJ). (2017). *The number of foreign stayers in Japan as of the end of 2016.* http://www.moj.go.jp/nyuukokukanri/kouhou/nyuukokukanri045873750-368300000065.html
Ministry of Justice (MOJ). (2023). *Todōfuken betsu Ukuraina hinan-min zairyū shasū* [Number of Ukrainian Evacuees by Prefecture]. https://www.moj.go.jp/isa/content/001373694.pdf
Nonaka, C., & Phillips, S. (2017). Higher education reforms in Japan. *Comparative & International Education, 9*, 15–18.
Pathways Japan. (2022). *Japan–Ukraine education pathways.* https://pathways-j.org/ukraine-edu
Rothschild, E. (1995). What is security? *Daedalus, 124*(3), 53–98. http://www.jstor.org/stable/20027310
Saldaña, J. (2021). *The coding manual for qualitative researchers* (4th ed.). Sage.

Sarmiento, K. (2014). *Cartagena +30/International protection and effective integration: recommendations from civil society for the current state of asylum and statelessness in Latin America and the Caribbean*. Asylum Access Ecuador. https://asylumaccess.org/route-cartagena-30-challenges-protection-latin-america/

Sontag, K. (2019). Refugee students' access to three European universities: An ethnographic study. *Social Inclusion, 7*(1), 71–79.

Takahara, K. (2022, March 10). Are Ukrainians who flee "refugees" or "evacuees"? For Japan, it's complicated. *Japan Times*. https://www.japantimes.co.jp/news/2022/03/10/national/ukrainian-refugees-evacuees-japan/

Tamrat, W., & Habtemariam, S. (2020). Self-financing as a new stream of refugee higher education: The case of Eritreans in Ethiopia. In L. Unangst, H. Ergin, A. Khajarian, T. Delaquil, & H. de Wit (Eds.), *Refugees and higher education: Transnational perspectives on access, equity, and internationalization* (pp. 225–240). Brill Sense.

Tarumoto, H. (2019). Why restrictive refugee policy can be retained? A Japanese Case. *Migration and Development, 8*(1), 7–24. https://doi.org/10.1080/21632324.2018.1482642

Unangst, L., & Barone, N. (2019). Operationalizing "internationalization" in the community college sector: Textual analysis of institutional internationalization plans. *Journal for the Study of Postsecondary and Tertiary Education, 4*, 177–196. https://doi.org/10.28945/4435

Unangst, L., Casellas Connors, I., & Barone, N. (2022). State based policy supports for refugee, asylee, and TPS-background students in US higher education. *Refuge: Canada's Journal of Refugees, 38*(1), 95–110. https://doi.org/10.25071/1920-7336.40819

Unangst, L., & de Wit, H. (2021, March). *Refugees and higher education: Selected themes and research questions* (Centre for Global Higher Education Working Paper Series No. 61). https://www.researchcghe.org/publications/working-paper/refugees-and-higher-education-selected-themes-and-research-questions/

Unangst, L., Harrison, L., Bah, S., Abdoulaye Balarabe, O., & Dunson-Dillard, T. (2022). *"Is anybody doing anything?" Policy actors discuss supports for displaced learners at Ohio's colleges and universities*. Journal of Thought. http://journalofthought.com/wp-content/uploads/2023/04/08unangstetal.pdf

UN News. (2022). *UNHCR: A record 100 million people forcibly displaced worldwide*. https://news.un.org/en/story/2022/05/1118772

UNHCR Global Focus. (2022). *Contributions*. https://reporting.unhcr.org/contributions?srcfund=GOVEU

Villegas, P., & Aberman, T. (2019). A double punishment: The context of post-secondary access for racialized precarious status migrant students in Toronto Canada. *Refuge, 35*(1), 72–82. https://doi.org/10.7202/1060676ar

Webb, S., Dunwoodie, K., & Wilkinson, J. (2019). Unsettling equity frames in Australian universities to embrace people seeking asylum. *International Journal of Lifelong Education, 38*(1), 103–120.

Woldegiyorgis, A. (2020). Higher education for refugees in Ethiopia. In L. Unangst, H. Ergin, A. Khajarian, T. Delaquil, & H. de Wit (Eds.), *Refugees and higher education: Transnational perspectives on access, equity, and internationalization* (pp. 209–224). Brill Sense.

Yonezawa, Y. (2019). Internationalization management in Japanese Universities: The effects of institutional structures and cultures. *Journal of Studies in International Education, 21*(4), 375–390.

PART II

Refugees and Asylum Seekers in Japan and Taiwan: Media Representations and Public Opinion

CHAPTER 7

Media Political Leanings: Polarised Depictions of Hong Kong Migration in Taiwan

Cody Wai Kwok Yau

Introduction

Immigrant and political asylum issues in Taiwan have become more prominent since the protests in Hong Kong as growing numbers of Hong Kong's residents seek life opportunities or protection in Taiwan. According to the data from Taiwan National Immigration Agency, the number of Hong Kong people in residency and settlement with citizenship in Taiwan increased from 8203 in 2014 to 10,240 in 2022 (National Immigration Agency, n.d.). There were a total of 76,245 successful cases through various investment, dependent, and asylum channels.

The growing trend of Hong Kong migration has sparked contentious debates within Taiwanese society because of the China factor (the PRC recovered Hong Kong in 1997 and Taiwan is the next in line for Chinese unification). The two major political camps in Taiwan exhibit contrasting

C. W. K. Yau (✉)
Department of Political Science, Soochow University, Taipei, Taiwan
e-mail: codyyau@scu.edu.tw

L. Momesso and P. Ivanova (eds.), *Refugees and Asylum Seekers in East Asia*, Palgrave Macmillan Studies on Human Rights in Asia,
https://doi.org/10.1007/978-981-97-2867-1_7

viewpoints, despite both initially claiming to support Hong Kong residents based on their humanitarian stances. The Green Camp is inclined towards Taiwan's independence, Taiwan's nativist values, and resisting the influence of the PRC. The leading party in this camp is the Democratic Progressive Party (DPP, the ruling party). The Blue Camp is inclined towards unification with the mainland China and making mitigating gestures to the PRC. The leading party in the Blue Camp is the Kuomintang (KMT). Due to the current DPP government's view towards China, the Hong Kong immigration issue has become intertwined with Taiwan's national security. Thus, Article 12 (for residency applicants) and Article 18 (for political asylum seekers) of *Regulations Governing the Relations with Hong Kong and Macao* (hereafter, the Hong Kong & Macao Regulations) are stringent and are implemented with caution. This circumstance is further reflected in a petition case to Control Yuan (a constitutionally mandated authority with a supervisory and auditory role) over Hong Kong residency in Taiwan.

As part of this case, the authorities, including the Immigration Agency, were criticised not only for the opaque, time-consuming, case-by-case review process but also for frequently rejecting applications for reasons of national security (by Article 22 (1) of *Hong Kong and Macao Residents Entering Taiwan and Residence and Settlement Permit Measures*). In addition, the petition blamed the government for drastically and unexpectedly raising the threshold of the applications for residency and settlement with citizenship. This places petitioners in a dilemma: whether to return to Hong Kong or wait without a definite date for their case to be settled in Taiwan. The Control Yuan's press release about this petition case stated that the matter of petitioners involves the protection of human rights because it stems from the 2019 Anti-Extradition Law Amendment Bill Movement (the 2019 Protests) (Chi et al., 2022). Arguably, this press release shows the tension between human rights when they are related to migration (the human rights of Hong Kong immigrants seeking life prospects and protection in Taiwan), and national security (such as alleged Chinese spies entering through immigration), in Taiwan. What, however, exactly are the specific security interpretations of Hong Kong immigrants in both the Blue and Green Camps?

Media outlets frequently play an active role in framing migration coverage, using a particular political perspective (Caviedes, 2017). This coverage includes editorials, letters, and columns, which look at the security and human rights aspects of migration from different points of view.

Some studies imply that all media outlets are complicit in the securitisation of migration (referring to a process of threat identification that is declaratory in nature, in which referent objects became securitised, which in turn legitimises urgent measures to tackle that perceived threat), and that the media's political leanings, such as those of conservative newspapers, tend towards greater securitisation (Benson, 2013).

This is the case in Taiwan because the political environment of Taiwan's media is mainly made up of two political camps, the "Green Camp" and the "Blue Camp" (Sullivan et al., 2018). Most studies on Taiwanese media representation, with regard to migration, focus on migrants' identities (Chung, 2000), media framing (Liu, 2021), and discrimination (Chu, 2007), while factors relating to the media's partisan leanings on migration are collectively an issue which has not received as much attention.

To fill this research gap, this chapter argues that Taiwanese media's partisan leaning towards the Blue Camp or the Green Camp plays a main role in shaping the portrayal of the migration issue. To address the questions, this chapter examines the perspectives of the Green Camp and the Blue Camp on the subject of Hong Kong migration in Taiwan by analysing news articles from the major pro-Blue/Green printed media. The rest of the chapter is structured as follows. The second section presents the context of Taiwanese media's partisan political leanings, which encourage media politicisation on the subject of Hong Kong migration. The third section presents the data and methods. The fourth section illuminates the results of the structural topic modelling (STM) (Roberts et al., 2016), including STM-identified topics, the trends, the proportions, conceptual categorisations, and the factorial effects on topic proportion. In the fifth section, the results of the sentiment analysis are highlighted. Concluding remarks and implications for Hong Kong migration are provided in the concluding section.

Partisan Leaning in Taiwanese Media

Since political liberalisation in the 1980s lifted the ban on opening media such as newspapers in Taiwan, independent newspapers have been allowed to open, shaping two major partisan media camps (Chen, 1998). One typical example of independent newspapers is the *Liberty Times*. The *Liberty Times* was founded in 1987. Its political stance is anti-KMT and anti-authoritarian rule, it emphasises Taiwan's nativist value and affirms Taiwan's independence. These are all compatible with the DPP's political position on Taiwan. For example, the *Liberty Times* arranges the China news in the international section, as opposed to the pro-Blue newspapers, who put such news in the national section. In contrast, the pro-Blue newspapers, the *United Daily News* and the *China Times* were both founded in 1950. The launch year implies that both newspapers met the KMT's requirement, and, in actual fact, for example, the founder of the *United Daily News* was a mainland Chinese man and also a core member of the KMT Central Committee (Guo, 2012, p. 4). Therefore, the pro-Blue newspapers generally empathise with a revival of Chinese culture and reunification with mainland China. As a result of Guo's study (2012), it was found that the news narrative in Taiwan exhibited ideological bias. In this regard, it can be said that party-leanings have always fuelled Taiwan's media polarisation, particularly when China-related issues arise.

One typical case of this polarisation is embodied in the issue of migration from mainland China. With the increase in transnational marriage (National Security Council, 2006), the issue of marriage migrants became a talking point in Taiwan. The media outlets in the pro-Blue Camp media tended to view mainland spouses through a lens of human rights, such as the right to residency in Taiwan. In contrast, the pro-Green Camp media tended to report on the spouses negatively, for example, suggesting that they were United Front conspirators (referring to those who assist the CCP in politically infiltrating the target countries by establishing friendly networks of groups and key individuals, Chao, 2004). For instance, one editorial in the *Liberty* Times (2008) stated that the increase in the number of mainland China spouses was equivalent to increasing the risk of the PRC's United Front in Taiwan. The *United News Daily* (Lin, 2007) criticised the then-DDP government's strict quota of mainland spouses, which drew criticism from human rights groups.

As mass media can shape the linkage between immigration and security, a comparison of the two main media camps' depictions of Hong Kong migration can unpack the security concerns surrounding Hong Kong migration, as detailed in the next section.

Data and Methods

The primary textual data in this chapter was derived from news articles published in the five major Chinese newspapers in Taiwan (Renli Aikman Company, 2022): the *Liberty Times* (LT, *Ziyou shibao*); the *United Daily News* (UDN, *Lianhe bao*); the *China Times* (CT, *Zhongguo shibao*);

the *Economic Daily News* (EDN, *Jingji ri bao*); and the *Commercial Times* (CTEE, *Gongshang shibao*). This study chose these five newspapers because they are issued throughout Taiwan and have a clear political leaning towards the Blue and Green Camps. As such, they are able to situate the national political debate on Hong Kong migration. Data collection was accomplished using the digital news media database of the Parliamentary Library, Legislative Yuan (https://nplnews.ly.gov.tw/). The search was conducted using the terms "Hong Kong" (*Xianggang*), "migrants", (*yimin*) and "Taiwan" from 1 January 2014 to 5 December 2022. This period covered the political turbulence from the 2014 Hong Kong Occupy Central Movement (OCM), and included the 2019 Protests, and the implementation of Hong Kong National Security Law (NSL) in 2020. There were 259 pieces of news articles left after duplicates were removed, composing the corpus used in this study. Figure 7.1 shows the yearly number of news stories after the OCM, which peaked following the 2019 Protests. The news articles reached 31.6% (82 pieces) in 2020. Figure 7.3 illustrates the distribution of the news articles of our dataset. The LT represents 45% (117), the UDN 21% (55), the CT 14% (37), the EDN 11% (29), and the CTEE 8% (21). The LT represents the Green Camp with 45% (117 pieces), while the other four newspapers represent the Blue Camp with 55% (142 pieces), according to the classification of Sullivan et al. (2018, p. 114).

Data analyses were performed in STM. STM, which assumes that every document (including every news article) is a mixture of topics, is a word-clustering technique to identify latent topics. The benefit of STM is that it is able to extract a discursive structure comprised of exclusive and semantically coherent clusters of topics from unstructured textual data from within a period of investigation. For the objectives of this study, the term "topics" refers to particular discursive frames (Van Atteveldt et al., 2014). The topics include information on the topic's proportion (which is the summed prevalence of each topic selected in this study), a list of FREX terms (referring to terms or phrases in a topic that appeared frequently and with exclusivity relative to other terms in other topics), and the top-ranking news of each identified topic. Moreover, STM can include metadata, document-level variables such as the date of publication and author (one variable in this study is pro-Blue/Green) for topic analysis (Grimmer et al., 2022, p. 153). With these variables for analysis, STM can present an identifiable trend, an examination of event effects on a topic's patterns, and can form the basis of a comparison of pro-Blue

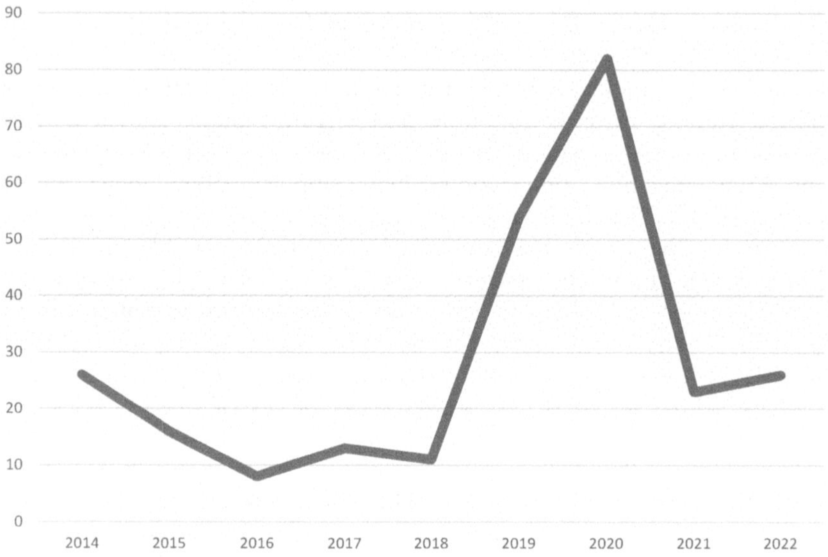

Fig. 7.1 Trend of news articles in our dataset

and pro-Green media content. All these advantages are not only helpful for finding evidence of the selected media's political leanings on the Hong Kong migration issue, but also present the general trends relating to this issue.

This study settled on a 12-topic model after processing the aforementioned corpus in STM. This study further selected and labelled the seven identified topics related to our research tasks for interpretation by carefully reading the top ten news articles about each topic (a total of 70 articles; for details of the topic model selection, see Appendix A, and see Grimmer & Stewart, 2013). The last step is to engage in topic interpretation, as elaborated in the following section.

The Results of STM

Table 7.1 shows the seven topic names used in this analysis and their proportions. By thoroughly examining the FREX terms and the top news stories, this study categorised the selected topics into two primary categories: "*Migration Safety*" and "*Political Security*". Three topics

(38.47%) fell in the category of *Migration Safety*, made of *Political Migration (Topic 2, hereafter, T represents Topic)*, *Insincere Assistance (T9)*, *Conditions Imposed on Migration (T1)*. The three topics in this category relate to human security, with protection of life opportunities (Persaud, 2022, p. 141) being a central requirement of Hong Kong migrants. The topic with the largest proportion in the category of *Migration Safety* is *Political Migration (T2)*, devoted to describing the lives of Hong Kong migrants in Taiwan and their reasons for migration. The four topics in the *Political Security* category (26.35%) include *Empty Promise of OCTS (T4)*, *Soft Penetration (T3)*, *Blur Jurisdiction (T8)*, and *Population Replacement (T12)*. Here this study adopts a wide definition of Political Security that refers to threats to both political stability and collective identity (Buzan et al., 1998, p. 141).

The Empty Promise of OCTS topic (OCTS means One Country, Two Systems, which was a unification model posed by the PRC for Taiwan that was used in Hong Kong first, and in which also promised that Hong Kongers can enjoy a high degree of autonomy that will remain unchanged for 50 years). It refers to the Hong Kong immigration issue and signifies the demise of OCTS in reality, implying that Taiwan has definitely rejected this political arrangement. The *Blur Jurisdiction* topic represented the conflict between Taiwan and Hong Kong over the question of jurisdiction or juridical sovereignty related to a Taiwan murder case that involved Hong Kongers. *Soft Penetration* and *Population Replacement* concerned the notion that the abrupt increase in Hong Kong immigrants posed a threat to Taiwan's political stability and social resource allocation. The topic with the largest proportion is *Empty Promise of OCTS*, which presents the political root of Hong Kong migration in Taiwan: Hong Kong's freedom is dramatically dwindling.

Figure 7.2 illustrates the thematic trend in Taiwanese mainstream media coverage that follows the two categories, *Migrant Safety* (the solid line) and *Political Security* (the dashed line), through the investigation period. It can be observed that the *Political Security* trendline decreased from a high point in 2014 (7.29%), shortly after the 2014 OCM, to a low point in 2015 (7.29%). Similarly, the *Migrant Safety* line went downward from the year of OCM (18.22%) to its lowest point in 2016 (12.80%). This implies that the media outlets' handling of the Hong Kong immigration issue became less intense after the OCM. Since then, however, the *Political Security* and the *Migrant Safety* trendlines rebounded, with fluctuations, respectively. The upward trends were maintained in both

Table 7.1 Categories and topics

Conceptual categories	*Topic name*	*Topic proportion (%)*	*FREX terms (translations from Chinese)*
Migration Safety	Political Migration (T2) Insincere Assistance (T9) Conditions Imposed on Migration	14.99 11.92 11.56	emigration, young people, today, migration, Hong Kong National Security Law, movement, Taiwan, Hong Kong, decision, living MAC, Project, assistance, humanitarian, related, Chen Ming-Tong, rescue, scheme, ordinance, service residence, settlement, application, permit, number of people, residents, passport, acquisition, this year, review
Political Security	Empty Promise of OCTS (T4) Soft Penetration (T3) Blur Jurisdiction (T8) Population Replacement (T12)	7.20 6.47 6.35 6.33	Kaohsiung, mayor, democracy, Han Kuo-Yu, Chief Executive, Beijing, One Country, Two Systems, parliamentarian, Kuomintang, today China, bookstore, Lam Wing-Kee, peace, infiltration, CCP, freedom, Xi Jinping, control, change Chen Tong-Jia, justice, police, Hong Kong Government, our side, immigration, operation, personnel, sovereignty, legislators refugee, UK, acceptance, Extradition Bill, CCP, incident, movement, local, extradition to China, asylum

trendlines until the 2019 Protests. Since then, the Political Security trendline has slumped, but the migrant security trendline has continued to boom to its peak (43.84%) in 2020, the year of the NSL legislation, and the gap between the two lines has been increasing. It shows that the NSL was probably the main driver of the re-politicisation of the issue of Hong Kong migrants.

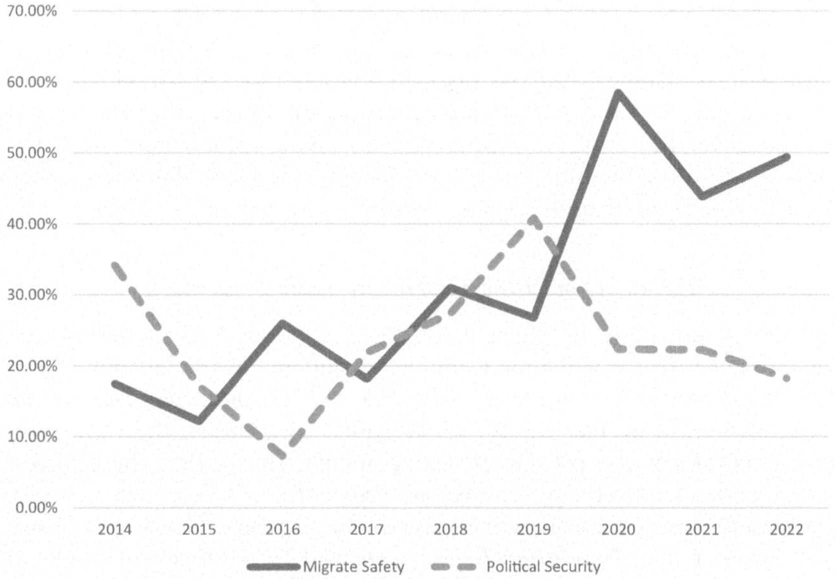

Fig. 7.2 Changing thematic proportion trends

Factors Affecting Topic Proportions

This section identifies the differences in news portrayals with a baseline of factors, including the implementation of NSL and Blue/Green as covariates, in order to observe any effects on the topic patterns. The NSL factor was established on the date the NSL went into implementation, 1 June 2020. This is when the trendline for migrant security attained its peak in 2020 (see Fig. 7.2). Blue/Green party affiliation was also considered in order to investigate the media's inclinations between *Migrant Safety* and *Political Security*.

The Effect of NSL on Topical Proportion

The result of the NSL effects on the topical patterns is shown in Fig. 7.3. The left plot and the right plot of the figure represent before and after the NSL's execution, respectively. This figure has two highlights. One is *Conditions Imposed on Migration (T1)*, which ranked third on the left plot, but climbed to the top in the right plot after the NSL's implementation. Another, *Soft Penetration (T12)*, ranked in fourth place in the right plot, a change from last place in the left plot. All in all, most of the discussion was focused on *Migration Safety* topics rather than *Political Security*. But look in depth: after the NSL's implementation, the focal point subtlety shifted to *Conditions Imposed on Migration*, while the *Political Security* topic, *Soft Penetration*, also gained attention.

The Effect of "Blue/Green" on Topic Proportion

Figure 7.4 illustrates the effect that the "Blue/Green" divide has on the topic pattern. In the pro-Blue Camp news outlets, on the left plot, *Political Migration* (T2), *Insincere Assistance* (T9), *Conditions Imposed on Applicants* (T1) occupy the top three spots. In contrast, the right plot, which represents the pro-Green Camp media, shows that the *Political Security* topics moved up. One is *Soft Penetration* (T3), which occupies the second position but is ranked last in the pro-Blue Camp plot. Similarly, another one, *Population Replacement* (T12), advances one ranks to the fifth position in the pro-Green Camp plot, compared to the one in the pro-Blue Camp plot.

Topic Content

This section closely examines the content of the high-ranking topics between pro-Green and pro-Blue media coverage. Both outlooks strongly engaged with the *Migration Safety* topics, that is, *Political Migration, Insincere Assistance,* and *Conditions Imposed on Migration*. We will look at these topics first.

Political Migration

First, regarding the topic of *Political Migration*, the two camps had no differences in their news report stances. Both emphasised that the political situation in Hong Kong in the aftermath of the OCM was the primary reason for Hong Kongers' emigration. Both camps' news outlets believed that Hong Kong immigrants desired to live in a liberal democracy, particularly after the NSL's implementation in July 2020. Moreover, the news articles on this topic reported on Hong Kong immigrants' living circumstances and exposed the risks of migrating to Taiwan, including low salaries, homesickness, and the sincerity of their loyalty to Taiwan

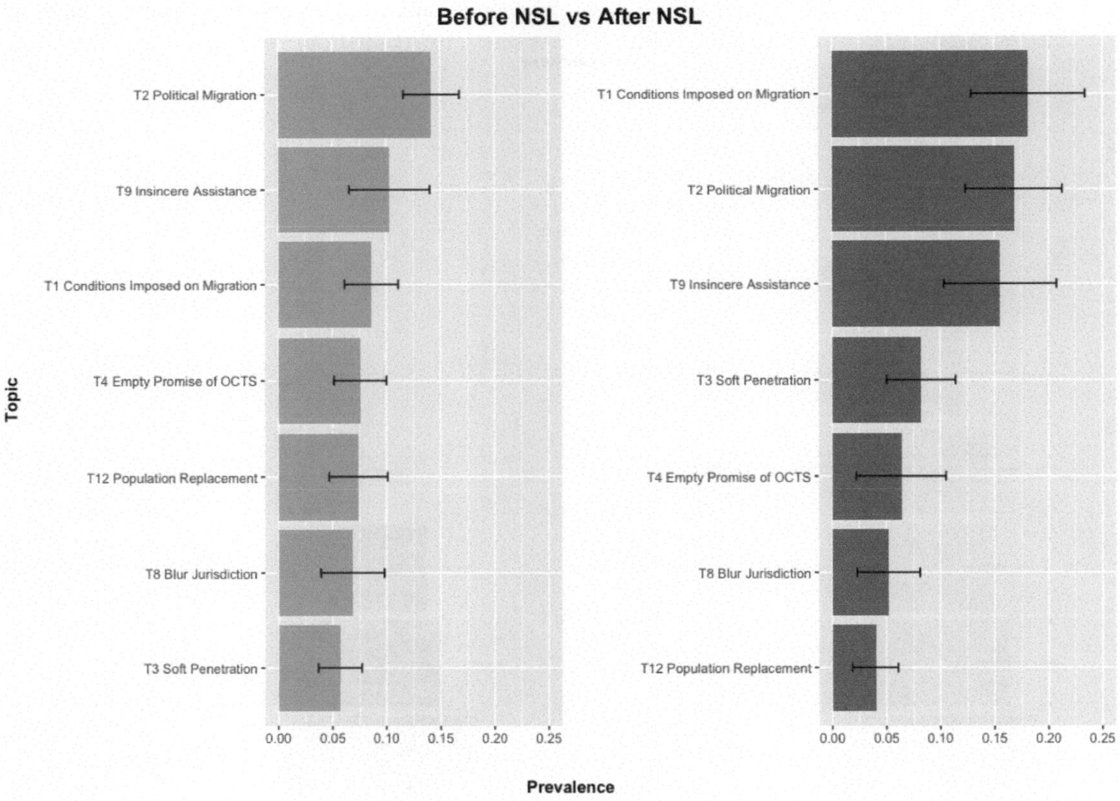

Fig. 7.3 The effect of NSL on topic proportion[1]

[1] The number below the plot is the mean score of topic prevalence. Here, the total of the topic prevalence is 1.

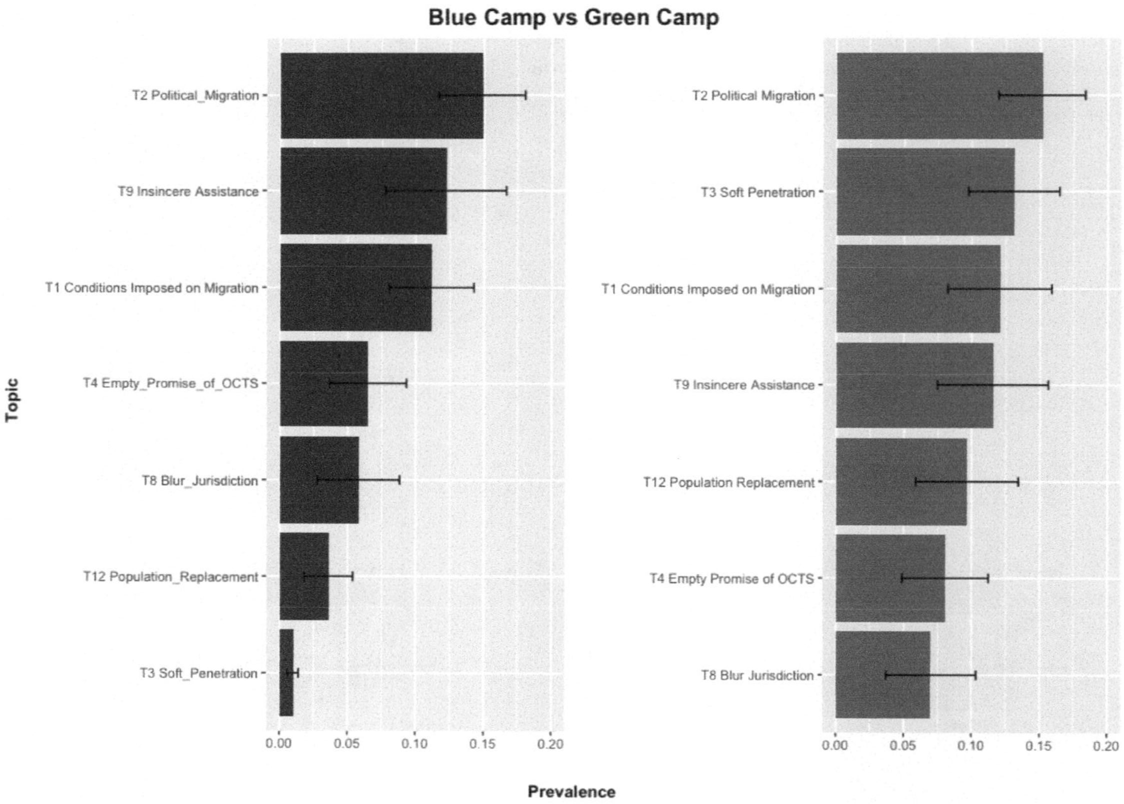

Fig. 7.4 The effect of "Blue/Green" on topic proportion

being doubted by local Taiwanese. In the interviews with Hong Kong immigrants, Chen, X.-Y. (2020) stated :

> Following the passage of the NSL, Alan and Joys [respondents] decided to speed up their actions [referring to emigrating to Taiwan]. Joys stated that they are looking forward to receiving their national ID cards soon in order to vote for the [Taiwan] president in 2024, and that 'this is a democratic experience that Hong Kong has never had before'. They also expressed concern about the situation in Hong Kong.
>
> Stella [another respondent] stated that the low salary is the main barrier to living in Taiwan, and that she must work multiple part-time jobs and invest in order to maintain her income levels.

In other interviews, a Hong Kong illustrator expressed anxiety about the Taiwan identity issue by asking "if a Hong Kong person falls in love with or marries a Taiwanese after coming to Taiwan, will it be considered that they are trying to save the six million dollars immigration fees?" (Lu, 2022).

Insincere Assistance

This topic mainly reflected the pro-Blue news media criticisms of the DPP's governmental assistance for Hong Kong migrants and political asylum seekers. News articles by the critics of the government's Hong Kong Humanitarian Assistance Action and Caring Project (hereafter, Assistance Project) referred to it as "old wine in new bottles", having no new or helpful mechanism for political asylum seekers, rather just intending to "handle them ambiguously". In a view presented in a news article in the *China Times* (Ji et al., 2020), the KMT Member of the Legislative Yuan, Chen Yu-Jen, stated that "the whole Project does not appear to differ from current regulations [targeting political asylum seekers]" (because the current regulations had been available through general immigration channels such as investment immigration). In the same news article, another KMT legislator, Chen I-Hsin, also questioned whether the Project only targeted legal immigrants:

> Chen Ming-Tong, Chairman of the Mainland Affairs Council, stated that this Project is not for rescue (received political asylum seekers) but rather assistance provided to those in need after entering the country. The question is, how can we help if there is no rescue plan (referring to taking

> in political asylum seekers from Hong Kong who entered Taiwan illegally first)? Furthermore, the targets of applicable assistance are confined to legal immigrants; could it be that we deport or detain Hong Kong and Macao residents who are under threat due to political factors and have entered Taiwan illegally? (Ji et al., 2020)

Professor Chen Yi-Xin, in an interview by the *China Times* (Cai, 2020), also stated that the Assistance Project was intended to handle the Hong Kong immigration wave in an ambiguous manner (using a case-by-case review) and thus did not detail the rescue targets due to political reasons. The reasons for this included an attempt to avoid angering mainland China, so Taiwan could not dramatically widen the definition of refugee for Hong Kong protesters as that could cause the over-acceptance of a large number of sensitive political activists. Professor Chen explained that the Taiwanese do not want "criminals" to enter, as the radical activists could undermine social order in Taiwan as they did in Hong Kong and thus would not lead to the government's public support. He concluded that the "ambiguous" strategy could somewhat please all parties, but this "narrowly-defined rescue" (termed by Professor Chen) is actually far away from the DPP's claim—that is, to "stand with Hong Kong".

Conditions Imposed on Migration

This topic contained news articles about the conditions imposed on immigration applicants as a result of the record number of applications received during the 2019 Protests. Coverage from both camps agreed that applications for residency in Taiwan had reached a record high, as shown in the news headlines, *Hong Kong people's residence in Taiwan hits a new high, 11,173 last year*, in LT, and, *The number of Hong Kong people who came to live in Taiwan increased by 1.5 times in the first four months*, in EDN (Chen, 2022a; Cheng, 2020). Nevertheless, there was a subtle distinction between the two media camps on this topic. The pro-Blue news outlets were likely to criticise the DPP administration's lack of sincerity in supporting Hong Kong, and its use of national security concerns as an for refusing Hong Kong immigrants' settlement in Taiwan. A UDN news story (Chen, 2022) raised inquiries regarding the "secret" imposition of a quota on Hong Kong applicants in immigration by the DPP government. The news story suggested that such a measure may have been implemented due to apprehensions that the immigration of individuals with affiliations to Chinese party organisations, government, and military, who had previously served in Hong Kong, may be utilised for the purposes of the "United Front" in Taiwan.

The LT does portray apprehension about migration issues. The phenomenon of "fake investment, true migration" (using investment in Taiwan as a pathway to residency without actually making the investment) was highlighted (Chen, 2022c). A similar concern also appeared with reference to applicants for professional migration, as exemplified in a news title, *People from Hong Kong and Macau who apply for professional migration should engage in business as opposed to retiring and enjoying medical insurance* (Chen, 2021). Furthermore, a news story on migration's national security implications prompted the DPP administration to reach a compromise (Chen, 2022b). One plan is issuing a permanent resident identification card to those Hong Kong immigrants in lieu of granting them citizenship. In the news article, an official explanation of this compromise measure was that it could lower the risks to Taiwan's security because the applicants would not have citizenship.

To summarise, the three topics about *Migration Safety* portrayed the risks for Hong Kongers of living in Taiwan (e.g., low salaries, doubt about the immigrants' loyalty to Taiwan), and also looked at the impact that the large flow of Hong Kong immigrants had on concerns such as national security, social welfare distribution, and administration resources, which caused or justified the DPP government's limited assistance to the applicants.

Soft Penetration

This subsection examines the difference between pro-Green and pro-Blue news outlets with regard to *Political Security* topics, focusing particularly on the pro-Green media. The *Soft Penetration* topic raised the possibility of Chinese cultural penetration through immigration. Most contributors to this topic took the situation in Hong Kong as an example of how Beijing took control of the city through immigration from mainland China. The contributors believed that the Chinese immigrants were filled with authoritarian beliefs. An LT editorial exemplified this phenomenon with Australian opinion poll results and discovered that the proportion of respondents (that is, Australian Chinese migrants) who identified with a democratic system (36%) was lower than the proportion who identified with a non-democratic system (41%). In an LT interview (He, 2021), Lam Wing-Kee, a Hong Kong immigrant and a book seller in Taiwan who had been detained in mainland China for selling prohibited books in

Hong Kong involving CCP General Secretary Xi Jin-Ping, said that the concept of the human rights was lacking due to Confucian culture (He, 2021). It is, he added in another interview (Yang, 2019), because Confucian ethics do not talk about human rights, being based on the idea that people are born unequally and have different social statuses.

Most articles on this topic suggested that Taiwan had to beware of Chinese penetration and thus should cut the cultural tie between Taiwan and China. One solution, as Lin proposed, was to transform the Confucian-centric perspective in Taiwanese society through education. Another was to prohibit any plan for mainland Chinese immigration. As a Hong Kong resident claimed in a letter to the LT's editor (Chen, M.-Y., 2019), the reasons the notion of human rights should not apply to China's "emigration penetration strategy" were because a huge influx of Chinese immigrants would "dilute" Taiwanese minds, and some of them could be spies, as happened in Hong Kong. The letter to the LT's editor was not only one person's view; it also projects society's mindset in Taiwan regarding Hong Kong immigration, as discussed in the following section, about the topic *Population Replacement*.

Population Replacement (Topic 12)

Like the *Soft Penetration* topic, contributors in this topic examined the Hong Kong case; that is, the daily quota of 150 mainland Chinese immigrants entering Hong Kong (Yang, 2011, pp. 10–11), which had resulted in an estimated more than one million new immigrants entering Hong Kong from mainland China since the 1997 Hong Kong handover (*Hong Kong Economic Times*, 2019). This situation was discussed in a letter to the LT's editor (Chen, Z.-G., 2019), stating that, "[the 1.5 million mainlanders] have crammed into a tiny place, Hong Kong, making it like a sardine can containing more than seven million individuals. Public facilities, medical resources, and educational resources are depleted. How can any hope for human rights exist?".

The alert mindset of the contributors regarding the issue of "fake immigrant, true Chinese spy" (Chen, Y.-C., 2020) reflected a cautious stance towards Hong Kong asylum seekers. Lin Pao-Hua (2019), a senior LT columnist, took a conservative stance on the refugee law for two reasons, in the news article titled "The refugee law and the spies in the background". First, he said it would incur a large-scale influx of Hong Kong refugees entering Taiwan, potentially exhausting Taiwan's human resources and management costs. As Lin pointed out, the worst-case scenario for Taiwan would be to become like Hong Kong was in the 1980s with the Vietnam refugee issue (also called the Vietnamese boat people) or as happened with the pre-handover illegal immigrants from mainland China. Second, and even more significantly, Lin believed that China would use the refugee law to conduct spying. Someone pretending to be a pro-democracy supporter could intent to incite rebellion—a personal experience he shared. Lin suggested that Taiwan should handle Hong Kong immigrants in a different way, by enacting more relaxed regulations to allow Hong Kong youth to study or work. In addition, political asylum regulations should be improved, according to Lin, but taking national security into account to cover investment immigrants.

The examination of topic contents in this section demonstrates that pro-Blue media tended to report on the situation of Hong Kong immigrants in Taiwan and to criticise the DPP government's assistance, whereas the pro-Green media tended to highlight potential national security and management cost issues related to immigrants.

The Results of the Sentiment Analysis

Sentiment analysis is a dictionary-based text-mining technique for extracting opinions (Lei & Liu, 2021), which has been used to grasp the public sentiment towards refugees (Backfried & Shalunts, 2016; Öztürk & Ayvaz, 2018) or migration (Heidenreich et al., 2020). This chapter uses sentiment analysis to identify tendencies in the media's partisan leanings and to look at the portrayals related to them.

The technique involves using a sentiment dictionary to count the words in the news articles that match those in the established dictionary. To improve the accuracy of word identification, the sentiment dictionary used in this study is a combination of two sentiment dictionaries created by National Taiwan University and the Dalian University of Technology from mainland China (translating from simplified Chinese into traditional Chinese when used). The calculation is straightforward. One word (e.g., "assistance", *yuanzhu*) with a positive meaning in the dictionary is counted 1, whereas one word (e.g., "illegal", *feifa)* with a negative meaning in the dictionary is counted -1. When the sum of the positive and the negative words in a news article is a positive number (i.e., 1 or above), the document is considered to contain positive sentiment. A negative sum (i.e., −1 or below) indicates that the document is considered to contain negative sentiment. Words are not counted if they are not listed in the sentiment dictionaries used in the chapter.

To conduct sentiment analysis, the same dataset used in this study was divided into two subsets: the pro-Blue Camp dataset (composed of UDN, CT, EDN and CTEE) and the pro-Green Camp dataset (represented by LT). By doing so, we returned 117 and 142 hits, respectively. The results of pro-Green and pro-Blue news outlets are depicted in Fig. 7.5. For the group of pro-Green news outlets, the number of news articles (41 of 117, or 35.04%) expressing negative sentiments regarding Hong Kong immigration was greater than the number of news articles (76 of 117, or 64.96%) expressing positive sentiments regarding Hong Kong immigration. For the pro-Blue group, only 31 out of 142 (21.83%) expressed negative sentiments, while 111 out of 142 (78.17%) expressed positive sentiments. This pattern indicates that the proportion of pro-Green news outlets having negative sentiments covering Hong Kong migration is greater (13.21%) than that of the pro-Blue news outlets.

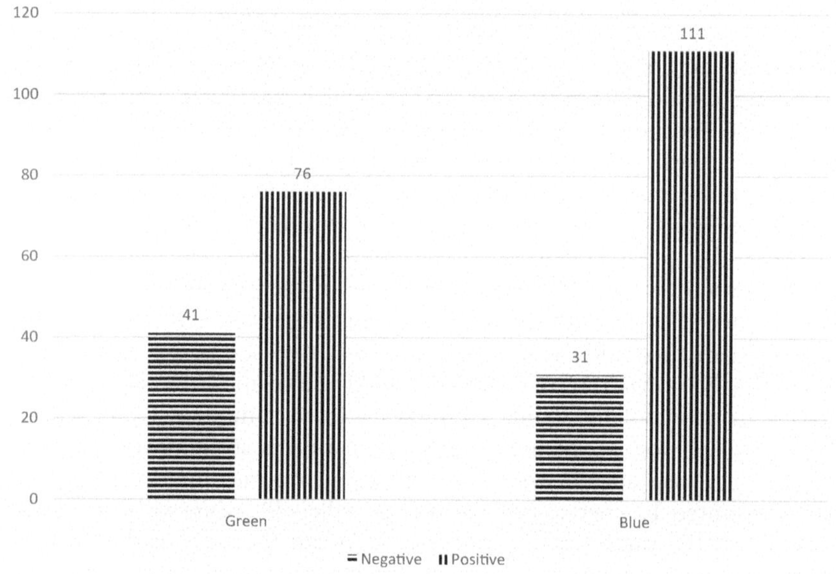

Fig. 7.5 Sentiment analysis of the pro-Green and pro-Blue news outlets

The most positive and negative news articles from each camp were then selected based on sentiment scores, with the top ten news articles on each topic being included in the selection. For the pro-Blue media, the most positive (39 marks) news report (in the *Insincere Assistance* topic) was titled *The Hong Kong Assistance Project has been announced; Chen Ming-Tong: Protesters seeking asylum must enter legally, and the law allows for assistance for Hong Kong students studying in Taiwan* (Lu et al., 2020). This news story, from UDN, positively affirmed that the DPP government established a "Taiwan-Hong Kong Office for Exchanges and Services to Provide Necessary Assistance to Hong Kong Citizens". Phrases used in the news report included, for example, "affirm the government's specific approach" and "the information provided to protesters entering Taiwan has become more specific".

The most negative news story was a CT editorial within the topic of *Empty Promise* of OCTS titled *Hsu Guo-Yong "self-slaps" Hsu Guo-Yong* (minus 42 points; Hsu was Minister of the Interior and in charge of immigration at the time). This editorial criticises the DPP government for "abandoning juridical sovereignty" in the "Chen Tong-Jia" case (a Hong Kong citizen suspected of murdering his Hong Kong girlfriend in Taiwan and then fleeing back to Hong Kong; both Taiwan and Hong Kong had no agreement for fugitives) in order to win the 2020 ROC presidential elections. The reason of this criticism is that this case would strengthen the case for the highly controversial Extradition Law, which was questioned for its violation of human rights and which sparked unprecedented protests in Hong Kong. If the party's candidate had claimed support of the Extradition Law bill, it could have harmed the DPP's chances of winning the presidency. Therefore, as the editorial added, the DPP government would not accept Chen's surrender to Taiwan's police.

For the pro-Green media, the most positive (23 marks) news report (in the *Conditions Imposed on Emigration* topic) was titled *Hong Kong people's residency cases in Taiwan hit a new high of 11,173 last year*. This news story affirmed the DDP government's effort to assist Hong Kong people settling down in Taiwan. As stated, "the government is revising immigration regulations for Hong Kong and Macau residents who wish to reside and settle in Taiwan, as well as enhancing the policy for assisting Hong Kong". As to the most negative news story, it was also mentioned in *Population Replacement*, that is, titled *the refugee law and the spies in the background* (minus 29 points).

Conclusion

In contrast to studies either of traditional migration border security or of progressive–conservative media, this chapter's text-mining findings contribute to an understanding of how subjective perceptions, that is, the Blue/Green partisan leanings of Taiwanese media, influence the portrayal of the migration issue. It can especially be seen when the migration issue involves the PRC, which intensified the politicisation of the Hong Kong migration issue and the divergent portrayal of Hong Kong migration. It is evident that the pro-Green media outlets offer more of a security narrative (such as cultural Sinicization and the possibility of Chinese infiltration through Hong Kong migration), which serves to justify the DDP's restrictive migration policy.

This chapter contends that while the media may aid in justifying such government policy actions, it also exacerbates the contradictions between human rights and national security. In other words, this tension calls the political legitimacy of the DPP and Taiwan into question, because they purportedly uphold the value of human rights while disadvantaging Hong Kong residents (especially those who are without full citizenship) who wish to reside and settle in Taiwan with ease. The side effect of the restrictive policies on Hong Kongers will impact social coherence in the long term. This chapter suggests that the matter of Hong Kong migration ought to be de-securitised and efforts by the Control Yuan should be redirected towards policy implementation concerns, such as administrative efficacy or the authories' violations of the Hong Kong & Macao Regulations.

Last but not least, this chapter highlights that fear of the PRC motivates the pro-Green media's negative portrayal of Hong Kong migration. However, it must be noted that this chapter has not delved comprehensively into the political roots of what structures the securitisation issue with regard to the Hong Kong migration. This includes an examination of Green Camp's normative framing and political identity such as Taiwan's subjectivity. These need further study but have already exceeded the scope of this chapter.

Acknowledgements The author thanks Bo-Yu Chen, Department of International Studies and Regional Development, Niigata University, for his warm collegiality and insightful guidance.

Appendix: A discussion of the Topic Model Selection

We used a package stm (version 1.3.6) operating in R, specifically designed to produce the structural topic model used in this chapter. We worked in R. There are several steps in the two main stages: the pre-processing stage (Stage 1), and the topic model-building stage (Stage 2).

In Stage 1, we pre-processed the news data. First, we retrieved and downloaded news articles as textual data and converted them into a machine-readable UTF-8 format compatible with the RStudio platform. Next, we stored the data in a document database, MongoDB, using Studio 3T, a graphical user interface, to tidy the data according to the news page, date, title, main text, and so forth. We then underwent two text processing stages, word segmentation and stop-word removal. We used the R package jibea (a popular dictionary-based Chinese word segment module, version 0.11) to segment the news articles into a corpus. We then removed the stop-words (i.e., common words such as "others" [*qi ta*]). Once the corpus had been established, we went to the next stage.

In Stage 2, we first used the R package STM to convert the corpus into a document-term matrix. Our matrix contained 259 documents. We then had to determine a "correct" number of topics (number of word clusters) because there is no overarching gold standard. To find the best and most substantive model, we referred to the methods used by Quinn et al. (2010, pp. 215–216) and Lucas et al. (2015, p. 264), first narrowing down the searching scope. We thus set the number of topics, ranging from five topics to 40 topics in 5-topic increments.

After referencing the model's diagnostic scores for "exclusivity" (the top words in a topic that significantly differ from others) and "semantic coherence" (the top words in a topic that are most likely to co-occur in a passage) (Fig. 7.6), the author independently close read the top news articles and top words in each candidate's topic model to validate the candidate models.

We chose the 12-topic model for our research task. In the topic selection step, we chose relevant topics and discarded uninterpretable or useless topics to avoid overwriting the selected model (e.g., fragmented, over-low prevalence). For example, Topic 6, *Hong Kong Culture*, was not closely related to our research tasks, and Topic 5 was an over-fragmented topic mixing economic strategy, conflict among generations and tourism,

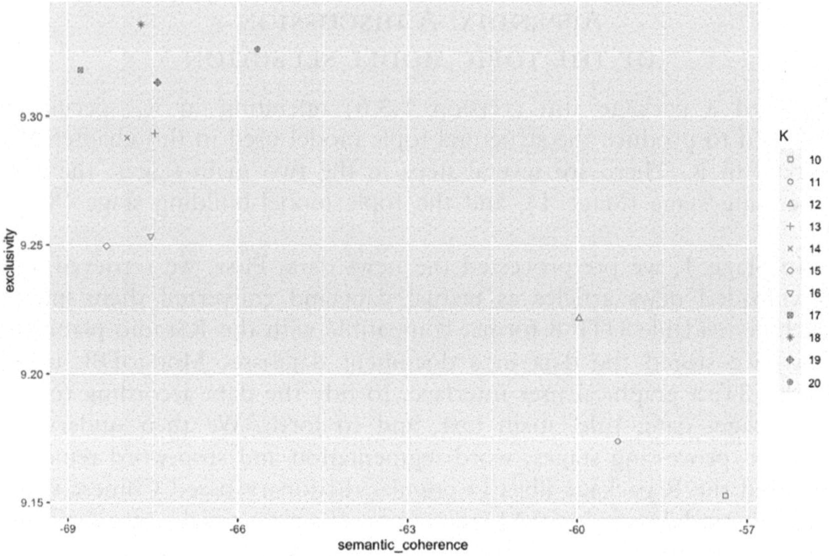

Fig. 7.6 Diagnostic values by number of topics in the candidate models

so the topics dropped. This step resulted in the seven topics used in our study for further interpretation. The author assigned corresponding labels in accordance with the core meanings of the top ten news articles for each topic.

References

Backfried, G., & Shalunts, G. (2016, October 26–28). Sentiment analysis of media in German on the refugee crisis in Europe. *Information Systems for Crisis Response and Management in Mediterranean Countries: Third International Conference, ISCRAM-Med 2016, Madrid, Spain, Proceedings, 3*, 234–241.

Benson, R. (2013). *Shaping immigration news: A French–American comparison*. Cambridge University Press. https://doi.org/10.1017/CBO9781139034326

Buzan, B., Wæver, O., & Wilde, J. D. (1998). *Security: A new framework for analysis*. Lynne Rienner Publishers. https://doi.org/10.2307/2586187

Cai, Z.-L. (2020, June 19). Zhu an an shen cha xue zhe zhi zheng fu mo chu li [Case-by-case review; scholars accuse the government of ambiguous handling]. *China Times*, p. A2.

Caviedes, A. (2017). Media agents. In P. Bourbeau (Ed.), *Handbook on migration and security* (pp. 296–315). Edward Elgar Publishing.

Chao, A. (2004). Imagined modernities, transnational migration, and border control: A case study of Taiwan's 'mainland brides.' *Taiwanese Journal of Sociology, 32*, 59–102.

Chen, M.-Y. (2019, January 7). Yi ming Xiang gang nu xingji Taiwan de si dianjian yi [Four pieces of advice for Taiwan from a Hong Kong female]. *Liberty Times*, p. A15.

Chen, S. Y. (1998). State, media and democracy in Taiwan. *Media, Culture & Society, 20*(1), 11–29.

Chen, X.-Y. (2020, December 14). Dan shui you Xiang gang de fu qi dang sheng huo pin zhi bian hao [Tamsui's Hong Kong feeling; husband-wife team: life quality has improved]. *Liberty Times*, p. A04. https://news.ltn.com.tw/news/politics/paper/1418924

Chen, Y.-C. (2020, December 25). Li zhi ying xiang hua qiang yi min fa [Lai Chee-Ying, Heung Wah-Keung, Immigration Law]. *Liberty Times*, p. A19.

Chen, Y.-F. (2021, April 26). Gang ao ren yi zhuan ye shen qingju liu xu zhi ye er fei tui xiu xiangjian bao [People from Hong Kong and Macau who apply for professional migration should engage in business as opposed to retiring and enjoying medical insurance]. *Liberty Times*, p. A04.

Chen, Y.-F. (2022a, January 30). Gang ren lai tai ju liu zai chuang xin gao qu nian11173 ren [The number of Hong Kong residents in Taiwan reached a new high of 11,173 last year]. *Liberty Times*, p. A02.

Chen, Y.-F. (2022b, August 2). Fang kuan Gang ren lai Tai ni yu chang qi ju liu [Lifting the limitation on Hong Kong residents in Taiwan; intended to permit long-term residence]. *Liberty Times*, p. A05.

Chen, Y.-F. (2022c, December 5). Bu xiao yi min gong si cao ban Gang ren jia tou zi zhenyi min [Manipulated and handled by unscrupulous immigration firms; Hong Kong residents arrived in Taiwan by 'fake investments; true migration']. *Liberty Times*, p. A04.

Chen, Z.-G. (2019, June 14). Song Zhong yu teng long huan niao [Extradition to China and 'population replacement']. *Liberty Times*, p. A17.

Chen, Z.-L. (2022, March 16). Gang ren lai Tai ding ju Lu wei hui: jue wu yin xing pei e [People from Hong Kong settle in Taiwan; Mainland Affairs Council: There's no secret quota]. *United Daily News*, p. A8.

Cheng, S.-H. (2020, June 8). Ren lai Tai ju liu qian si yue duo 1.5 bei [The number of Hong Kong residents relocating to Taiwan increased 1.5-fold in the first four months]. *Economic Daily News*, p. A5.

Chi H.-J., Yeh T.-H., & Shih C.-F. (2022, September 26). *According to complaints, Hong Kong resident applications over residency and immigration, political asylum, frequently rejected*. Press release of the Control Yuan of Republic of China, Taiwan. http://www.cy.gov.tw/News_Content.aspx?n=125&s=25411&Create=1

Chu, H. (2007). *An analysis on the representation of 'Asian bride' on newspapers in Taiwan: A case study of the United Daily and the Liberty Times* [Master Thesis]. Shih Hsin University. https://ndltd.ncl.edu.tw/cgi-bin/gs32/gsweb.cgi/login?o=dnclcdr&s=id=%22095SHU05383009%22.&searchmode=basic

Chung, P. (2000). The cultural other and national identity in the Taiwanese and South Korean media. *Gazette (leiden, Netherlands)*, *62*(2), 99–115.

Grimmer, J., & Stewart, B. M. (2013). Text as data: The promise and pitfalls of automatic content analysis methods for political texts. *Political Analysis, 21*(03), 267–297. https://doi.org/10.1093/pan/mps028

Grimmer, J., Roberts, M. E., & Stewart, B. M. (2022). *Text as data: new framework for machine learning and the social sciences* (1st ed.). Princeton University Press. https://press.princeton.edu/books/hardcover/9780691207544/text-as-data

Guo, S.-H. (2012). Yu yan yu yi shi xing tai: Taiwan mei ti lun shu fen xi *[Language and ideology: an analysis of Taiwanese media discourses]*. Mainland Affairs Council, Republic of China, Taiwan (No. NSC91-2411-H-007–023). https://archive.ph/DKC0

He, X.-X. (2021, March 11). Min zhu guo jia bi xu cu shi Zhong guo zhuan bian [Democracies must prompt China to transform]. *Liberty Times*, p. A02.

Heidenreich, T., Eberl, J.-M., Lind, F., & Boomgaarden, H. (2020). Political migration discourses on social media: A comparative perspective on visibility and sentiment across political Facebook accounts in Europe. *Journal of Ethnic and Migration Studies, 46*(7), 1261–1280.

Hong Kong Economic Times. (2019, March 20). Hui gui hou yu 103 wan nei di ren chi dan cheng zheng lai Gang Li jia chao: nei di wu yong jin mei ri 150 ge pei e [After the reunification, more than 1.03 million people from the mainland came to Hong Kong with one-way permit; The daily quota of 150 has not been used up by the mainland China, say Li Jia-Chao]. *Hong Kong Economic Times*. https://topick.hket.com/article/2302340

Ji, J., Lin, J.-M., & Cui, C.-T. (2020, June 19). Lü shuo zan Lan pi wei de bu zu [Green applauds; Blue criticises that a good thing was not done thoroughly]. *China Times*, p. A2. https://www.chinatimes.com/newspapers/20200619000503-260118?chdtv

Lei, L., & Liu, D. (2021). *Conducting Sentiment Analysis*. Cambridge: Cambridge University Press.

Liberty Times. (2008, September 26). Xiao xin tun xia you er bian cheng gong die [Watching out swallowing the bait and becoming a spy]. *Liberty Times*, p. A02.

Lin, P.-H. (2019, December 16). Nan min fa ji qi bei hou de die ying [The refugee law and the spies in the background]. *Liberty Times*, p. A15.

Lin, X-H. (2007, July 26). Ren kou zheng ce bai pi shu da lu pei ou pei e quan mian jin suo chang qi ju liu cong bu she xian gai wei1 lien 7220 ren Nei zheng bu: shang fei zui hou zheng ce [Population policy white paper: The quotas for mainland spouses will be fully tightened. Long-term residency will be reduced from no limits to 7,220. Not yet the finalised policy, says the Department of the Interior]. *United Daily News*, p. 15.

Liu, Sarah S.-J. (2021). Framing immigration: A content analysis of newspapers in Hong Kong, Taiwan, the United Kingdom, and the United States. *Politics, Groups, and Identities, 9*(4), 759–783.

Lu T.-H. (2022, March 15). Jiu ba ju shou zhi wei kan Xiang gang jie jing... wei zi you er lai you kun yu xiang chou [Gathering in a bar is just for the purpose of viewing Hong Kong's Street View; Came for freedom but got stuck in homesickness]. *Economic Daily News*.

Lu, J.-R., Lin, J.-Y., & Li, Z.-W. (2020, June 19). Yuan Gang zhuan an gong bu Chen ming tong: Kang zheng qiu bi hu xu he xu he fa ru jing fa lu shou quan yuan zhu Gang ren lai Taijiu xue, jiu ye, ding ju [The Hong Kong Assistance Project Has Been Announced; Protesters Seeking asylum must enter legally, and the law allows for assistance for Hong Kong students studying in Taiwan, says Chen Ming-Tong:]. *United Daily News*, p. A12.

Lucas, C., Nielsen, R. A., Roberts, M. E., Stewart, B. M., Storer, A., & Tingley, D. (2015). Computer-assisted text analysis for comparative politics. *Political Analysis, 23*(02), 254–277. https://doi.org/10.1093/pan/mpu019

National Immigration Agency, Republic of China, Taiwan. (n.d.). Statistics. https://www.immigration.gov.tw/5475/5478/141478/141380/

Renli Aikman Company. (2022). *The first quarter of 2022 [Renli Aikman Company] media survey report*. https://anm.frog.tw/wp-content/uploads/2022%E5%B9%B4%E7%AC%AC%E4%B8%80%E5%AD%A3%E3%80%90%E6%BD%A4%E5%88%A9%E8%89%BE%E5%85%8B%E6%9B%BC%E5%85%AC%E5%8F%B8%E3%80%91%E5%AA%92%E9%AB%94%E5%A4%A7%E8%AA%BF%E6%9F%A5%E5%A0%B1%E5%91%8A.pdf

National Security Council. (2006). *2006 National security report*. https://www.mac.gov.tw/public/Data/05271047271.pdf

Öztürk, N., & Ayvaz, S. (2018). Sentiment analysis on Twitter: A text mining approach to the Syrian refugee crisis. *Telematics and Informatics, 35*(1), 136–147.

Persaud, R. B. (2022). Human security. In A. Collins (Ed.), *Contemporary Security Studies* (4th ed., pp. 139–154). Oxford University Press.

Quinn, K. M., Monroe, B. L., Colaresi, M., Crespin, M. H., & Radev, D. R. (2010). How to analyze political attention with minimal assumptions and costs. *American Journal of Political Science, 54*(1), 209–228. https://doi.org/10.1111/j.1540-5907.2009.00427.x

Roberts, M. E., Stewart, B. M., & Tingley, D. (2016). stm: R package for structural topic models. *Journal of Statistical Software, VV*(2), 1–40. https://doi.org/10.18637/jss.v000.i00

Sullivan, J., Rawnsley, M.-Y. T., Feng, C.-S., & Smyth, J. (2018). The media in democratic Taiwan. In *A new era in democratic Taiwan*. Routledge. https://doi.org/10.1080/13439006

Van Atteveldt, W., Welbers, K., Jacobi, C., & Vliegenthart, R. (2014). LDA models topics.... But what are 'topics'. In *Big data in the social sciences workshop*. http://vanatteveldt.com/wpcontent/uploads/2014_vanatteveldt_glasgowbigdata_topics.pdf

Yang, C.-R. (2011). *Gang ao xin yi min yan jiu: da lu ren min fu Xiang gang Ao men ding ju dui wo Gang Ao zheng ce zhi ying xiang [The study of new immigrants in Hong Kong and Macau: The impact of mainlanders settling in Hong Kong and Macau on the ROC's Hong Kong and Macau policies]*. Mainland Affairs Council, Republic of China. https://ws.mac.gov.tw/001/Upload/OldFile/public/data/227915171.pdf

Yang, Y.-T. (2019, May 19). "Duan bi" mai shu lang Lin rong ji: xiang shou min zhu han tong yi shisi xiang wen ti "Severe arm" bookseller Lin Wing-Kee: Enjoying democracy but calling for unification is a matter of thought]. *Liberty Times*, p. A13.

CHAPTER 8

The Role of Nationalism and Political Identity in Shaping Japanese People's Perceptions of Immigrants and Refugees

Zdenka P. Kyselova and Kristina Kironska

Introduction

While anti-immigration sentiments are on the rise in many parts of the world, the case of Japan is specific in several aspects. With the world's oldest population (European Parliament, 2020), Japanese society will likely face pressing socio-economic problems, if it does not start accepting more foreign nationals. On the other hand, a strong sense of cultural uniqueness makes it difficult both for foreigners to integrate but also for Japanese people to accept them. Furthermore, as a democratic country which ratified the United Nations (UN) Convention Relating to the Status of Refugees, Japan is among the countries with the lowest rates of refugee acceptance.

Z. P. Kyselova (✉) · K. Kironska
Department of Asian Studies, Palacky University Olomouc, Olomouc, Czech Republic
e-mail: z.kyselova10@gmail.com

L. Momesso and P. Ivanova (eds.), *Refugees and Asylum Seekers in East Asia*, Palgrave Macmillan Studies on Human Rights in Asia,
https://doi.org/10.1007/978-981-97-2867-1_8

Japan has been tackling demographic issues related to its ageing society since the end of the twentieth century. Until that time, words such as immigration, migrants, or refugees were hardly present in the government discourse. With the ageing population and declining birth rate, the Japanese government has searched for means to secure economic and social stability, e.g. by involving more women in the job market, enhancing childcare facilities, and broadening the range of working visas. However, domestic issues are not the only reason for accepting immigrants and refugees. Japan has become a vocal promoter of human security and ratified the United Nations (UN) Convention Relating to the Status of Refugees in 1981. Despite all the commitments to international norms and rational reasons to open itself up, Japan continues to struggle to adapt its internal policy and bureaucratic processes towards modern immigration and asylum systems. In 2021, only 2.2% of residents are foreign (Statistic Bureau of Japan, 2021), which contributes to demographic issues and labour shortages. The low rate of refugees accepted yearly, together with harsh conditions in detention facilities and strict acceptance rules, has caused the worsening of Japan's international reputation.

With regard to Japanese perception of foreigners in general, the traditional view of Japan as a homogeneous nation prevailed as a common reason for its unfriendliness towards immigrants (Koizumi, 1992). However, in recent decades, the relevance of the notion of Japanese homogeneity has been questioned (Flowers, 2009; Mukae, 2022). The homogeneity of Japan, at least from the Asian perspective, is regarded by many as a myth, for there are numerous Asian minority groups of ethnic Koreans and Chinese, but also ethnic groups native to Japanese islands, such as the Ainu and Ryukyuan people. On the other hand, the period of isolation during the Tokugawa era, the efforts to assimilate ethnic groups such as the Ainu during the Meiji period, and the limited inflow of immigrants after World War II due to the focus on post-war reconstruction, gave rise to the notion of homogeneity in Japanese society. As Burgess (2010) argues, such discourse has influenced Japanese perceptions of foreigners and the country's stringent immigration policy.

The adoption of international norms related to human rights protection and refugees was a crucial step for Japan to fit into the global society. Conformity with such norms is, however, based on domestic standards and national identity, which have been traditionally anti-immigration

(Flowers, 2009). Public perception is another area where national identity matters. Existing research studies on the Japanese public attitude towards immigrants have focused on the impact of media framing, personal contact with foreigners, and the connection with threat perception (Cheng & Fraser, 2022; Green, 2017; Horiuchi & Ono, 2022). Indeed, mass media and threat framing play a significant role in shaping public opinion, especially in Japan where public safety is highly valued. As such, safety can be considered a constituent part of social harmony, which has historically been a strong element of Japanese national identity.

While considering harmony as an important aspect of Japanese national identity, it is vital to ask to what extent national identity impacts domestic discourse and public perception of foreigners. While national identity can be defined from many perspectives, depending on the field of study, one of the unifying features is the group's perception of specific aspects that distinguish them from others (Münch, 2002; Smith, 2001). In the past two decades, the discourse of historical revisionism and the endorsement of pride in Japanese society have been on the rise (Yamaguchi, 2017). The nationalist sentiment was remarkably present under the late Prime Minister Shinzo Abe's administration. It is therefore our ambition to reveal how such nationalist tendencies determine Japanese public opinion towards immigrants and refugees. In our study, we have tested whether Japanese society esteems Japan over other countries and how such feelings impact Japanese views of foreigners. In our study, we have built part of our argument on an experiment to see if there is a correlation between blind nationalism (see below) and views on immigration and refugees.

Given the general presumption that conservative right-wing ideology is prone to anti-immigration tendencies (Brooks et al., 2016; Hainmueller & Hopkins, 2014), we also tested attitudes towards immigrants and refugees against political leanings (conservative v. liberal) and voter/party preferences. While the definition of conservatism and liberalism can be blurry in the Japanese context (McCormack, 2008), we hypothesise that the respondents who identify themselves as conservative rather than liberal also have a sceptical view towards immigration and refugees. Conservatism in Japan is associated with revisionism, changing the pacifist clause of the constitution, and the support of a more robust defence policy. In other words, conservatives actually support a change in Japan's trajectory, rather than the conservation of the post-war democratic order in Japan (McCormack, 2008). Because the support for restoring some of the pre-war values, which were built on the notion of superiority towards others, especially Asian countries, is intertwined with conservatism and nationalism, we have examined how these two types of political identity correlate with anti-immigration sentiments. As scholars have already pointed out in their studies of Japanese perception of immigrants and refugees, the exceptionally low number of the latter makes it difficult to completely distinguish between the two categories, although the legislative differences are quite crucial. As Horiuchi and Ono (2021) reflect, it cannot be presumed that Japanese citizens recognise the difference between work-related immigrants, refugees, and short-term visitors. Also, the Japanese legal system does not provide special measures for refugees, as international law stipulates (Fujibayashi, 2020). Instead, refugee status is recognised under the Immigration Control and Refugee Recognition Act, which also defines the rights of foreign workers. This can also stir up legislative differences and can confuse assumptions about foreign workers and refugees. Due to the relatively small number of non-Japanese groups in Japan, both foreign workers and refugees might evoke the same feelings.

To reveal the Japanese views towards refugees, we selected the Rohingya as a concrete group (case study). The Japanese so-called special relations with Myanmar and Japan's particular efforts to economically mitigate the refugee crisis might create a surmise that Japan would be welcoming towards the Rohingya refugees. Nevertheless, only a few hundreds of Rohingya reside in Japan, despite the generally positive attitude toward their resettlement (see below in the survey results).

This chapter is organised as follows. In the following section, the methodology is explained. After that, the historical perspective of Japanese attitudes towards foreigners is introduced, followed by the theoretical framework, built on national identity, nationalism, and political leaning. The next section presents the data on how Japanese people feel about the current situation related to immigrants and refugees, with a special focus on Rohingya refugees, and how nationalism and political identity impact their views. The last section provides conclusions.

Methodology

This book chapter presents the results of the Sinophone Borderlands Indo-Pacific Survey (Turcsanyi et al., 2022), co-convened by one of the authors. The survey investigated global views of China and other issues, such as people's stances towards immigration and refugees, through a series of large-scale representative online public opinion surveys in many (selected) parts of the world, including Japan. Participants responded online to approximately 60 questions. Only a subset of the data related to the goals of the current paper, however, is reported in this research.

We analysed survey statements related to nationalism, such as: *The world would be a better place if people from other countries were more like the Japanese*, and, *Generally speaking, Japan is a better country than most other countries*. Furthermore, questions about political identity were analysed, including voting/party preference and conservative/liberal leaning, such as: *When it comes to politics, do you consider yourself more liberal or conservative? If there were parliamentary elections this weekend, which party would you vote for*? These questions and statements have been inspired by other surveys, such as the International Social Survey Programme (ISSP).

For assessing Japanese people's attitude towards immigrants and refugees (including a case study on the Rohingya), the following statements and questions have been selected and analysed: *The presence of migrant workers is beneficial for Japan*; *It is difficult for foreigners to fit into Japanese society*; *Chinese migrants face discrimination in Japan*; *Asian migrants (excluding Chinese) face discrimination in Japan*; *Japan is open to refugees*; *The Rohingya people are a persecuted Muslim minority in Myanmar. Do you support the resettlement of the displaced Rohingya people in your country*? Attitudes towards selected groups of people have also been considered. Additionally, all these questions have been disaggregated by socio-demographic data obtained from the survey.

The Japanese sample is national representative (in terms of age, gender, and region) with 1219 respondents. The responses were collected in Japanese from participants registered in national online panels by the survey agency Cint between 11 April and 17 June 2022. The main data about the respondents are shown below in Table 8.1. Most questions use a 7-point answering scale (in the analysis below sometimes recalculated into three categories for easier understanding of the results), while some are so-called thermometer questions, where the answering scale goes from 0 to 100.

In our research, we focused on people's attitudes towards immigrants and refugees in Japan through the lens of political identity, more specifically through voting/party preference, liberal/conservative leanings (see Table 8.1), and nationalism (see Figs. 8.1 and 8.2).

Table 8.1 Data about the survey respondents

Gender distribution	
Female	47%
Male	52%
Other	0%
I don't want to answer	1%
Age distribution	
18–25	20%
25–34	21%
35–44	24%
45–54	22%
> 55	13%
Education level	
Primary	1%
Secondary	28%
Tertiary	71%
Voter/party preference	
Liberal Democratic Party	27%
Constitutional Democratic Party	4.8%
Komeito	2.5%
Japanese Communist Party	4%
Nippon Ishin no Kai	7.2%
Social Democratic Party	0.5%
Reiwa Shinsengumi	1.5%
Democratic Party for the People	2.2%
NHK Party[1]	0.3%
Other political party	1.6%
I don't know	28.7%
I would not vote	19.7%

Liberal/conservative leaning

1 = Very liberal	*2*	*3*	*4*	*5*	*6*	*7 = Very conservative*	*I don't know*
3%	5%	13%	12%	25%	13%	5%	24%

When asked about liberal or conservative leanings, a large portion of the respondents opted for the option "I don't know" (24%). More

[1] *Nippon Hosōku Kyōkai. The NHK Party has been renamed to Seijika Joshi 48 Party.*

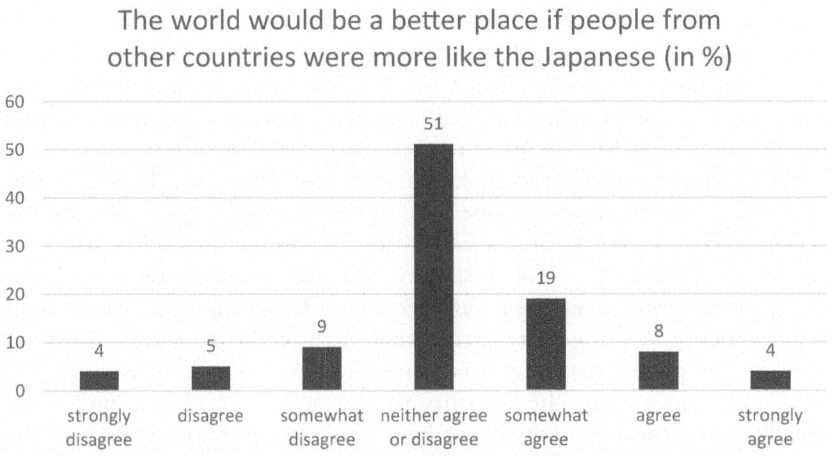

Fig. 8.1 Measuring nationalism in Japan—item 1

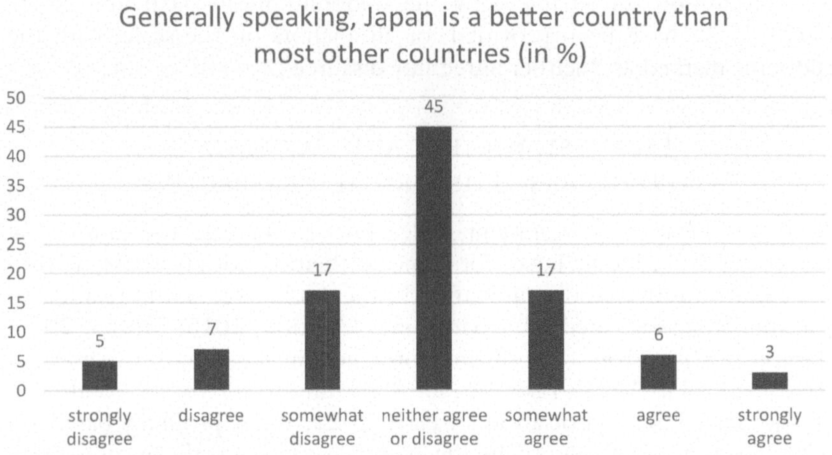

Fig. 8.2 Measuring nationalism in Japan—item 2

people see themselves as conservative (43%) than liberal (21%) and 12% are neutral.

To measure voter/party preference, we asked which political party people would vote for if parliamentary elections took place the following weekend. About 29% of the respondents said they didn't know which party they would vote for, 20% would not vote, 27% would vote for the Liberal Democratic Party, 7% for the Nippon Ishin no Kai, 5% for the Constitutional Democratic Party, 4% for the Japanese Communist Party, and the remainder for the other parties (with each 2% or less).

We measured nationalism in Japan with two items (see Figs. 8.1 and 8.2), using the theory developed by Davidov (2009), outlined in the section "What shapes people's perception of immigrants and refugees – theoretical framework". The first item was *The world would be a better place if people from other countries were more like the Japanese,* with which Japanese people slightly more agreed than disagreed (mean 4.1—in which 1 means completely disagree, 4 is in neither agree nor disagree, and 7 is completely agree), but the majority of the people chose the midpoint, signalling that the Japanese do not have very strong opinions on this. To the second item—*Generally speaking, Japan is a better country than most other countries*—the response was slightly more on the disagree side (mean 3.9), but again, the majority of the respondents chose the midpoint. To avoid confusion on what exactly the midpoint means (Chyung et al., 2017), labels have been provided for all anchors on the scale, with the midpoint marked as "neither agree nor disagree".

Japanese Society and Accepting Foreigners—Historical Perspective

While the Japanese government endeavours to increase the number of foreign workers, life in Japan for some of them is not effortless, as they face racially motivated discrimination in the workplace, and in relation to housing, shopping, medical services, etc. (Arudou, 2015; Morita, 2015; Shimoji, 2023). More than 60% of foreigners in Japan have experienced police control in 2022 (Take, 2022). According to the survey conducted by the Tokyo Bar Association in early 2022, racial profiling based on appearance was experienced in the past five years mostly by non-Asian nationals. The fear of a rise in criminality has been a common reason for xenophobia and anti-immigration tendencies in Japan. To what extent has Japanese society been welcoming of foreigners? What are Japan's experiences with accepting refugees and immigrants, and how has the opinion on these issues evolved?

To better anchor current trends in public opinion towards immigrants and refugees, as well as the policy debate and legislative framework, this part of the chapter presents the main obstacles in Japanese immigration and refugee policy through selected cases.

Japan and Refugees

As has already been explained in the introduction of this book, Japan ratified the UN Refugee Convention in 1981 and the related Protocol in 1982. However, Japan has its own legislation that defines the status of immigrants and refugees under the Immigration Control and Refugees' Recognition Act of 1951. The law follows a strict interpretation of the UN Refugee Convention, meaning that only those in danger of persecution due to religious, national, political, social, and racial reasons can be considered refugees. Simply put, those fleeing war conflicts are not considered refugees according to Japanese legislation. This represents one of the main reasons why Japan accepts so few refugees.

Nevertheless, there have been a few occasions when Japan showed flexibility and permitted exceptions. In this section, we will address the most significant events and shed light on public opinion towards these cases.

The first event that forced Japan to face a refugee crisis was the Second Indochina War of 1955–1975. Thanks to exponential economic growth during the period, Japan was able to financially contribute to the resettlement of refugees from Indochina in third countries (Havens, 1990). When it came to meeting the refugees' requests for asylum in Japan, the situation was much more complicated due to legislative issues, and because public opinion towards resettlement was divided between exclusionist sentiments and humanitarian tendencies. At the same time, if there was any sympathy among the Japanese towards people who were forced to flee from their homes, it was oriented towards Indochinese, especially those who took the most dangerous way, on the sea (Mizuno, 1990). Partly due to international pressure, Japan decided to extend the scope of aid beyond financial assistance and started accepting people fleeing the battlefield. According to Strausz (2012), another reason was that accepting Indochinese refugees was not seen as a precedent for a potential refugee influx, simply because the Indochinese were not exactly considered refugees from Japan's legal perspective.

As for public opinion towards the Indochinese refugees, Japanese government-commissioned surveys show that while in 1980 only 22.8% would be in favour of increasing the quota of accepted refugees from Indochina, in 1982 it was almost 50% (Dasgupta, 2021; Strausz, 2012;

Takeda, 1998). Interestingly, despite the disapproval of the public in 1980, the government decided to increase the quota for Indochinese refugees that year and again in 1981, 1983, and 1985. Moreover, in 1981 the UN Refugee Convention was ratified. Most of the judiciary and parliamentarians, along with public supporters of the resettlement pointed to the low number of Indochinese refugees accepted in comparison with other states, hence arguing for the importance of international prestige. Humanitarian reasons for the support were given much less emphasis (Strausz, 2012). Furthermore, the governmental surveys mentioned above only asked about the attitude towards Indochinese refugees, who were treated in a distinct way from other asylum seekers. Non-Indochinese refugees and political asylum seekers had to undergo a complicated process of acceptance following a rigid interpretation of the UN Refugee Convention. Only 43 officials from the Ministry of Justice were appointed to the agenda of such refugees, while in the case of Indochinese people, the intergovernmental committee consisted of several ministries, including the Ministry of Foreign Affairs, Justice, Labour, etc., who were involved in establishing the processes. Moreover, number of NGOs were engaged in the resettlement itself. (Takeda, 1998). Until 2005, Japan only accepted 330 "convention" refugee applicants (Iwasaki, 2006), while more than 11,000 Indochinese refugees found their new home in Japan as of 2009 (Refugee Assistance Headquarters, 2019).

Another example of flexibility in the Japanese legal framework concerning refugees is the Refugee Resettlement Programme established in 2010 in reaction to the Myanmar refugee crisis. The original idea was to accept 30 refugees each year (150 refugees in total), selected by the United Nations High Commissioner for Refugees (UNHCR) based on their potential for smooth integration into social and working life in Japan. According to the criteria established by the Japanese Ministry of Justice, the applicants would have to be members of the Karen ethnic group, members of a small nuclear family, and have high chances of finding a job (Hatcher & Murakami, 2020). Importantly, the UNHCR explicitly prohibits any form of discriminatory criteria.

Despite the expectations that the Refugee Resettlement Programme would represent a breakthrough in Japanese refugee policy, no legal shifts in the acceptance of asylum seekers happened. Nevertheless, according to government statistics, there were more than 37,000 Myanmar refugees living in Japan as of 2021, comprising the largest group of immigrants with humanitarian and refugee status. Approximately 300 of them belonged to the Rohingya minority, which has established a large community in Tatebayashi (Gunma prefecture) (Begum, 2021). Not many voices have been raised during the events related to the Myanmar refugees in Japan. There were protests for a stronger Japanese reaction to the 2021 coup organised by the Myanmar people and students ("Thousands March in Tokyo", 2021), but there was not any strong public voice to support refugee acceptance.

When the Syrian civil war erupted in 2011, millions of people were forced to leave their homes, resulting in a massive influx of migrants in Europe. Japan accepted only a handful of refugees. Instead, Japan opted to provide financial support and emerged as the second-largest contributor to the UNHCR. The late Prime Minister Shinzo Abe told reporters that Japan had to solve the domestic issues of an ageing population and a labour shortage first by engaging more women in the labour market (McCurry, 2015). In 2017, Japan experienced its highest peak of asylum applications with more than 19,000 applications, while only 20 of the applicants were successful (UNOCHA—Reliefweb, 2018). As for Syrian refugees, only seven were granted refugee status in Japan (Yamagata, 2017). Instead of refugees, the Japanese government decided to take in 150 Syrian university students in 2016 for a period of five years.

Public opinion polls conducted by news agencies did not show any strong support during the Syrian refugee crisis. Only 24% of respondents were favourable to refugees' resettlement, whereas 58% disapproved according to the Asahi Shinbun 2015 survey (Yamagata, 2017). In the 2017 *Mainichi Shimbun* survey, the proportion of those supporting the refugee intake was merely 15% (Yamagata, 2017). The results are not surprising if we look at anti-immigration sentiments in Europe and the terrorist attacks which happened in France, Belgium, and other countries. In his media and political analysis, Yamagata (2017) revealed that supporters of refugee acceptance generally used Japan's international reputation to bolster their arguments, along with the country's low rate of refugee acceptance in comparison with other developed countries. Similar narratives were present also during the Indochinese refugee crisis.

When Russia invaded Ukraine in February 2022 and millions of people fled the country, a massive wave of solidarity started to spread worldwide. Hundreds of Ukrainians found refuge in Japan, though they are not referred to as refugees, but "evacuees", since they are expected to return to Ukraine eventually. Nevertheless, the Ukrainian evacuees received unprecedented support in Japan and a legal status which allowed them to stay and work for one year (Immigration Services Agency in Japan, 2022). As such, the government's reaction to the Ukrainian refugees is comparable to the Indochinese crisis in the 1980s. It reopened the questions around Japanese refugee policy and the country's double standards with regard to people from Ukraine compared to other nationals, such as people from Myanmar, be they Rohingya or from other groups.

In light of the inconsistencies, the Japanese government resumed the debate over the amendment of the Immigration Control and Refugee Recognition Act in early 2023, with an additional stipulation that would allow war refugees similar legal rights to "convention" refugees under supplementary protection. The amendment also aims to put an end to prolonged detentions, however, by allowing for the deportation of those who have applied three times or more, even during the process of refugee status acceptance, which might be considered a violation of international law. The amendment has become a subject of criticism by the UN Office of the High Commissioner for Human Rights (OHCHR) (2023) and several Japanese NGOs (Han Hinkon Network, 2023).

Japan and Immigrants

As for immigrants, until the amendment of the Immigration Control and Refugee Recognition Act in 2019, only high-skilled professionals were eligible to work in Japan, with two exceptions. First, since the 1990s, the descendants of Japanese emigrants (Nikkeijin) have been allowed to work and reside in Japan. Second, when the Technical Intern Training Programme (TITP) started in 2004, 75,000 foreign workers were allowed in (Kashiwazaki & Akaha, 2006). The programme allows trainees to have contracts for three to five years and the official discourse states that trainees gain new skills which they then use to improve industry back home. Moreover, the Technical Intern Training Act of 2016 stipulates that "Technical intern training shall not be conducted as a means of adjusting labour demand and supply". However, many foreigners engaged in the TITP experienced harsh working conditions, exploitation, and harassment, and have clearly been used as a cheap labour force. The number of complaints received by the Organisation for Technical Intern Training doubled in 2020 from the previous year (Nara, 2022). At the time of writing, there has recently been a debate about abolishing TITP and creating a new system of training programmes, which would prevent human rights abuse (Tauchi, 2023).

With the deepening labour shortages, Japan established a new category of unskilled workers in 2019. The original aim was to bring 345,000 blue-collar workers within five years (Takizawa, 2021), but only 1621 foreigners came to Japan under the new visa system in the first ten months (Milly, 2020). Meanwhile, public support for the increase of foreign workers has been growing in the past years. According to a survey by the Japanese Trade Union Confederation in 2018, 55% of respondents viewed the increasing number of foreign workers as a positive development, while 22% disagreed. A year later, the approval rate increased to 74% (Kono, 2019). In their research on Japanese public opinion towards immigration, Davison and Peng (2021) conducted in-depth in-person interviews with 21 participants of higher education and social status. Their findings show that most of the interviewees did not have any particular antipathy towards immigrants if they were only short-term workers. The participants showed significant concerns about long-term or permanent immigrants for fear of losing the Japanese culture (Davison & Peng, 2021).

This section introduced several refugee and immigration issues Japan has been tackling for decades. Both foreign workers and refugees in Japan face a substantial level of prejudice, discrimination, and human rights abuse. Japanese public opinion towards the two categories has been shifting from strictly negative at the beginning of the 1980s to more accepting. Nevertheless, the Japanese official stance has not improved significantly over recent years. On several occasions, the Japanese government has acceded to the liberalisation of refugee and immigration policy but mostly under the combination of domestic and international pressure.

What Shapes People's Perception of Immigrants and Refugees—Theoretical Framework

Several researchers have dealt with the question of the driving forces behind people's perceptions of immigrants and refugees. Among the approaches, some researchers have applied contact theory, which hypothesises that contact between the locals and immigrants leads to a positive view towards foreigners (Green & Kayoda, 2017; McLaren, 2003; Oliver & Wong, 2003). Others have researched "threat" as a factor in perceiving refugees (Blinder & Lundgren, 2019; Semyonov et al., 2004). In our study, we build our argument on the role of nationalism and political identity in people's perceptions of foreigners. While Japanese society has been regarded as highly homogeneous, which emphasises its cultural values, we argue that nationalist sentiments and conservatism have an impact on anti-immigration sentiments in Japan.

National Identity and Nationalism

In the past few decades, Japan has experienced a revival of nationalist sentiments. In the early 2000s, a law acknowledging symbols associated with the imperial era as national symbols was enacted, despite the opposition. In 1999, a teacher committed suicide in protest against the forceful singing of the Kimigayo anthem (Tolbert, 1999). Moreover, former Prime Minister Shinzo Abe, who was assassinated in 2022, became almost a synonym for the term nationalism. His ideology was closely associated with the revival of a "beautiful Japan" ("Towards a Beautiful Country: My Vision for Japan" is the title of Abe's (2007) book), which ought to be much more assertive both politically and militarily. The reinterpretation of the Constitution, allowing the dispatch of self-defence forces, was understood by China and South Korea to be a clear indication of the rise of Japanese nationalism, whereas, for the USA, such progress was much welcomed because it implied a greater self-reliance and less dependence on protection from Washington (Ali, 2015). Besides political nationalism, Japan has experienced increasing anti-Korean and anti-Chinese sentiment with the rise of the ultra-right wing (Martini Grimaldi, 2022).

To better understand the nature of nationalism and national identity in the context of Japan, an introduction to some of the theoretical approaches is necessary. Both nationalism and national identity, which are often intertwined, have many possible meanings. The previous paragraph shows some examples of how national identification leads to particular political decisions or beliefs. As Greenfeld (1992) puts it, nationalism is first and foremost a way of creating identities, and only secondarily a political movement. The concept itself is built on the apprehension of the nation which, in its modern sense, came to be understood in early sixteenth-century England (Doak, 2007). Since then, nationalism has gained various forms depending on the context. Nevertheless, in all contexts, nationalism revolves around a shared sense of community, common history, culture, language, and often a perceived shared destiny among the people within a nation (Smith, 2010).

In our study, we aim to reveal how a certain level of attachment to the nation can shape Japanese public opinion towards immigrants and refugees. It is thus important to first understand the broader context of Japanese national identity. In their studies, many political scientists have distinguished between civic type of national identity, stemming from self-regarding and belonging to one's nation, and an ethnic type of national identity, which is represented by shared culture, language, history, and ancestry (Brubaker, 1996; Jeong, 2016; Kohn, 1944; Taniguchi, 2021). In that sense, Tanabe (2021) suggests that Japan as a nation can be described as an ethnic type and that Japanese society has strong political and national pride, which is connected to exclusionism and ethnocentrism. The presumption of Japan as an ethnic type of nation is in contradiction to Sasaki's research (2004), where he revealed that having Japanese citizenship and regarding oneself as Japanese are the most significant parameters of national identity as opposed to those notions of a shared culture, language, history, and ancestry. Furthermore, Jeong (2016) compared the results of a survey conducted in three Western countries (the USA, Norway, and Sweden) and three Asian countries (China, Taiwan, and South Korea) and found that in contrast to the Western countries, neither ethnic nor civic identities were associated with immigration attitudes in the respective Asian countries.

Because of these contradictions, we decided to build our theoretical grounds of nationalism on the approach of political psychology, which understands nationalism as a pride in one's nation and a feeling of superiority over other states (Kosterman & Feshbach, 1989). To distinguish from the type of nationalism connected to people's identity, which we introduced above, we address nationalism based on the political psychology approach as *blind nationalism*.

Some political thinkers, such as Bunzo Hashikawa, linked this notion of blind nationalism with the ethnic type of nationalism (Doak, 2007). In contrast to blind nationalism, constructive patriotism is defined as a feeling of love for the country and attachment to its democratic values, but with the ability to see the country's drawbacks (Davidov, 2009; Schatz et al., 1999). There is also a difference in how the blind nationalism and constructive patriotism correlate with fear of others. According to Raijman et al. (2008), blind nationalism correlates more with antipathy towards immigrants than constructive patriotism. Based on the above, to find whether nationalist tendencies play any role in the perception of immigration and current Japanese political and societal attitudes towards foreigners, we selected the following questions on nationalism: *The world would be a better place if people from other countries were more like the*

Japanese; and *Generally speaking, Japan is a better country than most other countries.*

Lind and Ueki's survey research (2021) found that while patriotism has a continuing presence in Japanese society, the sense of superiority and other nationalist tendencies are rather ambiguous factors (Lind & Ueki, 2021). Around 80% of the respondents in 1995, 2003, and 2013 ISSP surveys agreed that Japan is better than other countries. However, opinion was split in half on the question of whether the world would be a better place if people were more like the Japanese. The results of Lind and Ueki's research (2021) are similar to the results of our survey, which shows that 26% of the respondents agree with the idea that Japan is better than other countries, 29% disprove this claim, and 45% do not have a firm opinion. Since the survey was conducted in the spring of 2022, it is likely that the Covid-19 pandemic and the Russian war in Ukraine impacted Japanese nationalist tendencies. One-third of the respondents think that the world would be a better place if more people were like the Japanese, while 18% do not agree with this statement. Over half of the participants did not specify their feelings.

Political Identity

The Japanese political environment is characterised by stability and long-lasting regimes. With short periods of exception, the Liberal Democratic Party (LDP) has been ruling Japan since 1955. Shinzo Abe led the country for eight years (2012–2020), making him the longest-serving prime minister in Japanese history. Again, we find a certain amount of Japanese identity based on harmony. Paradoxically, in a country renowned for its innovation and ability to evolve rapidly, there is a fairly strong conservatism on many issues. Even after Abe and his successor Yoshihide Suga's resignation, and after strong criticism for failing to manage the pandemic, the LDP and its coalition partner Komeito retained a majority in the lower house election of 2021 (Obe, 2021).

When looking at the LDP's politics, there is not much space for discussion about accepting refugees. The government has, however, agreed to raise the financial contribution to mitigate the Rohingya refugee crisis in Bangladesh and has accepted an unusually high number of "evacuees" from Ukraine. In the past, only Indochinese refugees surpassed the number of Ukrainian refugees. However, it has done little to counter international criticism of its stringent rules for accepting asylum seekers.

The LDP attempted to enforce a revision of the Immigration Law introduced in 2021 but decided not to submit it officially in 2022. The draft was a reaction to international criticism of prolonged detentions and it would have stated the number of times one could apply for refugee status, but it was not generally welcomed by the UNHCR and numerous NGOs (more on that in the section "Japanese society and accepting foreigners – historical perspective"). Even with the passing of the bill, the main problem would remain—the strict recognition conditions and the near-impossibility of proving the legitimacy of someone's refugee status (Ara, 2021).

At the same time, the party was very interested in dealing with the country's ageing population and its labour shortage. In 2019, the government enacted a new law enabling "Specified Skilled Workers", promising to accept at least 345,000 foreign workers in the following five years (Takizawa, 2021). Although business organisations welcomed the step, human rights and immigration organisations opposed the legislation due to concerns that the rights of workers would not be protected (Milly, 2020).

In contrast to the conservative LDP, the Constitutional Democratic Party (CDP) with other progressive and left-oriented parties, proposed a bill to the government, which should secure the protection of refugees and prevent them from arbitrary detentions based on decisions of immigration officers (Rikken Minshutō, 2022). The bill was left on the table without any significant debate. In that sense, we expect that voters for the CDP would be more positive in their views of immigrants and refugees in Japan.

When considering the Japanese political parties' programme on refugees and immigrants, what can we assume from the political leanings and party/voting preferences of Japanese society? First of all, it is important to shed some light on the nature of Japanese political participation. As some studies have showed, left-wing citizens tend to be much more politically engaged than right-oriented people (Finkel & Opp, 1991; Torcal et al., 2016). Given the fact that the conservative right-oriented LDP has repeatedly gained the majority of votes in elections to Japan's Diet in the last decade, it might explain, why political engagement among Japanese citizens is usually low (Jou & Endo, 2017).

It is not surprising that the issue of refugees does not resonate much in Japan. If the society is rather conservative (conservatism in Japan is understood rather as traditionalism [Quo, 1966; Tanaka, 1989]) and prefers to stick to the proven consensus, then people are more likely to support the LDP, for whom the main issue is to improve the economic and demographic situation. Moreover, in his study, Strausz (2018) reveals that the majority of candidates and Diet members, and also respondents of media-conducted public surveys, did not have any strong opinion on whether Japan should accept more foreign workers during the elections of 2009, 2012, 2014, and 2017. This has already started to change. *Mainichi Shimbun*'s opinion poll from 2018 showed, that 47% of respondents agree with higher numbers of foreigners, while 32% oppose it. A year later, almost two-thirds of respondents to the Nikkei survey were in favour of the rising number of foreigners (Kono, 2019). What the Japanese people think about accepting refugees remains so far uncovered as there have not been many surveys on the issue, as the next section will show.

This research draws on the above and measures political identity through both voting/party preference and liberal/conservative leaning focusing on how political identity affects public opinion towards immigrants and refugees.

The next section will dive into the specifics of the survey data and will analyse Japanese people's attitudes towards foreigners, both immigrants and refugees, based on the two categories described in this section: nationalism and political identity.

Japanese Perceptions of Immigrants and Refugees—Survey Results

The General Attitude Towards Foreigners

In line with previous studies, the Sinophone Borderlands Indo-Pacific Survey results confirm that Japanese people are not so open towards foreigners in general. When asked how positively or negatively Japanese people perceive certain groups of people (on a scale 0 to 100, with 0 representing cold, negative feelings; 50 representing neutral; and 100 representing warm, positive feelings), the results show that Japanese people are most positive about Taiwanese people (mean 64), followed by Americans (mean 62), and Europeans (mean 60) (see Table 8.2), although the mean values are not very high. On the other hand, the Japanese are least positive towards the Chinese (mean 38), which is not surprising as there have long been animosities due to wars and historic competition between the two countries.

Table 8.2 Japanese people's attitudes towards various groups of people on a scale 0 to 100 (with 0 representing cold, negative feelings; 50 representing neutral; and 100 representing warm, positive feelings), depicting the mean value (rounded up)

Group of people	*Mean value (0–100)*
Taiwanese	64
Europeans	60
Americans (from USA)	62
Africans	55
Indians	54
Uyghur	53
Rohingya	52
Immigrants	50
Muslims	46
Chinese (from PRC)	38

The negative stance towards mainland Chinese is not new among the Japanese. In the 2013 Public Survey on Political Participation of Citizens and Internationalization, Chinese were the least favourable foreign nationals (Zhang, 2018). Anti-Chinese sentiments are common in Japan and usually have direct links to threats that China has come to bring over time. Chinese military spending is the second largest in the world. Japan lost its economic primacy in Asia and the US-China rivalry brings new challenges for the Japanese diplomacy. The disputed Senkaku/Diaoyu Islands add another friction and World War II also remains as an open wound. Needless to say, the dislike is both-sided. In contrast, Japanese relations with Taiwan are built on mutual trust, economic partnership, shared values, a common enemy and a common friend. As the first Japanese colony, Taiwan was forced to implement some of the Japanese cultural norms including language, but for the country's economic and technological development, the Japanese colonial rule brought much-welcomed innovations. In this sense, Taiwanese representatives have never been critical towards the Japanese colonial past and the Japanese appreciate this form of restraint (Peng-Er, 2004).

This question deliberately contained a mix of various groups—national, ethnic, and religious—to be able to see which resonated the most. The groups that most interested us regarding this research were immigrants, Muslims, Rohingya (refugees in Bangladesh), and Uyghurs (potential refugees from China). Out of these groups, Japanese people are most favourable towards the Uyghurs (mean 53), followed by the Rohingya (mean 52), and immigrants (mean 50). The category of immigrants was chosen because the term labels a group that is usually understood as a whole, regardless of nationality, with a certain connotation that can differ from country to country. In the case of Japan, immigrants are often understood as temporary workers. As Davison and Peng (2021) found out in their study, Japanese people have neutral or slightly positive attitudes towards short-term workers. Least favourable feelings among the Japanese are held towards Muslims (mean 46). Towards the Uyghurs and the Rohingya, Japanese people have a rather positive attitude, towards immigrants in general a neutral one, while Muslims are seen rather negatively (although not as negatively as the Chinese). Interestingly, the first two groups—the Rohingya and the Uyghurs, who are predominantly Muslims—are seen much more favourably than the religious group of Muslims.

Attitude Towards Immigrants and Refugees

To find out Japanese people's views on foreigners, including immigrants and refugees, we put forward various statements related to: the presence of immigrants in general; Chinese immigrants (as they are among the most numerous groups of foreigners coming to Japan for work); other Asian immigrants (there are predominantly Asian migrant workers in Japan); and refugees in Japan (see Table 8.3). In all these statements, the midpoint is the most prevalent, again pointing to what has been mentioned above—that people in Japan tend to not have strong options on certain issues, views on foreigners being one of them. Nevertheless, more people agree than disagree that the presence of migrant workers is beneficial for Japan. Also, the majority believe that it is difficult for foreigners to fit into Japanese society. More respondents disagree rather than agree that Chinese as well as other Asian migrants face discrimination in Japan. On the question of refugees, Japanese people clearly acknowledge that Japan is not open to refugees (49%).

According to 30% of the survey respondents, the presence of migrant workers is beneficial for Japan, 22% disagree, and 47% are unsure. When looking at this question through the lens of other variables—voting/party preference, nationalism, and demographics—only voting/party preference had any effect. Voters for the CDP (mean value 4.6 out of a scale 1–7) and the Democratic Party for the People (mean value 4.4 out of a scale 1–7) had the highest agreement rate, which confirms the hypothesis of the study.

Table 8.3 Agreement or disagreement with various statements related to immigrants and refugees

	The presence of migrant workers is beneficial for Japan	*It is difficult for foreigners to fit into Japanese society*	*Chinese migrants face discrimination in Japan*	*Asian migrants (excluding Chinese) face discrimination in Japan*	*Japan is open to refugees*
Disagree	22%	19%	27%	26%	49%
Neither agree not disagree	47%	39%	52%	50%	38%
Agree	30%	42%	21%	24%	13%

Respondents believed it is difficult for foreigners to fit into Japanese society—42% agreed, 18% disagreed, and 39% of the respondents did not have an opinion on this. Those who have been in higher education were slightly more likely to agree than less educated respondents.

In general, the survey participants did not think that Chinese immigrants in Japan face discrimination. Only about 21% of Japanese thought Chinese migrants face discrimination in Japan, 27% disagreed, and 52% were neutral. Women believed more than men that the Chinese face discrimination. More educated people believed this statement slightly less than people with lower education. Also, liberal leaning people tended to perceive the Chinese as being discriminated against slightly more than conservative leaning people. Also, the less nationalistic sentiments someone had (based on the item *The world would be a better place if people from other countries were more like the Japanese)*, the more the person tended to believe that Chinese face discrimination in Japan. From the analysis of attitudes towards various groups of people, we found that the Chinese are viewed as the least popular. Not only Chinese but other Asian nationals, namely Koreans, have reportedly faced some sort of discrimination (Goto, 2021).

Survey participants were divided on whether Asians (excluding the Chinese) are discriminated against or not. 23% thought they are, 25% did not think so, and half of the respondents were neutral. Women agreed slightly more than men that the Asian migrants face discrimination. Respondents leaning towards liberalism tended to be more convinced that Asians are discriminated against in Japan. Moreover, the less nationalist sentiments someone had (based on both items *The world would be a better place if people from other countries were more like the Japanese*, and, *Generally speaking, Japan is a better country than most other countries*, the former with a weak correlation and the latter with a very strong correlation), the more the person tended to believe that Asians face discrimination in Japan.

Japanese surveyees agreed that Japan is not open to refugees: 49% agreed, 13% did not believe that to be true, and 38% were neutral on this. When looking at this statement (*Japan is open to refugees*) through the other variables, what stood out was that women, young people, less educated, and conservative leaning people tended to agree with this more. Since Japan has a very complicated process of accepting refugees and only dozens of the applicants succeed yearly, we can argue that those with conservative leanings are more satisfied with the number of refugees and do not wish for Japan to open more. Moreover, the more nationalist leaning one is (based on the two nationalism items—*The world would be a better place if people from other countries were more like the Japanese*, and, *Generally speaking, Japan is a better country than most other countries)*, the more he or she agrees that Japan is open to refugees.

Our study demonstrates that, albeit in a limited way, nationalism and political identity affect Japanese nationals' perception of foreigners and refugees. At least of the two items of nationalism correlated with three out of the statements, namely the *Chinese migrants face discrimination in Japan, Asian migrants face discrimination in Japan*, and *Japan is open to refugees*. As for political identity, we found that voting preferences have an impact on people's belief in the benefits of having migrant workers in Japan. Liberal-minded people are more likely to perceive that Chinese and Asian migrants face discrimination and that Japan is not open to refugees.

Case Study: Opinion on Rohingya Resettlement

We wanted to expound on Japanese people's attitudes towards a concrete group of refugees and chose the Rohingya as a case study. When asked whether they supported the (hypothetical) resettlement of the Rohingya people to Japan, about 36% of respondents did not support the idea, 16% chose the midpoint option, and the majority of the survey participants, about 48%, supported resettlement (see Fig. 8.3.). Since we were not sure if Japanese people knew who the Rohingya were, we gave an explanation in brackets in the survey (*The Rohingya people are a persecuted Muslim minority in Myanmar*). These findings are very meaningful because they show that once a very concrete group is addressed (and their plight described), people tend to be more compassionate (Newman, 2003). Compared to other questions related to immigrants and refugees in our survey, the question on Rohingya resettlement had the least number of neutral responses. Moreover, this directly contradicts the long-held belief that Japanese people are essentially anti-refugees.

When tested against other variables, we found that none except for voter/party preference had any effect. Although NHK Party voters seemed to be in favour of resettling the Rohingya to Japan, the results are not significant (as in our sample we have only three such voters). Those who said they would not vote (20% of our respondents) oppose the idea of resettlement (see Table 8.4). Voters for the Liberal Democratic Party (27% of our sample) are somewhere in the middle, with a mean value 4.3 (on a 1–7 scale, where 1 means total disagreement and 7 total agreement); Nippon Ishin no Kai voters (7% of our sample) were slightly more in favour of resettling the Rohingya, with a mean value 4.6; CDP voters (5% of our sample) 4.4; and Japanese Communist Party voters (4% of our sample) 4.9. There was no correlation with the nationalism items, meaning that nationalism did not have any influence on people's choices in this case.

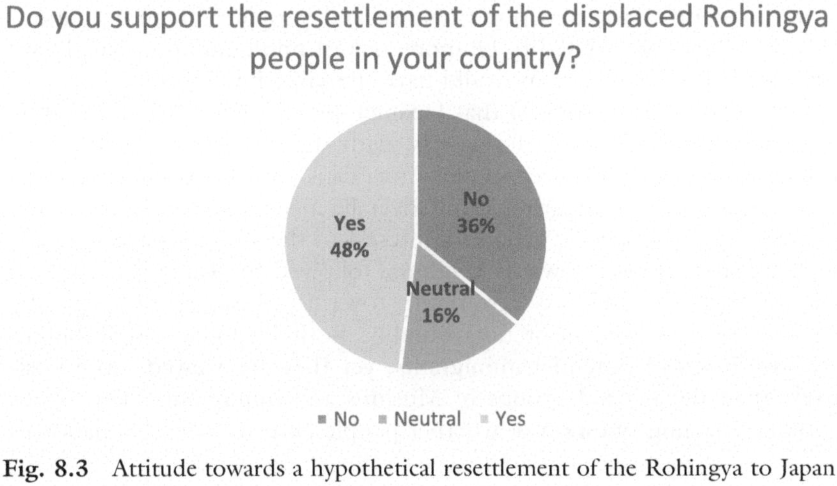

Fig. 8.3 Attitude towards a hypothetical resettlement of the Rohingya to Japan

Table 8.4 Attitude towards a hypothetical resettlement of the Rohingya to Japan through the lens of party/voting preference, measured by the mean value (on a 1–7 scale, where 1 means total disagreement and 7 total agreement), ordered from lowest to the highest mean value

Voting/party preference	*Mean value*
I would not vote	3.7
Komeito	4.1
I don't know	4.1
Social Democratic Party	4.2
Reiwa Shinsengumi	4.2
Other political party	4.2
Liberal Democratic Party	4.3
Democratic Party for the People	4.3
Constitutional Democratic Party	4.4
Nippon Ishin no Kai	4.6
Japanese Communist Party	4.9
NHK Party	5.7

Conclusion

This chapter aimed to investigate Japanese public perception towards immigrants and refugees. Since the Japanese government only recently revealed new guidelines for accepting refugees, and new legislation that would acknowledge people fleeing conflicts as "quasi-refugees", the understanding of the public's view is of great importance. More specifically, our goal was to explain how nationalism and political identity influence people's opinions in Japan. Nationalism is understood as a blind attachment towards one's nation, and people with more nationalist tendencies are argued to be more against immigration. Similarly, we suggested that conservatism would have the same implications.

Our survey results suggest that Japanese people generally have slightly negative attitudes towards foreigners, with the Chinese being the least favoured group. Taiwanese people, Americans, and Europeans were the most positively viewed groups, but overall, mean values were not very high. Among the specific groups of interest to the study, Japanese people were most favourable towards Uyghurs, followed by Rohingya refugees, and immigrants, and less favourable towards Muslims, although the Chinese were viewed most unfavourably. Both Uyghurs and Rohingya are Muslims and potential immigrants, yet they are viewed more positively than the general groups of Muslims and immigrants. This opens another puzzling question of whether people perceive concrete nationals and ethnic groups more positively than the same groups when described by their religion.

The results also showed that Japanese people tend to have a neutral opinion towards the presence of foreigners in Japan. While more people agree than disagree that the presence of migrant workers is beneficial for Japan, Japanese people believe that it is difficult for foreigners to fit into Japanese society. Additionally, Japanese people acknowledge that Japan is not open to refugees.

Both nationalism and political identity have an impact, if limited, on people's opinions towards refugees and immigrants. As shown in our study, a stronger nationalist sentiment correlates with people thinking that Chinese and other Asian nationals do not experience discrimination in Japan. People with nationalist and conservative tendencies also believe that Japan is open to refugees. We can interpret this to mean that such people are satisfied with the current refugee policy and with the number of refugees Japan accepts.

We have also learned that those referring to themselves as liberals acknowledge that Chinese and other Asian nationals face discrimination in Japan. Voters for the CDP and Democratic Party for the People which are typecast as progressive centrist parties, agreed most with the statement that immigrant workers are beneficial for Japan. Still, most of the respondents identified themselves as conservative, which shows that liberal views on foreigners are not common.

Finally, our research sheds light on people's perception of the potential resettlement of Rohingya in Japan. While the Japanese government welcomed Ukrainians fleeing the war, Rohingya people are only rarely accepted as refugees. However, public opinion towards their resettlement is rather positive. The study contradicts the belief that Japanese people are a priori anti-refugee and found that none of the variables except for voter/party preference had any effect on people's attitudes towards the resettlement of refugees.

Funding The work on this article was supported by funding from the European Union's research and innovation programme HORIZON-WIDERA-2021-ACCESS-03-01 under grant agreement No. 101079069, entitled "The EU in the Volatile Indo-Pacific Region" (EUVIP).

Disclaimer Funded by the European Union. Views and opinions expressed are however those of the authors only and do not necessarily reflect those of the European Union. The European Union cannot be held responsible for them.

References

Ali, I. (2015, March 19). More assertive Japan seen positively in Washington. *Voa News*. https://www.voanews.com/a/more-assertive-japan-foreign-policy-seen-positively-in-washington/2687973.html

Amnesty International. (2023, March 14). *Japan: 'Endless detention': Migrants speak out as government proposes harsh immigration bill*. https://www.amnesty.org/en/latest/news/2023/03/japan-endless-detention-migrants-speak-out-as-government-proposes-harsh-immigration-bill/

Ara, T. (2021). *Statement on the bill for amendments to the immigration control and refugee recognition act submitted by the government*. Japan Federation of Bar Association. https://www.nichibenren.or.jp/en/document/statements/210226.html

Arudou, D. (2015). *Embedded racism: Japan's visible minorities and racial discrimination*. Lexington Books.

Begum, K. (2021). Challenges of Rohingya refugee women in Japan. *Journal of Human Security Studies, 10*(2), 153–168. https://doi.org/10.34517/jahss.10.2_153

Blinder, S., & Lundgren, L. (2019). Roots of group threat: Anti-prejudice motivations and implicit bias in perceptions of immigrants as threats. *Ethnic and Racial Studies, 42*(12), 1971–1989. https://doi.org/10.1080/01419870.2018.1526392

Brooks, C., Manza, J., & Cohen, E. D. (2016). Political ideology and immigrant acceptance. *Socius: Sociological Research for a Dynamic World*, 2. https://doi.org/10.1177/2378023116668881

Brubaker, R. (1996). Civic and ethnic nations in France and Germany. In J. Hutchinson & A. D. Smith (Eds.), *Ethnicity* (pp. 168–173). Oxford University Press.

Burgess, C. (2010). The 'illusion' of homogenous Japan and national character: Discourse as a tool to transcend the 'myth' vs. 'reality' binary. *The Asia-Pacific Journal*. http://www.japanfocus.org/-Chris-Burgess/3310

Cheng, J. W., & Fraser, N. A. R. (2022). Japanese newspaper portrayals of refugees—A frame analysis from 1985 to 2017. *Journal of Refugee Studies, 35*(3), 1364–1385. https://doi.org/10.1093/jrs/feac007

Chyung, S. Y., Roberts, K., Swanson, I., & Hankinson, A. (2017). Evidence-based survey design: The use of a midpoint on the Likert Scale. *Performance Improvement, 56*(10), 15–23. https://core.ac.uk/download/pdf/147014152.pdf

Dasgupta, A. (2021). Human security and Japanese refugee policy: Explaining the 'Flux.' *Japan Forum, 152–171*,. https://doi.org/10.1080/09555803.2021.1990985

Davidov, E. (2009). Measurement equivalence of nationalism and constructive patriotism in the ISSP: 34 countries in a comparative perspective. *Political Analysis, 17*(1), 64–82. https://doi.org/10.1093/pan/mpn014

Davison, J., & Peng, I. (2021). Views on immigration in Japan: Identities, interests, and pragmatic divergence. *Journal of Ethnic and Migration Studies, 47*(11), 2578–2595. https://doi.org/10.1080/1369183X.2020.1862645

Doak, K. M. (2007). *A history of nationalism in modern Japan: Placing the people*. Brill.

Finkel, S. E., & Opp, K. (1991). Party identification and participation in collective political action. *The Journal of Politics, 53*, 339–371. https://doi.org/10.2307/2131763

Flowers, P. (2009). *Refugees, women, and weapons: International norm adoption and compliance in Japan*. Stanford University Press.

Fujibayashi, H. (2020). When public opinion drives national asylum policy-making: The case of Kurdish asylum seekers in Japan. *Asia & the Pacific Policy Studies, 7*(2), 204–216. https://doi.org/10.1002/app5.301

General Contact Point for Government Statistics. (2022, July 23). *Zairyū gaikokujin tōkei (kyu tōroku gaikokujin tōkei)/Zairyū gaikokujin tōkei* [Statistics on Foreign Residents (formerly Statistics on Registered Foreigners)/ Statistics on Foreign Residents], No. 00250012. https://www.e-stat.go.jp/stat-search/files?stat_infid=000032212359

Goto, Y. (2021, February 2). *Nichijō ni hisomu heito. "Nihon ni sabetsu wa nai" wa honto ka?* [Hate hidden in everyday life. Is it true that there is no discrimination in Japan?] Mainichi Shinbun. https://mainichi.jp/articles/20210212/k00/00m/040/027000c

Green, D. (2017). Immigrant perception in Japan. *Asian Survey, 57*(2), 368–394. https://doi.org/10.1525/as.2017.57.2.368

Green, D., & Kadoya, Y. (2015). Contact and threat: Factors affecting views on increasing immigration in Japan: Public opinion on immigration in Japan. *Politics & Policy, 43*(1), 59–93. https://doi.org/10.1111/polp.12109

Greenfeld, L. (1992). *Nationalism: Five roads to modernity*. Harvard University Press.

Hainmueller, J., & Hopkins, D. J. (2014). Public attitudes toward immigration. *Annual Review of Political Science, 17*, 225–249. https://doi.org/10.1146/annurev-polisci102512-194818

Han Hinkon Network. (2023, January 26). *"Kyōdō seimei" nyūkan-hō kaitei-an sai teishutsu ni tsuyoku hantai shimasu—seizon-ken ni kokkyō wa arimasen* ["Joint Statement" We strongly oppose the resubmission of the Immigration

Law Amendment Bill—The right to life knows no borders. https://hanhinkonnetwork.org/archives/1367

Hatcher, P., & Murakami, A. (2020). The politics of exclusion: Embedded racism and Japan's pilot Refugee Resettlement Programme. *Race & Class, 62*(1), 60–77. https://doi.org/10.1177/0306396820917068

Havens, T. R. H. (1990). Japan's response to the Indochinese refugee crisis. *Asian Journal of Social Science, 18*(1), 166–181. https://doi.org/10.1163/080382490X00105

Hirabayashi, Y. (2018, October 7). *47% support more foreign workers in Japan, while 32% opposed: Mainichi poll*. Mainichi Shinbun. https://mainichi.jp/english/articles/20181007/p2a/00m/0na/045000c

Horiuchi, Y., & Ono, Y. (2021). Social contact and attitudes toward outsiders: The case of Japan. *SSRN Electronic Journal*. https://doi.org/10.2139/ssrn.3985522

Horiuchi, Y., & Ono, Y. (2022). Susceptibility to threatening information and attitudes toward refugee resettlement: The case of Japan. *Journal of Peace Research, 60*(3), 459–473. https://doi.org/10.1177/00223433221079455

Immigration Services Agency in Japan. (2022). *How to apply for a change in status of residence to "Designated Activities (1 Year, Work Permitted)"*. https://www.isa.go.jp/en/support/fresc/01_00252.html

Iwasaki, A. (2006). Open the door—Japan's policy of exclusion of refugees (Part 2). *The Asia-Pacific Journal, 4*(2). https://apjjf.org/-Iwasaki-Atsuko/1788/article.html

Jeong, H. O. (2016). A new comparison of the East and West: National identity and attitudes toward immigration. *Asian and Pacific Migration Journal, 25*(2), 206–219. https://doi.org/10.1177/0117196816640972

Jou, W., & Endo, M. (2017). Political participation in Japan: A longitudinal analysis. *Asian Journal of Comparative Politics, 2*(2), 196–212. https://doi.org/10.1177/2057891116677349

Kashiwazaki, C., & Akaha, T. (2006). *Japanese immigration policy: Responding to conflicting pressures*. Migration Policy Institute. https://www.migrationpolicy.org/article/japanese-immigration-policy-responding-conflicting-pressures

Kohn, H. (1944). *The idea of nationalism: A study in its origins and background*. Collier Books.

Koizumi, K. (1992). Refugee policy formation in Japan: Developments and implications. *Journal of Refugee Studies, 5*(2), 123–135. https://doi.org/10.1093/jrs/5.2.123

Kono, S. (2019, January 21). *Survey: Two-thirds of Japanese view rise in foreigners as 'good'*. Nikkei Asia. https://asia.nikkei.com/Spotlight/Japan-immigration/Survey-two-thirds-of-Japanese-view-rise-in-foreigners-as-good

Kosterman, R., & Feshbach, S. (1989). Toward a measure of patriotic and nationalistic attitudes. *Political Psychology, 10*(2), 257–274.

Lind, J., & Ueki, C. K. (2021). Is Japan back? Measuring nationalism and military assertiveness in Asia's other great power. *Journal of East Asian Studies, 21*(3), 367–401. https://doi.org/10.1017/jea.2021.20

Martini Grimaldi, C. (2022, September 29). Anti-Korean sentiment simmers in Japan. *The Diplomat*. https://thediplomat.com/2022/09/anti-korean-sentiment-simmers-in-japan/

McCormack, G. (2008). "Conservatism" and "nationalism". The Japan puzzle. *The Asia-Pacific Journal, 6*(6). https://apjjf.org/-Gavan-McCormack/2786/article.html

McCurry, J. (2015, September 30). Japan says it must look after its own before allowing in Syrian refugees. *The Guardian*. https://www.theguardian.com/world/2015/sep/30/japan-says-it-must-look-after-its-own-before-allowing-syrian-refugees-in

McLaren, L. M. (2003). Anti-immigrant prejudice in europe: Contact, threat perception, and preferences for the exclusion of migrants. *Social Forces, 81*(3), 909–936. http://www.jstor.org/stable/3598180

Milly, D. (2020). *Japan's labor migration reforms: Breaking with the past?* Migration Policy Institute. https://www.migrationpolicy.org/article/japan-labor-migration-reforms-breaking-past

Mizuno, T. (1990). The refugee quandary. *Japan Quarterly, 37*(1), 89–93.

Mori, H. (1997). *Immigration policy and foreign workers in Japan*. Macmillan.

Morita, L. (2015). Some manifestations of Japanese exclusionism. *SAGE Open, 5*(3). https://doi.org/10.1177/2158244015600036

Mukae, R. (2022). Refugee policy. In T. Endoh (Ed.), *Open borders, open society? Immigration and social integration in Japan* (pp. 71–102). Verlag Barbara Budrich.

Münch, R. (2002). *Nation and citizenship in the global age: From national to transnational ties and identities*. Palgrave Macmillan.

Nara, R. (2022, July 26). FOCUS: Abuse of foreign trainees continues under technical internship. *Kyodo News*. https://english.kyodonews.net/news/2022/07/c5e9af8e7f16-focus-abuse-of-foreign-trainees-continues-under-technical-internship-program.html

Newman, T. B. (2003). The power of stories over statistics. *BJM, 327*(7429), 1424–1427. https://www.bmj.com/content/327/7429/1424

Obe, M. (2021, October 31). Japan's ruling LDP secures sole majority in lower house election. *Nikkei Asia*. https://asia.nikkei.com/Politics/Japan-election/Japan-s-ruling-LDP-secures-sole-majority-in-lower-house-election

OHCHR. (2023). *Mandates of the Special Rapporteur on the human rights of migrants; the Working Group on Arbitrary Detention and the Special Rapporteur on freedom of religion or belief.* https://spcommreports.ohchr.org/TMResultsBase/DownLoadPublicCommunicationFile?gId=27995

Oliver, J. E., & Wong, J. (2003). Intergroup prejudice in multiethnic settings. *American Journal of Political Science, 47*(4), 567–582. https://doi.org/10.2307/3186119

Peng-Er, L. (2004). Japan-Taiwan relations: Between affinity and reality. *Asian Affairs: An American Review, 30*(4), 249–267. https://doi.org/10.3200/AAFS.30.4.249-267

Quo, F. (1966). Jiyushugi: Japanese liberalism. *The Review of Politics, 28*(4), 477–492. http://www.jstor.org/stable/1405283

Raijman, R., Davidov, E., Schmidt, P., & Hochman, O. (2008). What does a nation owe non-citizens? National attachments, perception of threat and attitudes towards granting citizenship rights in a comparative perspective. *International Journal of Comparative Sociology, 49*(2–3), 195–220. https://doi.org/10.1177/0020715208088912

Refugee Assistance Headquarters. (2019, March 1). *Acceptance of refugees in Japan*. https://www.rhq.gr.jp/acceptance-of-refugees-in-japan/

Rikken Minshutō. (2022). *Seichō: "Nihon no nanmin seido wo kokusai hyōjun ni" Nanmintō hogohō—nyūkanhō kaiseian wo teishutu* [Political affairs: 'Bring Japan's refugee system up to international standards'. Proposed amendments to the Protection of Refugees and Others Act and the Immigration Control and Refugee Recognition Act]. https://cdp-japan.jp/news/20220422_3554

Sasaki, M. (2004). Globalization and national identity in Japan. *International Journal of Japanese Sociology, 13*(1), 69–87. https://doi.org/10.1111/j.1475-6781.2004.00054.x

Schatz, T., Staub, W., & Lavine, H. (1999). On the varieties of national attachment: Blind versus constructive patriotism. *Political Psychology, 20*(1), 151–174. https://doi.org/10.1111/0162-895X.00140

Semyonov, M., Raijman, R., Tov, A. Y., & Schmidt, P. (2004). Population size, perceived threat, and exclusion: A multiple-indicators analysis of attitudes toward foreigners in Germany. *Social Science Research, 33*(4), 681–701. https://doi.org/10.1016/j.ssresearch.2003.11.003

Shimoji, Y. L. (2023, February 3). *Why does Japanese society overlook racism?* Public Books. https://www.publicbooks.org/why-does-japanese-society-overlook-racism/

Smith, A. D. (2001). Interpretations of national identity. In A. Dieckhoff & N. Gutiérrez (Eds.), *Modern roots: Studies of national identity* (pp. 21–42). Routledge.

Smith, A. D. (2010). *Nationalism: Theory, ideology, history* (2nd ed.). Polity.

Statistics Bureau of Japan. (2021). *Basic complete tabulation on population and households of the 2020 population census of Japan was released*. https://www.stat.go.jp/english/info/news/20211228.html

Strausz, M. (2012). International pressure and domestic precedent: Japan's resettlement of indochinese refugees. *Asian Journal of Political Science, 20*(3), 244–266. https://doi.org/10.1080/02185377.2012.748966

Strausz, M. (2018). Does the LDP want to build a wall too? Immigration and the 2017 election in Japan. In R. J. Pekkanen, S. R. Reed, E. Scheiner, & D. M. Smith (Eds.), *Japan Decides 2017* (pp. 203–218). Springer International Publishing.

Take, S. (2022, September 15). *Many people with foreign roots stopped by police in Japan: Survey*. Nikkei Asia. https://asia.nikkei.com/Spotlight/Society/Many-people-with-foreign-roots-stopped-by-police-in-Japan-survey

Takeda, I. (1998). Japan's responses to refugees and political asylum seekers. In M. Weiner, & T. Hanami (Eds.), *Temporary workers or future citizens?* Palgrave Macmillan.

Takizawa, S. (2021). Japan's immigration policy 2015–2020: Implications for human security of immigrant workers and refugees. *Journal of Human Security Studies, 10*(2), 51–78. https://doi.org/10.34517/jahss.10.2_51

Tanabe, S. (2021). Sociological studies on nationalism in Japan. *International Sociology, 36*(2), 171–182. https://doi.org/10.1177/02685809211005347

Tanaka, H. (1989). The development of liberalism in modern Japan: Continuity of an Idea—From Taguchi and Kuga to Hasegawa. *Hitotsubashi Journal of Social Studies, 21*(1), 259–268. http://www.jstor.org/stable/43294592

Taniguchi, H. (2021). National identity, cosmopolitanism, and attitudes toward immigrants. *International Sociology, 36*(6), 819–843. https://doi.org/10.1177/0268580921994517

Tauchi, K. (2023, April 10). *Japan proposes to end problem-filled technical intern program*. Asahi Shimbun. https://www.asahi.com/ajw/articles/14882268

The International Organization for Migration. (2010, September 27). *First refugees from Myanmar arrive in Tokyo*. https://www.iom.int/news/first-refugees-myanmar-arrive-tokyo

The Japanese Trade Union Confederation. (2018). *Gaikokujin rōdōsha no ukeire ni kansuru ishikichōsa 2018* [Survey on the Reception of Foreign Workers 2018]. https://www.jtuc-rengo.or.jp/info/chousa/data/20181018-02.pdf

Think Tank: European Parliament. (2020, December 15). *Japan's ageing society*. https://www.europarl.europa.eu/thinktank/en/document/EPRS_BRI(2020)659419

Thousands march in Tokyo to protest Myanmar coup, biggest Japan demonstration so far. (2021, February 14). *Reuters*. https://www.reuters.com/article/us-myanmar-politics-japan-protests-idCAKBN2AE087

Tolbert, K. (1999, September 1). Japan's rising sun rises again. *The Washington Post*. https://www.washingtonpost.com/archive/politics/1999/09/01/japans-rising-sun-rises-again/13b83078-b9dd-476e-9129-35077a6b6d13/

Torcal, M., Rodon, T., & Hierro, M. J. (2016). Word on the street: The persistence of leftist-dominated protest in Europe. *West European Politics, 39*, 326–350.

Turcsanyi, R. Q., Kironska, K., Gerstl, A., Arnez, M., Čeněk, J., Chen, J., Chen, R., Chubb, A., Gries, P., & Wang, T. (2022). *Sinophone borderlands Indo-Pacific survey*. Palacky University Olomouc.

UNHCR Working Group on Arbitrary Detention. (2020). *Opinions adopted by the Working Group on Arbitrary Detention at its eighty-eighth session*. https://www.ohchr.org/sites/default/files/Documents/Issues/Detention/Opinions/Session88/A_HRC_WGAD_2020_58_Advance_Edited_Version.pdf

UNHCR. (2021). *JAPAN Fact Sheet-June 2021*. https://reporting.unhcr.org/sites/default/files/JAPAN%20Fact%20Sheet-June%202021.pdf

UNOHCA Reliefweb. (2018). *Despite global refugee crisis, Japan accepts only 20 refugees in 2017*. https://reliefweb.int/report/japan/despite-global-refugee-crisis-japan-accepts-only-20-refugees-2017

Yamagata, A. (2017). Conflicting Japanese responses to the Syrian refugee crisis. *The Asia-Pacific Journal, 15*(2). https://apjjf.org/2017/24/Yamagata.html

Yamaguchi, T. (2017). The "Japan Is Great!" boom, historical revisionism, and the government. *The Asia-Pacific Journal, 15*(3). https://apjjf.org/2017/06/Yamaguchi.html

Zhang, Y. (2018). The less favored foreigners: Public attitudes toward Chinese and South Korean residents in Japan. *Journal of Asia-Pacific Studies (Waseda University), 33*. https://core.ac.uk/download/286958599.pdf

CHAPTER 9

Formosa as a Safe Haven? Taiwan's Public Opinion on Potential Asylum Mechanisms and Refugees

Kristina Kironska

Introduction

Taiwan, officially the Republic of China (ROC), is considered to be one of the most progressive countries in terms of human rights in Asia, but it has no asylum law. Due to the political status of Taiwan, the challenges it faces in regard to this topic are quite different from other countries. Because the ROC was replaced in the United Nations' (UN) China seat by the People's Republic of China (PRC), Taiwan has not signed UN treaties on the handling of asylum seekers and refugees. However, not being a member of the UN is not a hindrance per se to the adoption of an asylum law. Taiwan has proven in the past that it can work around the system and adhere to international human rights standards.

K. Kironska (✉)
Department of Asian Studies, Palacky
University Olomouc, Olomouc, Czech Republic
e-mail: k.kironska@gmail.com

L. Momesso and P. Ivanova (eds.), *Refugees and Asylum Seekers in East Asia*, Palgrave Macmillan Studies on Human Rights in Asia,
https://doi.org/10.1007/978-981-97-2867-1_9

Although not able to become party to most human rights treaties, Taiwan has "ratified" five international human rights treaties, among them are the 2009 *International Covenant on Civil and Political Rights* and the *International Covenant on Economic, Social, and Cultural Rights*. These human rights protection provisions (including the *non-refoulement* obligations, which under international humanitarian law guarantees that no one should be returned to a country where they would face torture, cruel, inhuman, or degrading treatment or punishment) now have domestic legal status in Taiwan, and the state is bound to respect civil and political rights (such as the rights to life, and freedom of religion or speech) and to work towards granting people economic, social, and cultural rights (including labour rights, the right to health, education, and an adequate standard of living). Adopting an asylum law in Taiwan should thus be seen as a continuation of a broader push to bring Taiwan's legal system in line with international human rights law.

It is an important topic because although Taiwanese politicians claim that the regulations currently in place are sufficient, research has shown they are not. There are several groups that would benefit from an asylum law in Taiwan, from Hong Kong protesters facing persecution, through Chinese dissidents or descendants of the ROC army from the Thailand-Myanmar border region, to Turkish people with revoked passports (Kironska, 2022a). Despite the need for an asylum law, in political circles there is no rush for the adoption of such a law as this is a complex issue due to Taiwan's complicated relationship with China.

There are several legitimate and often repeated concerns surrounding this topic. These concerns have much weight. Firstly, most of the refugees seeking asylum in Taiwan are from China, Hong Kong, or Tibet, and technically they are ROC citizens according to the 1946 Constitution, which is still valid in Taiwan. Thus, it is unclear whether they would even qualify as refugees. According to the definition of a refugee under the 1951 Refugee Convention, a refugee must have crossed an international border. Secondly, it is unclear whether designating them non-citizens would be seen by China as claiming de jure independence, in which case China could use force against the island. Thirdly, there are national security concerns surrounding the issue of potential Chinese spies being sent to Taiwan (although there are much simpler avenues to enter the country) or the fear of "being flooded" by large numbers of people. However, there are clear reasons why having systems to manage such scenarios is better than not having them having systems to manage such scenarios is better than not having them. For example, an actual asylum law would allow for a proper vetting system with clear review mechanisms. To avoid conflicts with China, a dual system could be introduced. South Korea could serve as an inspiration, as it deals with North Koreans differently (by their Constitution they are considered citizens) than foreigners from other parts of the world (Wolman, 2012). This is, however, beyond the scope of this research, and could be examined in future research.

This chapter aims to shed light on Taiwanese public opinion on the refugee issue—towards refugees and towards a potential asylum law in Taiwan. In general, there is a very limited discussion on these topics within Taiwanese society, with many Taiwanese even being unaware of the absence of an asylum law in Taiwan. To address this gap, this chapter presents the findings of the first-ever comprehensive, nationally representative survey exploring Taiwanese views on the refugee issue. While the chapter employs mixed methods, the survey results add the most value. The survey covers various aspects—from stances on the eventual adoption of an asylum law in Taiwan and its potential form (inclusive or exclusive of Chinese nationals), through the perceived concerns in doing so (including potentially worsened relations with the PRC), to attitudes towards different groups of people facing persecution. While online forums may be dominated by negative comments about refugees, creating an impression that Taiwanese oppose granting asylum to refugees in their country, the research results paint a different picture.

Why is this important? Firstly, because public perception could have real-world implications. Some scholars argue that a strong consensus in public opinion should be enough to ensure a shift in policy (Petry, 1999), while others have pointed out that issue salience is key (Soroka, 2002). So, although the direct causal role of public opinion in shaping decision-making is disputed, it is still important and (in democratic societies) it has become part of the public policy-making process (Rouce, 2004). For political actors, consulting the public and paying attention to its opinions is an important part of democracy (Noelle-Neumann, 1993). In Taiwan, political actors heavily depend on public opinion, especially on sensitive topics that involve Taiwan's relationship with China, and discussing a potential asylum law in Taiwan inevitably touches on cross-strait relations. However, in the case of asylum in Taiwan, increasing its salience is of great importance, as, until now, there has been a lack of discussion on this issue. Secondly, the topic of asylum has not been very thoroughly explored in the arena of Taiwan studies, although with the new draft of an asylum law submitted to the Legislative Yuan for review in 2023, it is gaining relevance.

The chapter is organised as follows. After the introduction, the methodology is explained. In the next section, the lack of social dialogue on the refugee issue, including the lack of representative surveys on this matter, is described. It is followed by an analysis of the Sinophone Borderlands Indo-Pacific Survey data (2022) on Taiwanese people's opinion on a potential asylum law and on various groups in need of protection. The last part sums up the findings of this chapter.

Methodology

This research is based on a mixed method, both quantitative data (survey questions) and qualitative data (interviews) have been applied.

For the purpose of providing context on the refugee situation in Taiwan, especially the little social dialogue there has been on the topic, interviews were conducted with organisations that work on the refugee issue in Taiwan, namely Amnesty International Taiwan, Refugee Network Taiwan, and one other organisation that is directly involved in helping Hong Kongers in Taiwan, which prefers to stay in anonymity. In each of these organisations one person has been interviewed. Interviewees were selected based on purposive non-probability sampling, on the assumption that they represent interesting cases for the study. The interviews were conducted in the form of open-ended questions, loosely organised, focusing on the participants' professional opinions and experience with the asylum topic in Taiwan, be it from an advocacy or activist perspective. Two of the interviews were conducted before the survey data collection and one afterwards.

Quantitative data for this research was obtained from the 2022 Sinophone Borderlands Indo-Pacific Survey (Turcsanyi et al., 2022), part of the wider Sinophone Borderlands Surveys (2020–2022), which investigates global views of China through a series of large-scale representative surveys of public opinion in many (selected) parts of the world. The author is one of the conveners of the survey project and herself designed the Taiwan survey questions on the asylum/refugee issue in Taiwan, including several experiments using the split ballot technique. The Indo-Pacific Survey was conducted in 15 countries, with Taiwan as one of the surveyed countries.

The Taiwanese part of the survey data was collected by the survey agency Cint between April and June 2022. The sample is nationally representative in terms of age, gender, and regions, involving 1350 respondents. Participants registered in online panels operated by the agency responded, in Mandarin Chinese, to an online survey. The author is aware that there may be differences as a result of using data collected online rather than if the data had been collected offline (Saloniki et al., 2019). The questionnaire consisted of approximately 60 questions, many of which investigated people's views on topics other than China, such as asylum, the death penalty, and religion (while the overarching theme was "views on China"). For the purpose of this research, the author has worked with only a part of the Taiwanese dataset: the refugee issue questions (described below). In addition, information on a range of key demographic variables (e.g. age, gender, education, region, and political leaning) has also been collected. Data obtained from the survey was analysed in the open-source statistics software JASP and the results visualised in Infogram, a software which helps with visualising data. The percentage numbers have been rounded in the text and answers have been grouped together (on a 5-point scale, answers 1 and 2 are negative and 4 and 5 are positive; on a 7-point scale, answers 1, 2, and 3 are negative and 5, 6, and 7 are positive) for an easier understanding of the results.

The survey questions related to the topic of asylum in Taiwan included the stance on the eventual adoption of an asylum law in Taiwan, and in what form (including or excluding the Chinese); the perceived drawbacks in doing so (including potentially worsened relations with the PRC); and feelings towards different groups of people that are often on the move due to some form of persecution—Hong Kongers, Tibetans, Uyghurs, Syrians, or the Rohingya. Religious and ethnic groups have been grouped in the question on purpose, especially including "highly charged" group names (such as "Muslims"), to see if there would be any strong reactions from the respondents.

Additionally, the data has been analysed by disaggregating it based on demographic characteristics, which will be further reported in the data analysis section whenever correlations with gender, age, education, region, and/or party preference were found.

While the author uses the term "asylum" throughout this chapter, in the survey data used in this chapter the preferred term in English was "refugee" (in Chinese *nanmin*), such as, for example, "Refugee Law" (in Chinese *nanmin fa*), on the assumption that the wider public is more familiar with this term.

Lack of Public Dialogue and Opinion Polls on the Refugee Issue in Taiwan

Taiwan today, with its so-called small nation mentality ("*Who would want to come to Taiwan?*"), is not used to having to accept refugees or even discussing this issue very widely (Yoshin Wang, Refugee Network Taiwan, personal communication, March 2023). Most Taiwanese are not even aware there is no asylum law in Taiwan. It is also not a topic often seen in the media and Taiwanese politicians also refrain from such discussions. Thus, with the relative lack of experience or knowledge of the topic, it is hard to have any meaningful discussion.

According to the interviewees, what first brought awareness about people on the move requiring protection was the European refugee crisis in 2015. There were many articles in the Taiwanese media describing the events in Europe.

While the European crisis seemed a distant reality, the arrival of protesters from Hong Kong in 2019 and 2020 brought the issue somewhat closer. Still, it did not prompt the adoption of an asylum law. Instead, the Hong Kongers first got visa extensions, as the government was undecided as to what to do with them before the presidential elections in January 2020 (Taiwanese NGO activist, NGO in anonymity, personal communication, December 2022). Later, they were encouraged to seek other pathways to receive residency, such as working, investing, or studying in Taiwan (Davidson, 2022). The work of NGOs in helping individuals (legal and financial support, as well as counselling) was invaluable as there were no set rules, and Hong Kongers were handled on a case-by-case basis (Nachman & Hioe, 2019).

The refugee topic resurfaced again with the Russian invasion of Ukraine. Taiwan joined the ranks of Ukraine supporters with substantial financial and medical aid, as well as announcements of easier access to visas for Ukrainians (for which only a very limited amount of people were eligible—those who have relatives in Taiwan, whether Taiwanese or foreigners holding a residency certificate) (Kironska, 2022b).

Besides the media covering the refugee topic (mostly on refugee crises abroad), social dialogue on the refugee issue in Taiwan—small in its scale—has been led mostly by NGOs, such as the Taiwan Association for Human Rights, Covenants Watch, Asia Pacific Refugee Rights Network, and Amnesty International Taiwan, or by individuals who have hands-on experience with the issue (Chiu, 2022). Such is the case for an Egyptian activist and former political refugee who applied for asylum in South Korea, but then met his future Taiwanese wife, and now lives in Taiwan—he often speaks about his situation at various events (one such event was organised by the author herself in Taipei, "Amnesty Talks: Refugees", on 20 February 2020). Also, there is a new platform, Refugee 101 Taiwan, which is educating Taiwanese people about refugees, and there are other organisations, such as the Refugee Network Taiwan, which conducts work outside of Taiwan, including providing online teaching of internally displaced Syrians. Such organisations, working inside or outside Taiwan, also have an impact on the domestic Taiwanese audience (Yoshin Wang, Refugee Network Taiwan, personal communication, March 2023). Amnesty International Taiwan is also working on the refugee topic, introducing individual cases and educating their supporters. Perhaps the most visible and vocal on the topic of asylum and refugees is the Taiwan Association for Human Rights, which provides accommodation, medical treatment, and psychological counselling to asylum seekers in Taiwan and is also involved in advocacy work, including drafting an asylum law several times and submitting it to the Legislative Yuan (without it ever being passed).

While there has not been a nationally representative survey on the opinions of the general public, the above-mentioned organisations have encountered some responses from certain segments of the public in their work. According to Zak Huang (Amnesty International Taiwan, personal communication, December 2020), who works as a campaigner at Amnesty International Taiwan, there is a tendency among some people to believe that refugees would have a negative impact on society. Examples of such comments can be found in the comments section under Amnesty International Taiwan's Facebook posts from summer 2020. Some people shared concerns about security for such a small island ("Taiwan is too small, it would be unable to accept a large number of these refugees, and public security would deteriorate".), others about social issues ("Refugees can go to whichever country they want just because their children are innocent? Do you realise refugees are illegal and they can easily bring over many social issues?" and "Do not cause any trouble to Taiwan. These refugees won't be able to adapt to our culture – this is what caused the mess in Europe".) or financial concerns ("Let me ask you, has your organisation thought of who will pay for taking care of the refugees?") (Amnesty International Taiwan Facebook, 2020). Many also referred to the European refugee crisis as a comparison ("Stop causing trouble to more countries. Europe's public security deteriorated. Every country should help itself". And "Look at Paris in France, how dirty and messy it became due to refugees".) and suggested refraining from helping refugees ("Everyone has their own destiny, being a busybody means you are taking up other's karma. Helping others will get you in trouble".) (Amnesty International Taiwan Facebook, 2020). Also frequently observed on social media platforms are harsh and often racist comments comparing refugees to criminals ("No. Damn! After Europe accepted a crowd of trashy refugees the crime and unemployment rate increased. Don't Taiwanese know that?"), along with Islamophobic remarks (Amnesty International Taiwan Facebook, 2020). However, it should be noted that the prevalence of negative comments on social media cannot necessarily be seen as representative of society at large, and should be perceived as merely illustrative rather than conclusive. Nevertheless, based on such comments, one might assume that the Taiwanese people are not very receptive to accepting refugees in their country. However, the data presented in the next section contradicts this assumption.

Moving from the general public to Taiwanese elites, the picture remains somewhat similar. In the past, only a handful of Taiwanese politicians, such as Mei You-nu or Freddy Lim, have been vocal about the adoption of an asylum law. Also, after the start of Russia's war in Ukraine, the Taiwan People's Party spoke out in favour of the adoption of an asylum law in Taiwan, but these are exceptions rather than a systematic approach (Guo, 2022).

Since there is not much discussion on the topic of asylum in Taiwan (neither generated by the grassroots nor by the elites), national sample surveys on people's attitudes towards refugees and an asylum policy are also lacking. In 2016, the Foreign Relations Association commissioned a poll on National Attitudes towards International and Diplomatic Affairs, which contained questions on people's attitudes towards refugees. Only 2% of the respondents said they were willing to fully accept refugees, 11% accepted them with conditions, and 40% accepted them with conditions but with less openness. 37% were against accepting refugees (Chen, 2016). With Hong Kongers arriving in Taiwan, there were a few more polls focusing on the issue. In May 2020, the New Power Party (NPP) commissioned a poll about whether people supported amending the "Laws and Regulations Regarding Hong Kong and Macao Affairs" to help the arriving protesters, with over 60% support (Wu, 2020). However, a July 2020 survey conducted by ETtoday News Cloud showed that half of the public was not ready to support a significant relaxation of immigration to Taiwan for people from Hong Kong (Zhang, 2020). According to a 2021 poll, 28% of the people thought Taiwan was doing enough to assist Hong Kongers and 40% believed Taiwan had no obligations in this regard. 36% of Taiwanese people supported Hong Kongers immigrating to Taiwan while only 23% opposed it. The largest group, however, at 42%, was ambivalent (Nachman et al., 2021).

The following section attempts to fill this gap by providing a comprehensive picture of Taiwanese people's preferences (based on Sinophone Borderlands Indo-Pacific Survey data) when it comes to refugees and a potential asylum law.

Taiwanese People's Stance on Potential Asylum Mechanisms and Refugees

According to the data regarding potential asylum mechanisms in Taiwan, more respondents agreed than disagreed (see specific numbers below) with having to pass some kind of a refugee act, but most actually did not have an opinion on this (see Fig. 9.1). This lack of stance was evident from the respondents' choice of the neutral midpoint. Including a midpoint gave respondents the opportunity to express a neutral opinion, especially on obscure topics (Johns, 2005). However, research has shown that respondents do not always interpret and use a midpoint in the way that scale developers intended (Chyung et al., 2017). Labels have been provided for all the anchors on the scale, with the midpoint marked as "neither agree nor disagree". The lack of stance reflects what was described in the previous section, that discussions about asylum are missing in Taiwanese society.

The question on the asylum law was split into three groups (split ballot), with each group having to agree or disagree with a slightly different statement—about a refugee act in general, about a refugee act that would exclude the Chinese, and about a refugee act that would include the Chinese. Interestingly, while the percentual difference in the answers to these different statements did not differ much: 22–25% agreed, 30–35% disagreed, and 41–45% neither agreed nor disagreed with adopting an asylum law, there was a clear trend of feeling anxious about including the Chinese in the refugee law. The answer that explicitly stated that the refugee act would also include the Chinese prompted the highest

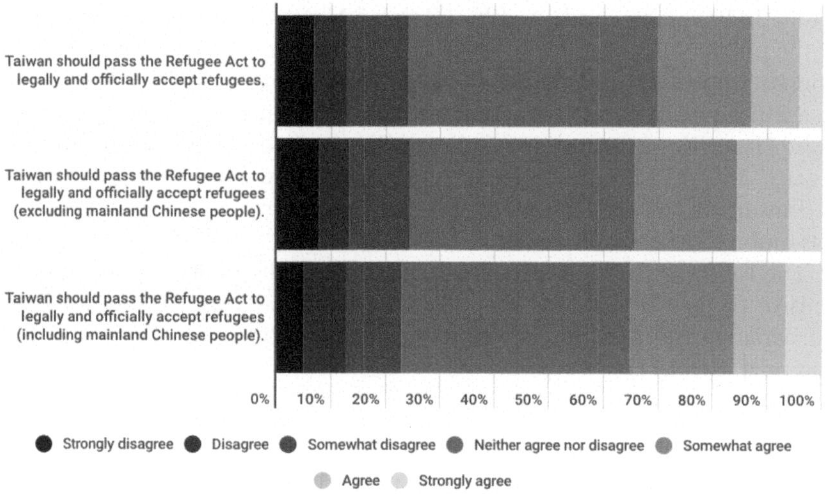

Fig. 9.1 Public opinion on adopting (different kinds of) an asylum law

number of respondents to disagree (25%), the lowest number of respondents to agree (30%), and ultimately also had the most midpoint answers (45%). The author did not find any correlations with other variables, meaning that gender, age, education, region, or political leaning did not have any influence on the people's opinion.

If Taiwan were to pass an asylum law, 33% of the people believed it would worsen relations between Taiwan and China, 19% believed it would not, while 47% did not seem to have an opinion (see Fig. 9.2). There was no correlation with any other variables. These findings suggest that cross-strait relations did not seem to be the main issue.

If Taiwan passed such a law, 56% of the people believed it would be too financially costly for the Taiwanese state budget (see Fig. 9.2). The older the respondent (slight correlation) and the more educated (some correlation) the respondent, the more he or she was convinced of it. Also, political leaning was found to have slight correlation. This item was measured on a 1–7 scale from deep green to deep blue, with the Democratic Progressive Party (DPP) leading the pan-green camp and the Kuomintang (KMT) the pan-blue one. The KMT is considered a pro-Chinese party and the DPP a party that wishes to limit Chinese influence in Taiwan. In this case, the more the respondent was bluer leaning, the

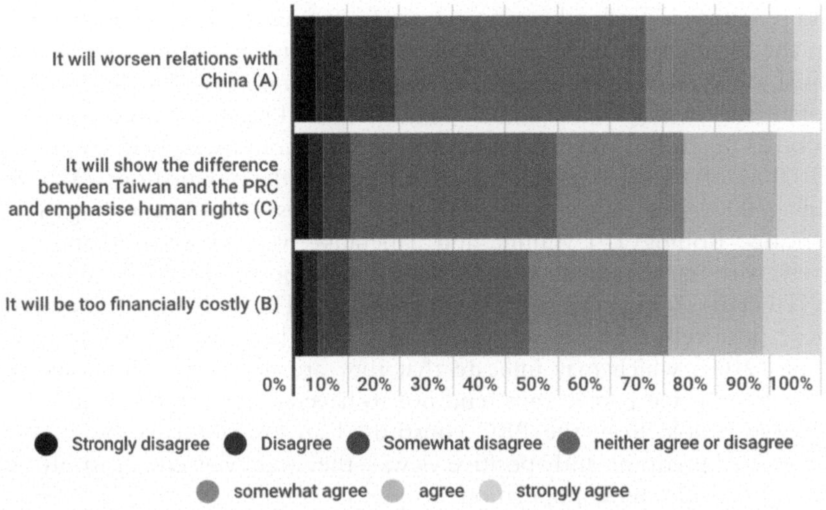

Fig. 9.2 Public opinion on the consequences of passing an asylum law

more he or she was convinced that passing such a law would be financially costly.

On the other hand, 50% of people also believed passing such a law would highlight the human rights values of Taiwan and the difference between Taiwan and China (see Fig. 9.2). Men more than women thought so (slight correlation), and so did more educated people (slight correlation). A strong correlation was found for age and political leaning, with younger people and green-leaning voters more strongly believing that adopting an asylum law would highlight the human rights values of Taiwan and show the difference between Taiwan and China.

In all these three questions, the dominant answer was "*neither agree nor disagree*", which can be interpreted, as has been explained above, as people not really having clear opinions on the issue.

When it came to potential beneficiaries of an asylum law in Taiwan (people who would/could be recognised as refugees under an asylum law), we asked Taiwanese citizens to indicate how positively or negatively they felt about various groups of people on a scale of 0 (cold/negative), through 50 (neutral), to 100 (warm/positive). Higher scores indicate more positive perceptions. Included were various groups, ethnic and religious, as well as known groups of refugees (such as the Rohingya) on the assumption that some of these could trigger a stronger reaction based on typical stereotypes. The category "immigrant"—which could potentially overlap with other categories—in Taiwan is mostly understood as migrant workers from Southeast Asian countries (there are about 720,000 of them, representing about 3% of the population) (Yen & Shih, 2023). Nevertheless, most of these groups—Muslims, immigrants, Africans, Rohingya, Uyghurs, and Tibetans—were viewed rather positively, with immigrants in general viewed most positively (63%), followed by Tibetans (62%), and then Uyghurs (59%). The Rohingya are viewed more positively than negatively but they had the most neutral answers of all (20%), which may indicate that they are not very well-known in Taiwan, and that people thus tend not to have an opinion (see Fig. 9.3). Chinese people from the PRC constituted an exception to the above-mentioned predominantly positive views—they were viewed negatively by 49% of the Taiwanese population.

When examining the data in relation to demographic variables, in the case of the Chinese, Uyghurs, and Tibetans, age was found to be

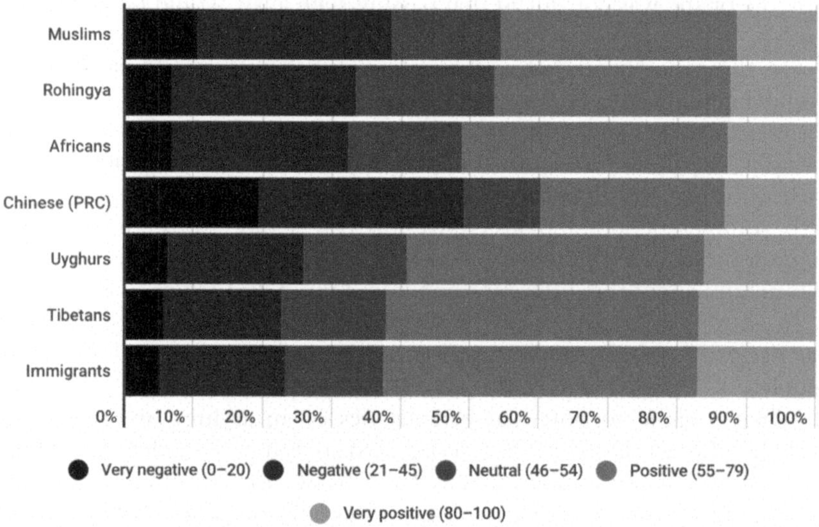

Fig. 9.3 Feelings towards selected groups of people—Muslims, immigrants, Africans, Rohingya, Uyghur, and Tibetans

a predictor of attitude—with older respondents having been more positive about them, especially in the case of the Chinese (strong correlation). For the latter two, gender was also found to correlate, with men having been more positive than women, especially about the Tibetans (strong correlation). Education was found to be factor only in one case—immigrants—with educated people having had a more positive image of them (slight correlation).

When looking at the data through the lens of voter/party preference (measured by the question "If there were parliamentary elections this weekend, which party would you vote for?"), what stood out was that the coldest feelings towards all these groups, with the exception of the Chinese, were held by the respondents that said they would not vote. When not considering those who would not vote or don't know who to vote for—only looking at the five listed parties (DPP, KMT, TPP, NPP, and TSP)—then the Taiwan People's Party (TPP) voters were very negative in comparison with other party voters, holding the most negative views towards Muslims, Africans, Tibetans, and immigrants. On the other side of the spectrum, in all cases except for the Chinese, it was the Taiwan Statebuilding Party (TSP) voters who had the warmest feelings towards the listed foreigners. On the other hand, in the case of the Chinese, it was the same TSP voters who held the coldest feelings of all (mean value 34, on a scale 0–100 with 0 being very negative and 100 very positive feelings), followed by DPP voters (mean value 37). Not surprisingly, the KMT voters had the warmest feelings towards the Chinese (mean value 58).

In order to have a more nuanced understanding of the above-mentioned negative view of the Chinese people by the Taiwanese respondents, the author looked closely at their attitudes/feelings towards various segments of the Chinese population. The Taiwanese were most critical of Chinese politicians (76%), surprisingly followed by Chinese dissidents (57%) and tourists (57%). They were the least critical of Chinese students (33%) and spouses (32%) (see Fig. 9.4). While politicians did not come as a surprise, the dissidents did—they were not seen as negatively as the politicians but still, the majority of the respondents perceived them negatively. When explored further (as the data does not provide an answer to the "why"), in the interviews and other informal discussions, the word "dissident" (in Chinese *yiyi fenzi*, direct translation "someone who disagrees", which is common vocabulary and is understood as dissident) was found to have a negative connotation, as it is connected to politics and politicians. Chinese tourists, while the biggest spenders in the tourism industry, were not seen positively. On the more receptive side were students from the PRC (known as *lusheng*)—increasingly a rare sight since the Chinese government announced a ban on new degree applicants to Taiwanese universities (Hayme, 2023)—and spouses from the PRC—predominantly Chinese women who have migrated to Taiwan through marriage over the last two decades. The latter two categories are people with whom the Taiwanese come in to contact with and may even interact with (more than with tourists who are confined to some certain touristic areas).

When asked explicitly about *accepting* certain groups/nationalities of refugees, Taiwanese people were very favourable towards people from Hong Kong (66%), Tibet (58%), and also towards war refugees (e.g. from Syria) (55%), but again they were rather unfavourable towards refugees from China (44%) (see Fig. 9.5). These four categories of refugees were chosen based on the author's previous research on the refugee topic, highlighting the groups of people that constitute the most common cases in Taiwan (Kironska, 2022a). This was an experimental split ballot question, with each respondent only answering one question about the four types of refugees (the full number of respondents, 1350, was divided between the four categories). Thus, it did not make much sense to disaggregate the data, as the number of respondents in the disaggregated categories would be too low to represent a statistically significant case.

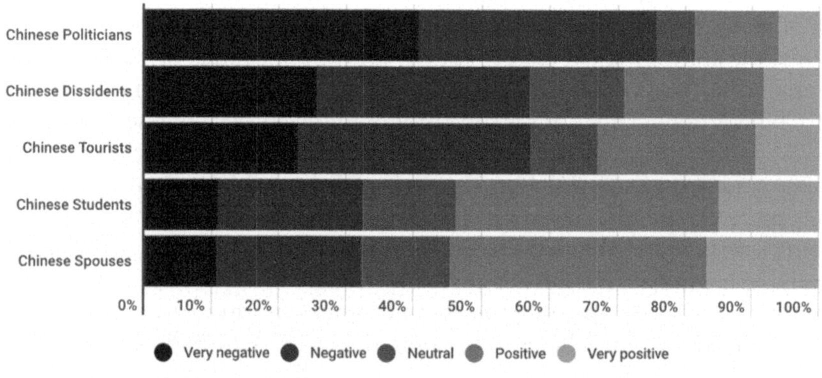

Fig. 9.4 Feelings towards different groups of Chinese people

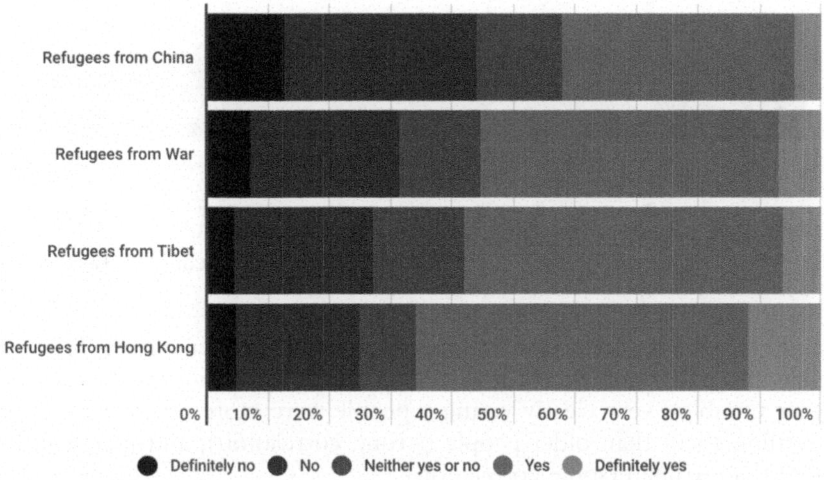

Fig. 9.5 Willingness to accept refugees from selected countries—China, Hong Kong, Tibet, and war refugees from other countries

The last question—on the resettlement of the Rohingya—was highly hypothetical but inspired by real events. It was hypothetical because there are no Rohingya in Taiwan and Taiwan is a rather impossible destination for them. Besides the fact that Taiwan does not have an asylum law, most Rohingya would, first of all, not have a legal way to get to Taiwan as they are stateless and do not possess identification documents such as a passport. Secondly, even if granted a special entry permit, according to Taiwanese law stateless persons who enter with a visitor visa are not eligible to apply for residency (Ministry of the Interior, 2018). Thus, Taiwanese people do not have any particular experience with this group of refugees and the assumption was that they would not be biased towards them. In one of the previous questions, described above, Taiwanese people, while having more positive than negative feelings towards the Rohingya, did not know them well, as evidenced by the large middle point percentage (see Fig. 9.3). When asked whether Taiwanese people supported the resettlement of the Rohingya to their country (the question contained a short explanation who the Rohingya were—a displaced minority from Myanmar, currently living in refugee camps in Bangladesh—in case the respondents were not familiar with the

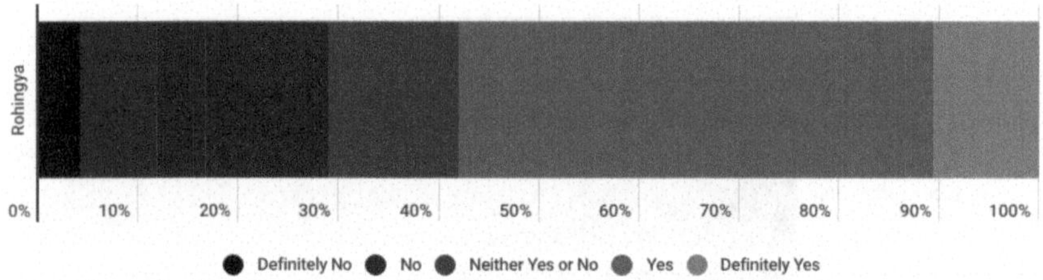

Fig. 9.6 Public opinion on resettlement of the Rohingya people in Taiwan

name), most Taiwanese (58%) supported their resettlement to Taiwan, while 29% did not (see Fig. 9.6). When looked at through the lens of other variables, very clearly younger people were more inclined towards resettling them than older people (strong correlation), and men a little more than women (some correlation).

Conclusion

Although Taiwan has accepted international human rights treaties as domestic law and thus has the obligation of *non-refoulement*, in the absence of an asylum system the island has not been able to handle people coming to Taiwan seeking protection. The International Review Committee on the Implementation of the International Human Rights Covenants, that Taiwan has adopted as domestic law, has repeatedly recommended a "speedy adoption of a refugee act, which should also include the principle of non-refoulement" (International Review Committee, 2022). There has, however, been little political will to implement such a system, likely because it is a complex issue involving the issue of cross-strait relations.

At the same time, there has been very little social dialogue on the issue and the political elites might have purposely kept it that way. There have been only very few surveys on public perceptions of refugees and a potential asylum law in Taiwan. This chapter fills this gap by presenting nationally representative data on the said issues.

While it is apparent from the data that there has long been a lack of discussion about asylum (a large part of the respondents chose the neutral answer, indicating that they do not have strong opinions on the issue), the data has also shown that people tend rather to agree that Taiwan needs a proper asylum system instead of dealing with incoming people on a case-by-case basis as has been done until now. Also, refugees are seen rather more positively than negatively—with people from China being an exception—and Taiwanese people are willing to accept refugees in Taiwan.

The results from this survey should, nevertheless, be understood in the context of the political climate in which the data has been collected—between April and June 2022—which was only a few weeks following the Russian invasion of Ukraine, which fuelled concern over China's plans for Taiwan (Lin & Culver, 2022). Many in Taiwan have speculated that the odds of an invasion by China have increased—with more people considering the likelihood of a Chinese invasion in the next ten years possible than not (61% see it as likely, 31% unlikely, and 8% are unsure) (see Fig. 9.7). With such fears for their own future, people tend to be more compassionate towards other people who are forced to leave their country of origin and seek refuge elsewhere (Banulescu-Bogdan, 2022). Moreover, the social desirability bias—the tendency of survey respondents to answer questions in a manner that is viewed favourably by others—might have also played its role in such positive-leaning survey results (Phillips & Clancy, 1972). Whether potential refugees in Taiwan would be accepted by Taiwanese society or not is beyond the scope of this chapter but would certainly be an interesting topic to explore in a future research project.

At the same time, the relatively low willingness to accept Chinese people as refugees compared to the other groups brings us back to the issue of the complicated relations between Taiwan and China, highlighting the need for social dialogue before any solution—an asylum system either including or excluding Chinese nationals—is accepted.

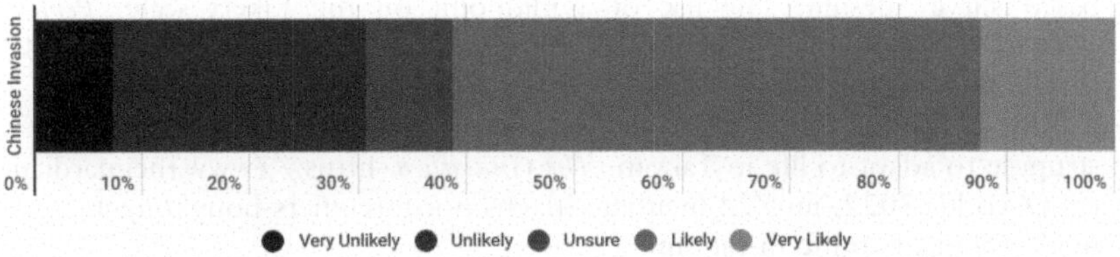

Fig. 9.7 Public opinion on the likelihood of a Chinese invasion in the next ten years

Acknowledgements The author would like to thank Chen Yiju and James Habersham Iocovozzi for their excellent research assistance.

Funding The work on this chapter was supported by funding from the European Union's research and innovation programme HORIZON-WIDERA-2021-ACCESS-03-01 under grant agreement No. 101079069, entitled "The EU in the Volatile Indo-Pacific Region" (EUVIP).

Funded by
the European Union

Disclaimer Funded by the European Union. Views and opinions expressed are however those of the author only and do not necessarily reflect those of the European Union. The European Union cannot be held responsible for them.

References

Banulescu-Bogdan, N. (2022). *From fear to solidarity the difficulty in shifting public narratives about refugees*. Migration Policy Institute. https://www.migrationpolicy.org/sites/default/files/publications/refugee-narratives-report-2022_final.pdf

Chen, Y. F. (2016, August 19). *Credibility poll: 53.1% of Taiwan people willing to accept international refugees*. Liberty Times Net. https://news.ltn.com.tw/news/politics/breakingnews/1800177

Chiu, E. L. (2022, January). *How should NGOs in Taiwan respond to the current refugee policy?* In P. Ivanova & L. Momesso (Eds.) "Refugee protection in East Asia: Taiwan and Japan in comparison", NEPCAP Policy Brief 2022/01. https://www.docdroid.net/TFgCpl7/nepcap-2022-01-full-pdf

Chyung, S. Y., Roberts, K., Swanson, I., & Hankinson, A. (2017). Evidence-based survey design: The use of a midpoint on the Likert scale. *Performance Improvement, 56*(10), 15–23. https://core.ac.uk/download/pdf/147014152.pdf

Davidson, H. (2022, June 22). Neither citizens nor foreigners: Hongkongers struggle to adapt to life in Taiwan. *The Guardian*. https://www.theguardian.com/world/2022/jun/22/neither-citizens-nor-foreigners-hongkongers-struggle-to-adapt-to-life-in-taiwan

Guo, J. S. (2022, March 11). *Russia–Ukraine war sees refugee waves, Taiwan People's Party calls for refugee law*. CNA. https://www.cna.com.tw/news/aipl/202203110169.aspx

Hayme, J. (2023, March 14). Why Chinese students are an increasingly rare sight in Taiwan. *Aljazeera*. https://www.aljazeera.com/news/2023/3/14/why-chinese-students-are-disappearing-from-taiwan

International Review Committee. (2022, May). *Review of the Third Reports of the Government of Taiwan on the implementation of the International Human Rights Covenants: Concluding observations and recommendations adopted by the International Review Committee*. https://www.humanrights.moj.gov.tw/media/20211673/concluding-observations-and-recommendations_taiwan-international-review-2022.pdf?mediaDL=true

Johns, R. (2005). One size doesn't fit all: Selecting response scales for attitude items. *Journal of Elections, Public Opinion and Parties, 15*(2), 237–264. https://www.tandfonline.com/doi/abs/10.1080/13689880500178849

Kironska, K. (2022a). Taiwan's road to an asylum law: Who, when, how, and why not yet? *Human Rights Review, 23*(2), 241–264. https://doi.org/10.1007/s12142-021-00644-y

Kironska, K. (2022b, April 19). Ukraine visas welcome, but lacking. *Taipei Times*. https://www.taipeitimes.com/News/editorials/archives/2022/04/19/2003776827

Lin, B., & Culver, J. (2022, April 19). China's Taiwan invasion plans may get faster and deadlier. *Foreign Policy*. https://foreignpolicy.com/2022/04/19/china-invasion-ukraine-taiwan/

Ministry of the Interior. (2018, December 5). *Regulations governing visiting, residency, and permanent residency of aliens*. https://law.moj.gov.tw/ENG/LawClass/LawAll.aspx?pcode=D0080129

Nachman, L., & Hioe, B. (2019, October 23). Friends from Hong Kong: Taiwan's refugee problem. *The Diplomat*. https://thediplomat.com/2019/10/friends-from-hong-kong-taiwans-refugee-problem/

Nachman, L., Rigger, S., Mok, C. W. J., & Chan, K. M. N. (2021, August 5). Taiwanese are sympathetic but uncertain about Hong Kong refugees. *Foreign Policy*. https://foreignpolicy.com/2021/08/05/taiwanese-sympathetic-uncertain-hong-kong-refugees/

Noelle-Neumann, E. (1993). *The spiral of silence: Public opinion—Our social skin*. The University of Chicago Press.

Petry, F. (1999). The opinion–policy relationship in Canada. *The Journal of Politics, 61*(2), 540–550. https://www.journals.uchicago.edu/doi/10.2307/2647516

Phillips, D. L., & Clancy, K. J. (1972). Some effects of "social desirability" in survey studies. *American Journal of Sociology, 77*(5), 921–940. http://www.jstor.org/stable/2776929

Refugee 101 Taiwan. (n.d.). Facebook. https://web.facebook.com/Refugee-101-Taiwan-104676894801001?_rdc=1&_rdr

Rouce, A. D. (2004). *Political actors' perception of public opinion: Assessing the impact of opinion on decision making*. Canadian Political Science Association's Annual Meeting, 2004. https://www.cpsa-acsp.ca/papers-2004/Rounce.pdf

Saloniki, E.-C., Malley, J., Burge, P., Lu, H., Batchelder, L., Linnosmaa, I., Trukeschitz, B., & Forder, J. (2019). Comparing internet and face-to-face surveys as methods for eliciting preferences for social care-related quality of life: Evidence from England using the Ascot Service User Measure. *Quality of Life Research, 28*(8), 2207–2220. https://doi.org/10.1007/s11136-019-02172-2

Soroka, S. N. (2002). *Agenda-setting dynamics in Canada*. UBC Press.

Turcsanyi, R. Q., Kironska, K., Gerstl, A., Arnez, M., Čeněk, J., Chen, J., Chen, R., Chubb, A., Gries, P., & Wang, T. (2022). *Sinophone Borderlands Indo-Pacific Survey*. Palacky University Olomouc.

Wolman, A. (2012). North Korean asylum seekers and dual nationality. *International Journal of Refugee Law, 24*(4), 793–814. https://academic.oup.com/ijrl/article-abstract/24/4/793/1568392

Wu, S. W. (2020, May 27). Poll conducted by New Power Party: Over 60% support amending the "Laws and regulations regarding Hong Kong & Macao Affair" to save Hong Kong people. *Liberty Times Net*. https://news.ltn.com.tw/news/politics/breakingnews/3179253

Yen, W., & Shih, H. (2023, January 23). Migrant workers in Taiwan lean on communities for comfort. *Focus Taiwan*. https://focustaiwan.tw/society/202301230006

Zhang, L. G. (2020, July 20). More than half of the public do not support the significant relaxation of immigration to Taiwan for Hong Kong people. *China Times*. https://www.chinatimes.com/realtimenews/20200720002467-260407?chdtv

CHAPTER 10

Kurdish Diaspora in Japan: Navigating Kurdish Identity and Activism on Social Media

Sohrab Ahmadian

Introduction

The definition of diaspora is still being debated among academics. Some academics claim that diasporas are populations that have lived abroad from their country for centuries as a result of tragic events, have a strong national identity, and are involved in active social and cultural activities (Cohen, 1997; Gilroy, 1993). Others, however, propose a broader vision that includes various transnational groups with fluid identities and hybrid cultural practices (Brah, 1996; Vertovec, 1999). This ongoing argument shows the complexities and diversity of diasporic experiences (Brah, 1996; Cohen, 1997; Gilroy, 1993; Vertovec, 1999).

In recent years, a significant number of Kurds have personally experienced migration, becoming actively engaged in the process of leaving their homeland and settling in new countries. The study of the Kurdish

S. Ahmadian (✉)
Tokyo University of Foreign Studies, Tokyo, Japan
e-mail: ahmadian@tufs.ac.jp

L. Momesso and P. Ivanova (eds.), *Refugees and Asylum Seekers in East Asia*, Palgrave Macmillan Studies on Human Rights in Asia,
https://doi.org/10.1007/978-981-97-2867-1_10

diaspora generally is an introduction to understanding transnational relations as well as identity and the desire to return as strategies of immigrants in relation to the country of origin.

In today's information era, diasporas are no longer defined solely by territorial claims, but rather by the preservation and reconstruction of cultural assets, shared imaginations, and the collective consciousness of their members (Cohen, 1997). The advent of the internet and other modern communication platforms has significantly influenced the contexts and practices surrounding diasporic identity. Through the internet, diasporas gain access to a rich and intricate symbolic environment, enabling them to connect, interact, and express their cultural identities in complex ways (Keles, 2015; Kissau & Hunger, 2010). While the internet provides a platform for diasporas to imagine and establish virtual homes, it also facilitates the clash of national and transnational political ideologies and cultural expressions, leading to counter-expressions of identity (Bucy & Gregson, 2001; Georgiou, 2006).

Online diasporic communities provide an ideal environment for individuals to explore and reassess their cultural identity and political perspectives (Georgiou, 2006). Meanwhile, members of the diaspora may share characteristics such as homeland, language, cultural traditions, history, ancestry, values, and religious practices (Bernal, 2006; Chuang, 2004). However, it is critical to recognise that diaspora groups are varied and incorporate distinct identities within these wider categories. Diasporas are also using cyberspace as a means of voicing political opposition and developing a sense of political identity through participation in political debates (Adamson, 2002; Diamandaki, 2003). There is a growing recognition, among diaspora activists and political organisations, of the internet's pivotal role as a vital tool in fostering the development of diasporic behaviours within immigrant communities. This is facilitated through the sharing of information and the amplification of political claims (Ekici, 2014). Diasporic societies often have more than one type of a sense of belonging, involving political, ethnic, and cultural identities, as is evidenced by the prominence of political culture in the diaspora (Aghapouri, 2018). Some diasporas place a higher priority on building a political identity due to political concerns, while others place a greater weight on building an ethnic identity. The weighting of each can be changed with context and over time (Karim, 2003).

Through this research, the author analysed approximately 200 Facebook posts from public accounts belonging to individuals and civic organisations associated with the Kurdish diaspora in Japan. The method of post-selection involved examining the last five posts for individuals and the previous ten posts for associations and organisations. Specifically, this chapter analyses the role Facebook plays in the development and representation of Kurdish diasporic identity in Japan and what kind of insight it provides in the transnational space. This chapter argues that everyday transnational communication on Facebook, as a social media, plays an important role in fostering cultural and political identity among Kurdish diasporic community members. This research has been designed based on several stages, such as general monitoring of public online communications, thematic categorisation, content analysis, and determining the frequency of topics and variables within the content that has been shared on Facebook at different times and in response to diverse events.

In summary, the findings presented in this chapter provide evidence that offers support for the hypothesis that Facebook plays a unifying role rather than promoting division and conflict within the Kurdish diaspora in Japan, by facilitating communication and fostering a sense of togetherness.

Kurdish Diaspora in Japan

In the 1990s, Japan lifted visa restrictions for some countries, especially for Iran and Turkey, allowing many young people from these countries to enter Japan without visas. The visa-free entry for Turkey came at a time when the situation of Kurds in Turkey was deteriorating due to political conflicts and unbalanced economic conditions. Japan became a destination for Kurds seeking to improve their situation and find a better life for themselves and their families. However, Japan did not officially open its labour market to unskilled foreign workers, but instead created some "side-doors" to allow them in, such as the status of residence for permanent residents of Japanese descent from South America and the trainee and technical intern programmes (Mori, 1997). However, these side-doors did not apply to Kurds from Turkey, as Turkish citizens and most of the migrants who came to Japan in the 1990s entered as tourists or students and overstayed their visas or worked illegally.

1990 was the starting point for Turkish Kurds to migrate to Japan (Nakajima, 2003). The news spread that Japan was full of job opportunities and easy money could be made. Unskilled labour from low-income Kurdish regions of Turkey travelled to Japan in search of high-paying jobs

(Ahmadian, 2020). Looking for a job was one of the common features of many immigrants from different countries coming to Japan in that period, but the situation was more complicated in the case of the Kurds and the reasons for their migration. The Kurds who migrated to Japan during that time had previously moved within Turkey due to political pressure and to escape conflicts between the Kurdistan Workers' Party and the Turkish army. They relocated from regions near the conflict to safer areas. It was during that period that young people from the rural areas of the cities of Gaziantep and Kahramanmaraş in the southeast of Turkey, who suffered from many deprivations such as economic and political problems, tried desperately to get a ticket to Japan (Ahmadian, 2020). Young people who did not even understand the basics of the Japanese language chose to immigrate to a country with strict refugee laws and entered Japan with a three-month visa-free travel, which was enough to enter Japan.

While Kurds have been present in Japan since the 1990s, their numbers have experienced significant growth in recent years. As per most estimates, there were more than 2000 Kurds residing in Japan in 2019, with a majority concentrated in the Kawaguchi and Warabi cities of southern Saitama Prefecture (Ahmadian, 2023). Nearly 30 years have passed since Kurds first arrived in Japan in the 1990s, and, around the region, young Kurds who were born or raised in Japan can be seen (Tokizawa, 2019, p. 5). Legal stays in Japan, such as through marriage, work, or other reasons, have allowed some Kurds to remain in the country for years. However, some Kurds entered Japan without applying for asylum and avoided immigration control (Ahmadian, 2023). Previously, asylum seekers could repeatedly renew their applications, extending their stay and living in uncertainty until a decision was made. But with the new amendment to the Immigration Control Act, passed on June 9, 2023, deportation is no longer suspended after the third application unless "sufficient reasons" are provided (Asada & Sendō, 2023).

Kurds in Turkey have had very difficult periods and painful experiences over the long history of their political struggles and freedom movements. In the late 1980s, as fighting broke out between the Kurdistan Workers' Party (PKK) and the Turkish military, unrest intensified, leaving the southeastern part of Turkey in a state of near-civil war (Yilmaz, 2016). In the 1990s, the Turkish government repeatedly bombed and destroyed the area with tanks, claiming that towns and villages in the southeast supported the PKK. Turkish military bombings peaked between 1994 and 1995, displacing more than 3 million Kurds and destroying more than 3000 towns and villages (McDowall, 2021). Many Kurds, whose houses, agricultural lands, and livestock were burned and destroyed, also were forced to migrate to the cities of Turkey and other countries. Many refugees fled to European countries, while some Kurds also emigrated to Japan, because was easier for them to enter Japan during that period due to visa exemptions with the Republic of Turkey (Beşikçi, 2002; Nakagawa, 2001; Nakajima, 2003).

Most Kurds who eventually made it to Japan came from those aforementioned areas of southeastern Turkey. These areas have a history of political violence, including the tragic Marash massacre in 1978. The combination of violence, discrimination, and assimilation policies has contributed to the migration of people from these areas to other parts of the world, including Japan. In rural parts of Turkey, Kurdish communities maintain their tribal, kinship, political, and religious affiliations. Likewise, the Kurdish community in Japan, which originates from similar tribes and neighbouring regions in Turkey, also maintains and strengthens its social bonds over time. The regions they come from in Turkey face many environmental problems at the same time. Its lands are also almost uncultivable due to being covered with thick black stones. Preparing these lands for cultivation is very costly and beyond the means of the residents there. During my field research trip to some of these areas around Gaziantep city in February 2022, I obtained detailed information about the demographic characteristics of the regions in Turkey where the Kurdish diaspora members originated from. During my visit to rural areas in Kahramanmaraş (Marash) and Gaziantep, specifically among the Makhakan (Maxikon) clan, I observed a strong connection between them and the Kurdish community in Japan. Many members of the Makhakan clan, who reside in a village complex located 30 kilometres from Gaziantep, have immigrated to Japan, either with their families or individually. It is worth noting that some of them eventually returned to their hometowns after their time in Japan. Based on the observations made during the fieldwork, it was found that even after returning from Japan, many of the returnees have retained their ability to speak Japanese. Furthermore, their children, who grew up in Japan and attended Japanese schools, can still speak Japanese.

Based on fieldwork and exploration of the Kurdish diaspora's Facebook usage, the analysis of their posts revealed the intended audiences. Results show that a notable portion, 53.5%, targeted the Kurds in their homeland (see Fig. 10.1). This suggests successful maintenance of a connection

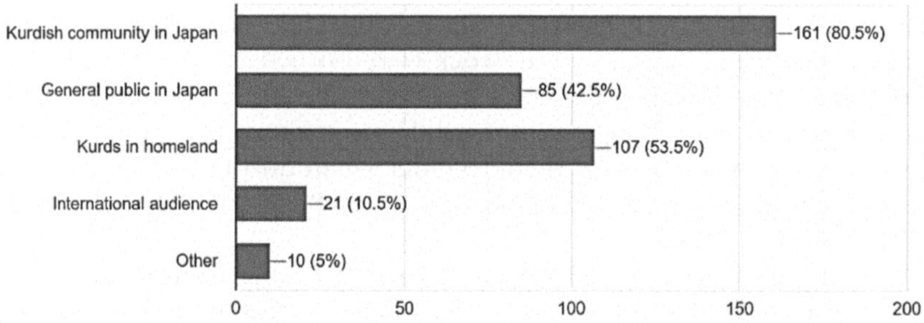

Fig. 10.1 Distribution of targeted audiences in the Facebook posts of the Kurdish diaspora in Japan (calculations and graph made by the author)

between the Kurdish community in Japan and both their community in Japan and their homeland.

The Turkish government is generally opposed to the presence and expansion of the Kurdish community in Japan and labels the process of political mobilisation of the Kurds as terrorism, separatism, and extremism (Kyodo, 2022; Rich, 2016). Until 2022, no Kurds had ever been granted refugee status in Japan, which would allow them to settle in Japan permanently (Kyodo, 2022; Rich, 2016). However, on 28 July 2022, a Kurd from Turkey, who was living in Hokkaido, was granted refugee status after an appeals court ruled in May that he would be at risk of persecution if he returned to Turkey, according to the lawyer Koji Yamada (Kyodo, 2022).

The dissatisfaction of the Kurds with the political and social conditions in Turkey, and the numerous conflicts of the Turkish government with the political factions of the Kurds, led to various waves of migration in the nineteenth and twentieth centuries, which began with migration to neighbouring countries in the Middle East, followed by a large number of people emigrating to European countries, North America, and East Asia, including Japan.

The emergence of the internet and social media has become for members of the Kurdish diaspora a means of gathering and civic participation at the transnational level (Ekici, 2014). Diasporic Kurds have been able to attract greater and wider support from international organisations at the governmental and non-governmental levels through online communication, especially social networks. Social networks have provided a suitable platform for the voices of political leaders and elites to be better heard among members of the Kurdish diaspora, and to provide the necessary potential for cultural identity representation and political mobilisation (Aghapouri, 2018).

Building upon be background described in this section, the levels and types of participation exhibited by members of the Kurdish diaspora on the Facebook social network platform have been further explored. This exploration sets the stage for the next section, where a deeper dive into these aspects will be conducted, and a comprehensive analysis will be provided.

Methodology

Social media has become an important source of data and methodology for social research because it allows researchers to access and analyse the online activities and interactions of many groups and communities (Sloan & Quan-Haase, 2016; Staff et al., 2016). With a focus on this understudied group, this study examines how the Kurdish diaspora in Japan uses Facebook to negotiate their Kurdish identity and activism. As one of the most well-known and widely used social media sites among the Kurdish community in Japan, Facebook was chosen as the focus of the study because it provides a rich variety of content types, including text, images, videos, and links, that can reveal different facets of their online expression and engagement (Wills, 2016, p. 50).

During the monitoring of the online activities of this community, I concluded that the TikTok social network is also common among the members of this community, but preliminary investigations showed that the activities of the community members in the TikTok space are not serious enough to answer the questions used to analyse social media posts created by the Kurdish community in Japan. However, as the primary and preferred social network within the community, Facebook has a prominent role. The vast majority of Kurds in Japan maintain active Facebook accounts and regularly engage with the platform, as do civic organisations associated with the Kurdish community.

In the first stage of this study, ten public pages/groups belonging to Kurdish civil society organisations and institutions on Facebook were identified by searching for keywords such as "Kurds in Japan" in Kurdish, Japanese, English, and Turkish (see Fig. 10.2). This was done in order to get an overview of the level and sentiment of participation on Facebook by diaspora members. The number of followers of each Facebook group was checked separately. Public pages and group pages that are affiliated with Kurdish organisations in Japan, and those that focus more on the promotion of Kurdish political and cultural identity, were found to be more followed by Kurds in Japan.

In the context of social media research, snowballing is a technique used to identify additional participants or sources of information through referrals or connections within a network (Dosek, 2021). In this study, the snowball method was used to collect a comprehensive list of Facebook accounts associated with Kurdish individuals and civic organisations in Japan. After the initial set of public Facebook accounts was identified, the author searched among the likes, followers, and comments of the initial sources and discovered additional public Facebook accounts and added them to the list.

In the second stage, in order to gain a comprehensive understanding of the community's online activities in the Facebook space, the author

GROUP/PAGES NAME	ENGLISH TRANSLATION
Kuridisutan Ryouri Mesopotamia クルディスタン料理メソポタミア	Kurdistan Cuisine Mesopotamia
Ippan shadan Houjin Nihon Kurudo Yuoko Kyoukai 一般社団法人 日本クルド友好協会	Japan Kurdish Friendship Association
Kurudo Bunka Kyoushitsu クルド文化 教室	Kurdish Culture Class
Kurudo Nihongo Kyoushitsu クルド日本語 教室	Kurdish Japanese Class
Zainichi Kurudojin to tomo ni 在日クルド人と 共に	Together with Kurds in Japan
Kurudisutan Aka Tsuki クルディスタン 赤月	Kurdistan Red Moon (Japan)
Ippan Shadan Houjin Nihon Kurudo Bunka Kyoukai 一般社団法人日本クルド文化協会	Japan Kurdish Cultural Association
Kurudo wo Shiru Kai クルドを知る会	Society for Understanding Kurds
Nihon Kurudo Gakusei Renmei 日本クルド学生連盟	Kurdish Students Association of Japan

Fig. 10.2 List of institutional groups and pages on Facebook associated with the Kurds in Japan

selected 100 Facebook posts from personal accounts of Kurdish users and 100 posts from institutional accounts of Kurdish civil society groups. However, due to the fact of applying some filters in the selection of pages and persons, the composition of this selection finally came out as follows (see Fig. 10.3).

One of the filters that was applied in the selection of Facebook accounts was to select only people and members who were active on Facebook. For example, individuals whose last Facebook posts were over a year old were excluded from the study as less active users. Since the aim of this research was to obtain the latest status of the Kurdish diaspora members' online activities in Japan, the publication date of the last Facebook posts was used as a criterion to distinguish between active and inactive users (Fig. 10.4). As an additional criterion for selecting Facebook pages belonging to Kurdish associations and civil organisations in Japan, the frequency of updates, their popularity, and the number of followers were also considered. In general, the public pages that were selected had 200–3000 likes and followers. To protect participants' information and safety, this study will not disclose names of individual account holders, while the list of institutional pages and groups on Facebook is provided in Fig. 10.2.

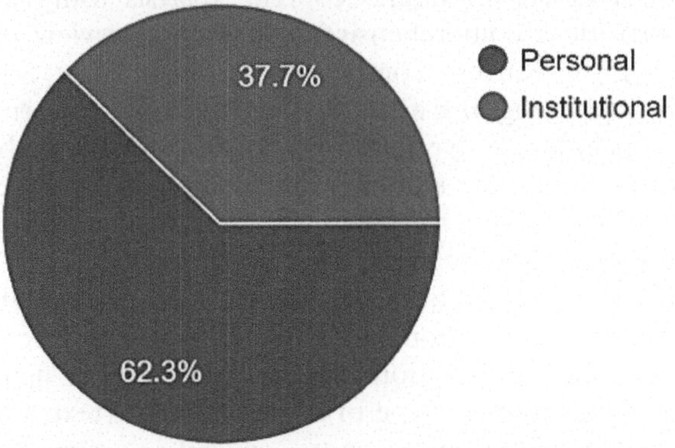

Fig. 10.3 Distribution of selected Facebook accounts/pages by types

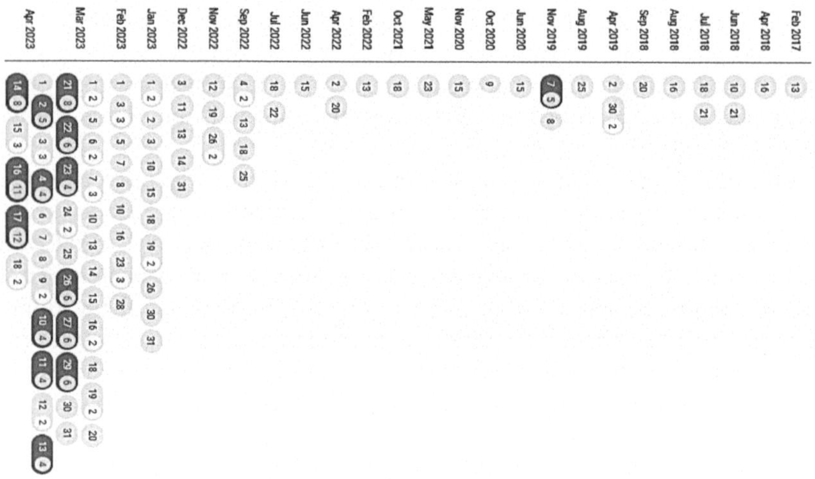

Fig. 10.4 The frequency of publication dates of Facebook posts

The Challenge of Data Collection

This research is based on online content analysis using a qualitative method, to provide a comprehensive and visual overview of Facebook activities among the Kurdish community in Japan. Data collection was conducted through designing a database on the Google Forms platform. This database included twelve questions. Before designing the database, the author spent some time scanning and skimming the Facebook posts of the community members to obtain the correct categories and themes. During data entry, after opening each post and checking its quality, the author answered twelve questions for each post separately. For each post, the following information was screened and submitted in Google Forms: post number, publication date, account owner name, account type (personal/institutional), type of shared content (text, image, video, mixed, etc.), general topic of the post, general impression of the post (positive/negative), representation of identity in the posts, representation of activism in the posts, the level of interaction with the community, the language in which the post is written and the type of audience of the posts.

In general, the checkbox field option in Google Forms was used to address the main research questions, which encompassed multiple aspects. This option allows for multiple choices, as each item may not necessarily fit into a single category, and a category may encompass multiple characteristics that need to be included in the responses at the same time. By using checkboxes that allow for multiple choices, it is possible to capture multiple topics, views, languages, or audiences associated with each post. In addition, drop-down menus were used for certain questions to provide options for single selections. These structured question formats allowed for easier and more efficient data analysis, so that responses could be used and analysed to produce quantitative results.

The data collected from Google Forms was then subjected to qualitative analysis, with visual and quantitative data results presented. It is important to note that since this research follows a qualitative approach, the graphs presented below are the result of qualitative data analysis to give a visual and broader perspective on the Kurdish community in Japan.

Identity Representation on Facebook

Facebook is one of the most influential social networks that, despite the emergence of other competitors such as Instagram, Twitter, TikTok, etc., still maintains its position as a main platform for online activities (Meta Platforms, 2023; Statista, 2023a, 2023b). Considering the structural features of Facebook compared to other social networks, at least by observing the Facebook posts of Kurd users, it became clear that Facebook posts provide more offer more possibilities for analysis with regard to everyday issues than Instagram and TikTok. The greater freedom that Facebook has given users to post text, video, and image content simultaneously could be one of the reasons for this. Since Facebook is older than other social networks, this media has become a centre of nostalgic memories and a place to recover and reread memories (Davalo et al., 2015; Zhao et al., 2013). Facebook serves as a virtual space for Kurds in Japan to engage with their past, present, and future identities. They repost photos and videos of their homeland that Facebook has archived and retrieved for them, such as landscapes, monuments, festivals, or historical events. These posts illustrate some of the ways that Kurds use Facebook to interact with their memories and culture. The development of the interactive and network level of this media, along with its other features, has given the users of this media have access to an interactive space where they can express their sense of belonging to a group.

Since the Kurdish diaspora space is far from the original homeland, Facebook has become a key space in the interaction of diaspora members with each other and with their hometowns. The meanings of "being Kurdish" are actively represented in this virtual space. This section discusses the distinct manifestations of diasporic identity among the members of the Kurdish online community in Japan. Examining the Facebook posts of members of the Kurdish diaspora and civil organisations in Japan, first, required a thematic classification to achieve a general and comprehensive analysis of the content of the posts.

Figure 10.5 shows that about 36% of the posts examined had political content, which is the highest rate, as shown on the chart. In other words, 72 out of 200 Facebook posts that were analysed had political features, references, and elements. After the posts with political content, the second place was dedicated to events related to the Kurdish community in Japan with a value of 32% and 64 posts out of 200 posts. The third position (29.5%) was occupied by posts that represented solidarity, and the largest part of this solidarity was related to events that occurred in Kurdish regions in different countries. A category named "Neutral" was included among the post types to allow for ranking or categorising posts that were not directly related to the research topic or did not align with any specific theme.

In another question, the representation of the elements, signs, and factors that had the closest overlap with the issue of Kurdish identity was investigated. In response to this question, it was possible to choose several

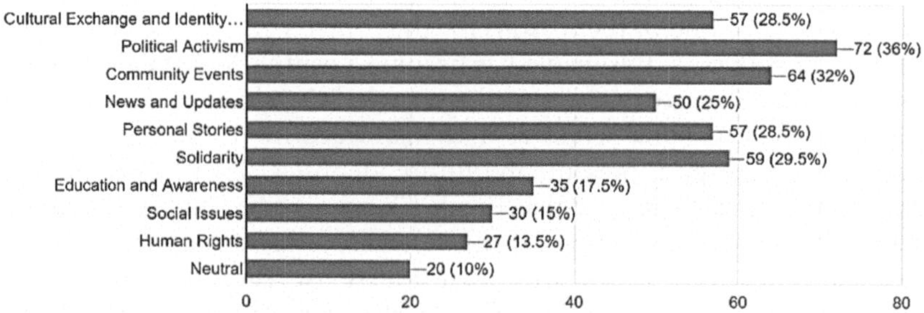

Fig. 10.5 Distribution of content categories in Facebook posts

options. As can be seen in Fig. 10.6, the content of 84 posts out of 200 posts had identity stimuli. The "identity stimuli" indicate that there were specific signals, inputs, or factors that influenced or provoked a response related to identity. It suggests that various elements or aspects play a role in shaping or triggering identity-related experiences or behaviours among diaspora members. Some of the identity stimuli are considered below.

- Use of Kurdish language in posts and comments.
- Sharing news and events related to Kurdistan issues.
- Sharing of cultural content such as music, art, and literature.
- Using Kurdish symbols, flags, or other visual elements.
- Participating in online discussions and debates about Kurdish identity and politics.
- Networking with other Kurds on Facebook.
- Sharing stories and personal experiences related to being Kurdish.
- Expressing pride or solidarity with the community.
- Criticism of negative images of Kurds in the media or society.

By posting photos, videos, stories, and news articles that showcase the diversity, richness, and resilience of Kurdish culture and people, Kurds in Japan seek to create a positive image of Kurds in Japan and foster mutual understanding and respect. Figure 10.6 illustrates the subsets of "Identity Stimuli", such as: Language, History, Culture, Religion, Symbols, Ethnicity, Nationalism, and Identity Struggles. The inclusion of the heading category (Identity Stimuli) and its subsets (Language, History,

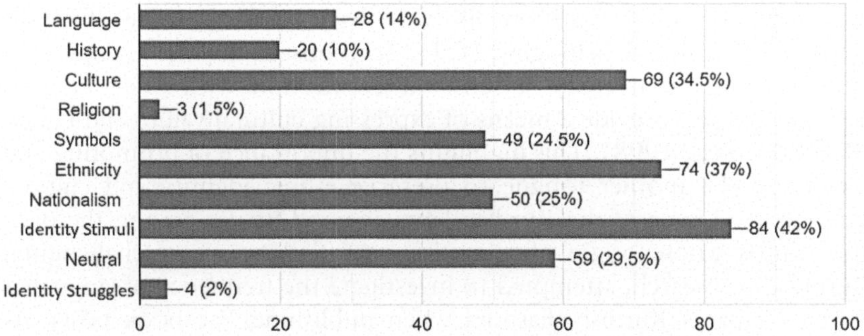

Fig. 10.6 Frequency of identity variables in Facebook posts

Culture...) in the database ensured that all possible identity stimuli were separately accounted for. Additionally, this allowed for further investigation into the level of engagement with specific subsets of identity stimuli. The general result of the question about identity shows that "identity stimuli" were generally observed in 84 posts out of a total of 200 posts (42%). Among the more detailed subsets of identity stimuli, we saw that the topic of "ethnicity" (being Kurdish) was visible in 74 posts (37%) and the topic of "culture" was visible in 69 posts (34.5%), in contrast to a topic of "religion" which had the lowest value (1.5%). Religion featured in only three posts out of a total of 200 Facebook posts, two of which introduced positive aspects of religion and one video post related to publishing negative aspects of religion. Although the majority of Kurds in Turkey follow Sunni Islam, some Turkish Kurds are Alevis, a religious minority repeatedly subjected to persecution and discrimination in Turkey (Gezik, 2021). Given that some Alevi refugees live in Japan, it would be logical to expect some religious activism in their Facebook posts; however, no signs of Alevism in the online activities of the Kurds in Japan have been found.

The Role of Language in Maintaining Ethnic Identity

The mother tongue plays a vital role in maintaining ethnic identity, as it is often the primary means of transmitting cultural values, traditions, and beliefs across generations. Therefore, promoting and supporting the use of the mother tongue among migrants/emigrants can have positive effects on their well-being, integration, and cultural diversity (UNESCO, 2022). Research also has shown that emigrants who are able to speak their mother tongue are more likely to have a strong sense of ethnic identity and cultural belonging (Giles & Johnson, 1987). Using one's mother tongue can create a sense of connection with one's cultural heritage and can provide a means of expressing cultural values and beliefs (Baker & Jones, 1998). This highlights the importance of promoting and preserving the mother tongue to preserve ethnic identity and cultural heritage. The issue of the Kurdish language and its use among the diaspora Kurds whose origin of migration was Turkey is very challenging. During this research, attempted to investigate the frequency of languages used by Japan's Kurdish diaspora when publishing Facebook posts. As can be seen in the results of the answers to this question in Fig. 10.7, the language used in the community's Facebook posts was Japanese with a frequency of 47.4%, followed by Turkish, with a frequency of 25%, Kurdish with a frequency of 20%, and finally English with a frequency of 7%.

This chart also includes a column for Arabic, which has a frequency of 0.4% and has the lowest scale.

The Japanese language has the highest percentage (47.4%) of use in published posts. However, this does not mean that the majority of members of the Kurdish community in Japan are fluent in Japanese. A field study, as well as a review of Facebook posts, shows that few Kurds in the diaspora in Japan are fluent in Japanese. The high percentage of Japanese language in Fig. 10.7 is due to the frequency of use of the Japanese language by Facebook pages related to Kurdish associations and civic institutions. Most of the Kurdish leaders of civic organisations in Japan can communicate effectively in Japanese, and they publish their posts in Japanese or in multiple languages to raise awareness of Kurds among the Japanese community. In contrast, posts published by individuals are usually a combination of photos and videos without text or with a short text. For this research, the photos and the languages used in

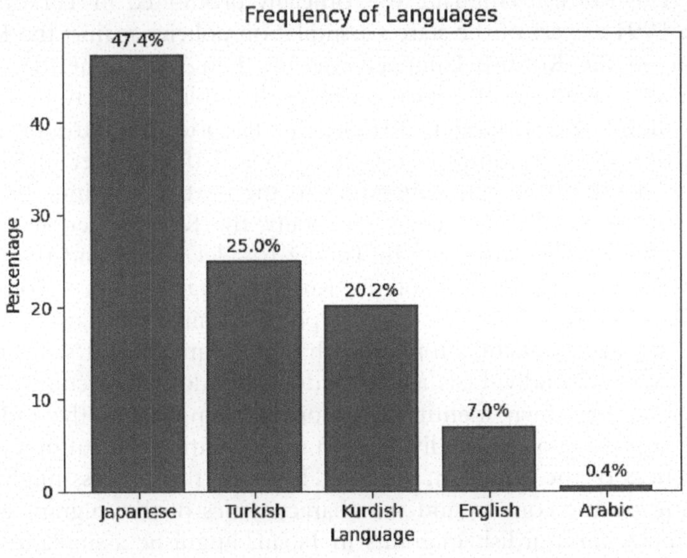

Fig. 10.7 Frequency of languages used in Facebook posts

the videos were also recorded, and the most used language by personal accounts was the Turkish language (25.0%).

The representation of Kurdish ethnic identity is strong among members of the Kurdish diaspora who are active on Facebook, as shown in Fig. 10.6. But it can be concluded that the emphasis on a collective responsibility to preserve the Kurdish identity is not manifested in the use of Kurdish language. The author also conducted field studies during the field research trip to areas of origin of Kurds in Japan, especially Gaziantep city and its rural areas of Makhakan (Maxikon) in southeastern Turkey, in February 2022. Observations based on the fieldwork showed that Kurds in Turkey and Kurds from Turkey in the diaspora generally are politically mobilised.

Kurdish people in Japan have a strong sense of political and national identity that is distinct from the Turkish state. This is evident from their use of Kurdish symbols, culture, and history, as well as their resistance to assimilation and oppression by the Turkish authorities but the Turkish language is the dominant language among members of Kurdish society, even for daily conversations. This issue has several reasons that are rooted in Turkey's policies in assimilating the Kurdish language throughout history. The Kurdish language was officially prohibited in Turkey from 1937 to 1991 as part of the state's assimilation policies against the Kurds. The ban on the Kurdish language was lifted in 1991, but the use of Kurdish as a language of education in both public and private schools remains illegal (Zeydanlıoğlu, 2012). This historical background and a combination of many other factors have caused the transfer of Kurdish linguistic identity from one generation to the next to continue to move away from the Kurdish language. Generally, the Kurdish people's proficiency in the Kurdish language in Turkey has decreased, and the use of the Turkish language instead of the Kurdish language has become the daily habit. Today, we can see a new type of assimilation that the author named "self-driven assimilation", which is a voluntary and self-directed process by which individuals actively adopt the dominant culture while maintaining their own identity. This process emphasises the independent agency and choice of individuals in incorporating the cultural norms and practices of the dominant society. However, this process might vary depending on the context and the characteristics of the migrant group. For example, for Kurdish migrants in Japan, linguistic assimilation in a style of "self-driven assimilation" has persisted even after they arrived in

Japan, because their daily habit of using a native level of Turkish, a prominent language in their homeland, could not be replaced by Kurdish, a language that they had not spoken widely before or even in Japan.

In some cases, the Turkish language has paradoxically become the language of Kurdish nationalism in Turkey. In general, the issue of Kurdish language among Kurds in Turkey raises a new question of how or to what extent it is possible to represent Kurdish identity and reproduce Kurdish nationalism without the Kurdish mother tongue.

Facebook as a Platform for Political Activism

Facebook groups and pages run by Kurdish non-governmental organisations in Japan have become a central place for discussion of the political issues facing Kurdish immigrants. Some of the major political debates involve: the immigration policies of the Japanese government; criticising the policies of the Turkish government during various events; expressing political solidarity with the opposition parties in Turkey; and showing solidarity with the victims of political and ethnic violence and discrimination in the Kurdish regions. They are published and promoted both on Facebook pages and groups by Kurdish organisations and on the personal accounts of Kurdish community members. As shown in Fig. 10.8, posts containing political engagement have the highest frequency. In other words, 32.5% or 65 of the 200 reviewed posts had content that represented political engagement. In addition, the number of posts that showed solidarity was 63, and the number of posts that represented activities to preserve Kurdish culture was 54.

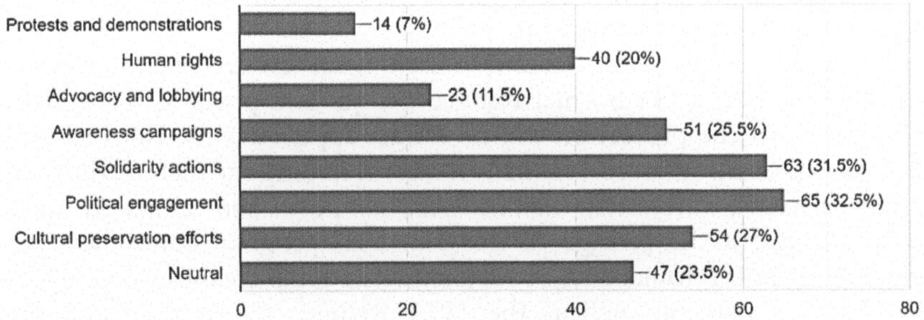

Fig. 10.8 Frequency of activism variables within Facebook posts

The online activities of Kurdish users and their Japan supporters also contribute to creating and spreading a coherent and inclusive political discourse on behalf of the Kurdish diaspora. One of the reasons for the high number of political posts was the publication of posts in support of the opposition party and the supporter of Kurdish rights in Turkey called "Left Green Party" which were reposted and shared among members of the community. Due to the general election in Turkey on 14 May 2023, the advertising campaigns of the Green Left Party (Turkish: Yeşil Sol Parti, YSP), which were represented by some Kurdish organisations in Japan, increased their political activity on Facebook. Examining the Facebook pages of members of the Kurdish community in Japan showed that advertising banners supporting the Green Left Party were published on the accounts of many members of this community.

The Kurds in Japan showed solidarity with their compatriots in Turkey, who suffered from a big earthquake in February 2023. They started a campaign on Facebook to help the victims and raised about 30 million yen in donations. They also got media attention and cooperation from the Japanese public and the People's Democratic Party (HDP) in Turkey (Gulbahçe, 2023). This case shows how the Kurds in Japan used Facebook to mobilise their resources and express their solidarity with their fellow Kurds in Turkey.

They use Facebook to establish contacts and relations with Japanese politicians and activists who are sympathetic or supportive of the Kurdish cause. Among the pages and groups that are associated with institutions and civil society organisations with Japanese leaders, many posts are in Japanese, and a significant part of them are related to the launch of campaigns and awareness-raising against the policies of the Japanese government in the revision of the immigration law, which is targeting asylum seekers and their situation.

While the current law ensures that asylum seekers are protected from deportation during the normal refugee recognition process, the revised bill means that the protection will no longer apply after the third asylum claim is closed. For this reason, many issues, including the increased risk of forced evictions, were mentioned in Facebook posts, and campaigns were launched against the passage of this bill. This proposal contradicts the principle of non-refoulement of major international treaties on refugees that Japan is part of, such as the 1951 Refugee Convention and the Convention against Torture (Kasai, 2023). Opposition to the new immigration bill intensified when news of the torture of some Kurdish asylum seekers in Japanese immigration detention centres and the death of a Sri Lankan woman were widely reported in the Japanese news and social media (Slater & Barbaran, 2020; Tauchi, 2023).

Conclusion

This chapter has investigated how and to what extent Facebook can serve as a useful tool for Kurdish diaspora members to explore and represent their Kurdish identity and political awareness. Many of the Kurdish community members in Japan originated from rural areas surrounding the cities of Gaziantep, Kahramanmaraş, and Adyaman in southeastern Turkey. For them, social networks such as Facebook provide a way to interact and connect with their homeland, to negotiate their identities, and to expand and strengthen their "Kurdishness". Facebook also facilitates political and cultural mobilisation among the Kurdish community members and their supporters among Japanese nationals. Kurdish diaspora elites and activists have established Kurdish associations in Japan to promote Kurdish interests and rights, and they have used social media and mass media simultaneously to influence public spheres and produce and represent online content that matches "Kurdishness" in Japan.

The findings of this study help to understand how social networks such as Facebook enable Kurdish diaspora members in Japan to explore and negotiate their identity and culture online. Although this study reveals a paradoxical nature of identity stimuli in online interactions, in which "Kurdish language" and "Religion" occupy the last position while "Kurdish ethnicity" and "nationalism" get high scores, this does not imply a lack of attachment or commitment to the Kurdish heritage. Rather, analysis of the online content shows that the Kurds in the Japanese diaspora primarily use the Turkish language as a borrowed tool to represent their Kurdish identity and nationalism in a context where they face linguistic and cultural barriers.

Social media influences public opinion in Japan, and it can bring attention to shortcomings within the current system, such as deportations, prolonged detention periods, and the low rates of asylum recognition for migrants in Japan. Examples from the findings of the case of Kurdish asylum seekers in Japan clearly show that social media platforms have the potential to increase public awareness and generate empathy towards the challenges faced by Kurdish asylum seekers who experience persecution and violence in Japan as well as their home country (Fujibayashi, 2020).

Based on the findings, the Kurdish community in Japan exhibits unique characteristics and behaviours compared to many other diaspora communities. Unlike those communities that have their own nation-state, the Kurds do not possess a recognised sovereign territory, which intensifies their quest for identity. This distinct feature influences their actions and motivations within the diaspora. For instance, the case of campaigns launched on the Facebook pages of the Kurdish community in Japan to aid earthquake victims in southeast Turkey in February 2023 illustrates their strong sense of solidarity. They collected and sent significant amounts of cash and non-cash donations to support their fellow Kurds in need. Furthermore, the utilisation of the Facebook platform by members of the Kurdish diaspora in Japan to rally political support for the Turkish opposition party, the Green Left Party, during the 2023 general election campaigns showcases their active engagement in virtual campaigns. Additionally, they leverage Facebook to disseminate information and raise awareness among opponents of Japan's immigration law revision bill. These examples clearly demonstrate how social media has amplified public awareness and fostered empathy for the challenges faced by immigrant minority groups.

The Kurdish community in Japan stands out due to their circumstances of being a stateless group, which strengthens their quest for identity and drives their active engagement in social and political activities within the diaspora. The examples mentioned, such as their support campaigns and political mobilisation through Facebook, highlight the distinctiveness of their experiences and their concerted efforts to address the issues impacting their community.

In summary, this study uncovered the various impacts resulting from the online activities of Kurdish users and their Japan supporters, which primarily revolve around Kurdish cultural identity and political mobilisation in Japan. These activities have three main effects: firstly, they contribute to fostering public awareness and actively combating discrimination within the host society. Secondly, they produce and disseminate a coherent and inclusive political discourse on behalf of the Kurdish diaspora. Lastly, these online activities provide a valuable platform for public diplomacy, facilitating enhanced relations between Kurdish political elites and Japanese politicians and activists.

References

Adamson, F. B. (2002). Mobilizing for the transformation of home: Political identities and transnational practices. In N. Al-Ali & K. Koser (Eds.), *New approaches to migration? Transnational communities and the transformation of home* (pp. 155–168). Routledge. https://doi.org/10.4324/9780203167144-13

Aghapouri, H. (2018). *Nationalism and diaspora in cyberspace: The case of the Kurdish diaspora on social media* [Doctoral dissertation, University of Auckland]. ResearchSpace@ Auckland. https://researchspace.auckland.ac.nz/handle/2292/35845

Ahmadian, S. (2020). *Kurudo-jin, furusato kara no koe* [Kurdish Diaspora, Voices from Homeland]. In M. Kobayashi & H. Koami (Eds.), *Hen'yō suru imin komyuniti jikan. kūkan. kaisō* (pp. 38–41). Akashi. https://www.akashi.co.jp/book/b612447.html

Ahmadian, S. (2023). Zainichi Kurudo-Jin no Diaspora Taiken nikansuru Shitsuteki Kenkyu [Qualitative Study on the Diaspora Experience of Kurds in Japan]. (Unpublished doctoral dissertation).

Asada T., & Sendō K. (2023). Nyūkan-hō kaisei-an seiritsu ni 'machigatta ketteida' Saitama no Kurudo hito ni rakutan no koe: Asahishinbun dejitaru [News]. *Asahi Shimbun Digital*. https://www.asahi.com/articles/ASR696KL6R69UTNB003.html?iref=ogimage_rek

Baker, C., & Jones, S. P. (1998). *Encyclopedia of bilingualism and bilingual education*. Multilingual Matters.

Bernal, V. (2006). Diaspora, cyberspace and political imagination: The Eritrean diaspora online. *Global Networks, 6*, 161–179. https://doi.org/10.1111/j.1471-0374.2006.00139.x

Brah, A. (1996). *Cartographies of diaspora: Contesting identities*. Routledge.

Bucy, E. P., & Gregson, K. S. (2001). Media participation: A legitimizing mechanism of mass democracy. *New Media & Society, 3*, 357–380.

Chuang, R. (2004). Communicating ethnic and cultural identity. In M. Fong & R. Chuang (Eds.), *Communicating ethnic and cultural identity* (pp. 3–18). Rowman & Littlefield.

Cohen, R. (1997). *Global diasporas: An introduction*. University of Washington Press.

Davalo, S., Merchant, A., Rose, G. M., Lessley, B. J., & Teredesai, A. M. (2015). 'The good old days': An examination of nostalgia in Facebook posts. *International Journal of Human-Computer Studies, 83*, 83–93. https://doi.org/10.1016/j.ijhcs.2015.05.009

Diamandaki, K. (2003). Virtual ethnicity and digital diasporas: Identity construction in cyberspace. *Global Media Journal, 2*, 1–14.

Dosek, T. (2021). Snowball sampling and Facebook: How social media can help access hard-to-reach populations. *PS: Political Science & Politics, 54*(4), 651–655. https://doi.org/10.1017/S104909652100041X

Ekici, D. (2014). Kurdish identity, discourse, and new media. *Critical Discourse Studies, 11*, 135–138. https://doi.org/10.1080/17405904.2013.793045

Fujibayashi, H. (2020). When public opinion drives national asylum policy-making: The case of Kurdish asylum seekers in Japan. *Asia & the Pacific Policy Studies, 7*, 204–216. https://doi.org/10.1002/app5.301

Georgiou, M. (2006). *Diaspora, identity and the media: Diasporic transnationalism and mediated spatialities.* Hampton Press.

Gezik, E. (2021). The Kurdish Alevis: The followers of the path of truth (Raa Haq/Riya Heqi). In H. Bozarslan, C. Gunes, & V. Yadirgi (Eds.), *The Cambridge history of the Kurds* (pp. 560–580). Cambridge University Press. https://doi.org/10.1017/9781108623711.023

Giles, H., & Johnson, P. (1987). Ethnolinguistic identity theory: A social psychological approach to language maintenance. *International Journal of the Sociology of Language, 68*, 69–99. https://doi.org/10.1515/ijsl.1987.68.69

Gilroy, P. (1993). *The Black Atlantic: Modernity and double consciousness.* Harvard University Press.

Gulbahçe, E. (2023, February 16). *Kurdên Japonyayê çûn hewarê* [Kurdish people in Japan went to help their compatriots]. https://kurmanci.ozgurpolitika.com/nuceya-kurden-japonyaye-cun-heware-173519

Karim, K. H. (Ed.). (2003). *The media of diaspora.* Routledge.

Kasai, T. (2023, June 14). Japan Immigration Law Creates New Obstacles for Asylum Seekers: Heightened Risk of Refugee Applicants Being Returned Home to Harm. Human Rights Watch. https://www.hrw.org/news/2023/06/15/japan-immigration-law-creates-new-obstacles-asylum-seekers

Keles, J. (2015). Diaspora, the internet and social capital. *Migrant Capital: Networks, Identities and Strategies*, 102–116.

Kissau, K., & Hunger, U. (2010). The internet as a means of studying transnationalism and diaspora In R. Bauböck & T. Faist (Eds.), *Diaspora and Transnationalism: Concepts, Theories and Methods* (pp. 245–265). Amsterdam University Press.

Kyodo. (2022, August 1). *Japan recognizes Turkish Kurd as refugee.* Kyodo News+. https://english.kyodonews.net/news/2022/08/93675dd4ff0e-japan-recognizes-turkish-kurd-as-refuge.html

Meta Platforms. (2023). *Audience insights: Explore interactive Facebook insights tool.* https://www.facebook.com/business/insights/tools/audience-insights

McDowall, D. (2021). *A Modern History of the Kurds.* I.B. Tauris.

Mori, H. (1997). Immigration policy and foreign workers in Japan. *Palgrave Macmillan.* https://doi.org/10.1057/9780230374522

Nakagawa, K. (2001). *Kurudojin to kurudisutan: Kyozetsusareru minzoku kurudogaku josetsu* [The Kurds and Kurdistan: An introduction to the ethnology of the rejected people]. Nanpō Shinsha.

Nakajima, Y. (2003). *Shingetsu no yoru ga akeru toki: Kita Kurudisutan no hitobito* [When the night of the new moon dawns: The people of northern Kurdistan]. Shinsensha.

Rich, M. (2016, August 16). Ethnic Kurds find haven, but no home, in insular Japan. *The New York Times*. https://www.nytimes.com/2016/08/17/world/asia/japan-kurds-refugees.html

Slater, D. H., & Barbaran, R. (2020). The whole block goes down: Refugees in Japan's detention centers during the pandemic. *Asia-Pacific Journal-Japan Focus*, *18*(18), 1–16.

Sloan, L., & Quan-Haase, A. (Eds.). (2016). *The Sage handbook of social media research methods*. Sage Publications.

Staff, C., King, H., Cooper, A., & Mann, R. (2016). *Using social media for social research: An introduction*. Social Media Research Group. https://assets.publishing.service.gov.uk/government/uploads/system/uploads/attachment_data/file/524750/GSR_Social_Media_Research_Guidance_-_Using_social_media_for_social_research.pdf

Statista. (2023a). *Facebook—Statistics & facts*. https://www.statista.com/topics/751/facebook/

Statista. (2023b). *Global social networks ranked by number of users 2023*. https://www.statista.com/statistics/272014/global-social-networks-ranked-by-number-of-users/

Tauchi, K. (2023, March 7). Cabinet approves bill to speed up deportations of illegal stayers. *The Asahi Shimbun*. https://www.asahi.com/ajw/articles/14855500

Tokizawa, T. (2019). *Nihon de ikiru kurudojin* [Living as Kurds in Japan]. Buna no mori.

UNESCO. (2022). *Why mother language-based education is essential*. https://www.unesco.org/en/articles/why-mother-language-based-education-essential

Vertovec, S. (1999). Conceiving and researching transnationalism. *Ethnic and Racial Studies, 22*(2), 447–462.

Wills, C. (2016). Social media as a research method. In L. Sloan & A. Quan-Haase (Eds.), *The Sage handbook of social media research methods* (pp. 49–64). Sage Publications.

Yilmaz, Ö. (2016). Germany's Kurdish and PKK Policy: Balance and Strategy. *Insight Turkey*, p. 98.

Zhao, X., Salehi, N., Naranjit, S., Alwaalan, S., Voida, S., & Cosley, D. (2013). The many faces of Facebook: Experiencing social media as performance, exhibition, and personal archive. In *Proceedings of the SIGCHI Conference on*

Human Factors in Computing Systems (pp. 1–10). https://doi.org/10.1145/2470654.2470656
Zeydanlıoğlu, W. (2012). Turkey's Kurdish language policy. *International Journal of the Sociology of Language, 217*, 99–125. https://doi.org/10.1515/ijsl-2012-0051

PART III

Lived Experiences of Refugees and Asylum Seekers in Taiwan and Japan

CHAPTER 11

The Lived Experience of Tibetan Refugees in Taiwan: Contesting Rights to Work, Residence, and Citizenship

Mei-Lin Pan and Dolma Tsering

Making Tibetan Refugees

On 1 October 1949, the Communist Party of China (CPC) proclaimed the foundation of the People's Republic of China and declared the incorporation of Tibet into China. By the end of 1959, The People's Liberation Army of the CPC successfully defeated the Tibetan army and had complete control over Tibet. Thousands of Tibetans were forced to escape to India and Nepal by becoming refugees, including its leader the 14th Dalai Lama (Shakya, 1999).

In India, the Dalai Lama announced the establishment of the Tibetan government in exile with two key purposes: the first was the rehabilitation of Tibetan refugees and the other was to work for the freedom movement against the CPC (The 14th Dalai Lama, 1977). According to a demographic survey conducted by the Central Tibetan Administration (CTA

M.-L. Pan (✉) · D. Tsering
National Yang Ming Chiao Tung University, Hsinchu, Taiwan
e-mail: mlpan@nycu.edu.tw

L. Momesso and P. Ivanova (eds.), *Refugees and Asylum Seekers in East Asia*, Palgrave Macmillan Studies on Human Rights in Asia,
https://doi.org/10.1007/978-981-97-2867-1_11

aka the Tibetan government in exile) in 2009, the population of Tibetans outside Tibet stood at 127,935. There were 94,203 in India, 13,514 in Nepal, 1298 in Bhutan, and 18,920 elsewhere (Office of Planning Commission, 2010, p. 13).

In 1960, upon the request of the Dalai Lama, various countries, such as Canada, Switzerland, and the United States, provided asylum for the Tibetan refugees in India and Nepal based on humanitarian reasons (Buchser, 2010; Contenta, 2010). The dispersal of Tibetan refugees outside India and Nepal began as early as 1959, with Taiwan becoming the first country to receive Tibetan refugees from India and Nepal. The first group of Tibetan refugees migrated to Taiwan in September 1959 (Liu, 1996, p. 129). Taiwan received its first group of Tibetan refugees not at the request of the Dalai Lama but due to political motives, especially those Tibetans recruited by government agencies like the Mongol and Tibet Affairs Commission (MTAC). We will discuss this in a following section. Since then, Tibetan refugees from India and Nepal have continued to enter Taiwan for various purposes including education, marriage, job opportunities, and religion. According to the data submitted by the Mongolian and Tibetan Cultural Centre as of December 2022, there were 649 Tibetans in Taiwan, 559 being citizens of Taiwan, and the rest having residence permits called Alien Residence Certificates (ARC) (Mongolian and Tibetan Cultural Centre, 2022). If we include those who do not have an ARC residency permit as well as those who do not have any connection with MTCC, then there currently will be approximately around 850 Tibetans in Taiwan.[1]

The number of Tibetans in Taiwan is usually only a few hundred, so they do not receive too much attention from the Taiwanese. Since the MTAC has been the official agency in Taiwan responsible for Tibetans, publications from commission including annual reports and policy compilation provides the historical accounts and policy guidelines about Tibetans coming to Taiwan through this agency (Hsu, 2001; Liu, 1996). In early 2000, the MTAC in collaboration with scholars

[1] The total number of registered Tibetans in Taiwan is 649 as mentioned above. In addition to this number, the Office of the Religious Foundation of the Dalai Lama, in 2022, had records of about 200 plus Tibetans in Taiwan, the majority of them being monks with Indian ICs. There are also four to five students with Indian ICs. Inshort, in addition 649, the number provided by Mongol and Tibet Culture Center, there are about 200 Tibetans with ICs. Based on these data, at the most conservative term, the total number of Tibetans in Taiwan is about 850 or more.

from academic institutions conducted survey to obtain data on the lived experience of Tibetan refugees in Taiwan through questionnaires and interviews. The resulting two reports help us to understand the various challenges encountered by Tibetan refugees living in Taiwan at that time (Shen & Chen, 2005; Zhang et al., 2002).

Okawa (2007) observed that Tibetan refugees have been in an invisible situation in Taiwan. He studied Tibetans in Taiwan through two political stages: the ideology of Chinese nationalism and democratisation. According to the time when Tibetan refugees came to Taiwan, he divided them into six categories, emphasising that Tibetan refugees are not a homogeneous group in Taiwan. Okawa placed the history of Tibetans coming to Taiwan in the context of world politics, and emphasised the importance of continued attention on this issue.

Pan (2015) adopts the perspective of international human rights and uses the concept of "double liminality" to explain the particularity of Tibetan refugees in Taiwan. She points out that the Taiwan government neither treats Tibetan refugees in Taiwan as compatriots nor accepts their status as refugees, reflecting the ambiguity of the identity of Taiwan. Placed in this double liminal status, exiled Tibetan refugees in Taiwan have been discriminated against and have been denied their entitlement to human rights (Pan, 2015). The policy of denying residence to Tibetan refugees holding Indian Identity Certificates (ICs) lacks human rights considerations, while the certificate is recognised by many countries as a valid travel document (Pan, 2023).

These studies illustrate the particularity of Tibetans in Taiwan and why they deserve attention. However, the lived experiences of Tibetans in Taiwan are usually only reported by newspapers and magazines, or by a single group, such as Taiwanese-Tibetan families in Taiwan (Kung et al., 2020; Pan, 2016), which cannot provide a whole picture of the lived experience of Tibetan refugees in Taiwan.

This chapter examines the experiences of Tibetan refugees living in Taiwan, focusing particularly on Tibetans' rights to work, live, and hold Taiwanese citizenship. The first section explains the history of Tibetan refugees' migration from Nepal and India to Taiwan. In the second section, the chapter looks at Tibetan lives in Taiwan during three distinct periods. The final section examines human rights issues facing Tibetan refugees, and shows how Taiwan's changing politics has been a key factor in determining Tibetan refugees' rights, and their status in Taiwan.

Data were collected from personal experiences, interviews with authors, and existing scholarship available as secondary sources. The archives and research reports published by the MTAC provided important information for understanding the policies. Different experiences were analysed and presented through various case studies and authors choose these cases based on their time of arrival in Taiwan as well as to reflect the different phases. To protect the personal information and privacy of our interviewees, pseudonyms are used throughout the chapter to present the various case studies.

Historical Connection of Tibetan Refugees to Taiwan

The relationship between Taiwan and Tibetan refugees began after the CPC's occupation of Tibet and the Kuomintang (KMT) relocated to Taiwan. In Taiwan, the Kuomintang reinstated the ROC (Republic of China) government, along with its historical claim over Tibet. Subsequently, the MTAC continued its function to affirm the historical claims over Tibet.[2] According to MTAC websites, it aims:

> To defend the aim of the ROC constitution, ensure the equal status of various ethnic groups, promote the regional autonomy of Mongolia and Tibet, enhance the economic and educational reforms in Mongolia and Tibet, foster Mongolian and Tibetan cultures, and respect their religious beliefs and social customs, in the hope of achieving harmonious ethnic relationships and protecting the ROC's sovereignty. (MTAC, 2011)

The MTAC, therefore, served as an important channel for allowing Tibetan refugees to move to Taiwan. It also operated as an institution under the Executive Yuan, the highest administrative organ in Taiwan, making the MTAC responsible for managing Tibet and Tibetan affairs in Taiwan until it was transformed into the Mongol and Tibet Culture Center (MTCC) with the abolishment of the Organisational Act of the

[2] Qing Dynasty established Mongol and Tibet Affairs bureau to handle the issue related to Tibet and Mongolia. The ROC succeeded it and transformed it into Mongol and Tibet Affairs Commission. After relocated to Taiwan, it reestablished various former government bodies and the MTAC was one of them.

MTAC in 2017 (Laws and Regulations Database of the Republic of China [Taiwan], 2017; Ministry of Culture, Republic of China, 2017).

In the late 1950s, the KMT government in Taiwan proposed that several Tibetan resistance force leaders from Kham and Amdo, who had become refugees in India, relocate to Taiwan (Gyari, 2022, p. 121). Since then, different kinds of Tibetan refugees, such as resistance forces, students, monks, and Tibetan government officials from India and Nepal, have migrated to Taiwan and continue to travel to Taiwan. The historical trajectories of Tibetan refugees in Taiwan can be divided into three phases reflecting Taiwan's transformation from authoritarian to democratic governance.

The first phase, lasting from 1959 to the mid-1980s, is characterised by the authoritarian regime. This is an era in which Chinese nationalist ideology was espoused. Two agendas largely dominated Taiwan's national interest during this period, one was to defeat the CPC and unify China, and another one was to preserve the ROC-Taiwan as the only legitimate ruler of China.

The second phase, characterised by economic and political transformation, began in the mid-1980s and lasted until the end of the 1990s. During this period, in light of the realisation that recovering and unifying mainland China was unfeasible, the government abandoned its military focus and the political ideology of unifying China, and shifted towards strengthening the economic prosperity of the island. In these years, a major democratic transition occurred, involving the lifting of martial law, and the legalisation of the right to freely form political parties and to directly vote for the president. In the meantime, Taiwan's manufacturing sector grew, which created a demand for foreign labour. While facing dramatic political, economic, and social change, Taiwan had to renounce many outdated laws and enact laws to cope with the new reality, such as enacting the Employment Service Act to incorporate foreign workers and the implementation of Immigration Law. The economic and political transformation evolving in Taiwan had a direct impact on Taiwan's approach, attitude, and policy towards Tibetan refugees in India and Nepal. Before the Dalai Lama's visit in 1997, Taiwan and the CTA shared hostile relations resulting from the MTAC's pursuit of policy and activities that challenged the legitimacy of the CTA. For instance, as we discuss in the following section, the MTAC recruited Tibetan refugees from India and Nepal to Taiwan and propagated them as Tibetan ethnic minority representatives of the ROC-Taiwan. A condition that helped with the reconciliation was Lee Tung-hui's agreement with the Dalai Lama that the MTAC would not be involved in the further development of Taiwan and CTA relations (Su & Wei, 2012, p. 186).

The third phase began in the early 2000s and has continued to the present time. It is defined as the era of post-democratic transformation. The Democratic Progressive Party that won the election in 2000 did not abide by the political ideology and claims of the KMT. In 2000, Chen Shui-bian of the Democratic Progressive Party was elected as the president, becoming the first elected president from an opposition party. Compared with the KMT's consistent policy of treating Tibet as an inalienable part of China, the Democratic Progressive Party advocates for the recognition of Tibet's independence and right to self-determination, and also does not recognise Tibetan refugees as overseas Chinese (President Office of the ROC, 2003). In 2003, to strengthen ties with the CTA, the DPP government established the Taiwan and Tibet Exchange Foundation. It was meant to replace the MTAC, however, due to its constitutional link, the MTAC could not be abolished. From 2003 to 2008, until the election of the KMT government in 2008, the Taiwan and Tibet Exchange Foundation played a central role in engaging with the CTA. Another important change witnessed during the Chen Shui-bian period was that Tibetan refugees from India and Nepal could directly apply for visas from the Ministry of Foreign Affairs without the support of the MTAC. Considering that Taiwan does have a refugee law and the majority of Tibetans who migrated to Taiwan during this period were those with Indian ICs, Tibetans faced the situation of not being able to secure rights to residence and work. They encountered more challenges than people in the previous two phases.

In short, Tibetan refugees in India and Nepal have been migrating to Taiwan for over 60 years. The lived experiences of Tibetans in Taiwan, especially in the context of rights to residence, work, and citizenship, are different in these three phases, based on Taiwan government policy towards Tibet and Tibetan refugees. In the following section, we will examine how Tibetan refugees have been treated differently as compatriots, cheap labour, and stateless people, in each of the phases.

Lived Experiences of Tibetans in Taiwan Based on Three Different Phases

First Phase, 1949–mid-1980s: Tibetan Refugees as Compatriots

During the era of the authoritarian regime, with its Chinese nationalist ideology, three sets of Tibetan refugees entered Taiwan via two prominent institutions: the KMT's Intelligence Bureau and the MTAC. Their arrival in Taiwan was driven by a larger political motive to defeat the CPC and to assert Taiwan's ROC sovereignty over Tibet.

1. Members of the Tibetan resistance force

Soon after the Tibetan uprising on 10 March 1959, President Chiang Kai-shek issued a letter to Tibetan compatriots titled "Message to Tibetan Compatriots" (*Gao Xizang Tongbao Shu*), which outlined Taiwan's policy towards Tibetan refugees in India. The letter reads as follows:

> You are now shedding your blood in fighting against the Communist tyranny. Although I am now in Taiwan, my heart has been always with you in your war against Communism. The Government of the Republic of China is making every possible effort to give you continuous and effective aid.
> The Government of the Republic of China has always respected Tibet's traditional political and social organisation and guaranteed the freedom of religious belief and traditional life of the Tibetan people. I would now like to solemnly declare that Tibet's future political system and political status will be fulfilled by our government based on the principle of self-determination of its people. (Chin, 1984, pp. 222–223)

The letter confirmed that the KMT in Taiwan had not given up the policy of claiming sovereignty rights over Tibet. Following the letter, Taiwan launched a programme called "Support the Tibetan Resistance Movement against the CPC" and started mobilising resources and the general public to extend support for the Tibetan resistance movement. Upon the invitation of the KMT's Intelligent Bureau, in September 1959, Taiwan received the first group of Tibetan refugees from India. These included, Chama Samphe, his wife Dolkar and their three daughters, and Mingyur Rinpoche's assistant Thinley Phuntsok, and Asha (Liu, 1996, pp. 129–130). The Taiwanese government chose this group because its members were connected with the Tibetan resistance force (*Chushi*

Gangdruk). For instance, Chama Samphe was one of the former administrative heads of the resistance force. Mingyur Rinpoche was an influential Buddhist master from Kham-Lithang,[3] the place with the largest membership of the Tibetan resistance forces. The KMT extended invitations to them solely because of their affinity with the Tibetan resistance force (The Welfare Society of Dhokham Chushi Gangdru, 2022, p. 110.)

The KMT hoped to use them to influence guerrilla operations undertaken by the resistance force in Nepal (Okawa, 2007). After their arrival, Chama Samphe was offered the position of Major General within the Taiwan army and Taiwan also established a branch office of the Tibetan resistance force in Taiwan (Lin, 1999). Whether the group was efficient in helping Taiwan against the CPC is not known but their arrival had high propaganda value for the KMT.

2. Frontier Cadre Training Class

In 1961, following the first group, the KMT initiated Project "National Glory" (*Guoguang*) which was a secret guerrilla war plan against the CPC. As part of the project, it launched a secret operation to recruit Tibetans from India and Nepal under the programme called Frontier Cadre Training Class (Liu, 1996). A total of 32 Tibetans were recruited for this particular programme. The government abandoned the secret operation in 1970 after many failures, and trainees were allowed to join various government units. Among 32 trainees, only ten remained in Taiwan; some of them returned to Tibet and some returned to India (Wu, 1999). Some of them continued to work as secret service agents for the Taiwan government in India and Nepal (Wu, 1999). Many of them has passed on and one of them, aged 87, lives with his Taiwanese family (Pseudonym, personal communication, December 22, 2022).

3. Tibetan Children's Home

By the end of the 1960s, it was becoming more apparent that the KMT's ambition to defeat the CPC was not realistic. The KMT had to terminate Project National Glory; however, it remained committed to the

[3] Tibet traditionally has three regions; U-Tsang, Kham, and Amdo. Lithang is part of Kham region, with the Tibetan resistance force originally being founded by a famous trader from Lithang. As a result, many of the resistance forces were from Lithang.

Chinese nationalist ideology, holding that the ROC (Taiwan) is the legitimate ruler of China. This led to a shift in the approach towards Tibetan refugees. The Taiwanese government started a new project of educating the younger generation of Tibetan refugees in Taiwan as part of a larger project to create ethnic cadres in Taiwan. In 1970, it implemented a programme titled "Cultivating Next-generation Tibetan Ethnic Cadres". According to the MTAC:

> Tibet and Mongolia, given their distinct culture, religion, and ethnic identity, and principally due to geographical location, remained isolated from the rest of China. Therefore, recruiting more ethnic cadres from these regions is crucial to integrating and unifying the country. It further asserted that 'these young children must not only learn about their own inherent culture but should learn about national (Chinese-the KMT) history and language'. (MTAC, 1971, p. 152)

The project was initially undertaken by the China Mainland Famine Relief Association and only dozens of young Tibetans joined as students in the programme. However, the project was discontinued in 1978 because many students did not want to remain in Taiwan and could not master the Chinese language (Liu, 1996, p. 164). The government realised that it would be easier for children to start learning the Chinese language from a younger age. The project was transferred from the China Mainland Famine Relief Association to the MTAC. In 1980, the MTAC implemented a project called the Tibetan Children's Home. From 1980 to 1992, about 107 Tibetan refugee children from India and Nepal took part in this project. According to the programme, once a student was accepted, all of his or her expenses were guaranteed, including cost-of-living fees, educational fees from primary school through college, and a round-trip ticket to return home every four years. Through this project, on the one hand, the government aimed to enable more Tibetan children to receive a complete modern education in a stable society and to help them maintain traditional Tibetan culture and religious beliefs; on the other hand, through such a programme, the Taiwanese government aimed to foster nationalistic feelings amongst members of Tibet's younger generation, so that they would identify with the ROC and so that Taiwan could use these educated ethnic cadres to disseminate Taiwan's influence among Tibetans in exile, as well as in a future Tibet (Liu, 1996, pp. 164–165).

An interview report published by *Taiwan Panorama*, a bilingual magazine run by Taiwan's government, presents the living conditions of the children who came to the Taiwan as apart of the Tibetan Children's Home at that time,

> These Tibetan children range from six to fourteen years old. They go to school, watch TV cartoons, and go to parks and children's playgrounds on holidays, like ordinary children in Taiwan. In addition, they also learn Tibetan and recite Buddhist scriptures ...
>
> Exposed to a new world that is rich in variety and with lots of things to do and see, these children's little hearts are full of wonderful excitement, but their hearts are also sometimes heavy when they think of their parents far away. "Sometimes when we get homesick, we hug each other and cry", says one little fellow. "But you get used to it after a while". (Hsu, 1981)

Parents sent their children to Taiwan with the hope that their children could get a better education, and most of the parents who sent their children were economically less privileged (Pseudonym personal communication, March 28, 2021). However, these children were thousands of miles away from their parents and lived in a different linguistic and cultural environment. Although the aim was to pursue a better life, these Tibetan children who grew up in Taiwan often had a lonely and painful childhood, and developed feelings of alienation (Shen & Chen, 2005, pp. 27, 124). They felt alienated both from Taiwanese and Tibetan communities because of a lack of language proficiency and due to their different physical appearance (Pseudonym personal communication, December 22, 2022).

Tibetan refugees recruited during this phase were treated as compatriots and were provided with Taiwan nationality cards because the government in both principle and practice endorsed a policy of Tibet as part of China (ROC). The project was implemented without support from the CTA. As a result, a credibility gap was created, along with a hostile relationship between Taiwan and the CTA. The CTA criticised the MTAC for manipulating poor Tibetans and buying their influence through such a programme (Tethong, 2006). Parents of these children also faced severe criticism from the Tibetan refugee community in India because of their alliances with the MTAC. A Tibetan in Nepal revealed that in the 1970s and 1980s, the MTAC officers would visit Nepal and offer to relocate Tibetans to Taiwan because they were part of the ROC and, as such, were citizens of the ROC-Taiwan (Chiu, 2023). However, this was not the case later when the MTAC launched a programme of vocational training, discussed in the next section (Pseudonym, personal communication, April 28, 2023). Therefore, the MTAC's efforts to advocate for Tibet as part of the ROC were more aggressive during the first phase.

The TCH project was not successful because many children were not able to master the Chinese language and did not perform well academically, except when studying the English language because it was easier to learn. Moreover, children also suffered discrimination and bullying at school because of their appearance and their lack of proficiency in the Chinese language. In addition, many children also forgot the Tibetan language and gave up on their education, which ended up with them joining the low-skilled workforce in Taiwan (Shen & Chen, 2005, p. 1). Since the overall outcome did not meet the original expectation, the project was discontinued by 1992 (Liu, 1996, pp. 167–168). Some of the students returned to India and Nepal while some continued to work in factories and the construction sector, and some graduated from university. They were treated as overseas Chinese and through the overseas Chinese scheme they were able to obtain Taiwan citizenship after arriving in Taiwan.

Second Phase mid-1980s–1990s: Tibetan Refugees as Cheap Labour

During this phase, the MTAC was still a major formal channel for Tibetans in exile to migrate to Taiwan, but the motives of Tibetan refugees migrating to Taiwan during this phase were more focused on economic rather than political reasons. Taiwan was also going through a major political and economic transformation, including the change from an authoritarian to a democratic system.

1. Vocational training programme

In 1983, the MTAC started a project called "Tibetan and Nepalese returning to home country for vocational training program". The primary purpose of this project was to help Tibetan refugees in India and Nepal gain some skills and training that could eventually help them secure a job or pursue entrepreneurial opportunities in India and Nepal.

Even though the Taiwanese government continued to use Chinese nationalist ideology rhetoric such as "returning to the home country" and identified Tibetans as "overseas Tibetans" or "Chinese minority nationalities", it stopped providing citizenship for Tibetan refugees as it had done in the first phase (Liu, 1996, pp. 187–188). The government issued a regulation titled "Items governing the occupational training for Tibetan youths emigrated from India and Nepal", which clearly stated the changed status of Tibetans in Taiwan. For instance, the Ministry of the Interior was no longer in charge of matters concerning ethnic minorities, including Tibetan refugees. The selected candidate's application for training was to be forwarded to the Ministry of Foreign Affairs (MFA), which would issue a visitor visa. The items also mentioned that the duration of the course should not be longer than one year at the most. After finishing the course, trainees must return to India or Nepal within one week, and they were not eligible to apply for long-term residence in Taiwan under any circumstances (Hsu, 2001, pp. 134–135). The government also abolished the "regulation of applying for the overseas certificate" which could potentially help them apply for long-term residence or for the Taiwan national identity card. With this, the government stopped treating Tibetan refugees as Chinese nationals but as foreigners (Mongolian and Tibetan Affairs Commission, 2011).

In 1983, MTAC received the first batch of six Tibetans from Nepal for a car repair course, joined by a second batch in the same year for a cooking course (Hsu, 2001, pp. 134–135). The duration of the first sixteen batches was limited only to three months, and was later extended to six months and then to one year. From 1983 to 1989, 235 Tibetans over 16 years old, from India and Nepal, entered Taiwan via this vocational training programme (Liu, 1996, pp. 186–191). Gradually, when labour shortages became a serious concern in Taiwan in the 1990s, the MTAC started providing internships after training was completed. Consequently, the training period was extended up to one year or more. From 1990 to 1993, in batches 17–20, 179 trainees were sent to work in various factories. These internship programmes were aimed at helping the government with the labour shortage problem and also at helping Tibetans earn money to start businesses in India or Nepal. In 1992, the government announced the Employment Service Act and, according to the regulation,

MTAC's internship programme did not meet requirements.[4] Tibetan refugees working in factories through the internship programme become illegal. The MTAC found it hard to sustain the internship programme and had to end it that year (Liu, 1996, pp. 192–194).

However, some Tibetan trainees, after completing the training programme and working in factories, refused to return to India and Nepal and stayed in Taiwan in the hope that they could seek asylum there. There were several cases where Tibetan refugees were forced to become illegal residents because the MTAC had collected their passports after they landed in Taiwan and, when it was returned to them after completion of the course, their visa had already expired (Taiwan Association for Human Rights, 1999; Zhang et al., 2002, p. 63). Some, furthermore, went on to accuse the MTAC of forcing them to come to Taiwan with fake promises to provide jobs and citizenship (Shen & Chen, 2005, p. 18). There are also the some cases where MTAC rejected Tibetan requests to return to India due to labour exploitation.

Tsering was a farmer in one of the Tibetan settlements in South India. He came to Taiwan in 1989 with his wife, together with 40 other Tibetans, to join the vocational programme. After completing some training, he and his wife were sent to a glass factory in Hsinchu to work. They had no experience of working in a factory and did not speak any Chinese language. They worked long hours at hundreds of degrees Celsius making glass, earning 7000 NT dollars each as a monthly salary. At that time, a young Tibetan woman died suddenly by accident in the factory. This incident caused panic among Tibetan workers, plus there were some Tibetans who also got sick because of the poor environment at the workplace. Tsering and other Tibetans did not want to continue working in the factory anymore and wanted to go back to India. When the MTAC rejected their request, they decided to escape the factory together (Pseudonym, personal communication, February 13, 2011).

During those years, Taiwan's economy was booming, and factories were facing labour shortages. The government opened up Taiwan to foreign labour to solve the problem. The situation was favourable for Tibetans looking for another job as there was high demand for labour in Taiwan. Tsering and his wife easily found another job at a motor factory.

[4] The Employment Service Act defines only nationals, foreigners, and mainlanders as being eligible to be employed in Taiwan. The government does not include Tibetan refugees from India and Nepal in any of these categories.

They worked ten hour and could earn up to 800 NT dollars a day. This income was much better than for farming in India. They lived in the factory's hostel and seldom went out because they feared that the police might catch them and send them back to India. They did not have any residence permit documents. Therefore, they wanted to make the most of their time in Taiwan to earn money so that they could send their children to a better school to study (Pseudonym, personal communication, February 13, 2011).

Those overstayed Tibetans had found their way to survive and make money in Taiwan. However, for the Tibetan community in exile, coming to Taiwan with the MTAC was not a sanctioned act and so they were labelled as traitors (Tsering, 2022). Even though there were good economic opportunities in Taiwan, the burden of being despised also weighed heavily on Tibetan refugees.

2. Working illegally in Taiwan

When the MTAC stopped the vocational programme, the official channel for Tibetans coming to Taiwan to work in factories was also closed. However, in 1997, Taiwan's first democratically elected president, Lee Teng-hui, bypassed the MTAC and invited the Dalai Lama to Taiwan through "The Buddhist Association of the Republic of China". On this occasion, the Taiwanese people's courtesy and respect for the Dalai Lama contributed to changing the Tibetan exiles' perception of Taiwan from suspicion to trust. This reversed the image of Tibetans in Taiwan amongst the exile community (Bawa, 2020, p. 43). On 16 April 1998, the CTA established the office of Religious Foundation of the Dalai Lama in Taipei, which was a concrete political achievement resulting from the Dalai Lama's visit to Taiwan (Tsering, 2022). In addition, the visit of the Dalai Lama to Taiwan also washed away the stigma of those Tibetans who came to Taiwan through the MTAC. The improvement of the relationship between the Taiwan government and CTA created the illusion that Tibetan refugees could just take tourist visas to work in Taiwan and earn money (Tashi, 1997, pp. 80–81).

Inspired by the Dalai Lama's visit to Taiwan, Tsering and other overstayed Tibetans appealed to the MTAC and the Taiwan government for citizenship rights. In 1999, with the help of the Taiwan Association for Human Rights, Tibetans who had overstayed their visas came to the

MTAC to deliver their petition and to ask the MTAC to keep their promise of citizenship, which was long overdue. The petition reads as follows:

> From 1989 to 1992, MTAC officials came to South India, North India, and Nepal to recruit Tibetan refugees to work in Taiwan. They explicitly said that 'if you wish to come to Taiwan, we will arrange everything for you, including passports. In Taiwan, we will find a job for each of you and help you apply for ID cards with permanent residency'. So we left our parents and family, with only a passport (that was given by the MTAC) and an immigration certificate in hand, and a dream of a better life in Taiwan. At that time, only a few of us were told to take the training programme here. Most of us were informed that we would have a good job and live a better life. The MTAC even promised to grant us ROC ID cards. However, our passports and immigration certificates were taken away by the MTAC after arriving in Taiwan. We were sent to factories to work in poor conditions. From then on, we became cheap labourers and lived an ambiguous life in Taiwan.
>
> Although we did not have nationality in India or Nepal, we were refugees and at least were admitted as legal foreigners. In Taiwan, however, we are neither citizens of Taiwan nor refugees, and at worse we became illegal. We cannot go back to our family in India or Nepal because we have no passports. Thus, we are trapped and have had to live the past decade in fear and with no protection. We can only do odd jobs; we cannot ask for medical help even when we need it; we are afraid of the police in the streets, as we cannot explain to people our absurd situation. We cannot seriously develop a relationship because having a legal marriage under such circumstances is impossible (Taiwan Association for Human Rights, 1999).

In 2001, 139 Tibetans received Taiwan's ID with the help of local human rights organisations and official legislators (Hsu, 2001). The Dalai Lama, during his second visit to Taiwan in 2001, also appealed to President Chen Shui-bian about these Tibetans. Although protests and petitions solved the legal problem of Tibetans in Taiwan at that time, it caused misunderstanding among Tibetan refugees that they could come to Taiwan to work and earn money. Some people even borrowed money to apply for passports to come to Taiwan through a human trafficking ring (Shen & Chen, 2005). After they arrived in Taiwan, they often found out that the reality was not what they had imagined. It turned out that they were trapped in Taiwan, living a life hiding from the police by holding fake passports or overstaying (Shen & Chen, 2005) (Pseudonym, personal communication, May 12, 2023).

Tibetan refugees did not have the required qualifications for higher-skilled jobs. Although it was easy for them to find work in factories, it was difficult for them to negotiate better wages or benefits because they were illegal workers. Tibetan workers were often mistaken for foreign workers or aboriginals due to their appearance, and were assigned to rough or dangerous jobs (Shen & Chen, 2005, p. 90).

Kalsang's working experience in Taiwan is a typical case among Tibetans in the 1990s. He was born in India and his parents sold sweaters during the winter in an Indian city. He helped with his parents' business before coming to Taiwan. After the Dalai Lama's first visit to Taiwan in 1997, Kalsang came to Taiwan in 1998 with an Indian passport bought on the black market and 600 US dollars. His first job was in a textile factory introduced to him by a Tibetan he knew in Taiwan. However, he found it too difficult to keep up with the pace of the other workers and quit on the first day. He then worked in another factory but had to leave because the police came to check. Finally, he worked in another textile factory and earned 30,000 NT dollars a month(Pseudonym, personal communication, February 25, 2011).

In Kalsang's experience, Tibetan refugees are amongst the hardest-working group in the factory compared to other foreign workers from South Asian countries. Kalsang said, "This is not because Tibetans are necessarily more diligent, but because we are working illegally. I never know when I will be caught, so I try my best to make money every day" (Pseudonym, personal communication, February 25, 2011). Fortunately, Kalsang was able to obtain a Taiwan ID in 2001 with the help of a petition group in 1999[5] (Pan, 2015, pp. 50–52).

After getting the Taiwan ID, the 139 Tibetans could finally live without fear and with no need to hide when working in Taiwan. While

[5] In December 2008, another group of Tibetans came forward to turn themselves into the police. This group was composed of runaway Tibetans who were not part of the petition group in 1999 due to poor dissemination of information. These overstayed Tibetans came to Taiwan with tourist visas or fake IDs from India and Nepal. This group of Tibetans was not as fortunate as the group in 1999. There were some new regulations in applying for ROC citizenship, and this group of Tibetans was treated as foreigners in having to obtain an ARC. To obtain ROC ID, they had to provide evidence that they had stayed for 183 days in Taiwan per year for more than five consecutive years or more (Pan, 2015, pp. 50–52).

Tibetan refugees had been actively seeking visas or legal residency in Taiwan, the MFA pointed out that the situation of Tibetans staying in Taiwan illegally was becoming quite serious, had "reached the level of threatening border security and social peace" (Merit Times, 2007), and violated the original intention of the policy of lenience towards Tibetans. The government at the time was compelled to re-examine the applicable laws for Tibetans coming to Taiwan (Merit Times, 2007).

Third Phase, 2000–Present: Tibetan Refugees as Stateless People

The third wave of Tibetan refugee migration to Taiwan occurred in the post-democratic reform period. The experiences of Tibetans who migrated to Taiwan during this period were different from those who migrated during the first two phases, mainly because of the changed political situation in Taiwan. This phase had a number of distinct features. First the great majority of Tibetans travelled to Taiwan without the involvement of the MTAC. This meant that they were not recruited by the MTAC and there was no political agenda behind their migration to Taiwan. Second, instead of using fake Indian and Nepal passports, they travelled using ICs issued by the Indian government. Third, since the Dalai Lama's first visit to Taiwan, there was a new demand for Tibetan Buddhist masters (Fraser, 2018). The total number of Tibetan Buddhist centres increased from 82 in 1996 to 473 in 2018. Also, the total number of Tibetan Buddhist followers increased to approximately half a million (Own, 2018, pp. 3–4). The numbers of Taiwanese visiting Dharamsala, headquarters of the CTA and the Dalai Lama's residence in exile, for both religious and other purposes such as tourism, also increased, and, as a result, there were growing cases of transnational marriage between Taiwanese and Tibetan refugees. The Director of the Dalai Lama's Office in Dharamsala disclosed that every year for the Dalai Lama's teaching, about 1000–1500 Tibetan Buddhist followers from Taiwan visit Dharamsala (T. Ngawa, personal communication, October 19, 2020). Earlier on, visits to Dharamsala from Taiwan were only limited to a few officers from the MTAC (Tethong, 2006). In addition to monks and marriage migrants, there are a few students from India who have also migrated to Taiwan for educational purposes (D. Tsering, personal communication, January 11, 2020). Therefore, in the post-democratic transformation period, Tibetan migration to Taiwan largely constitutes monks, marriage migrants, and students.

Although Tibetan refugees can visit Taiwan with an IC, the Taiwan government has tightened its borders for the migration of Tibetan refugees. When the KMT regained power in the presidential election of 2008, the government amended the "Regulations Governing Visiting, Residency, and Permanent Residency of Aliens" (RGVRPR): The new Article 6 of the residency regulation stated that

> Stateless persons who entered Taiwan with a visitor visa may not apply for residency. If a particular individual holds a valid visa whose duration of stay is at least 60 days and has not been prohibited from extending the duration of stay or any other restriction, or has special circumstances verified by other government agencies commissioned by competent authorities, then this individual shall not be excluded. (Ministry of Interior, 2008)

With this resolution, the status of Tibetan refugees was reduced from foreigner to stateless. With the exception of staff members of the office of the religious foundation of the Dalai Lama, visitor visas that are issued to Tibetans with ICs, and also some with Indian and Nepalese citizenship, contain an additional note which states that the visa cannot be changed to other visas such as those for residence or work. This means that Tibetan refugees in Taiwan cannot have the right to apply for a residence permit, which causes complex problems while living in Taiwan (Pan, 2023). In this section, we will illuminate those challenges.

1. Tibetan refugee students in Taiwan:

We explore the challenges that Tibetan refugee students face in Taiwan through a personal experience shared by one of the authors of this chapter. We use the auto-ethnography[6] method to reflect on Taiwan's immigration process and law related to Tibetan refugees who hold Indian ICs.

After completing my PhD degree in India, I obtained a scholarship from an NGO in Taiwan for studying the Chinese language. I visited the Taiwan Economic and Culture Center in New Delhi for a visa application.

[6] It is a research method that involves critical observation of a personal or individual experience and connecting those experiences to study a particular situation or broader political, cultural, or social concept. More about the method (Reed-Danahay, 2009).

The office denied my application, reasoning that study visas are not applicable for IC holders according to Article 6 of the residency regulations. Of course, there is no guideline available on government websites about Tibetan refugees seeking to travel to Taiwan for education purposes.

Fortunately, I have a friend who had earlier faced the same problem. With their help, I contacted the Taiwan and Tibet Human Rights Networks (TTHRN), an NGO that works advocating for human rights in Tibet and Taiwan. The NGO helps students connect with legislative members in Taiwan who are willing to help Tibetan refugees. The legislative member will issue a letter of guarantee stating he/she will be responsible for students while in Taiwan. This letter of guarantee is used by the NGO to apply for a visa for Tibetan refugee students at the MFA. Based on the letter of guarantee, the MFA will issue a visitor visa. If the MFA accepts the visa application, the office will notify the applicant, in this case the legislative member, and will provide the visa number. After securing the visa number, the student can visit the Taiwan's Taiwan Economic and Culture Center residency in Delhi to apply for a visa. The problem here is while some students are aware of the TTHRN, many are not. Therefore, those who do not have an opportunity to contact the TTHRN fail to obtain the visa. During one conversation, a Tibetan student in Taiwan revealed that he wasted six months on a visa application as he was not aware of the TTHRN. The TECC does not provide any clear guidelines on how to process the visa application, and does not give reasons for declining a visa (Pseudonym, personal communication, June 12, 2020).

After securing a visitor visa with the help of the TTHRN, I was able to join a Chinese language class. Generally, after three months in Taiwan, foreigners are eligible to apply for an ARC residence permit, which provides, in addition to a one-year residence permit, access to the government's healthcare service, which is probably one of the most affordable healthcare services in the world (Numbeo, 2019). An ARC also allows the foreign student the right to take a part-time job and it serves as an identification certificate for foreigners in Taiwan. However, the visitor visa that I obtained had a note stating "This visa is not changeable for a resident visa". Based on Article 6 of the residency regulations, I am not eligible for the right to residency and consequently I am not allowed to have a part-time job and do not have access to affordable medical insurance provided by the government.

Additionally, regardless of the duration of the language programme, I was eligible only for six months visa, which meant I had to leave Taiwan every six months and come back with a new visa. This costs me about 3000 US dollars every year only in travel expenses. Therefore, for people like me, the Covid pandemic was a blessing in disguise because, after the closure of the border, I did not have to leave Taiwan every six months. This saved me huge amount of travel expenses and meant I could avoid another lengthy bureaucratic process in India for exit permits to travel outside India. However, the Covid pandemic left stateless people like me among Taiwan's most vulnerable groups of foreigners. The ARC, residence permit was a prerequisite for foreigners seeking to apply for vaccines and even for Covid tests. Taiwan's government later used the Unique Identity number to allow foreigners without an residence permit to apply for a Covid vaccine, but it was delayed for the first few months of the Covid pandemic outbreak.

After completing two years of Chinese language courses, I joined National Cheng Kung University as post-doctoral researcher. Even after the Ministry of Labour provided me with a work permit, the immigration office and the Ministry of Foreign Affairs denied me residence permit, reasoning that I was stateless. After several months petitioning various institutions, such as Executive Yuan, the MFA, and the immigration office, with the help of the CTA representative office in Taiwan and legislative members, I became the first Tibetan refugee who was not an employee of the CTA to be able to work in Taiwan with both a work permit and an ARC residence permit.

2. Tibetan refugee monks in Taiwan: The case of Geshe Tenzin

In contrast to Tibetan refugee students, the Taipei Economic and Culture Center provides clear guidelines for the application of visas for Tibetan monks (Bureau of Consular Affairs of the Ministry of Foreign Affairs, ROC-Taiwan, 2023). However, they are entitled only to a two to three months visa. This means, regardless of the duration of their religious activities in Taiwan, every two months Tibetan refugee monks should leave Taiwan and come back with a new visa. They are also not eligible to apply for the residence permit. Additionally, monks should go for a visa interview that is not required for other applicants like students.

Geshe Tenzin (Tenzin, personal communication, April 25, 2023) entered Taiwan with an IC in early 2016 to take part in religious teaching organised by a Taiwanese-Tibetan Buddhist centre. Since then, he continued to receive invitations from various centres and has been living in Taiwan with a visitor visa that is valid only for two to three months. This means that every two months, he has to leave Taiwan and come back with a new visa. Generally, he travelled to Thailand because it was cheaper and because this did not require an exit permit from the Indian government, which in itself takes about two months to obtain. It was financially difficult for Geshe to travel five or six times a year, and also sometimes caused psychological distress.

As a consequence of these visa troubles, Geshe applied for an Indian passport in 2019 after surrendering his registration certificate (aka refugee certificate) and IC issued by the Indian government. Geshe hoped that after obtaining Indian citizenship, he would be able to apply for an residence permit as a foreigner, but the government refused to give him a residence permit. Geshe continued to face similar problems those of stateless Tibetans in Taiwan.

Taiwan has already granted resident visas for other religious practitioners but Tibetan monks with Indian, Nepalese, and Bhutanese citizenships continue to face the same challenges as stateless citizens (Bureau of Consular Affairs, Ministry of Foreign Affairs, ROC [Taiwan], 2017). On 6 June 2023, Tibetan monks launched a press conference which called for the Taiwan government's fair treatment of Tibetan Buddhist monks (Taiwan International Tibetan Buddhist Association, 2023). American Institute in Taiwan publishes annual reports about human rights in Taiwan and unfair treatment of Tibetan monks was mentioned as one of the issues (American Institute in Taiwan, 2019).

3. Taiwan-Tibet transnational marriage: The case of Tsai Yung-ching and Lhundup Tsering

In November 2020, a group of non-governmental organisations in Taiwan including the TTHRN, Students for a Free Tibet (Taiwan), and the Association of Visual Arts in Taiwan, organised a talk that discussed transnational marriage between Tibetan refugees and Taiwanese.[7] The main speaker Tsai Yung-ching, a documentary filmmaker, married her Tibetan husband Lhundup Tsering. She visited Dharamsala in 2004 to interview the Dalai Lama. Tsai made her second visit to India in 2005 and met her future husband, Lhundup Tsering, who was living in India as a refugee. After their marriage in 2008, Tsai Yung-Ching and Lhundup Tsering were preparing to relocate to Taiwan; however, because of his status as "stateless", Lhundup Tsering was only able to acquire a visitor visa to Taiwan, which allowed him to stay with his family for only six months a year. The lack of a right to residential status for Tibetan refugee spouses triggered a forceful separation of the family (Pan, 2016).

In 2011, Tsai, along with twelve other Taiwanese-Tibetan families, formed the Taiwan-Tibet Family Human Rights Alliance (Taiwanese and Tibetan Family Rights Association, n.d.), and started petitioning for residential rights for Tibetan spouses. In July 2012, the government set up guidelines for the review of applications filed by Tibetan spouses who hold Indian ICs, to allow them to apply for residency under certain conditions. The conditions that holders of Indian ICs must meet to qualify for this type of visa were: being in a registered marriage of at least three years and having been in the country for more than 183 days in each of the three most recent years. Those who have biological children in Taiwan only needed to meet a two-year condition.[8]

After seven years of petitions and demonstrations, the Executive Yuan repealed the regulation for Tibetan spouses with Indian ICs in 2017 (Immigration Services, Ministry of Interior, ROC-Taiwan, 2017). Finally, Tibetan refugee spouses in Taiwan were eligible to apply for the ARC and, after staying in Taiwan continuously for three years, could apply for citizenship. It was originally a right enjoyed by foreign spouses in Taiwan, but it took a long time for Taiwan and Tibetan families to obtain it (Kung et al., 2020; Pan, 2016).

[7] Dolma Tsering took part in the talk and later published a report of the talk (Tsering, 2020).

[8] The Executive Yuan has stipulated the "Joint Review Guidelines of the Application of Residence by Tibetan Spouse with Indian IC Married with Taiwanese" to deal with the problem (https://themefile.culture.tw/file/2019-04-17/2259a6ae-f96b-499c-98f5-9cc6161a95fa/06%20政府放寬持印度IC旅行證之國人藏族配偶在臺居留條件......藏事處.pdf).

Conclusion

Tibetan refugees holding Indian ICs can apply for political asylum following international refugee laws in Europe and the United States, and can then become citizens of those countries (Hess, 2009). Due to historical and political factors, Tibetan refugees have had certain links with Taiwan. Considering that Taiwan does not have a refugee law and is not a signatory member of the United Nations' 1959 convention on refugees and its 1969 protocols, the lived experiences of Tibetan refugees in Taiwan are unique compared to other countries. This chapter underscores various experiences of Tibetan refugees in Taiwan with a particular focus on rights to residence, work, and citizenship. Different stages of the political system present different ways in which Taiwan treats Tibetans, and it also directly affects the lives of Tibetans in Taiwan.

As shown in the first phase of Tibetan migration to Taiwan, Tibetan refugees were able to obtain citizenship rights because of the KMT government's policy that advocated Tibet as part of the ROC-Taiwan and Tibetan as one of the ethnic minorities. The first two groups, the Tibetan resistance force and the secret 32 guerrilla forces, were recruited with the plan to launch a military attack on the CPC. The TCH aimed to create an ethnic minority cadre for the future ROC. The Tibetan refugees were used by the KMT government as propaganda for its anti-communist missions and also to legitimise the ROC-Taiwan as the sole representative of China.

When Taiwan entered the stage of democratic transition and economic development, in addition to propaganda value, Tibetan refugees became an important source of cheap labour to support labour shortages in Taiwanese factories. As discussed in the second phase, the government abandoned the overseas Chinese category for Tibetan refugees and subsequently revoked their right to obtain citizenship. Tibetans recruited by the MTAC during this phase were treated as foreigners and had to get a visa from the Ministry of Foreign Affairs to enter Taiwan. Fake promises to provide jobs and citizenship forced refugees to become illegal immigrants and cheap labour in Taiwan's booming factories.

Due to the Dalai Lama's visit to Taiwan and the democratisation of Taiwan, which have brought a breakthrough in the relationship between Taiwan and CTA, Tibetan refugees no longer need to come to Taiwan through MTAC. However, the Taiwan government started treating Tibetan refugees as stateless. In consideration of national security concerns, the government imposed strict scrutiny and restrictions on Tibetan refugees entering Taiwan. The government enacted a law that prohibited Tibetans from obtaining the right to residence, work, and citizenship. With their new status as stateless, Tibetan refugees were denied residence visas, working rights, and access to healthcare, as showed in the experiences of Geshe Tenzin, Tibetan students, and marriage migrants.

In conclusion, the Taiwan government has treated Tibetan refugees as compatriots, overseas Chinese, foreigners, and stateless people in different political stages. While Tibetan refugees have gained citizenship by serving the state's Chinese nationalist ideology, they have also been considered stateless and unable to obtain a residence visa due to national security concerns. This chapter illustrated the lived experience of Tibetan students, economic migrants, and Tibetan Buddhist monks, who encounter discriminatory treatment by the government. Although national security is an important consideration, human rights protection is the responsibility of a modern democratic country. Therefore, under the consideration of national security, it is also necessary to take into account the protection of human rights. That is a problem that Taiwan, as a modern democratic country, must face and solve.

Acknowledgements This research is supported by the National Science and Technology Council, NSTC-112-2811-H-A49-500.

References

American Institute in Taiwan. (2019). *Taiwan 2018 international religious freedom Report*. https://www.ait.org.tw/2018-report-on-international-religious-freedom-taiwan/

Bawa, D.T. (2020). *Tibet and Taiwan go together: The 20th-anniversary book of the Dalai Lama Tibetan Religious Foundation*. Snow Land Publisher.

Buchser, C. (2010, April 9). *Why the Swiss accepted Tibetans with open arms?* https://www.swissinfo.ch/eng/why-the-swiss-accepted-tibetans-with-open-arms/8643062

Bureau of Consular Affairs, Ministry of Foreign Affairs, ROC (Taiwan). (2017, July 31). *Resident visas for religious work*. https://www.boca.gov.tw/fp-166-286-0ce3e-2.html

Bureau of Consular Affairs of the Ministry of Foreign Affairs, ROC-Taiwan. (2023, May 26). *Supplementary precautions for foreign monks (Tibetan monks)*

of Tibetan Buddhism to come to Taiwan to promote the Dharma. https://www.boca.gov.tw/cp-36-192-55163-1.html

Chin, S.-y. (1984). *The collection of President Chiang Kai-shek's thoughts and speeches vol. 33*. http://www.ccfd.org.tw/ccef001/index.php?option=com_content&view=article&id=593:0002-90&catid=238&Itemid=256

Chiu, T. (Host, 2023, May 13). *Tibetans in exile in Nepal—Memories of the coup in Nepal, the KMT and master Thubten* (No. 7) [Audio podcast episode]. 南亞小閣樓 ཨེ་ཤྱོ་གླིང་ཁང [South Asia Loft]. https://podcasts.apple.com/tw/podcast/%E5%8D%97%E4%BA%9E%E5%B0%8F%E9%96%A3%E6%A8%93-%E0%BD%A8-%E0%BD%A3-%E0%BD%A3-%E0%BD%84-%E0%BD%81%E0%BD%84/id1669969751?i=1000612884290

Contenta, S. (2010, October 23). *For Tibetan refugees, Canada was the new world*. Thestar.com. https://www.thestar.com/news/world/2010/10/23/for_tibetan_refugees_canada_was_literally_the_new_world.html

Fraser, S. E. (2018). Tibetan Buddhist temples in Taiwan: An exploration of transnational religious architecture. In *The hybridity of Buddhism: contemporary encounters between Tibetan and Chinese traditions in Taiwan and the Mainland* (pp. 43–65). EFEO, École française d'Extrême-Orient.

Gyari, L. G. (2022). *The Dalai Lama's special envoy*. Columbia University Press.

Hess, J. M. (2009) *Immigrant ambassadors: Citizenship and belonging in the Tibetan diaspora*. Stanford University Press.

Hsu, C. K. (Ed.). (2001). *A compilation of important policies of Mongolia and Tibet since the establishment of ROC*. Mongolian and Tibetan Affairs Commission.

Hsu, L. (1981, July). The Tibetan Children's Home. *Taiwan Panorama*. https://www.taiwan-panorama.com/en/Articles/Details?Guid=0c2a1da1-3bfa-4188-b0e8-db78ce010463&CatId=11&postname=The%20Tibetan%20Children%27s%20Home

Immigration Services, Ministry of Interior, ROC-Taiwan. (2017, February 7). *Tibetan spouses, Tibetans stranded in Taiwan, and minor children of Tibetans who fulfil human rights protection requirements can apply for special residence permits*. http://ws.mac.gov.tw/001/Upload/OldWeb/www.mac.gov.tw/ctdf03.html?xItem=116538&ctNode=5630&mp=1

Kung, Y. C., Jeng, H. T., & Chuang, H. L. (2020). Marriage in the political context: A case study of Tibetan spouses in Taiwan. *Taiwan: A Radical Quarterly in Social Studies, 15*, 285–309.

Laws and Regulations Database of the Republic of China (Taiwan). (2017, December 13). *The organizational activities of the Mongolian and Tibetan Affairs Commission—Legislative history—Laws & regulations database of The Republic of China (Taiwan)*. Law.moj.gov.tw. https://law.moj.gov.tw/ENG/LawClass/LawHistory.aspx?pcode=D0000044

Lin, C. C. 1999. *The lama killing: The tragedy of Tibetan 40-year exile*. Unitas.

Liu, S. C. (Ed.). (1996). A *short history of the Mongolian and Tibetan Affairs Commission*. Mongolian and Tibetan Affairs Commission.
Merit Times. (2007, July 16). Ministry of Foreign Affairs: Tibetans who come to Taiwan have seriously violated the law. *Merit Times*. https://www.merit-times.com/NewsPage.aspx?unid=54672
Ministry of Culture, Republic of China. (2017). *Mongol and Tibet Culture Center*. https://www.moc.gov.tw/en/information_85_75003.html
Ministry of Interior. (2008, December 5). *Regulations governing visiting, residency, and permanent residency of aliens*. https://www.rootlaw.com.tw/en/LawArticle.aspx?LawID=A040040110015000-1071205
Mongolian and Tibetan Affairs Commission. (1971). *A brief history of Mongolian and Tibetan Affairs Committee*. Mongolian and Tibetan Affairs Commission.
Mongolian and Tibetan Affairs Commission. (2011). *Aims of Mongolian and Tibetan Affairs Committee*. http://www.mtac.gov.tw/pages.php?lang=1&page=1. Accessed 4 August 2011.
Mongolian and Tibetan Cultural Center. (2022). *The number of households and population of Tibetans in Taiwan*. https://mtcc.moc.gov.tw/home/zh-tw/statistics/96664?mark=
Numbeo. (2019). *Health care index by country 2019 mid-year*. https://www.numbeo.com/health-care/rankings_by_country.jsp
Office of Planning Commission. (2010). *Demographic survey of Tibetan in exile–2009*. Central Tibetan Administration.
Okawa, K. (2007). Lesson from Tibetan in Taiwan: Their history, current situation and relationship with Taiwan nationalism. *The Memoirs of the Institute of Oriental Culture (Tokyo University), 152*, 581–608.
Own, S.-J. (2018). The development and mechanism of the *Gelug* sect in Taiwan: The boundary and integration of Sino-Tibetan in theocracy inheritance. In K.-H. Hsu (Ed.), *Proceedings of the symposium of Gelug sect and Sakya sect of Tibetan Buddhism* (pp. 27–51). Ministry of Culture.
Pan, M.-L. (2015). Neither compatriots nor refugees: Status discrimination of exiled Tibetans and the contradictory faces of the Republic of China (Taiwan). *International Journal of Asia Pacific Studies, 11*(2), 41–59.
Pan, M.-L. (2016). Misplaced displacement: Taiwanese-Tibetan families in Taiwan. *Taiwan Human Rights Journal, 3*(4), 69–89.
Pan, M.-L. (2023). 'Refusal to granting residence': Exiled Tibetan with Indian IC and Taiwan's border control policy. *Taiwan Human Rights Journal, 7*(1), 5–25.
President Office of the ROC. (2003, January 12). *President Chen meets with Tenzin Phuntsok Atisha, chairman of the Tibet Religious Foundation of the Dalai Lama*. https://english.president.gov.tw/NEWS/352

Reed-Danahay, D. (2009). Anthropologists, education, and autoethnography. *Reviews in Anthropology, 38*(1), 28–47. https://doi.org/10.1080/00938150802672931

Shakya, T. (1999). *The dragon in the land of snows: A history of modern Tibet since 1947*. Columbia University Press.

Shen, C. H., & Chen C. C. (2005). *A study on the development of Tibetan families in Taiwan and their social welfare resources network*. Mongolian and Tibetan Affairs Commission.

Su, C., & Wei, C. X. (2012). Taiwan's relations with the Central Tibetan Administration in exile. In C. X. Wei (Ed.), *China-Taiwan relations in a global context: Taiwan's foreign policy and relations* (pp. 174–198). Routledge. http://hdl.handle.net/20.500.11861/5878

Taiwan Association for Human Rights. (1999). *The overstayed Tibetans' petition to the government*. http://www.tahr.org.tw/site/case/passport.htm#a

Taiwan International Tibetan Buddhist Association. (2023, June 5). *The longest distance to Taiwan*. Taiwan International Tibetan Buddhist Association (Facebook Page). https://www.facebook.com/itbsi/

Tashi. (1997). Taiwan is a working paradise for Tibetans. *Business Weekly, 525*, 80–81.

Tethong, T. N. (2006). Tibet and Taiwan: History and prospects. *Bimonthly Newsletter on the Current Situation of Mongolia and Tibet, 15*(4), 59–70.

The 14th Dalai Lama. (1977). *My land and my people*. Potla Press.

The Welfare Society of Dhokham Chushi Gangdrug. (2022). *The Warriors of the snowland—A History of Chushi Gangdrug—Volume One*. Blue Rose Publishers.

Tsering, D. (2020, December 13). Reflecting on challenges of Taiwan's immigration law: A personal story of Taiwanese and Tibetan spouses. *New Bloom Magazine*. https://newbloommag.net/2020/12/13/tibet-spouse-discrimination/

Tsering, D. (2022, November 16). *Tibetan diaspora in Taiwan: Who are they and why They are invisible (1)*. Taiwan Insight. The University of Nottingham, The Taiwan Studies Programme. https://taiwaninsight.org/2022/11/16/tibetan-diaspora-in-taiwan-who-are-they-and-why-they-are-invisible-1/

Wu, P. C. (1999). *Scattered Dzi beads–Exiled Tibetans in Taiwan* [unpublished master's thesis]. National University of Taiwan. https://hdl.handle.net/11296/pp4cm7

Zhang, R., Chen, J., & Wu, Z. (2002). *Survey on living conditions of Tibetan compatriots in Taiwan and counselling measures*. Mongol and Tibetan Commission Review Committee.

CHAPTER 12

"I Am Still a Refugee!" Displacement and Transnational Activism

Shu-Fen Lin

Introduction

In the summer of 1979, Nguyễn Văn Hùng, who was born and raised in a family that had resettled in South Vietnam since 1954, successfully escaped Vietnam and was ultimately rescued by a Norwegian gas carrier in the treacherous South China Sea. Following his rescue, he resided in a refugee camp in Japan for two and half years before embarking on his studies at a Columban seminary in Sydney Australia. In 1988, he made his first visit to Taiwan to participate in a two-year Overseas Training Programme and returned again upon his ordination in 1991. Since then, he has become a prominent advocate for migrant rights and a respected community organiser.

Based on Father Nguyễn's life history, this chapter is divided into two parts, each delving into different aspects of his journey and activism. The first part chronicles Father Nguyễn and his family's experiences as they navigated a life of constant displacement and precarity in war-torn

S.-F. Lin (✉)
National Yang Ming Chiao Tung University, Hsinchu, Taiwan
e-mail: shufenlin@nycu.edu.tw

L. Momesso and P. Ivanova (eds.), *Refugees and Asylum Seekers in East Asia*, Palgrave Macmillan Studies on Human Rights in Asia,
https://doi.org/10.1007/978-981-97-2867-1_12

Vietnam during the late 1950s and 1970s. It illustrates their struggle for survival amidst the violence and their perilous sea voyage in search of a new life. Moreover, it explores Father Nguyễn's engagement in political activism as a refugee in Japan and Australia, shedding light on his resilience and determination.

The second part of this chapter shifts its focus to Father Nguyễn's dedication to advocating for migrant rights and his involvement in community-organising activities in Taiwan. It highlights his encounter with different waves of Vietnamese migrants, and the emergence of a Vietnamese diasporic community since the 1990s. Furthermore, it traces Father Nguyễn's persistent efforts in transnational networking, which have played a crucial role in fostering collaboration, support, and collective actions across national borders.

The primary source of material for this chapter is derived from extensive in-depth life history interviews. These interviews spanned 15 sessions, taking place between November 2019 and May 2023, with an average duration of two hours per session. As a result, approximately 33 hours of recorded and transcribed conversations were accumulated. It is important to acknowledge that while the chapter utilises the life history approach and centres on Father Nguyễn, it does not seek to generalise his individual life experience to represent Vietnamese refugees as a whole. Such a generalisation would oversimplify the complexities and variations within refugee communities. However, Father Nguyễn's life history offers a unique perspective that enables an exploration of the broader social and historical contexts in which not only his own journey but also the journeys of others have unfolded and intersected.

As Ken Plummer (1983) aptly argues, the life history approach requires a continuous interweaving "between the changing biographical history of the person and the social history of his or her life-span" (p. 70). To demonstrate how the personal and the social, or the micro and macro, interact and influence each other, and to provide a more contextualised analysis of Father Nguyễn's life experience, this chapter enriches the narrative by cross-referencing and supplementing his personal accounts with a carefully selected group of scholarly literature on the Vietnam War, along with research in the fields of refugee studies and migration studies. Additionally, relevant government documents, statistics, and newspapers are consulted whenever appropriate. By integrating these diverse sources, the chapter aims to provide a nuanced understanding of how the interplay between human agency, and the evolving geopolitical configurations and refugee/migration regimes in different historical contexts, has profoundly shaped the trajectory and experiences of Father Nguyễn and his contemporaries.

Displacement and Resettlement

Northern Immigrants in South Vietnam

In addition to the temporary division of Vietnam into the North and the South, and the agreement to hold national general elections before July 1956, the Geneva Accords, signed between France, the "Việt Minh" (League for the Independence of Vietnam), and other involved parties, included a provision that allowed civilians to freely move between the two Vietnams within 300 days after the signing of the agreement. Despite the fact that this provision was strongly influenced by the intervention of the Eisenhower administration, motivated by its anti-communist stance (Catton, 2015), it set off the "Great Migration" (Cuộc Di Cư Vĩ Đại), the largest population movement in Vietnam's history within the shortest period of time. From 1954 to 1956, with assistance from France, the United States, the Soviet Union, and Poland, over 800,000 northerners, predominantly Catholics, who later became known as "Northern immigrants" (Bắc Di Cư) or the "Northern fifty-four" (Bắc Năm Tư), migrated to the South. Simultaneously, approximately 120,000 individuals, mainly Việt Minh members and sympathisers, moved to the North (Goscha, 2016, p. 280; Hansen, 2009, pp. 178–79).

The division and subsequent Great Migration marked the beginning of an era characterised by what scholars have referred to as "internal transnationalism" (Hardy, 2004; Hansen, 2009, pp. 174–75). The phenomenon of internal displacement was further exacerbated by the direct military interventions of the US beginning in 1964. As the conflict escalated, urban residents in the North sought refuge in rural areas to evade bombing raids, while villagers in the South were displaced due to intensive bombings in mountainous regions and rural areas or were relocated to cities as part of counterinsurgency tactics (Dang et al., 1997, p. 318). Samuel Huntington, an American political scientist and proponent of the Vietnam War, referred to this process as "forced urbanisation" or "forced modernisation" through the "liquidation of the countryside", viewing it as a form of "creative destruction" (Biggs, 2018, p. 134; Gawthorpe,

2018, p. 315). Indeed, according to a report by the US Agency for International Development, during the peak years of the war between 1965 and 1969, approximately 3.2 million people, accounting for one-fifth of the South Vietnamese population, experienced displacement at some point (Vong, 2020, p. 76). Evidently, the "Operation Passage to Freedom" implemented by the US during the Great Migration did not shield Northern immigrants from the ravages of the war.

Both of Hùng's parents were typical Northern immigrants, originating from Nghệ An, a province located in central Vietnam which became part of North Vietnam (Democratic Republic of Vietnam) in 1954. Nghệ An had long been under the control of the Việt Minh. To resist the Việt Minh, many local Catholics were enlisted into the militia led by a Vietnamese Bishop, while also serving in the French military, which had led to accusations of collaboration (Hansen, 2009, p. 179). Hùng's father joined the French Navy in 1946 at the age of 16. Following the French defeat in 1954, he left the navy, briefly worked as a fisherman, and eventually relocated to the South alone.

In contrast to Hùng's father, Hùng's mother migrated to the South with her family. Motivated by the harrowing memory of the famine during the final days of the Japanese occupation (1940–1945), their Catholic background, and Hùng's grandfather's service in the French Navy, the family saw an opportunity for a new life in the South. Initially, Hùng's grandmother had to travel from Nghệ An to Hải Phòng, the major French naval base, with three children in tow, to join her husband. They had to travel at night under the cover of darkness to avoid being mistaken for Việt Minh members by the French. Despite the challenges, the family persevered and ultimately was reunited, boarding a French vessel bound for the South.

Notwithstanding the varied reasons for leaving the North (Hansen, 2009) and the mixed reception from the government of South Vietnam (Republic of Vietnam) towards northern Catholic refugees (Biggs, 2012, pp. 164–67; Nguyễn, 2017), people from the same parishes tended to stick together and provide mutual support. For instance, the family of Hùng's mother, along with fellow parishioners, received assistance from Missions Étrangères de Paris (M.E.P.) upon their arrival in the South and later established a new parish in the coastal city of Bình Tuy. As for Hùng's father, thanks to a connection from his village, he secured employment as a crew member on a transport ship for RMK-BRJ, a construction consortium established by the United States Navy to support military operations that involved a simultaneous process of "construction and destruction" on an unprecedented scale in South Vietnam (Carter, 2008, pp. 157–58).

Hùng was born in 1958 while his family resided in the fishing village of La Gi. In 1965, Hùng's father began working for RMK-BRJ, prompting the family to move to Gò Vấp, on the outskirts of Saigon. Hùng recalls that the forests surrounding their neighbourhood were teeming with Việt Cộng, an armed communist guerrilla force in South Vietnam, leading to occasional arrests of villagers suspected of affiliations with the Việt Cộng. Hùng frequently heard gunshots and stray bullets while playing with other children in the forests. The constant presence of helicopters and the sounds of falling bullets could also be clearly heard from his home. Most of the time, Hùng's school was occupied by allied troops from the United States, South Vietnam, South Korea, and Australia.

Gò Vấp was one of the targets in the 1968 Tet Offensive, a significant military campaign initiated by North Vietnam and Việt Cộng forces during the Vietnamese New Year holiday (Goscha, 2016, pp. 331–33). Around the same time, Hùng's father and his co-workers were attacked and narrowly escaped death during one operation. In the aftermath of these events, Hùng's family decided to return to La Gi around 1970. Unfortunately, even La Gi was not a safe place. Hùng vividly recalls the tense atmosphere during the two or three years leading up to his father's passing in mid-April 1975. Gunshots would echo in the sky nearly every night, and the village was constantly filled with the scent of burning incense for the deceased. It became commonplace to witness villagers donning white cloths on their heads as a symbol of mourning. To seek refuge from air raids, Hùng and his brothers often had to carry their ailing father to the fields.

Prior to the takeover of their province, Bình Tuy, by the Provisional Revolutionary Government of the Republic of South Vietnam (1969–1976) in late April 1975, the wealthier relatives of Hùng's family had already departed for Nha Trang, Phan Thiết, and other major US military sites, or had sought safer locations in the South. Although Hùng's father had previously worked for the RMK-BRJ, his family did not belong to the group of approximately 65,000 Vietnamese with the closest ties to the US who were "evacuated" in April 1975, nor were they among the other 65,000 Vietnamese who managed to escape on their own (Loescher & Scanlan, 1986, p. 111).

For those who remained or were left behind, life underwent a drastic change. In Hùng's case, he was denied the opportunity to attend college, likely due to his family's Catholic background and his father's "US connections". Additionally, his seminary studies were abruptly halted due to the new policy of household registration. Hùng observed his friends, one by one, starting to "vanish" as they fled abroad. Despite his own desire to leave, he lacked the financial means and was deterred by the terrifying sight of the "shark-man" (sharks that spit out human hands and legs) at the beach. Moreover, his mother repeatedly warned him against risking his life. However, driven by the lack of freedom in Vietnam and his brother's conscription into the war in Cambodia, Hùng eventually became determined to flee. Over the next two years, Hùng lived a life divided between farming and fishing, all the while making numerous attempts to escape with close relatives and friends. After seven or eight failed attempts, Hùng finally succeeded in the summer of 1979.

"Boat People" Across the South China Sea

On 27 July 1979, Hùng joined 55 fellow Vietnamese on a perilous journey across the South China Sea, desperately seeking freedom and a new life in a new land. They crowded onto a cramped fishing boat that was a mere eight and a half metres long and two and a half metres wide. With limited supplies of fuel, food, and drinking water, they had provisions that would last for about a week ("Shi mo kakugo shi ni shukkoku", 1979). For maritime Vietnamese refugees, the South China Sea was a treacherous and life-or-death liminal space they had to navigate. Regardless of the condition of their vessels, the chosen routes, or the ultimate destination, their survival hinged on safely reaching a neighbouring Southeast Asian country or being rescued by other ships in time.

As the Indochina refugee crisis unfolded in the late 1970s, the dangers of the sea became a grim reality for those fleeing the country. In response to the crisis, the International Chamber of Shipping, urged by the United Nations High Commissioner for Refugees (UNHCR), called on ship masters to fulfil their obligations in undertaking rescue operations at sea (Goodwin-Gill, 2017, pp. 17–18). At the same time, the UNHCR Executive Committee reiterated that "it is the humanitarian obligation of all coastal states to allow vessels in distress to seek haven in their waters and to grant asylum, or at least temporary refuge, to persons on board wishing to seek asylum" (Trevisanut, 2008, p. 210). However, despite these appeals, the chances of Vietnamese maritime refugees, commonly known as "boat people", being rescued by merchant ships were low. It was estimated that up to 10% of these refugees perished at sea, never reaching the shores (Wain, 1981, p. 83). As Patricia Nguyễn (2017) poignantly underscores, "Vietnamese refugees existed in a state of suspension, where the delicate balance between life and death was governed by the precarious conditions of the ocean and the conflicting claims of nation-states and multi-state entities" (p. 96).

In Hùng's case, as they ventured into the open sea, despite the efforts of some on the boat to attract attention by burning clothes, and the boat captain taking the risk of damaging the engine to catch up with the passing ships, Hùng and other refugees were still disregarded. Fortunately, after drifting at sea for about 36 hours, they were rescued by a Norwegian liquefied petroleum gas carrier named Mundogas Atlantic, which had recently departed from Singapore and was en route to Mizushima Port in Japan. Hùng remembers that when their boat was lifted several stories high by the storm and sank rapidly, they were unaware of the approaching super typhoon. It was an extremely close call. Hùng believes that had Mundogas Atlantic not reached out in time, they would not have survived the second night at sea. Ironically, the typhoon they narrowly escaped was the super typhoon "Hope". Just a few days after their rescue, Typhoon Hope struck Hong Kong and Macau. Reports indicate that five refugee boats were allowed to dock in Hong Kong ahead of the storm, while the Macau government rejected three other boats seeking refuge. Tragically, around 400 people, along with their hopes, perished in the storm (NOAA, 1979, p. 370; Ngai, 1979).

It is important to note that sea rescues often triggered a complex negotiation process involving multiple parties, including the country of departure, coastal states, port states, destination countries, and the countries or flag states of the ships carrying refugees. Each country held different perspectives on search and rescue operations in different maritime regions, leading to debates regarding the legal authority of individual nations to deny entry to refugees (Trevisanut, 2008, pp. 206–7). According to Hùng, with 56 Vietnamese refugees on board, Mundogas Atlantic was initially denied entry to Japan. Hùng and his fellow Vietnamese were only allowed to disembark under the condition that they all left Japan and resettled in third countries, and the Norwegian government had to ensure their resettlement.

Being a de Facto Refugee in Japan and Australia

Due to its geographical distance from Vietnam, the majority of maritime refugees who arrived in Japan during the Indochina refugee crisis were rescued at sea by Japanese or other foreign ships before being brought to Japan, including Okinawa. According to Hashimoto (2019), "the term 'refugee' did not exist in Japanese domestic law until accession to the Refugee Convention in 1981, and no public entity had the statutory authority, mandate, or budget to provide assistance for refugees or displaced persons. Assistance to Indo-Chinese refugees was almost entirely reliant upon private charities" (p. 134). Also, in the early stages, it was noted that refugees rescued by Japanese vessels were relatively more likely to receive special permission to land in Japan compared to those rescued by foreign vessels. For the latter, the country of registration of the vessel had to confirm its willingness to accept the refugees. The situation became even more intricate in cases involving "flags of convenience" ("Nanmin, yatto jouriku", 1977).

Consequently, refugees faced the risk of being denied entry into Japan without guaranteed resettlement in other countries. This was the case even when NGOs like Caritas Japan were volunteering to serve as guarantors and provide asylum facilities. A notable example of this occurred in 1976 when a cargo ship flagged by Malaysia, carrying Vietnamese fishermen and their families, was denied entry by the Yokohama Immigration Office due to the Malaysian government's refusal to guarantee it as a receiving country ("Chō no jōriku fukyoka", 1976). Furthermore, even in cases where the Japanese government agreed to offer temporary shelter, refugees were denied "permanent residence" status. This policy, however, began to change in 1978 ("Nanmin, hajimete teijū", 1978).

Prior to 1978 when the issue of maritime refugees, particularly those of overseas Chinese descent, escalated in Southeast Asian countries, and reports of deterred refugee boats became increasingly common, neither the United States nor the international community had adequately addressed the refugee crisis. However, as the internationalisation of the Indochina refugee problem started to gain momentum, Indochinese refugees, and the Vietnamese "boat people" in particular, became subjects of geopolitical and even geo-economic considerations (Loescher & Scanlan, 1986, pp. 102–46). This shift brought about competitions and collaborations in the realms of international humanitarianism, refugee diplomacy, geopolitical deployment, and economic developments, culminating in the UN conference on refugees in Geneva in July 1979. During this conference, alongside the implementation of the Orderly Departure Program (ODP), agreements were reached to establish first-asylums and processing centres in several Southeast Asian countries. Most notably, Indochinese refugees were granted an exceptional status. Rather than individually identifying each person fleeing Indochina as a Convention refugee, they were collectively recognised as prima facie refugees or "refugees of direct concern to the UNHCR" (Cutts, 2000, pp. 84, 86; Robinson, 1998, p. 51).

In response to growing international pressure, the Japanese government eventually collaborated with the UNHCR, the United States, and ASEAN countries to address the refugee crisis. As part of these efforts, Japan increased its contributions to the UNHCR's assistance programmes for Indochinese refugees and provided substantial financial and technical aid for establishing refugee processing centres in Indonesia and the Philippines (Loescher & Scanlan, 1986, p. 144). In addition, the UNHCR opened a branch office in Tokyo in August 1979 ("Nihon ni mo shibu kaisetsu", 1979), and the Japanese government took significant steps towards resettlement by enacting a series of cabinet approvals and setting up the Refugee Headquarters in the same year (Hashimoto, 2019, p. 134).

This initiative granted subsidies, allowances, and de facto refugee status to refugees, and it facilitated family reunification for resettled Vietnamese under the ODP framework. Between 1975 and 1995, Japan received 11,071 boat people and resettled 8,803 Indochinese refugees (Cutts, 2000, p. 98), bolstering its role as a prominent Asian country in refugee resettlement. Yet, as Hashimoto (2019) observes, Japan's refugee policy created a "stratification of rights and entitlements" (p. 128). Despite adhering to the Convention and Protocol Relating to the Status of Refugees in 1981, the Refugee Headquarters initially limited support to refugees from Indochina, only broadening its assistance to include Convention refugees in 2003 (p. 135).

Upon Hùng's arrival in Japan in 1979, the Japanese government had just recently begun adopting a more humanitarian, though still somewhat ad hoc, approach to refugee issues. Shortly after Hùng and the other refugees were transported to Caritas Japan-operated refugee camps in Fujisawa City and Kamakura, they were prompted to decide on their future destinations based on an agreement between Japan and Norway.

As Hùng's family had no relatives abroad, they were ineligible for the ODP. By the end of 1979, all of Hùng's family, except for him, were resettled in Norway. Hùng, having been accepted into the Missionary Society of Saint Columban, faced a choice of attending seminary in the United States, Ireland, or Australia. He ultimately chose Australia, the first country to offer him resettlement. Consequently, Hùng remained in Japan for another two and a half years before enrolling at Saint Columban seminary in Sydney in 1982.

During his time at the Misono refugee camp in Japan, Hùng and other refugees received limited support from the Japanese government and had to rely on their own efforts for livelihood. Hùng undertook various low-paying jobs, such as welding, machine operation, customer service, grave digging, and construction work. He faced workplace discrimination and other challenges, but found solace and support among the Vietnamese community in Japan. This included students who had arrived before 1975 and volunteered at refugee camps, as well as members of advocacy groups like the Free Vietnamese (Người Việt Tư Do), who championed the human rights of Vietnamese people.

Hùng engaged in these community activities, representing his camp, and later discovering that some senior students were part of the National United Front for the Liberation of Vietnam (NUFLVN), a political group of Vietnamese refugees in the US, advocating for liberation from communist rule. He actively participated in events organised by the Free Vietnamese, including protests at the embassy of the Democratic Republic of Vietnam in Tokyo on dates like International Human Rights Day and 30 April, the anniversary of the Fall of Saigon. Additionally, Hùng was involved in fundraising led by Father Cathal Gallaher, a Columban priest, to improve the Misono camp. His time in Japan was transformative, marking the start of his commitment to social and political advocacy.

On 12 April 1982, Hùng left Japan and embarked on his journey to Australia. At that time, Australia's refugee policies under Prime Minister Malcom Fraser, were lauded as proactive, generous, effective, and humanitarian (Stats, 2015, pp. 70–1). However, these policies were also viewed as "primarily motivated by fear of the political consequences of an uncontrolled refugee influx, and was a reactive rather than principled response" (Stats, 2015, p. 75). Despite its geographical proximity to Vietnam and its promises to provide "refuge, security, freedom, and hope" (Stats, 2015, p. 74), Australia had implemented a "forward selection" policy, prioritising refugees from first-asylum camps over those arriving directly at its borders. As Michael MacKellar, then Minister for Immigration and Ethnic Affairs, candidly expressed in 1978:

> We give first priority to family reunion, second priority to people who have been associated with or worked with Australians in the region, third priority to those with skills useable in Australia and fourth priority to special compassionate cases. (Stats, 2015, p. 80)

As noted, the Geneva conference agreement recognised Indochinese refugees collectively as de facto refugees, bypassing individual assessments. Nonetheless, this did not eliminate criteria or processes for transitioning from temporary to permanent resettlement. It is unclear under which category Hùng would have fallen for resettlement in Australia. However, had he not pursued priesthood and been accepted by the Columban Society, he would have been required to go to Norway with his family. Australia's practice of "forward selection" of refugees from first-asylum camps set a precedent for later policies such as the "outsourcing of asylums and offshore processing" (Stats, 2015, p. 84), assessing asylum seekers outside Australia before granting entry. As Jana Lipman accurately points out, "[re]settlement countries like the United States, Canada and Australia receive disproportionate attention in refugee crises at the expense of first-asylum sites" (2020, p. 5).

Arriving in Sydney in 1982, Hùng initially resided at the Endeavour Hotel, a Vietnamese refugee reception centre. Due to his involvement in the "Free Vietnamese" movement and other political and social activities during his time in Japan, Hùng quickly became a prominent figure within the Vietnamese community in Sydney. He was invited to speak at an annual commemorative event organised by overseas Vietnamese on 30 April, where he presented the NUFLVN statement. Despite efforts to clarify his role, many still mistakenly perceive him as a representative of NUFLVN. Nevertheless, these experiences significantly contributed to his political activism in Sydney.

In Australia, Hùng balanced seminary studies and English courses, funded by the Australian government, with community involvement. He helped organise a Vietnamese youth choir that symbolised solidarity and patriotism, while also participating in fundraising for community causes. Moreover, Hùng, along with a group of seven or eight friends, regularly contributed articles to *The Resistance*, a Vietnamese community newspaper based in the US but circulated monthly in Australia. Their articles covered cultural events and protests organised by the Vietnamese community in Sydney against Vietnam's human rights violations. Hùng consistently stressed the importance of remaining politically engaged and fostering unity within the Vietnamese community.

Hùng's role in building the Vietnamese refugee community and promoting transnational actions in Australia laid the foundation for his subsequent activism in Taiwan. He viewed his endeavours in Taiwan as a natural extension of his experiences in Australia, rather than an entirely new undertaking. However, as the following section will demonstrate Hùng's engagement with the Vietnamese community in Taiwan differed notably from his time in Japan and Australia.

Vietnamese Community Organising and Transnational Activism

The First Encounter

When Hùng first arrived in Taiwan in 1988 to participate in an Overseas Training Programme as part of his seminary education, the international community's stance towards Vietnamese refugees had undergone a noticeable shift since the consensus reached during the 1979 Geneva conference. The increasing number of refugees struggling to secure resettlement in third countries led to overcrowding in the first-asylums in Southeast Asia and a revival of the policy of pushing refugee boats back into international waters. The challenge was further compounded by the decision of Hong Kong government to individually screen refugee, effectively reclassifying "boat people" from de facto refugees to asylum seekers. Consequently, some were repatriated to Vietnam after being "screened out" (Lipman, 2020, pp. 161–200).

The situation in Taiwan reflected some aspects of these changes. Despite not being a United Nations member since 1972 and not directly involved in the international response to the Indochinese refugee problem in the late 1970s, the government of the Republic of China (ROC) expressed support for Vietnamese refugees and launched an anti-communist propaganda campaign due to its diplomatic setbacks at that time. While the actual efforts were relatively limited, approximately 15,284 refugees received assistance between 1975 and 1992 (Huang, 2019, p. 180). Among them were 3939 ethnic Chinese Vietnamese who fled Vietnam from April to July 1975, as well as 2740 overseas Chinese students from Vietnam, Burma, and Laos who were already in Taiwan (Huang, 2019, p. 171). They comprised the first group of returning overseas Chinese aided by the ROC government immediately after the war. Additionally, another group of 6777 Chinese Vietnamese were "repatriated" to Taiwan through chartered flights intermittently under the "Ren Der Project" between 1976 and 1992 (Huang, 2019, p. 173). The Indochina Refugee Reception Centre in Penghu, operational from 1977 to 1988, provided shelter to 2,098 Vietnamese refugees, both ethnic Chinese and Vietnamese, with 231eventually finding resettlement in Taiwan (Huang, 2019, p. 178).

The ROC government initially established task forces to assist Vietnamese refugees, offering affordable housing, allowances, and employment training to Chinese Vietnamese refugees who were evacuated with government support. Maritime refugees accommodated at the reception centre in Penghu received daily allowances and assistance for resettlement in third countries (Huang, 2019, pp. 94, 178). However, around 1982, the ROC government implemented the "Pacification Program" to counter the perceived exploitation of "refugee tactics" by mainland China, altering the perception of "boat people" from symbols of anti-communism to potential security threats. Unfortunately, this shift culminated in the tragic killing of 20 Vietnamese refugees by the Little Kinmen Garrison on 7 March 1987 (Control Yuan, 2022).

The difference in the backgrounds of the Vietnamese refugees Hùng encountered in Taiwan compared to those he met in Japan and Australia can be attributed to Taiwan's refugee policy. In Taiwan, a majority of the resettled refugees who arrived after the Vietnam War and the Sino-Vietnamese border conflicts were of Chinese descent. However, during his internship, Hùng still had the opportunity to meet a small group of non-Chinese Vietnamese boat people from South Vietnam. These encounters were facilitated by Vietnamese fathers and brothers already in Taiwan, allowing Hùng to share his experiences of activism and the efforts of Vietnamese communities in the US, France, Japan, and Australia. They even organised a commemoration event on 30 April 1989. Nevertheless, Hùng observed that this group was less engaged in activism compared to those he encountered in Japan and Australia, and after returning to Australia in 1990, he lost contact with them.

In addition to clergymen and refugees, Hùng also came across a group of Vietnamese workers employed at a towel factory in central Taiwan. These workers, primarily young men from South Vietnam, had been recruited under the pretext of participating in an "internship" by a Taiwanese company that had invested in South Vietnam. However, Hùng soon discovered the harsh working conditions they were subject to. Deeply concerned for their well-being, Hùng attempted to connect them with local clergy members to seek assistance. Unfortunately, the clergy members were uncertain about how to effectively address the situation. Taking matters into his own hands, Hùng met with the workers and reported their plight to the Council of Labour Affairs (the predecessor of the Ministry of Labour). He became their advocate, demanding improved living conditions and fair wages to rectify the injustices they were enduring.

Advocating for Migrant Rights

Hùng returned to Taiwan in 1992 following his ordination. It was also the year when the Taiwanese government implemented the Employment Service Act in response to labour shortages, rising wages, and the offshoring of manufacturing operations since the late 1980s. The Act opened Taiwan's door to Southeast Asian migrant workers, leading to a steady increase in their numbers.

Hùng, now known as Father Nguyễn, remained committed to advocating for the rights of migrant workers, alongside his work in assisting the homeless, youth, orphans, and individuals with mental disabilities. Around 1997, Father Nguyễn assisted a group of exploited Filipino migrant workers employed at a textile company. He reached out to companies that placed orders with the factory for support. Eventually, the compliance office of the GAP clothing brand in Hong Kong contacted him and sent representatives to assess the situation. Subsequently, Father Nguyễn established an organisation, Taiwan Independent Monitoring, conducting regular visits to the two factories to inspect their operations.

Regarding the Vietnam-Taiwan labour migration corridor, while Taiwan had started to receive migrant workers from Southeast Asian countries like Thailand, the Philippines, Malaysia, and Indonesia since the early 1990s, it was not until 1999 that the bilateral agreement between Vietnam and Taiwan was finally signed, underscoring the significance of "migrant worker diplomacy" (Tseng, 2004, p. 23). Following the implementation of the agreement, there was a rapid surge in the number of Vietnamese workers in both the manufacturing and social welfare sectors. Notably, even prior to the signing of the bilateral labour agreement, the number of Vietnamese marriage migrants in Taiwan had already surpassed those from other Southeast Asian countries as early as 1996 (Wang & Chang, 2002, p. 96). As a result, the Vietnamese community has emerged as the largest diasporic community in Taiwan, with marriage migrants and migrant workers being the two largest sub-groups within this community (Ministry of Labor, 2023; National Immigration Agency, 2023).

Southeast Asian marriage migrants in Taiwan have faced commodification, discrimination, and social stigma (Hsia, 2001; Wang & Chang, 2002). While some choose to migrate through marriage voluntarily for various reasons, there are cases of human trafficking victims. Similarly, while working abroad has been perceived as an opportunity to escape poverty and unemployment, it has also become a significant and risky financial investment within an exploitative system. Many migrant workers' families find themselves trapped in debt after borrowing money from loan sharks to cover migration expenses, and some workers are deceived into signing false contracts or loan agreements. Consequently, workers often endure harsh working and living conditions in their efforts to break free from the cycle of debt (Hoang & Yeoh, 2015, p. 289). Many workers would take further risks of entering "illegal" trajectories for better paid but no less exploitative jobs (Lan, 2007).

As Hoang and Yeoh accurately put it, "[i]n the race to increase the supply of labour and expand markets for labour exports, the state in labour-sending countries is often complicit in lending a helping hand to the 'migration industry' while failing to pay due attention to the protection of migrants' rights" (Hoang & Yeoh, 2015, p. 285). Rather than addressing the exploitative nature of the broker system, both the Taiwanese and Vietnamese governments tend to place the burden on the workers themselves. To tackle issues like worker "runaways" or overstays, workers are subjected to fines and various punishments, including criminalisation (Li & Cheng, 2014).

Against this backdrop, Father Nguyễn assumed the position of director at the Hope Workers' Centre in 2000. The centre, originally established by Columban Missionaries in 1986 to assist local Taiwanese workers, was transformed into one of the pioneering organisations dedicated to supporting migrant workers as their numbers grew. Moreover, in response to the increasing population of Vietnamese marriage migrants and migrant workers and prompted by a distressing incident in 2004 where three young Vietnamese women were advertised for sale on eBay

Taiwan ("EBay pulls 'women for sale' ad", 2004), Father Nguyễn made the decision to found the Vietnamese Migrant Workers and Brides Office.

Transnational Networking

Despite facing limited resources, Father Nguyễn actively sought support from church members and overseas Vietnamese communities during this period. He collaborated with Ms Lê, a Vietnamese refugee who had resettled in the US and volunteered at a refugee camp in Hong Kong, to combat human trafficking and advocate for anti-trafficking legislation. Through Ms Lê's networks, Father Nguyễn established connections with the Vietnam Alliance to Combat Trafficking (Viet Act), an anti-trafficking coalition in the US and Canada formed in 2004, as well as media outlets such as Saigon Broadcasting Television Network and Little Saigon Radio.

With the assistance of Viet Act, Father Nguyễn further engaged with Vietnamese diaspora groups in the US and Canada, who enthusiastically raised funds to aid his work in Taiwan. Thanks to these funds, he was able to establish a shelter in Taiwan, despite the government's initial lack of action. Over time, as Father Nguyễn collaborated with local NGOs and effectively advocated for the government to fulfil its responsibilities, he no longer relied on fundraising support from the overseas Vietnamese community.

Unexpectedly, while Father Nguyễn received support from the overseas Vietnamese community for his initiatives, concerns were raised regarding his work. Some questioned whether it inadvertently supported the Vietnamese government without effectively addressing the fundamental issues in Vietnam. This controversy reflects the differing visions and practices within the transnational Vietnamese community regarding the future of Vietnam. On the other hand, initially when Father Nguyễn took on cases such as the sexual assault of a group of Vietnamese female caregivers by brokers (Zheng, 2005), he was praised by the Vietnamese media for his efforts to assist these victims. However, shortly after, due to his connections with the Vietnamese community in the US and his outspoken comments, he was accused of exploiting these incidents to criticise the Vietnamese government.

Controversies aside, it is crucial to highlight that Father Nguyễn's initiatives went beyond providing rescue and shelter. He actively encouraged Vietnamese marriage migrants to establish the Vietnamese Women's Association, which became the first officially recognised Vietnamese organisation in Taiwan with the approval of the local government. Furthermore, Father Nguyễn played a pivotal role in organising the Vietnamese Migrant Workers' Union, aiming to support Vietnamese workers and their endeavours to form industrial unions, as demonstrated by the protests initiated by workers in two food factories in 2019. While the full impact of these initiatives may not have been realised, the primary objective was to empower Vietnamese migrants in Taiwan.

Notably, some migrant workers who received assistance from Father Nguyễn underwent transformative experiences, leading to an enhanced social consciousness and active involvement in organising protests and supporting others (Jian, 2020). Despite the risk of arrest by the Vietnamese government upon their return to Vietnam, some of them have persevered in their engagement with social activism. This serves as evidence of the enduring impact of Father Nguyễn's initiatives and the empowerment of Vietnamese migrants in Taiwan and aligns with recent scholarship on "social remittances" (Lacroix et al., 2016), which highlights the influence of migrants in transmitting ideas and practices that contribute to social change in their home countries.

The ongoing efforts to support the victims affected by the Formosa Hà Tĩnh steel plant disaster in Vietnam serve as another example of Father Nguyễn's involvement in transnational activism. The illegal discharge of wastewater by the Taiwanese corporation resulted in extensive coastal pollution, devastating fish deaths, and significant impacts on the livelihoods and health of local fishermen. In 2016, Father Nguyễn collaborated with the Environmental Jurists Association to establish a support platform, forging connections with overseas Vietnamese organisations, as well as international human rights and environmentalist groups. They also worked closely with local Catholic organisations and activists in Vietnam, forming a transnational network of action. Their efforts included pursuing transnational legal lawsuits to seek compensation for the victims' losses, protesting against the Vietnamese government's arrests of activists, and advocating for legislative reforms to regulate Taiwanese investments overseas. This initiative has been recognised as indicative of the emergence of a transnational public sphere (Jobin, 2020, pp. 108–9). However, when examining Father Nguyễn's trajectory of practice in Taiwan, it becomes evident that fostering transnational connections with various organisations, both within the Vietnamese diaspora and in the international community, has been at the heart of all his actions.

Conclusion

The life story of Father Nguyễn illustrates the profound impact of colonialism, the entanglement of the civil war and the Cold War, and the subsequent globalisation on ordinary Vietnamese. His passage through South Vietnam, Japan, Australia, and Taiwan poignantly reveals the politics of humanitarianism and the varied approaches adopted by different countries towards refugees in different regions and times. Initially viewed as "de facto refugees", "good refugees", "bona fide refugees", or "anti-communist warriors" (Espiritu, 2014), the Vietnamese "boat people" later faced stigmatisation as "fake refugees", "illegal immigrants", "smugglers" driven by economic motives. They were even perceived as potential threats to national security, reflecting shifting geopolitical reconfigurations.

By the late 1980s, as Southeast Asian countries started repatriating Vietnamese refugees, Vietnam experienced a new wave of outmigration, spurred by the country's economic reform and the rapid globalisation. This, in turn, led to the further transnationalisation and transformation of Vietnamese diasporic communities. Father Nguyễn's activism exemplifies the multifaceted and multidirectional nature of transnationalism, shaped by evolving migration patterns and border governance. It also underscores the emergence of transnational spaces and networks that connect Vietnamese individuals in their homeland to those overseas and foster mutual support among Vietnamese diaspora in various regions. The Formosa Hà Tĩnh incident is a particularly striking example of transnational activism that transcends national borders, facilitating collaborations among diverse groups irrespective of their original countries or national identities, and highlighting the tension between grassroots transnationalism and top-down transnationalism.

Lastly, as Lê Espiritu (2014, p. 11) reminds us, refugees are "intentionalised beings", who "possess and enact their *own* politics as they emerge out of the ruins of war and its aftermath". Father Nguyễn's life story is not merely one of escape and survival, it is a testament to his commitment to freedom through community organising and transnational activism. His determination reflects the resilience and agency of refugees in shaping their futures and challenging systems that perpetuate displacement and injustice. In Father Nguyễn's own words "I am still a refugee … I have no choice but to strive for change. I hope that through this change, I can undo and liberate the circumstances that turned me into a refugee ... Only then can I be released from my refugee status".

Acknowledgements I am grateful to Father Nguyễn Văn Hùng for his unwavering support, trust, and invaluable insights throughout the entire process. Special thanks are extended to Chihsiung Liu and Hunglin Liao for their collaborative efforts in conducting the interviews. I am also deeply thankful to my assistants, Christine Chow and Lixing Yang, for their meticulous work in transcribing the interviews, and to Zong-Kun Chang for his excellent editing of the interviews. Additionally, I wish to convey my sincere appreciation to both editors for their feedback, patience, and ongoing support.

This project received funding from the Ministry of Science and Technology, Taiwan, under the research project "Refugee Regimes and Biopolitics" (MOST 109-2410-H-009-017-MY3). Additionally, an expanded version of a portion of the first section of this chapter was previously published in my article titled "Lùdì yǔ hǎiyáng: Yuènán qīngnián Hùng de nànmín lìchéng yǔ lěngzhàn nànmín zhèngzhì" [Land and Sea: The Refugee Passage of Vietnamese Youth Hùng and Cold War Refugee Politics], in Shu-Fen Lin, Iam-chong Ip, and Lawrence Zi-Qiao Yang (Eds.). *Qiányán yǔ liúdòng: Chóng tàn lěngzhàn yàjì liánjiē* [*Frontiers on the Move: Revisiting Inter-Asia Connections in the Cold War*], National Yang Ming Chiao Tung University Press, 2024.

References

Biggs, D. A. (2012). *Quagmire: Nation-building and nature in the Mekong Delta*. University of Washington Press.

Biggs, D. A. (2018). *Footprints of war: Militarized landscapes in Vietnam*. University of Washington Press.

Carter, J. M. (2008). *Inventing Vietnam: The United States and state building, 1954–1968*. Cambridge University Press.

Catton, P. E. (2015). "It would be a terrible thing if we handed these people over to the communists": The Eisenhower administration, Article 14 (d), and the origins of the refugee exodus from North Vietnam. *Diplomatic History, 39*(2), 331–358.

Chō no jōriku fukyoka betonamu nanmin hongu to mukau [First denial of landing permission: Vietnamese refugees heading to Hong Kong]. (1976, October 16). *The Asahi Shimbun* evening edition, 13.

Cutts, M. (Ed.). (2000). *The state of the world's refugees, 2000: Fifty years of humanitarian action*. Oxford University Press.

Dang, A., Goldstein, S., & McNally, J. (1997). Internal migration and development in Vietnam. *The International Migration Review, 31*(2), 312–337.

EBay pulls "women for sale" ad. (2004, March 13). *ABC News*. https://www.abc.net.au/news/2004-03-13/ebay-pulls-women-for-sale-ad/150870

Gawthorpe, A. J. (2018). "Mad dog?" Samuel Huntington and the Vietnam War. *Journal of Strategic Studies, 41*(1–2), 301–325.

Goodwin-Gill, G. S. (2017). Setting the scene: Refugees, asylum seekers, and migrants at sea – the need for a long-term, protection-centred vision. In V. Moreno-Lax & E. Papastavridis (Eds.), *"Boat refugees" and migrants at sea: A comprehensive approach* (pp. 17–31). Brill Nijhoff.

Goscha, C. (2016). *Vietnam: A new history*. Hachette UK.

Hansen, P. (2009). Bắc di cư: Catholic refugees from the north of Vietnam, and their role in the Southern Republic, 1954–1959. *Journal of Vietnamese Studies, 4*(3), 173–211.

Hardy, A. (2004). Internal transnationalism and the formation of the Vietnamese diaspora. In B. S. Yeoh & K. Willis (Eds.), *State/nation/transnation: Perspectives on transnationalism in the Asia-Pacific* (pp. 218–237). Routledge.

Hashimoto, N. (2019). Stratification of rights and entitlements among refugees and other displaced persons in Japan. In S. J. Takahashi (Ed.), *Civil and political rights in Japan* (pp. 128–142). Routledge.

Hoang, L. A., & Yeoh, B. S. (2015). Transnational labour migration, debts and family economics in Vietnam. In L. Hoang & B. Yeoh (Eds.), *Transnational labour migration, remittances and the changing family in Asia* (pp. 283–310). Springer.

Hsia, H. C. (2001). "Wàijí xīnniáng" xiànxiàng zhī méitǐ jiàngòu [The media construction of the "foreign brides" phenomenon]. *Taiwan: A Radical Quarterly in Social Studies, 43*, 153–96.

Huang, J. Y. (2019). *Fúshēng suíbǐ Huáng Jǐnyú xiānshēng huíyì lù* [Memoirs of Mr. Huang Jinyu]. Self-Publishing.

Jian Y. D. (2020). *Wǒ zài Táiwān xué kàngzhēng zài Tái yígōng de gōngmín kè* [Learning protest in Taiwan: A citizenship lesson for migrant workers in Taiwan]. Mirror Media. https://www.mirrormedia.mg/premium/20200110pol001

Jobin, P., & Ying, Z. W. (2020). Táisù qù Yuènán "dǎ tiě"? Gōnghài shūchū nánxiàng jí kuàguó chàngyì liánméng [Formosa Plastics steels itself in Vietnam: Southbound export of industrial pollution and transnational advocacy initiatives]. In E. C. Chao (Ed.), *Nánfāng de shèhuì, xué – xíngdòng zuòwéi lǐlùn (xià) [Studying the South, the South studying: On the ethics of the social action]* (Vol. 2, pp. 213–241). Rive Gauche.

Lacroix, T., Levitt, P., & Vari-Lavoisier, I. (2016). Social remittances and the changing transnational political landscape. *Comparative Migration Studies, 4*(1), 1–5.

Lan, P. C. (2007). Legal servitude and free illegality: Migrant "guest" workers in Taiwan. In R. S. Parreñas & L. C. D. Siu (Eds.), *Asian diasporas: New formations, new conceptions* (pp. 253–278). Stanford University Press.

Lê Espiritu, Y. (2014). *Body counts: The Vietnam War and militarized refugees*. University of California Press.

Li, L. F., & Cheng, E. H. (2014, January 13). *Yuènán jì zhòng fá táo yì yuè láo zìshǒu duō 4 bèi* [Vietnam increases penalties: Fourfold increase in Vietnamese migrant workers voluntarily surrendering after escape]. Liberty Times Net. https://news.ltn.com.tw/news/society/paper/746316

Lipman, J. K. (2020). *In camps: Vietnamese refugees, asylum seekers, and repatriates*. University of California Press.

Loescher, G., & Scanlan, J. A. (1986). *Calculated kindness*. The Fre Press.

Ministry of Labor. (2023, April). *Chǎnyè yǔ shè fú yí gōng rénshù* [Number of migrant workers in manufacturing and social welfare sectors]. https://statfy.mol.gov.tw/index12.aspx

Ministry of the Interior National Immigration. (2023). *Tǒngjì zīliào* [Statistical data]. Agency. https://www.immigration.gov.tw/5382/5385/7344/7350/8887/

Nanmin, hajimete teijū Betonamu no Mai-san ikka, Hōmushō ga kyoka e [Refugees, first-time resettlement. Mr. Mai and his family from Vietnam, the Ministry of Justice grants permission]. (1978, August 31). *Asahi Shimbun*, Evening edition, 13.

Nanmin, yatto jouriku [Refugees, finally landed]. (1977, June 13). *Asahi Shimbun*, Morning edition, 3.

Ngai, J. (1979, August 3). *500 people feared dead as typhoon strikes*. Glasgow Herald. https://news.google.com/newspapers?id=DstAAAAAIBAJ&sjid=D6YMAAAAIBAJ&pg=3248,413337&hl=en

Nguyễn, P. (2017). Salt | Water: Vietnamese refugee passages, memory, and statelessness at sea. *Women's Studies Quarterly*, *45*(1/2), 94–111.

Nihon ni mo shibu kaisetsu nanmin kōtō benmu-kan jimusho [Establishment of Branch Office in Japan: Office of the High Commissioner for Refugees]. (1979, August 19). *Asahi Shimbun*, 13.

NOAA. (1979). *Mariners Weather Log*, *23*(1).

Plummer, K. (1983). *Documents of life: An introduction to the problems and literature of a humanistic method*. Allen & Unwin.

Robinson, W. C. (1998). *Terms of refuge: The Indochinese exodus and the international response*. Zed Books.

Shi mo kakugo shi ni shukkoku [Leaving the country with the preparedness to face death]. (1979, August 5). *Asahi Shimbun*, 13.

Stats, K. (2015). Welcome to Australia? A reappraisal of the Fraser government's approach to refugees, 1975–83. *Australian Journal of International Affairs*, *69*(1), 69–87.

The Control Yuan. (2022, July 28). *Xiǎo jīn mén shǒu jūn qiāng shā yuè nán nán mín jūn shì shěn pàn àn diào chá bào gào* [Investigation report on the military trial of Little Kinmen garrison's shooting of Vietnamese refugees]. https://www.cy.gov.tw/CyBsBoxContent.aspx?n=133&s=17946

Trevisanut, S. (2008). The principle of non-refoulement at sea and the effectiveness of asylum protection. *Max Planck Yearbook of United Nations Law* (vol. 12, pp. 205–46). Brill.

Tseng, Y. F. (2004). Yǐn jìn wàijí láogōng de guózú zhèngzhì [Expressing nationalist politics in guest worker program: Taiwan's recruitment of foreign labour]. *Taiwanese Journal of Sociology, 32*, 1–58.

Vong, S. (2020). "Assets of war": Strategic displacements, population movements, and the uses of refugees during the Vietnam War, 1965–1973. *Journal of American Ethnic History, 39*(3), 75.

Wain, B. (1981). *The refused: The agony of the Indochina refugees*. Simon & Schuster.

Wang, H. Z., & Chang, S. M. (2002). The Commodification of international marriages: Cross-border marriage business in Taiwan and Viet Nam. *International Migration, 40*, 93–116.

Zheng, H. Z. (2005, May 17). Zhòngjiè fùzǐ dàng shè xìngqīn 50 yú yuè láo [Father-son intermediary duo involved in sexual assault of more than 50 Vietnamese labourers]. *United Daily News*, A5.

CHAPTER 13

Japanese and Taiwanese Approaches to Future Climate Displaced People

Kate Hannah Martin

Introduction

Japan and Taiwan do not yet have a defined approach to climate displaced people. This can be explained by a combination of the perceived slow-onset nature of climate change and the reluctance of both nations to accept displaced populations. This situation is underpinned by both nations' current legal definitions failing to recognise such people. Whilst the discourse surrounding such migrants exists both on an international scale and within the limited domestic dialogue of Japan and Taiwan, there is no consensus as to how they should be referenced or what protections/aid they should be given (Apap & de Revel, 2021). Without a standardised approach, individual nations are left grappling with the issue of international climate displacement, a challenge which requires a whole new layer of administration, legal frameworks, and financial aid. As climate induced displacement transforms from a domestic issue into a global crisis, the Pacific Islands region, just a stone's throw from Taiwan

K. H. Martin (✉)
University of Central Lancashire, Preston, UK
e-mail: kmartin5@uclan.ac.uk

L. Momesso and P. Ivanova (eds.), *Refugees and Asylum Seekers in East Asia*, Palgrave Macmillan Studies on Human Rights in Asia,
https://doi.org/10.1007/978-981-97-2867-1_13

and Japan, is set to contribute the first to the climate migrant crisis. It is for this reason that we must consider possible outcomes, including those which result in climate displaced peoples from the Pacific Islands seeking asylum in nations like Japan and Taiwan. As such, this chapter investigates to what extent these nations are prepared and willing to accept Pacific Islanders. Learning from positive and negative experiences of Pacific Island migrants and those international refugees who now reside in Japan and Taiwan could help inform the migratory decision-making process of future climate displaced people from the Pacific Islands.

In a recent legal case brought to the New Zealand High Court by Ioane Teitiota who attempted to gain refugee status as he argued that his human rights were being infringed upon by the impacts of climate change on Kiribati (Climate Change Litigation Database, 2015), it became clear that climate induced displacement in the Pacific Island region is leading some to search for a more stable home, most likely in a new country. If the forecasts on climate migration are accurate 1.2 billion people could be displaced globally by 2050, the UN Human Rights Council and the White House is already suggesting a need for some form of protected status for climate refugees (McAllister, 2023). Developing the kind of protections for climate displaced peoples that are reflective of both the domestic discourse and acclimation requirements of receiving nations whilst creating attainable options that will provide a balance of community, opportunity and stability would require a unique and balanced approach. Japan and Taiwan offer an interesting case in this area because, when it comes to climate migration and asylum seeking, they are relatively blank slates. Both are highly developed post-industrial nations with the financial capacity and sturdy social infrastructure to accommodate climate displaced communities. However, willingness to offer sanctuary varies within the domestic discourse, with one showing acceptance coming from the top (Taiwan) (Kironska, 2022b) and the other seemingly more agreeable at grassroots level (Japan) (Uji et al., 2021). This chapter argues that as contributors to the global climate crisis who have the necessary financial capital, Japan and Taiwan have a moral obligation to offer refuge to climate displaced peoples from the Pacific Islands. This chapter also hopes to contribute to identifying new migratory pathways which reflect the changing needs and requirements of climate migrants from the Pacific Island region. In order to discover viable solutions and substantiate the given argument, this chapter will analyse secondary source materials, employing textual analysis to help explore the nature of refugee and migrant experiences and how those experiences could influence migratory decision-making. The use of textual analysis will be focused on both the accounts and experiences of existing Pacific Island migrants as well as the discourse within Japanese and Taiwanese society and politics related to migrants and refugees, whilst framing this within a wider context of global migration to and asylum seeking in Japan and Taiwan. The patterns revealed in the experiences of existing migrants or the perspectives of the receiving countries will be translated into constructive recommendations at the end of the chapter conveying the current trends surrounding climate displacement and displaced populations.

Climate Change and Future Climate Migrants and Displaced People from the Pacific Islands

Climate change is a concern that the governments and agencies of the Pacific Islands and beyond are attempting to tackle (Bafana, 2022; Harding, 2022). Biodiversity loss and extreme weather events are just a few of the ways Pacific Islanders experience climate change and those experiences influence their decisions to remain in place or to migrate abroad (Ferris, 2023; Taylor, 2023). Sea-level rise is often the focal point of climate discussions related to the Pacific with an "average sea-level rise of between 25 and 58 centimetres [...] predicted to occur by the middle of the century along the coastlines of Pacific Island countries" (Parsons, 2022). This poses a very real existential threat to those nations that sit just a few metres above sea level (Merga & Redl, 2023), and even for those on higher ground, the displacement and migration of coastal communities and a drastic reduction in tenable land (Albert et al., 2016; Singh, 2022) would still have an effect. Even though the Pacific Islands are responsible for only 0.3% of global carbon emissions (Natano, 2022), the list of climate-related impacts that threaten island systems, in some cases rendering them unstable during the twenty-first century (Parsons, 2022), is too long to detail here. The most serious changes to note would be the permanent loss of groundwater sources within the next few decades and the sea-level rise within the next 20 to 40 years (Parsons, 2022). Running parallel to one another, these factors will present human communities with intolerable levels of risk by 2060 (Parsons, 2022). Meanwhile, marine resources will continue to be depleted through ocean warming and acidification (United Nations, 2023a) whilst agriculture is crippled by higher tides, increasing storm intensity, heatwaves, and soil salination and erosion (Salem, 2020a), all leading residents to possibly contemplate leaving for a more stable and safer life elsewhere (UNU-EHS, 2017). In the words of Kausea Natano, Prime Minister of Tuvalu, "This (the impacts of climate change) is how a Pacific atoll dies. This is how our islands will cease to exist" (Natano, 2022), and though nations like Tuvalu are not yet in this state, they are heading towards it (Craymer, 2022).

For the people of the Pacific Islands "land and sea" are both of significant economic, political, and cultural importance. As US$474 million in revenue has been brought into the region in the form of fishing licences in 2016 alone, the "untouched" nature of Pacific Islands continues to draw in tourism which makes up to 70% of any given island's gross domestic product (GDP) (Salem, 2020a). Tourism is just one area of a nation's economy which will be affected by increased extreme weather events and a reduction in natural beauty spots such as coral reefs (Salem, 2020b).

On a community level, climate change is felt acutely, which is clearly exhibited by a recent UNU-EHS report based on fieldwork in Tuvalu, Nauru, and Kiribati. Researchers found that "in Nauru, 74% of households experienced one or more impacts of environmental change in the last decade … drought and irregular rains impacted 61% of the surveyed families", and in Kiribati 94% of households had been impacted by natural hazards over the preceding ten years, 81% of which having been affected by sea-level rise (UNU-EHS, 2015; UNU, 2017). It is clear that without a drastic reduction in emissions and a significant shift in the behaviours of developed and developing nations, countries across the Pacific will observe a marked decline in their economy over the coming decades, thereby further reducing their resilience to climate change and its impacts (IISD, 2019). Every year the region suffers from cyclones, flooding, and heatwaves, and larger and larger proportions of GDP are spent by Pacific Island nations on recovering and rebuilding from climate-related disasters and crises (Fouad, 2021). If such conditions continue unabated, the world would have to find solutions for the Pacific Island populations displaced by or unwilling to live with the constant bombardment of climate impacts.

Climate Induced Migration and Displacement in the Pacific Islands

Migration was repeatedly mentioned in the UNU-EHS report, when discussing climate change across the three islands. In Nauru over a third of households believed that "migration will be necessary in the future due to climate change... however, only a quarter of households believe that they would be able to afford to migrate in the future" (UNU-EHS, 2015; United Nations University, 2017). Meanwhile, in Kiribati migration had remained internal with people moving to the capital of South Tarawa "intensifying existing overcrowding and water shortages" (UNU-EHS, 2015; United Nations University, 2017). Tuvalu was also experiencing internal migration as "environmental conditions triggered 9% of recorded movements in 2005–2015" and the majority of households indicated that migration may become a necessary survival strategy as climate change impacts living conditions and quality of life (UNU-EHS, 2015; United Nations University, 2017). In all nations the combined or individual factors of "sea-level rise (76% of respondents), saltwater intrusion (74%), drought (72%) and floods (71%) are the most likely environmental factors to trigger future migration" (UNU-EHS, 2015; United Nations University, 2017). Most concerning was how 97% of the Tuvaluan households which were surveyed reported having been impacted by natural disasters between 2005 and 2015, yet just 53% believed that they could afford to migrate, if necessary, in the future (UNU-EHS, 2015; United Nations University, 2017). For many people on the ground, migration, or displacement due to climate change, is becoming a fact of life. Even so, there is a significant gap between those who believe that migration will be necessary and those who, when the time comes, will be financially able to move. The concern over whether one is able to afford to migrate could dictate the future patterns of migration decision-making if it proves true that those with the financial capacity will move voluntarily in advance of environmental disasters whilst those who lack the resources become the forcibly displaced post event.

Unmanaged rural to urban migration in the Pacific Islands is already observed, and this trend is only set to grow as outlying atoll islands are no longer able to sustain communities (Campbell & Warrick, 2014). Unfortunately, urban centres do not necessarily offer safe harbour as both urban and non-urban atolls are considered to be vulnerable to climate change's impacts and the impact of development pressure on the already struggling environment (Campbell & Warrick, 2014). Despite the UN reports which indicates that climate change is impacting migration trends and discourse in the Pacific Islands (UNU-EHS, 2015; United Nations University, 2017), some migration scholars remain unwilling to attribute a significant role in migration decision-making to climate change and environmental drivers (Campbell, 2014). Climate migration as we know it today is only just beginning and though there is a growing body of literature on the topic (Ghosh, 2022), we still do not possess enough empirical evidence for this phenomenon as climate change migration continues to be interwoven with other forms of migration which are more easily identified, i.e. escaping war, violence, or persecution.

This hesitancy to accept the looming climate displacement crisis is evident in the failure of international organisations and individual governments to come to a consensus on or provide legal provisions for climate displaced people (Prange, 2022). It is perplexing, particularly in light of several sovereign Pacific Island nations becoming uninhabitable due to climate change (Natano, 2022). Nevertheless, Pacific Island governments are taking radical actions such as launching the Rising Nations Initiative to fill in gaps in legal frameworks whilst pushing for increased awareness and political commitment (Natano, 2022).

Pacific Island Climate Migrants—Thoughts and Perspectives on a Displaced Future

The Pacific Islands are already struggling with the disproportionate impacts of climate change and for people residing in nations such as Tuvalu, the Marshall Islands, Kiribati, or Nauru, as adaptation options in situ become inadequate or too expensive in the face of "particularly severe, frequent or unrelenting" climate impacts (Campbell & Warrick, 2014) migration may become the only option. Such circumstances are being met with mixed feelings, particularly as migration for economic reasons is already so prevalent in the region (Tchounwou et al., 2022).

Today, Pacific Islanders are pushing for voluntary, dignified migration whereby migrants can actively contribute to the social and economic life of the country to which they move (ABC News, 2014). Across every level of society in Oceania, climate change is coming into focus and people, communities, and governments are taking action. These include national adaptation plans (Government of the Republic of Fiji, 2018); students campaigning and taking their message all the way to the International Court of Justice (PISFCC, 2023); and foreign ministers making impactful speeches at international conferences (Packham & Singh, 2021). The Pacific Islands are doing all they can to help stop climate change, primarily by working towards an aim of carbon neutrality for the region by

2050 (IISD, 2022). Meanwhile, the juxtaposition between the islanders' resilience and their understanding of the inevitability of migration, at least in some quarters (Doherty, 2017), exhibits a clear need for adaptation strategies which stretch across everything from food security (SPREP, 2023) to new migratory policies and opportunities (Plano, 2022).

The UNU-EHS report on Nauru, Kiribati, and Tuvalu provides one of the most significant insights into approaches to emigration, whilst telling very different stories for the three nations and identifying a common will to remain on the islands where possible. For those experiencing climate-related hazards Kiribati saw 1.3% of respondents move internationally (7.7% moved internally), Nauru saw 10% move internationally (no internal migration), and Tuvalu saw 15% move internationally (12% moved internally) (UNU-EHS, 2016). As a one-island state Nauruans have no choice but to move abroad, whereas I-Kiribati and Tuvaluans have the option to move to other islands that they perceive to be safer or more stable within the state (United Nations University, 2017). This displays their connection to their homeland and a wish to avoid external migration where possible, thereby avoiding being disconnected from their culture, a top concern in the UNU-EHS report (UNU-EHS, 2016).

It can be safely stated that Pacific Islanders prefer to have a choice to migrate, no matter their reasons, as opposed to being forcibly displaced and yet current statistics show an average of "50,000 people in the Pacific being forced to flee their homes due to the devastating impacts of disasters and climate change" each year (United Nations, 2021). Nauru have already shared their concerns that resettlement will no longer be a last resort as it is cheaper for the major polluters to move people than it is to shift to a green economy (United Nations, 2021), meaning that the receiving nations will have at least some if not all the input. It is of the upmost importance that the Pacific Island people have the strongest voice on migration that pertains to themselves; even so, questions remain as to the balance of power and decision-making when resettlement outside the region begins to occur.

For those people who are facing displacement, their thoughts, perspectives, and particularly their concerns are already being voiced. The Carteret Islands of Papua New Guinea play host to around 2500 islanders who have, until recently, lived relatively peaceful lives (Farrell, 2014). Unfortunately, the Carterets have experienced significant agricultural disruption lately as coastal erosion, destruction of sea walls, and inundation of saltwater have led to a rapidly depleting emergency food supply and relocation possibly becoming the only option readily available to resolve the situation (Farrell, 2014). The Papua New Guinea administration has since struggled to move the islands' populations, having already made several unsuccessful attempts as "many residents say they are worried about losing their culture and traditions and are uncertain as to how they will be received by the host community" (Farrell, 2014). For the Carteret Islanders migration and resettlement are their only choice; in some ways they are lucky in being able to move to land within the same nation state where they can retain, at least in part, their sense of community and their rights as citizens, a privilege other such migrants in Oceania may not enjoy.

Though Pacific Islands have growing political, economic, and trade connections with Japan and Taiwan, this is yet to translate into consistent migration. This may be due, in part, to linguistic and cultural challenges posed by migrating to Japan and Taiwan. With the exception of Tonga, the Japanese language does not appear in the high school curriculum and to experience Japanese culture one would need to attend events ran by the Japanese embassy in Fiji (Embassy of Japan in the Republic of Fiji, 2022). Whilst Mandarin and Cantonese speakers can be found in pockets across the Pacific Islands, the opportunities to learn either of the core Chinese languages remain limited to universities in countries such as Samoa, Fiji, and Tonga (JICA, 2009). The linguistic connections between the Pacific Islands and Japan/Taiwan are tenuous at best, even when taking into account the links between Indigenous Taiwanese languages and the related languages spoken in the Pacific Islands. The perceived lack of an existing community is also a barrier to migration, particularly when compared with Pasifika communities in nations such as New Zealand and Australia where Pacific Island migrants make up 8% (381,642 people) (New Zealand Foreign Affairs & Trade, 2023) and 1.3% (337,000 people) (Liu & Howes, 2023) of the population, respectively. Without this sense of community, which Pacific Islanders place so much emphasis upon (PICA-WA, 2022), it is easy to understand why previous trends in migration are linked to regions with an existing community and cultural connection to Oceania. Nevertheless, there are small grassroots Pasifika communities growing in both Taiwan and Japan, and the experiences of those migrants, as well as others from existing refugees, will be invaluable in informing the migratory decision-making process of other Pacific Islanders and in building ties between the islands and Taiwan/Japan (Schieder, 2021). With a larger community base, future displaced people may be able to transition to Japan or Taiwan more smoothly. Pre-emptive Pacific Islander trans-border mobility within the Pacific may go a long way to opening Japan and Taiwan up to future displaced peoples and ensuring that existing policies and frameworks are amended to meet the needs of future climate migrants.

Current Approaches to Migration and Refugees in Japan and Taiwan

Whilst Japan has a working legal framework to allow for refugees, Taiwan's policies remain complex and to an extent dictated by wider geopolitical constraints. The homogenous nature of Japan has meant that the door to migration is opened to a select few. In contrast to this, modern-day Taiwan is a product of continuous migration and colonisation. Its culture today reflects this; however, its difficulty in allowing larger-scale migration and accepting refugees in significant numbers is due to its unique political relationship with China.

Japan—Migration and Refugee Policy

Migration between the Pacific Islands and Japan is limited. Japanese immigration policy is particularly restrictive towards foreign unskilled workers, who in 2015 made up only 2.5% of the workforce (Saito, 2022) a statistic that remained the same five years later (CNBC, 2021). This practice of discriminating against so-called unskilled workers puts up a barrier to the many potential Pacific Islander migrants who are skilled in sectors such as agriculture, forestry, fishing, tourism, and business linked to natural resources (ILO, 2017). On those occasions when Japan does open its doors opportunities are often limited to specific sectors or for those willing to work the 3Ks jobs (Saito, 2022). One of the most interesting examples of such a job is that of a care worker. With a rapidly ageing population Japan has taken to recruiting migrant workers from Southeast Asia to fill caring positions. Though these migrant care workers often find themselves in a paternalistic system of control (Lan, 2022) prospective migrants from nations such as Indonesia continue looking to Japan for opportunities.

Recently, schools offering a mixture of vocational and Japanese language training have mushroomed across the region to channel more than 16,000 Indonesians into the Japanese special skilled worker scheme in 2022 alone. This growth in migration, which has "benefited both countries" (Matarani, 2023), provides a framework for future migration which could be copied by other Pacific Island nations (Matarani, 2023). The Australian Government has already set up a similar Pacific Australia Labour Mobility scheme to provide training in order to increase the number of Fijian aged care workers who can make the transition (APTC, 2022), proving that there is a demand within the Pacific Island region to train for such jobs and to migrate if the right opportunities exist.

Though adding in a language learning element to such training will have an added expense, recruiting from nations such as Fiji, where multilingualism is already prominent (Kaur, 2016), should not prove any more challenging to implement than in the training schools of Indonesia. There may be great potential in introducing vocational schools to the Pacific Islands which include a Japanese language course, as in 2019 a law took effect which introduced a new category of "specified skilled workers" in 14 sectors such as agriculture, sanitation, and construction, which is aimed at attracting 345,000 such workers over a five-year period. It is hoped that this policy will help primarily Vietnamese, Indonesian, and Filipino workers to continue living and working in Japan as well as offering the opportunity to bring their families with them (Lang, 2023). There is nothing to say that this could not also benefit Pacific Islanders, even if this still leaves the scope for migration relatively limited. Nevertheless, some business leaders have clearly stated that "if the country wants to remain competitive, redrafting its immigration policies is inevitable" (Barron, 2017). There is a clear will, at least within the business community, to have Japan open its doors to asylum seekers and refugees as potential future workers (Lewis, 2017). If Japan were to redirect funds into language and vocational programmes for communities in the Pacific Islands who are most likely to be affected by climate change, such a measure could give potentially displaced peoples a skillset that would allow them to apply for work in Japan, provide a fresh start for those who feel they would otherwise be displaced by climate change, and introduce migrant communities who have a head start in acclimating to the culture, ensuring that Japan retains a level of cultural homogeneity even in a growing multicultural society.

For refugees looking to find safe harbour in Japan, the path to asylum and eventual citizenship proves difficult and, for the majority, impossible. Japan still strictly adheres to the 1951 United Nations Refugee Convention definition (UNHCR, 1951). This means that those who are fleeing conflict, natural disasters, or possibly climate change do not qualify for asylum in Japan. Unfortunately, the measures which are currently in place have historically fallen short of providing for refugees who are both waiting in Japan for a visa and to be resettled in country, with reports of homelessness among refugees who are struggling to meet basic needs not uncommon (JAR, 2023). Refugees can wait anywhere up to ten years for a decision on their case and in that time the government funds they are eligible to receive can take several months to materialise and will only amount to two-thirds of the normal social welfare fund (JAR, 2023). Those who do not have the status of resident whilst seeking a refugee status could be seen as illegal (undocumented) and are at risk of being detained (Japan Association for Refugees, 2023).

Taiwan—Migration and Refugee Policy

Taiwan's migration and refugee policies are made complex by the strained relationship with China which has drawn a line in the sand blocking Taiwan from forming a comprehensive framework for migration and refugees. That is not to say, however, that Taiwan has become disinterested in or unwilling to act upon the refugee question, "Taiwan cannot ignore the refugee issue, because there are various groups of people that require protection and the government is not able to respond effectively in the absence of an asylum law" (Kironska, 2022a). The country has, in theory, a limited migration policy, and although there are a number of methods to sidestep its limitations, Taiwan's inability to effect further change to its policies even when the will might exist to do so leaves it at what initially appears to be a dead end. The three most common long-term categories of visa which are open to non-Chinese foreigners are "migrant workers, marriage immigrants and skilled workers" (Wang, 2011, p. 174). The treatment of migrants can vary depending on their category. Skilled workers receive the most favourable treatment, with an option for permanent resident status after six years, whilst less-skilled migrants have to leave Taiwan after their contracts expire (Wang, 2011, p. 174). Similar to Japanese migration policies, Taiwan places importance on retaining a relatively homogenous society by guarding "population quality" (*renkou suzhi*) with the added point of protecting "national security" (Wang, 2011, p. 182–83). However, such entrenched positions on migrants have been forced to change due to existing labour shortages.

In order to make up the shortfall in workers, Taiwan has recognised that "to maintain Taiwan's economic growth momentum, the foreign workforce needs to be increased by a net 400,000 from 2021 to 2030" (Taiwan Economic Forum, 2022) which is just over the total populations of Kiribati, Tuvalu, the Marshall Islands, Nauru, Cook Islands, Tonga, Niue, American Samoa, Wallis and Futuna, Tokelau and Easter Island (389,255). Attempts to meet the labour shortage are currently limited to "strengthening recruitment of foreign professionals, increasing the attraction and retention of foreign students and overseas compatriot students and retaining foreign technical manpower" (Taiwan Economic Forum, 2022) but is yet to extend to offering provisions for blue-collar workers to reside long term.

Unfortunately, refugees in Taiwan are often left in a legal grey area, even after Taiwan ratified and adopted sections of the international human rights convention into national law. Among the five international treaties that Taiwan has agreed to is the "International Covenant on Civil and Political Rights (ICCPR) which binds its signatories to respecting civil and political rights, such as the rights to life, freedom of religion or speech), which introduced the *non-refoulement* obligation in Taiwan" (Kironska, 2022a). Despite this, Taiwan has previously deported refugees including those who file an asylum application; various authorities pass refugees from one organisation to the next, leaving many reliant on support given by civil society groups to provide basic resources such as accommodation and medical treatment whilst they wait (Kironska, 2022a). The chasm in Taiwan's immigration system has the potential to be filled as soon as the 15-year-old draft refugee law, which recognised environmentally displaced people and is slated to be passed in 2024 (TaiwanPlus News, 2023), comes into force. This could contribute to Taiwan's already growing status as a leading regional figure in human rights (Amnesty International, 2023) and open the nation up a potential migration option for climate displaced people or environmental migrants coming from the Pacific Islands. Though this will present new challenges in providing the necessary infrastructure and aid for incoming refugees, an issue the nation already grapples with (Davidson & Lin, 2022), it does present a modicum of hope.

Experiences of Pacific Island Migrants Living in Japan and Taiwan

Though there are currently no climate displaced people living in Japan or Taiwan who originate from the Pacific Islands, we can use the experiences of those Pacific Island migrants currently living in the two nations. This chapter will focus on the community-building practices and experiences of Fijian migrants living in Japan, the highs and lows of life for Pacific Island students studying in Taiwan and Japan, the paternalistic systems and opportunities which influence the lives of Tongan sportsmen in Japan, and the transition from island life in Hawaii to the bustling metropolis of Taipei for a Hawaiian-Taiwanese family unit. Finally, this section will consider experiences of refugees from Myanmar which could inform the future policies that may affect displaced peoples from the Pacific Islands.

The literature on the experiences of Pacific migrants in Japan and Taiwan is not extensive; however, through Dominik Schieder's articles: "Fiji Islander trans-border mobility in the Pacific: The case of Fiji and Japan" (Schieder, 2021) and "Community Life and Discourses among Fiji Islanders in Kantō, Japan" (Schieder, 2015), we can gain a glimpse of the true reality of life for such migrants.

According to Schieder the number of Fijian migrants in Japan has grown steadily since the commencement of diplomatic relations in 1970 and as of 2019 there were 287 Fiji Islanders in Japan. This level of migration is significantly lower than the levels we see to New Zealand or Australia, but it does show that migration is viable, though assuredly more difficult. The age bracket of these migrants is particularly telling, with the vast majority (65%) being between 20 and 39 years of age, with education and professional rugby being the core reasons behind the decision to migrate. Between 2012 and 2019 the number of these migrants increased from 181 to 287, a sharp increase on previous migration levels, which indicates a strengthening of ties and a corresponding increase in access to student visas and engineer/specialist in humanities/international services visas. In 2021 students made up 74 of the 287 migrants to Japan and the Japanese government is actively encouraging this migration as part of a wider aid programme, which funnels Fijian students into degrees in agriculture, environmental conservation, management, pedagogy, and science education (Schieder, 2021). Fijians, among other Pacific Islanders such as Samoans, Tongans, and Rotumans, have also appeared in increasing numbers across sports in Japan such as rugby and to a lesser extent sumo.

Migration in this sector remains small and though it could grow in a similar way to sports migration in other parts of the world, it does rely on youth and possibly the willingness to give up one's citizenship if the sportsperson is hoping to compete internationally in events such as the Olympics. It also appears to be a stream of migration dominated by men, with limited prospects for female sports migration to Japan. This is due to the core recruitment coming from universities or companies looking to bolster their existing men's teams. In Schieder's view, these small migrant communities could grow and foster longer-term migration trends from Fiji to Japan. However, the trans-border mobility between the two nations remains limited and does not appear likely to expand, which calls into question Schieder's predictions of long-term migration trends between Fiji and Japan.

As part of Schieder's study on this community he took note of the trends in behaviour and social/cultural discourse that are beginning to form in diaspora communities. In particular, Schieder states that the term "community", a frequent topic of discussion even when physical social gatherings are infrequent, is playing a unique role in manifesting social bonding and creating a sense of belonging to a wider community when the regular community life which many Islanders are so familiar with is no longer open to them. What is of interest to an outsider is how Fijian Islanders have transformed their concept of community and built into their lives in Japan through their retention of the "community" term whilst disconnecting from the expectations typically associated with the term. In effect, "community discourses allow Fiji Islanders in Japan to circumvent socio-economic commitments without questioning their participation in a community as such" (Schieder, 2015). This taps into something not just of interest to researchers focusing on the changing perceptions of sociality among Indigenous Fijian migrants but also to those who are attempting to understand how a wider community of Pacific Islanders may cope if moved to a nation such as Japan. In understanding how Pacific Island migrants approach the discourse surrounding community" and all that term encompasses, the outcome of further research in this field could be of significance when contributing to any new policies linked to both migrants and displaced peoples/refugees from the wider Pacific region.

Community can be a crucial part of life for migrant and diaspora communities, particularly as they can be fed by a flow of new migrants joining already settled communities. However, that flow of migrants either relies on consistent, healthy diplomatic relations between two nations or on one nation being willing to take in migrants, refugees or displaced peoples from the other. When relations sour, whether that be for political, economic, or other such reasons grassroots communities can suffer. This is the case we have seen with new communities and groups such as the Pacific Islands Students Association (PISA, 2023). The ill feeling which resulted from the switch in diplomatic relations by the Solomon Islands and Kiribati has cost students studying in Taiwan their scholarships (91 being I-Kiribati and 35 from the Solomon Islands) and led to either repatriation or the decision to continue their academic journey in mainland China (Quinn, 2019). The "immediate and angry" response exhibited by Taiwan in light of the diplomatic switch has had devastating results for the students who found out about the loss of their scholarships after reading it in the newspaper and were left with sleepless nights as they tried to quickly organise a new plan and leave Taiwan within one month. With little to no communication from mainland Chinese universities or from the Solomon Islands government beyond a vague commitment to eventually take in these students many have been left worrying about having to move to universities in China. Some are having to dip into limited family savings to complete their tuition in Taiwan or to simply return home having not completed their degrees (Cavanough & Nielson, 2019).

These shifts in diplomatic relations have had ramifications for small grassroots Pacific Island communities in Taiwan and unfortunately this has meant that, whether they had a good experience of Taiwan or not, those who do not have the funds to continue will probably leave dissatisfied as they are no longer able to see out their scholarships and could, through word of mouth, put off other Pacific Islanders from viewing Taiwan as a future migration option. What we can see from those students who are attempting to stay is that the overall experience of Taiwan and its education system is a positive one, particularly as individual institutions attempt to find new scholarships for their Pacific Island students, which shows a level of care and acceptance at least from the academic world (Leung, 2019). The previous scholarship funding from the Taiwanese government will however now benefit other Pacific Islanders as Taiwan redirects funding into new scholarships for its remaining diplomatic partners in the region (Leung, 2019).

As mentioned previously the paternalistic system of control over migrant workers in Japan (Lan, 2022) has also been observed by Besnier

(Besnier, 2011) whose research on Pacific Islanders in Japan leads us to the experiences of Tongan rugby players whose treatment in Japan has recently come under criticism due to the players being controlled by the team managers, who are employed by the corporation who owns the team and not looking out for Tongan players best interests. Unfortunately, these relatively well-paid positions are still considered to be blue-collar work and so the Tongan migrants are scrutinised in all their actions both on and off the pitch. If they step out of line, they are often swiftly deported.

For Tongan rugby players in Japan this has led to a high "burnout" rate and shows how sport can offer opportunities for employment and migration but that such forms of migration are a double-edged sword. What rugby opportunities in Japan do offer to Tongan players, which goes beyond a monetary or migration value, is in the reproduction of the traditional social order and the introduction of possible stardom and wealth, a hope that we see repeated in those Tongans who migrate to Japan to train as future sumo wrestlers (Besnier, 2011).

The experiences of these Tongan sportsmen speak to one of the most prominent issues linked to migration in Japan, particularly for blue-collar workers, migrants coming from low-income countries, and refugees: Japan's innate need to control the activities and behaviour of such migrants. Though the system of paternalistic control over migrants is not necessarily unique to Japan, the simple fact that migrant numbers coming from the Pacific Islands are so low means that such control is felt most acutely when struggling with challenges linked to the workplace (Besnier, 2011). Such a feeling is compounded when a migrant does not have the resource of a community to draw on due to the geographic distance between existing Pacific Island migrants. This could be a source of concern for climate migrants or displaced peoples who do not wish to live under a microscope, having their choices questioned or risking deportation if they fail to assimilate. However, from Besnier's research it is also clear that the opportunities offered by Japan may, for some, outweigh the disadvantages of the paternalistic system and that such a system can prove a welcome reflection of the social norms of Tongan culture with which Tongan migrants are familiar.

A possible exception to this paternalistic system is in migration for education. In a series of YouTube video's documenting life in Japan as an international student, Philemon Maiennaka Nangu, originally from Papua New Guinea, shows his experiences in Japan whilst continuing to post videos linked to his home country. Though his videos do not verbalise his thoughts on life in Japan, it is clear from the imagery and content that there is a small "Pasifica family" (Nangu, 2020) in Nagoya and across the wider expanse of Japan. Nangu's choice to name another one of his videos "Pacific Island Family in Japan" (Nangu, 2020) exhibits a willingness to create a Pacific Island community as opposed to one solely based on his own nationality. This speaks to the community-building practices of Pacific Islanders living in Japan and shows that Pacific Islanders can find community connection points beyond Oceania. Even if Japan is unwilling to move on the matter of climate migrants (Kameyama & Ono, 2020), another possible option could be to filter more Pacific Islanders through the higher education system where possible, which will give them time to put down roots and learn the language before eventually transitioning into longer-term employment in Japan.

It is particularly important to remember that the Pacific Islands are home to people from a variety of mixed heritages. An interesting podcast by the Ka ʻiwakīloumoku Pacific Indigenous Institute interviewed a Hawaiian-Taiwanese family living in Taipei, showcasing the benefits and challenges of life in Taiwan (Kaʻiwakīloumoku, 2021). One of the family's major challenges came in the form of extreme changes in weather/ temperatures as well as the earthquakes which they had not experienced to such a level before. Though the family were jovial about it the mother did recognise how such events are dangerous and expressed some concern for the family's welfare. The major positives that come through in the interview were how Taiwan is more conducive to "new things, to new hobbies, to new experiences in general" and how moving to Taiwan opened the horizons of the younger generation and gave them a new perspective which they believe has had a positive influence on their lives. For the mother her experiences were more mixed as she noted how they missed loved ones in Hawai'i and the overall environment of the islands (Kaʻiwakīloumoku, 2021). Arguably the difficulties experienced by this Hawaiian–Taiwanese family could be the same as those of any new migrant in Taiwan as they reflect the challenges of daily life linked to language, education, and acclimating to the environment and culture. Yet, it is clear from the outset that the availability of opportunities, more so for the younger generation through improved access to extra-curricular activities and a multicultural educational experience, can make the move more bearable.

Although the migratory experiences of this family do not include the trauma of forced displacement, it does offer an insight into how it is possible to make a transition to Taiwan smoother by placing children in international schools, focusing on language training for adults to give them greater access to the society and culture, and also to possibly connect incoming Pacific Islanders with Taiwan's Indigenous community, which could prove to have some positive outcomes. For the Hawaiian-Taiwanese family in this interview, beyond the jabs made at their inadequate linguistic skills, the family did not have any further unpleasant experiences, however, researchers have questioned if the numbers of Pacific Island migrants with no Taiwanese ethnic heritage were to increase and remain on a more permanent basis, whether they may experience such discrimination. Naturally, questions will arise over the humane treatment of migrants and refugees as findings shed light on such experiences (Phillimore et al., 2021). It is no secret that Japanese and Taiwanese societies and the cultures at large are not as racially or culturally sensitive as they could be which can lead to misunderstandings and negative experiences being had by those of non-Japanese/non-Taiwanese heritage or even by those with a mixed heritage (Arudō, 2015; Illmer, 2020; Park, 2017).

Moving beyond migration to Japan or Taiwan, it is also crucial to glance at the experiences of those refugees who have settled and made these nations home. Within the literature it has already been recognised that there is an urgent need to "expand the scale and scope of refugee resettlement schemes" in Japan as the current approach focused on economic self-sufficiency lacks the more holistic aspects of community collaboration and integration (Phillimore et al., 2021). However, in a recent study comparing refugee approaches and experiences in the UK and Japan conducted by Jenny Phillimore and her team, which interviewed refugees from Myanmar currently residing in Japan, the self-sufficiency policy appears to prove more successful than the UK's more informal approaches.

The approach of transitioning refugees into paid employment after an initial settling in period appears to improve self-esteem and self-respect, particularly among men who, through taking financial responsibility for their families, felt that they were fitting into Japanese society. It is not only the independence which comes from this income which helps refugees to integrate but also the opportunity to build social connections and build new communities through a multicultural workplace, whilst also experiencing an interest in their own culture from their Japanese co-workers. These factors make integration feel more like a two-way process.

To strike a balance the study also highlighted the issues which have arisen. For example, some refugees experienced xenophobia, struggles with the language, and with social integration, particularly for women with school age children. Though Japan's model does offer early financial independence, the difficulty comes later as case workers do not help refugees access new employment if they do not like their first placement or wish for more social mobility. The dependence on a refugee's first employer and colleagues can prove challenging. They have cited the long working hours as a reason for why they have struggled to make connections within the local community (Phillimore et al., 2021).

Phillimore's study is crucial to understanding the positives and pitfalls of Japan's approach to refugees and the implications this may have for possible future climate displaced peoples from the Pacific Islands. The integration of refugees into any society is a complex and non-linear process. Japan's strength in its approach to refugees lies in its provision of employment opportunities. However, there is room for improvement in fostering positive community engagement. The community groups of Schieder's study, and of Philemon Maiennaka Nangu, as well as those many related groups on Facebook which can provide connections to Chamorro (Guam) dance and cultural exhibitions ran by the Guma' Famagu'on Tano' yan I Tasi (Guma' Famagu'on Tano' yan I Tasi, 2023) or other community events organised by Pacific Islanders serving in the United States military, can all provide a resolution and bridge the gap, allowing for a smoother, less traumatic transition for climate displaced peoples from the Pacific Islands.

Public Discourse on Accepting Climate Displaced People in Japan and Taiwan

Pacific Islanders may prove willing to migrate to Japan or Taiwan, and the latter countries may have the capacity to take displaced people, but do they have the willingness to do so? Literature available on the policies and public discourse surrounding climate displaced people arriving in Japan or Taiwan is difficult to attain and could offer a particularly interesting field of research for those who are looking to both understand their experiences and contribute to new and existing policies pertaining to such peoples. The available information does not shed much light on how Taiwan will process, provision for, and assimilate future climate displaced people should the new bill pass, nor does it articulate what possible actions the Japanese government is planning to take or even if the issue is on their radar. For both nations, efforts to create policies regarding displaced people will be implemented in preparation for the displacement of their own people as climate change and sea-level rise begin to impact upon these nations. In this regard Japan and Taiwan have much in common with their Pacific Island brethren as they are all islands, with limited amounts of tenable living space. All have varying levels of risk posed by rising seas, by extreme weather events, and by a rapidly changing climate; the only difference is their capacity to withstand the impacts of these events. It would be foolish to approach Taiwan and Japan as nations which will be untouched by the climate crisis and therefore capable of spending vast quantities on relief efforts or welcoming in large numbers of refugees without keeping in mind the significant domestic challenges linked to climate change they must themselves also face. Nonetheless, we cannot discount the carbon emissions and consumption patterns in these countries which have made a substantial contribution to the current climate crisis and that both Taiwan and Japan will need to shoulder some of the responsibility and provide aid to those most affected.

Japan's Public Discourse

Though awareness and discussions surrounding migration have increased in Japan, usually the topic is discussed in relation to replacing an ageing population, not in offering safe harbour to climate displaced people. Therefore, attempting to gauge locals' reactions to having a large number of climate displaced migrants arriving on their doorstep remains somewhat difficult to ascertain. In 2021, a team of researchers released their data produced from a survey-embedded joint experiment; the results of this experiment highlighted the responses of Japanese participants to possible future climate migrants and considering what has already been observed from Japan on an international level in relation to providing aid as opposed to opening its borders, the responses are telling (Uji et al., 2021). The results of the survey suggested that Japanese public opinion is not so much swayed by previous aid or immigration levels but by the support a nation gives to Japan whether that be in international forums or in purchasing Japanese exports to improve their economy. Japanese respondents did not see taking in migrants as an obligation, but they did show a bias towards taking Asian migrants (Uji et al., 2021). So, what does this mean for future climate migrants coming from the Pacific? It could mean for a time that if the affected countries continue to provide a block of political support to Japan at the international level, there may be some leverage through which they can open Japan's doors, however, it would also mean that when countries start to disappear from the map that leverage will dissipate, even if Pacific Island nations are able to retain some form of sovereignty without their islands. Their only saving grace may be in the latter part of the Japanese responses which showed that "sea-level rise and droughts, whose effect is gradual seem to generate more public support than dramatic events such as floods, typhoons, and wildfires" (Uji et al., 2021); this contrasts with Western support which often occurs after significant events. Japanese public support appears to rely on something that they can see is threatening a person's safety but does not necessitate quick and decisive action, in keeping with their slow adoption of refugee policies. This could explain why Japan has shown little to no interest in climate refugees or in how climate displaced people could present both a security risk to Japan and an opportunity to secure further economic growth. There is also the matter of how they could lose face due to their lack of prior action on the subject (World Economic Forum, 2021). In a meeting of the United Nations Security Council in February of 2023, the Japanese position on climate migrants became yet clearer as Japan's delegate likened the threat posed by sea-level rise to that posed by foreign invasion (United Nations, 2023b). The delegate also mentioned the need to work beyond the council with other entities to handle these issues (United Nations, 2023) which once again allows Japan to shift responsibility away from itself in relation to physically taking in displaced people (United Nations, 2023b). Though a limited number of "general refugees" have been allowed to enter the country, this poses no real threat to national security, but it is clear that there are concerns over future threats and instability caused by climate migrants moving to Japan, even though this is not yet something the Japanese government is discussing publicly (Kameyama & Ono, 2021). Though, for the time being, Japan's public discourse, at least within the bounds of the media, does recognise climate displacement as a burgeoning issue the manner in which media outlets address this issue shows quite plainly how the Japanese discourse perceives this to be an international problem which either they can help to relieve through finance or which needs to be resolved by the Western world (Naidoo, 2018; Uji et al., 2021).

Taiwan's Public Discourse

Surprisingly, the available information on how Taiwan is approaching international climate migration, beyond the possible changes to asylum law, appears to be thin on the ground. There are two possible reasons for this, the first of which is the difficulty in producing a comprehensive refugee framework and putting it into practice. Though human rights groups in the nation have consistently lobbied for a change to the law, this has often been in response to political turmoil in China (TaiwanPlus News, 2023). There has been no definitive discourse on doing so to aid climate migrants, which is baffling considering their recognition of such people in the new refugee law. Of course, such a move could possibly be taken as a sign to China that Taiwan is taking further steps towards sovereignty and autonomy and would possibly make an already fragile situation worse. In the knowledge of this, Taiwan may not be in the position to make policies or take in climate migrants at the time of writing (2023). However, any moves from them to do so would certainly send a message not just to China but to the world of their global standing and their ambitious human rights plans. It could also change the face of international refugee law, in being the first nation to accept environmentally displaced peoples. The second reason is that Taiwan is already beginning to handle the fallout from climate change as many of their own low-lying communities come under threat (Yuan Teng, 2022) and they recently experienced some of the worst droughts in history which has shown how easily their water supplies can be destabilised (Jensen, 2020). With discussions already arising that include Taiwan among the first nations that will produce climate refugees (Taiwan Today, 2006), Taiwan will require a modicum of understanding in any hesitance to take in climate displaced peoples from other nations. If this is the case, then any expectations one might have for Taiwan to take climate refugees simply due to its developed status and strong economy would need to be put aside whilst it directs its finances to protecting its own communities at risk and remaining strong. We cannot criticise Taiwan for not initiating further action to provide safe harbour for climate migrants but considering its past history of taking in refugees we also have little cause to believe that they would turn people away at this time.

Conclusion

This chapter aims to contribute to the conversations about climate displaced people from the Pacific Islands, examining the issues around possible migration routes to Japan and Taiwan. It has become clear through the development of this chapter that any decision to migrate would not be made lightly due to the existing restrictive and complex immigration systems of Japan and Taiwan, and that making and pursuing such a choice could prove strenuous and inconvenient in comparison with other more well-trodden migration routes to Australia, New Zealand, or the US. Yet, considering the unpredictable nature of climate change and its impacts on the Pacific Islands it is necessary to prepare for all possible migratory choices which result from the environmental damage anticipated.

We have seen how those nations involved retain relatively amicable ties, making it all the more puzzling as to why those relationships have not resulted in increased rates of migration. This does not necessarily need to be taken as an indication of Japan or Taiwan's unwillingness to accept Pacific Island people or of the Pacific Island people's lack of interest in migrating to these nations. Instead, we must look at what triggers migration and why Pacific Island people make the migratory choices that they do, so as to understand why Japan and Taiwan are not yet viewed as preferable choices for Pacific migrants. In this chapter, the current trends in migration from the Pacific Islands have been defined by education and potential work opportunities, largely in the sporting field. The experiences of these migrants have shown many positive aspects to life in Japan and Taiwan, whilst also recognising the drawbacks of how migrants can be impacted by changes in diplomatic relations or restricted by paternalistic systems of control placed on lower-skilled migrants. Meanwhile, the insight into refugee experiences shows how Japan's system of ensuring paid work for newly arrived refugees can provide stability and a sense of self-worth, yet there are challenges in providing refugees with a community. For Japan and Taiwan to become viable destinations for climate-displaced Pacific Islanders, they must offer language and cultural classes, educational and vocational training, and collaborate with existing Pacific Island communities to ensure community engagement and a sense of belonging. This combination would allow newly arrived people to access their receiving society, Japan or Taiwan, and provide them with a space to find common ground and community with other

Pacific Islanders. Pacific Islanders can become active, valuable members of Japanese or Taiwanese society if they so choose and in being given the ability to do so both Japan and Taiwan ensure migration with dignity for Pacific Islanders whilst also being able to resolve their own internal challenges of a reduced workforce and ageing populations. Time will show if Japan is able to transform its migratory frameworks and if Taiwan is willing to commit to its new refugee law in 2024 and set a new precedent for environmental migration.

References

ABC News. (2014, September 5). *Pacific Islanders reject 'climate refugee' status, want to 'migrate with dignity', SIDS conference hears*. ABC. https://www.abc.net.au/news/2014-09-05/pacific-islanders-reject-calls-for-27climate-refugee27-status/5723078

Albert, S., Grinham, A., Gibbes, B., Leon, J., & Church, J. (2016, May 9). *Sea level rise swallows 5 whole Pacific Islands*. Scientific American. https://www.scientificamerican.com/article/sea-level-rise-swallows-5-whole-pacific-islands/

Amnesty International. (2023, July 13). *Taiwan can play a leading regional role on human rights but sustained commitment needed, says Amnesty's Secretary General following visit*. Amnesty International. https://www.amnesty.org/en/latest/news/2023/07/taiwan-can-play-a-leading-regional-role-on-human-rights-but-sustained-commitment-needed-says-amnestys-secretary-general-following-visit/

Apap, J., & de Revel, C. d. P. (2021, 10 18). *The concept of 'climate refugee'*. European Parliament. https://www.europarl.europa.eu/RegData/etudes/BRIE/2021/698753/EPRS_BRI(2021)698753_EN.pdf

APTC. (2022, May 30). *Fijian aged care workers to benefit from new pilot program*. APTC. https://www.aptc.edu.au/news/news/2022/05/30/fijian-aged-care-workers-to-benefit-from-new-pilot-program

Arudō, D. (2015). *Embedded racism: Japan's visible minorities and racial discrimination*. Lexington Books.

Bafana, B. (2022, November 15). *Climate change is no 'future scenario' for Pacific Island Nations; Climate change is 'real' - world*. ReliefWeb. https://reliefweb.int/report/world/climate-change-no-future-scenario-pacific-island-nations-climate-change-real

Barron, L. (2017, July 6). *Japan has a labor crisis that refugees could fix, if only its government would let them*. Quartz. https://qz.com/1014031/japan-has-a-labor-crisis-that-refugees-could-fix-if-only-its-government-would-let-them

Besnier, N. (2011). *On the edge of the global: Modern anxieties in a Pacific Island nation*. Stanford University Press.

Campbell, J., & Warrick, O. (2014, 09 14). *Climate change and migration issues in the Pacific*. ILO. https://www.ilo.org/dyn/migpractice/docs/261/Pacific.pdf

Campbell, J. R. (2014). *Climate-change migration in the Pacific, 26*(1). The Contemporary Pacific.

Cavanough, E., & Nielson, J. (2019, December 7). When China came calling: Inside the Solomon Islands switch. *The Guardian*. https://www.theguardian.com/world/2019/dec/08/when-china-came-calling-inside-the-solomon-islands-switch

Climate Change Litigation Database. (2015). *Ioane Teitiota v. The Chief Executive of the Ministry of Business, Innovation and Employment - Climate Change Litigation*. Climate Change Litigation Databases. https://climatecasechart.com/non-us-case/ioane-teitiota-v-the-chief-executive-of-the-ministry-of-business-innovation-and-employment/

CNBC. (2021, November 17). *Japan looking to allow more foreigners to stay indefinitely in a major immigration policy shift*. CNBC. https://www.cnbc.com/2021/11/18/japan-could-allow-more-foreigners-to-stay-indefinitely-in-major-shift.html

Craymer, L. (2022, November 15). *Tuvalu turns to the metaverse as rising seas threaten existence*. Reuters. https://www.reuters.com/business/cop/tuvalu-turns-metaverse-rising-seas-threaten-existence-2022-11-15/

Davidson, H., & Lin, C. H. (2022, June 22). Neither citizens nor foreigners: Hongkongers struggle to adapt to life in Taiwan. *The Guardian*. https://www.theguardian.com/world/2022/jun/22/neither-citizens-nor-foreigners-hongkongers-struggle-to-adapt-to-life-in-taiwan

Doherty, B. (2017, May 13). 'Our country will vanish': Pacific islanders bring desperate message to Australia. *The Guardian*. https://www.theguardian.com/world/2017/may/14/our-country-will-vanish-pacific-islanders-bring-desperate-message-to-australia

Embassy of Japan in the Republic of Fiji. (2022, March 15). *Culture and Education (Information on Japan & Japanese Culture)*. Embassy of Japan in the Republic of Fiji. https://www.fj.emb-japan.go.jp/itpr_en/culture_and_education.html

Farrell, B. (2014, December 14). *Pacific islanders face the reality of climate change... and of relocation*. UNHCR. https://www.unhcr.org/uk/news/latest/2009/12/4b264c836/pacific-islanders-face-reality-climate-change-relocation.html

Ferris, E. (2023). *Countervailing pressures: climate change, migration and COVID-19...* Environmental Migration Portal. https://environmentalmigration.iom.int/blogs/countervailing-pressures-climate-change-migration-and-covid-19-pacific

Fouad, M. (2021, September 24). *Unlocking access to climate finance for Pacific Island Countries*. IMF eLibrary. https://www.elibrary.imf.org/view/journals/087/2021/020/article-A001-en.xml

Ghosh, R. C. (2022, April 16). A systematic review of climate migration research: gaps in existing literature. *SN Social Sciences, 2*(47). https://doi.org/10.1007/s43545-022-00341-8

Government of the Republic of Fiji. (2018). *Republic of Fiji National Adaptation Plan*. United Nations Climate Change. https://unfccc.int/documents/302826?gclid=CjwKCAjwm4ukBhAuEiwA0zQxkwA9LBTaXJnV5JV8bAqA8Ur9bQdEqqfsBq8_WRqIRDJKb_TN-n0hrBoCDQIQAvD_BwE

Guma' Famagu'on Tano' yan I Tasi. (2023). *Guma' Famagu'on Tano' yan I Tasi*. Facebook. https://www.facebook.com/gumafamaguontanoyanitasi

Harding, B. (2022, July 7). *Pacific Islands Forum: Leaders want to focus on climate change, not geopolitics*. United States Institute of Peace. https://www.usip.org/publications/2022/07/pacific-islands-forum-leaders-want-focus-climate-change-not-geopolitics

Higushi, E. (2019, December). *Climate change policies and migration issues of New Zealand and Australia*. Climate Change Policies and Migration Issues of New Zealand and Australia. https://www.spf.org/en/global-data/opri/perspectives/prsp_002_2019_higuchi_en.pdf

IISD. (2019, May 21). *Pacific Island Leaders, UN Secretary-General call for "Decisive and Transformative Action" to reduce emissions | News | SDG Knowledge Hub | IISD*. SDG Knowledge Hub. https://sdg.iisd.org/news/pacific-island-leaders-un-secretary-general-call-for-decisive-and-transformative-action-to-reduce-emissions/

IISD. (2022, July 27). *Pacific Island leaders declare climate emergency | News | SDG Knowledge Hub | IISD*. SDG Knowledge Hub. https://sdg.iisd.org/news/pacific-island-leaders-declare-climate-emergency/

Illmer, A. (2020, August 28). *Black lives matter pushes Japan to confront racism*. BBC. https://www.bbc.co.uk/news/world-asia-53428863

ILO. (2017, May 11). *A study on the future of work in the Pacific*. https://www.ilo.org/wcmsp5/groups/public/---asia/---ro-bangkok/---ilo-suva/documents/publication/wcms_553880.pdf

Japan Association for Refugees. (2023). *Refugees in Japan*. Refugees in Japan | Japan Association for Refugees (JAR). https://www.refugee.or.jp/en/refugee/

Jensen, S. (2020, December 21). *FEATURE-Taiwan may face fewer typhoons – but harsher drought – as planet warms*. Reuters. https://www.reuters.com/article/climate-change-taiwan-typhoon-idINL8N2IP5J7

JICA. (2009). *We are islanders!– For the future of the Pacific*. JICA. https://www.jica.go.jp/english/publications/jica_archive/brochures/pdf/islanders.pdf

Ka'iwakīloumoku. (2021, March 5). *Offshoot commentaries: Living as a Hawaiian-Taiwanese in Taipei – Ka'iwakīloumoku – Hawaiian Cultural Center*. Hawaiian Cultural Center. https://kaiwakiloumoku.ksbe.edu/article/pacific-conversations-offshoot-commentaries-living-as-a-hawaiian-taiwanese-in-taipei

Kameyama, Y., & Ono, K. (2020, September 25). The development of climate security discourse in Japan. *Sustainability Science, 16*, 271–281.https://doi.org/10.1007/s11625-020-00863-1

Kameyama, Y., & Ono, K. (2021). The development of climate security discourse in Japan. *Sustainability Science, 16*, 271–281. https://doi.org/10.1007/s11625-020-00863-1

Kaur, M. (2016, March). Multilingualism, the linguistic landscape of Fiji. *International Journal of Humanities and Cultural Studies, 2*(4), 625–631. https://www.researchgate.net/publication/327190543_Multilingualism_the_Linguistic_Landscape_of_Fiji

Kironska, K. (2022a, January 10). Taiwan's road to an asylum law: Who, when, how, and why not yet? *Human Rights Review, 23*, 241–264.https://doi.org/10.1007/s12142-021-00644-y

Kironska, K. (2022b, April 13). *Taiwan's asylum policy: A lack of political will to implement the law? – CEIAS*. Central European Institute of Asian Studies. https://ceias.eu/taiwans-asylum-policy-a-lack-of-political-will-to-implement-the-law/

Lan, P.-C. (2022, 09 13). Contested skills and constrained mobilities: migrant carework skill regimes in Taiwan and Japan. *Comparative Migration Studies, 10*(37). https://doi.org/10.1186/s40878-022-00311-2

Lang, E. (2023, April 25). *Japan eyes long-term stays for wider range of skilled foreign workers*. Nikkei Asia. https://asia.nikkei.com/Spotlight/Japan-immigration/Japan-eyes-long-term-stays-for-wider-range-of-skilled-foreign-workers

Leung, M. (2019, September 25). *Pacific Islands students caught in China-Taiwan standoff*. University World News. https://www.universityworldnews.com/post.php?story=20190925161021413

Lewis, L. (2017, November 16). *Japan business group chief calls for more foreign workers*. Financial Times. https://www.ft.com/content/9a55f006-caab-11e7-ab18-7a9fb7d6163e

Liu, H., & Howes, S. (2023, March 31). *Pacific Islanders in Australia: 2021 census results*. Devpolicy Blog. https://devpolicy.org/pacific-islanders-in-australia-census-results-20230331/

Matarani, Z. (2023, April 4). *As Japan ages, young Indonesians train to fill caregiver jobs*. Reuters. https://www.reuters.com/world/asia-pacific/japan-ages-young-indonesians-train-fill-caregiver-jobs-2023-04-04/

McAllister, S. (2023, June 3). *There could be 1.2 billion climate refugees by 2050. Here's what you need to know*. Zurich Insurance Group. https://www.zurich.com/en/media/magazine/2022/there-could-be-1-2-billion-climate-refugees-by-2050-here-s-what-you-need-to-know

Merga, R. D., & Redl, C. (2023, July 26). *Tuvalu Needs to Build Resilience Amid Threat from Rising Seas*. International Monetary Fund. https://www.imf.org/en/News/Articles/2023/07/26/cf-tuvalu-needs-to-build-resilience-amid-threat-from-rising-seas

Naidoo, K. (2018, May 28). *The coming wave of climate displacement*. The Japan Times. https://www.japantimes.co.jp/opinion/2018/05/28/commentary/world-commentary/coming-wave-climate-displacement/

Nangu, P. M. (2020, May 13). *Park games with Pacifica family*. YouTube. https://www.youtube.com/watch?v=0RPWH5coDN8

Natano, K. (2022, September 28). The climate crisis is making the Pacific Islands unlivable. *Time*. https://time.com/6217104/climate-crisis-pacific-islands-uninhabitable/

New Zealand Foreign Affairs and Trade. (2023). *Pasifika New Zealand*. New Zealand Ministry of Foreign Affairs and Trade. https://www.mfat.govt.nz/en/trade/free-trade-agreements/free-trade-agreements-in-force/pacer-plus/pasifika-new-zealand/

Packham, C., & Singh, K. (2021, November 9). *Tuvalu minister stands in sea to film COP26 speech to show climate change*. Reuters. https://www.reuters.com/business/cop/tuvalu-minister-stands-sea-film-cop26-speech-show-climate-change-2021-11-08/

Park, S. (2017). Inventing aliens: immigration control, 'xenophobia' and racism in Japan. *Sage Journals, 3*(58). https://doi.org/10.1177/0306396816657719?journalCode=racb

Parsons, C. (2022, May 23). *The Pacific Islands: The front line in the battle against climate change*. National Science Foundation. https://beta.nsf.gov/science-matters/pacific-islands-front-line-battle-against-climate

Phillimore, J., Morrice, L., Kabe, K., Hashimoto, N., Hassan, S., & Reyes, M. (2021, April 28). Economic self-reliance or social relations? What works in refugee integration? Learning from resettlement programmes in Japan and the UK. *Comparative Migration Studies, 9*(17). https://doi.org/10.1186/s40878-021-00223-7

PICA-WA. (2022, November 18). *Pasifika Narratives*. https://www.youtube.com/playlist?list=PLKESMBc5RpAo0raZrWkQX5pAQ9ZheM95F

PISA. (2023, June 22). *Pacific Island students in Taiwan – Our cultures our pride*. https://sites.google.com/site/ourculturesourpride/entertainment/pacific-island-students-in-taiwan

PISFCC. (2023). *Pacific Islands students fighting climate change | Seeking an advisory Opinion from the ICJ*. Pacific Islands Students Fighting Climate Change | Seeking an Advisory Opinion from the ICJ. https://www.pisfcc.org/

Plano, R. (2022, November 1). *Pacific Island states — Spotlight — Climate refugees*. Climate Refugees. https://www.climate-refugees.org/spotlight/tag/Pacific+Island+States

Prange, M. (2022, December 19). *Climate Change Is Fueling Migration. Do Climate Migrants Have Legal Protections?* Council on Foreign Relations. https://www.cfr.org/in-brief/climate-change-fueling-migration-do-climate-migrants-have-legal-protections

SPREP. (2023). *Pacific Adaptation to Climate Change (PACC) Programme | Pacific Environment*. SPREP. https://www.sprep.org/pacc

Quinn, C. (2019, September 27). *Pacific Island airplane argument costs students Taiwan scholarship*. The PIE News. https://thepienews.com/news/pacific-students-taiwan-scholarship/

Saito, J. (2022, June 15). *Historical background of the Japanese restrictive immigration policy*. Japan Centre for Economic Research. https://www.jcer.or.jp/english/historical-background-of-the-japanese-restrictive-immigration-policy

Salem, S. (2020a, January 9). *Climate change and the sinking island states in the Pacific*. E-International Relations. https://www.e-ir.info/2020/01/09/climate-change-and-the-sinking-island-states-in-the-pacific/

Salem, S. (2020b, February 18). *Climate change and food security in the Pacific*. E-International Relations. https://www.e-ir.info/2020/02/18/climate-change-and-food-security-in-the-pacific/

Schieder, D. (2015). Community life and discourses among Fiji Islanders in Kantō, Japan. *Anthropological Forum, 2*(25), 167–186. https://doi.org/10.1080/00664677.2014.995153

Schieder, D. (2021, August 21). *Fiji Islander trans-border mobility in the Pacific: The case of Fiji and Japan*. University of Siegen. https://pacific-geographies.org/wp-content/uploads/2021/08/PG56_DOI10.23791_561322_DS.pdf

Singh, V. (2022, November 28). *Blog: How Fiji is turning to nature to cope with climate change*. Commonwealth. https://thecommonwealth.org/news/blog-how-fiji-turning-nature-cope-climate-change

Taiwan Economic Forum. (2022). *Launching population and immigration policy, to maintain Taiwan's economic growth momentum* (2, 20th ed.). Xiàjì hào. https://ws.ndc.gov.tw/Download.ashx?u=LzAwMS9hZG1pbmlzdHJhdG9yLzEwL3JlbGZpbGUvMC8xNDg1OS85ZTMwMGJlZS1hZmU3LTRiZTAtYmJjNi0wN2M0ODAwZDc0MGEucGRm&n=MjAyMue2k%2Ba%2Fn%2BirluihoV8yMC0yXzItMi7mlL%2FnrZbnhKbpu55f5Y2U6Kq%2F5o6o5YuV5Lq65Y%2Bj5Y%2BK56e75rCR5pS%2F562

TaiwanPlus News. (2023, June 20). *Human rights activists call for new refugee laws for Taiwan*. https://www.youtube.com/watch?v=1-DOE5yqYKE

Taiwan Today. (2006, July 7). *Taiwan today*. Taiwan Today. https://taiwantoday.tw/news.php?unit=10,23,45,10&post=16154

Taylor, L. (2023, February 20). *Pacific islanders head to Australia for jobs as climate fears grow | Context*. Context News. https://www.context.news/climate-risks/pacific-islanders-head-to-australia-for-jobs-as-climate-fears-grow

Tchounwou, P. B., McNamara, K. E., & Westoby, R. (2022, 06 01). Emotions of the Anthropocene across Oceania. *International Journal of Environmental Research and Public Health, 19*(11). https://doi.org/10.3390/ijerph19116757

Uji, A., Dolšak, N., Song, J., & Prakash, A. (2021). Public support for climate adaptation aid and migrants: A conjoint experiment in Japan. *Environmental Research Letters, 16*(12). https://iopscience.iop.org/article/https://doi.org/10.1088/1748-9326/ac3b7b

UNHCR. (1951). *Convention and protocol relating to the status of refugees*. UNHCR. https://www.unhcr.org/media/28185

United Nations. (2021, February 11). *Pacific regional consultation on internal displacement | UN Secretary-General's high-level panel on internal displacement*. the United Nations. https://www.un.org/internal-displacement-panel/events/pacific-regional-consultation-internal-displacement

United Nations. (2023a). *How is climate change impacting the world's ocean | United Nations*. the United Nations. https://www.un.org/en/climatechange/science/climate-issues/ocean-impacts

United Nations. (2023b, February 14). *Climate change-induced sea-level rise direct threat to millions around world, Secretary-General Tells Security Council | UN Press*. UN Press. https://press.un.org/en/2023/sc15199.doc.htm

United Nations University. (2017, February 23). *Pacific islanders faced with climate-induced migration – Institute for Environment and Human Security*. UNU-EHS. https://ehs.unu.edu/blog/articles/pacific-islanders-faced-with-climate-induced-migration.html

UNU-EHS. (2015). *Climate change and migration in the Pacific: Links, attitudes, and future scenarios in Nauru, Tuvalu, and Kiribati*. https://i.unu.edu/media/ehs.unu.edu/news/11747/RZ_Pacific_EHS_ESCAP_151201.pdf

UNU-EHS. (2016). *How does climate change affect migration in the Pacific?* The United Nations University. https://unfccc.int/files/science/workstreams/research/application/pdf/part2_unu-ehs_oakes_vandergeest_poster.pdf

Wang, H. (2011). *Immigration trends and policy changes in Taiwan* (20th ed., Vol. 169–194). Asian and Pacific Migration Journal.

World Economic Forum. (2021, June 18). *Climate refugees – the world's forgotten victims | World Economic Forum*. The World Economic Forum. https://www.weforum.org/agenda/2021/06/climate-refugees-the-world-s-forgotten-victims/

yuan Teng, K. -. (2022, June 13). *Taiwan's first climate refugees/Politics & Society/2022–06–13/CommonWealth Magazine*. CommonWealth Magazine. https://english.cw.com.tw/article/article.action?id=3243

CHAPTER 14

Asylum Seeking as Survival Strategy: The Narratives of Indonesian Work Seekers in Japan

Firman Budianto and Yusy Widarahesty

Introduction

Dimas first came to Japan in 2012 as a trainee under Japan's Technical Internship Training Programme (TITP). After completion of his three years' training and work in Japan, he returned to Indonesia in 2015 and started looking for a job. As a high school graduate, he struggled to find a decent job in his hometown, Surabaya, which is the second largest city in Indonesia. His work experience in Japan did not help him to find a job in Indonesia. He then decided to continue his education at university, majoring in engineering while working part-time as an online taxi driver. Since he found his income as a taxi driver insufficient to financially support himself and his family, in 2019, he returned to Japan to

F. Budianto (✉)
National Research and Innovation Agency (BRIN), Jakarta, Indonesia
e-mail: firman.budianto@brin.go.id

Y. Widarahesty
Asia-Japan Research Institute, Ritsumeikan University, Kyoto, Japan

L. Momesso and P. Ivanova (eds.), *Refugees and Asylum Seekers in East Asia*, Palgrave Macmillan Studies on Human Rights in Asia,
https://doi.org/10.1007/978-981-97-2867-1_14

work. This time, he came to Japan via Osaka using a visa waiver for a short-term visit before ending up as an undocumented worker and an asylum seeker. Following his arrival in Japan, with the help of an Indonesian friend, Dimas managed to find a broker in Nagoya who introduced him to a company in need of workers. Not only that, but his friend also helped him to get a fake residence card and handled everything, from the apartment to the job. Dimas had a job interview with the broker, and eventually secured a job as an operator in a subcontractor company of a large corporation in Nagoya.

Dimas is only one example of an Indonesian who aspires to work in Japan but ends up seeking asylum status in the country. Many Indonesian young people find it hard to find a decent job in the country, especially if they do not have a university degree or vocational training. According to an Indonesian government survey in 2021 (Statistics Indonesia, 2021), about 8 million people in Indonesia were unemployed at that time. More than half of them were high school graduates or below and were between 20 and 29 years of age. It is not uncommon that some of these people would choose to find jobs abroad. In 2019, 277,489 Indonesian migrant workers went abroad to work in various sectors (BP2MI, 2022).

Emigration is not a new phenomenon in Indonesia. It began in the 1970s when the government tried to find overseas work opportunities for Indonesian people as part of a larger economic development policy (Palmer, 2016; Palmer & Missback, 2022). In its early phase, in the 1970s and 1980s, Saudi Arabia and Malaysia were the most preferred migration destinations for Indonesians, while Asia–Pacific countries, such as Taiwan, Japan, Hong Kong, and South Korea, emerged later. It is undeniable that working abroad can significantly improve the lives of many Indonesians and their families. As migrant workers provide the largest source of foreign exchange contributions, they are even referred to by the Indonesian government as "foreign exchange heroes" for their contributions through remittances to the nation. For many nations, including Indonesia, remittances from migrant workers have been a major source of foreign currency. The influx of funds from migrant workers has helped to strengthen Indonesia's current account, notably its secondary income account. Around US$3.2 billion in remittances were sent by the 3.2 million Indonesians who work abroad in 2021 (Faisal, 2022).

Nonetheless, it can potentially be risky to work abroad. Reports of mistreatment have led many people to believe that not enough is being done to protect Indonesian migrant workers abroad. The concerns involved—such as physical and sexual abuse, forced labour, and unpaid wages—have been highlighted by reported cases, particularly among female domestic employees (Bachtiar, 2011). As a result, the government responded to these problems by imposing a two-year prohibition on immigration to Malaysia starting in 2009 and by outlawing the mobility of female domestic migrant workers to Saudi Arabia starting in 2011 (Bachtiar, 2011). Twenty-one nations in the Middle East, North and East Africa, as well as Pakistan, had their moratoria extended in 2015 (The World Bank, 2017, p. 4). These various conditions eventually stopped Indonesian migrant workers, with an illegal or undocumented status, attempting to continue working abroad.

In addition to the numerous cases of violence that migrant workers encounter in their destination countries, the pre-departure administration procedure is viewed as a hardship by Indonesian migrant workers who seek to migrate legally. It can take up to three months to complete some of the arduous administrative steps required to become a legally recognised migrant worker, and there are 22 steps in total, which deter some potential migrants from choosing this route (The World Bank, 2017). By looking at the conditions of poverty, unequal education, and high inequality in Indonesia, various alternative strategies are used by Indonesian migrant workers to be able to migrate with the aim of improving their lives.

Japan is undoubtedly one of the preferred destinations for migrant workers from Indonesia. For young people in particular, Japan is one of the most attractive destination countries for Indonesians working abroad, thanks not only to the influence of Japanese pop culture but also due to Japan's changing labour market and the emerging migration channels that affect how they see Japan (Budianto, 2023). Indonesians comprise a significant number of foreign residents in Japan. From 2019 to 2021, there were, respectively, 486, 753, and 359 Indonesians newly employed in Japan (MHLW, 2023). In June 2016, there were 50,478 Indonesian nationals in Japan, and the number increased to 67,751 in December 2020 and had hiked up to 83,169 by the middle of 2022 (MHLW, 2023). By June 2022, technical trainees ranked at first place (38,863) among the group of Indonesian residents in Japan, followed by students (6330), working professionals (4926), healthcare workers (1618), and other visa categories (MHLW, 2023).

The opening up of various opportunities to become migrant workers in Japan started when Japan expanded its companies to developing countries in the 1960s, which led to work becoming available through the IET (Individual Enterprise Type) Technical Intern Trainee scheme. This development was followed by the emergence of the TITP (Technical Internship Training Programme) in 1993, with the goal of transferring technology and knowledge to developing countries (JITCO, 2017). In the 1980s, Japan began to face labour shortages that impacted both large corporations and small and medium-sized businesses. Consequently, in the 1980s and early 1990s, the number of migrants, both documented and undocumented, kept increasing. During the period of 1983 to 1993, the number of foreign residents rose by 62%, totalling 1.3 million, including around 300,000 undocumented immigrants (Goodman et al., 2003).

Although the Immigration Control and Refugee Recognition Act, which came into force in June 1990, was a response to increasing migrant inflows, it was never intended to formally welcome unskilled immigrants to help with the country's acute labour crisis. On the contrary, it effectively shuts the door to unskilled immigrants. Migrant workers, however, are only marginally present in policy approaches to Japan's demographic change, if it all. On the one hand, Japan does not openly promote a policy of accepting large, systematic influxes of foreign workers. There exists a tension between the notion of Japan as a homogeneous nation-state and the stark need for trans-border labour importation to supply the demand for a short-term labour workforce, something which also potentially could diversify the Japanese body politic (Onuki, 2015). On the other hand, immigration rules cover the Japanese economy's requirement for unskilled labour through side and back doors. First, *Nikkeijin*, or descendants of Japanese emigrants, primarily from Brazil but also from Peru and Bolivia, have been granted the right to long-term residence without limitations on employment. Second, the 1993 reforms to the trainee programme made it possible to import unskilled workers by using the immigration law (Yamanaka, 2004).

Foreign workers who aim to work in Japan face various problems, even before their departure. They have to pass the rigorous pre-departure stages, including administrative selection, competency tests, and medical and physical exams, before going through several months of pre-departure training (Widarahesty, 2022). Following their arrival in Japan, they continue experiencing problems, including human rights violations that cause Indonesian migrant workers to run away. For instance, there was one case of 7000 trainees running away and going missing in 2021 (Uemura, 2023).

As a result of these circumstances—the lengthy pre-departure process, the high departure fees, and the disadvantageous conditions in the destination country—the number of undocumented migrant workers in Japan has increased; some of these individuals were from Indonesia and they ended up requesting asylum status. Among them, as of December 2020, there were 250 Indonesians being considered for asylum status in Japan (MHLW, 2023).

The case of Indonesian asylum seekers is intriguing. On the one hand, although the country is seen to be economically growing and politically stable, there are not many job opportunities available and the unemployment rate is quite high. On the other hand, the lack of employment opportunities in the home country alone does not necessarily give grounds for asylum seeking or humanitarian protection in other countries, including Japan. All the influential factors, both in Indonesia and in Japan, should therefore be put into the spotlight.

Thus, this chapter aims to investigate and examine the phenomenon of asylum seeking from Indonesia to Japan, and it does so by discussing the narratives of Indonesian work seekers aiming to find employment in Japan, who end up seeking asylum status. This chapter explores their motivations and the migration routes they had taken. As this chapter focuses on the narratives of Indonesian work seekers and migrants who have sought Japan's asylum seeker status, it takes into account how their aspirations on asylum status and mobility impact their security. We will answer these fundamental questions: Why do Indonesian people seek asylum status in Japan? How do economic motivations affect the decision-making process? How do they choose the routes? In order to answer these questions this chapter consists of several parts. We examine some previous studies on precariousness in the context of labour migration to Japan, followed by an investigation of the various channels that contribute to the mobility of Indonesian work seekers to Japan. The next section contains the narratives of two categories of Indonesian asylum seekers, followed by a discussion of what asylum seeking in Japan means in the case of Indonesians, which will lead to the conclusion.

Methodology

This chapter uses a conceptual tool—namely, the regime of the migration industry—to explain the origin and driving force behind the phenomena of Indonesian asylum seekers in Japan. This chapter makes use of this conceptual framework to explain the causes and motivations underlying the phenomenon of Indonesian asylum seekers in Japan. This chapter draws on qualitative data collected between 2018 and 2023, including ethnographic field notes and in-depth semi-structured interviews, both in person and online.

We interviewed five Indonesian nationals who once aspired and applied for asylum-seeking status, both in Japan and Indonesia. In addition, we also interviewed fellow Indonesians in Japan from diverse backgrounds, such as Indonesian workers and members of the Indonesian diaspora in Japan, along with staff from related NGOs, offering a non-elite perspective to reflect the complex conditions and circumstances in the field. The fieldwork was done in the Kansai and Kanto area of Japan, between April 2018 and March 2023. In Indonesia, we also took part in interviews and observations in the West Java and Jakarta regions, in 2019 and 2020, in order to observe the overall effect of the Indonesian labour programme to Japan. Additional interviews were conducted by Zoom and LINE in 2022. The "snowball strategy" was used to engage the audience. We followed ethical research guidelines and, to preserve confidentiality, this project uses pseudonyms instead of interviewees' real names. Prior to interviews, we explained the aim of the research and received the consent of our interviewees to participate in this study. In the next section, in order to understand how this research is positioned, the perception of asylum seekers in academic literature will be considered.

The Precariousness of Labour Migration to Japan

Research on refugees and asylum seekers in Japan "has primarily concentrated on the analysis of legal concerns and the application procedure itself" (Koizumi, 2015, p. 241). If we look back in history, the end of the Cold War brought about significant changes and political unrest around the world, leading to new large-scale migrations, and increasing the number of persons seeking political asylum in all developed nations except Japan (Takeda, 1998, p. 431). While this phenomenon of increasing refugee numbers was going on, several studies examined the NGOs, national and international organisations, and grassroots movements in Japan that support and work with refugees and asylum seekers (Kuroda, 2003). Several studies have also been conducted on some issues related to detention centres, such as detention facilities, detention procedures, and detainee conditions. The studies on the relationship between refugees and detention centres have become increasingly important research topics. This is due to the many reports regarding Japan's treatment of refugees, asylum seekers, and migrants within its immigration detention centres, which, it was found, failed to protect the health of detainees (Kimiko & Wattles, 2019; Ichikawa et al., 2006; Miyauchi, 2015; Niitsu, 2012; Oh, 2017; Ohashi & Kodama, 2009).

Numerous studies have been done on refugees and asylum seekers in Japan, focussing particularly on the second generation of Vietnamese refugees in Osaka and Kobe. According to Takizawa (2018), even officially recognised refugees struggle issues relating to identity, economics, and education. Takizawa's study emphasises the value of Japanese language proficiency for overcoming difficulties, particularly for assimilating into Japanese society. In his ethnographic investigation exploring what it is like to be an asylum seeker in Japan, Avci (2020) shows how people perceive, deal with, and cope with life while in this liminal situation. Avci's study demonstrates how asylum seekers exhibit constrained but potent subjectivity inside the Japanese asylum procedure by drawing on their experiences in the prison, employment, love, and marriage spheres. Suzuki (2003) analyses Cambodian immigration to Japan in 1998 and 1999 as a case study to examine the problems that exist between the first and second generations of immigrants. She claims that the tragic experiences of war and being a refugee have inhibited generational communication.

As stated above, the available research has offered helpful insights concerning the state of Japan's immigration policy, particularly for refugees and asylum seekers in Japan. Additionally, the existing research on refugees and asylum seekers in Japan (e.g., Kalicki, 2019; Kondo, 2015) has primarily focussed on institutional issues, policy changes in immigration law, demographic changes in the country, the benefits and limitations of bringing in foreign workers, human rights abuses in detention facilities, and Japan's low acceptance rate for refugees and asylum seekers.

However, the existing literature on refugee and asylum seekers has predominantly looked at the issues as policy, legal, and institutional issues that create various problems and demonstrate Japan's resistance to taking in refugees and asylum seekers. Such research is indeed crucial to gauge Japan's disposition to fulfil its commitments as a developed nation that accepts refugees and asylum seekers. Nevertheless, we cannot ignore the fact that the asylum application process is extremely complicated, especially when considering the diverse backgrounds and motivations of the asylum seekers as they apply for asylum. These include economic motivations as a result of many factors stemming from conditions in their respective countries of origin. Thus, this study aims to further investigate and analyse the topic of asylum seekers who are driven by economic motivations, which has not been covered significantly in previous research involving asylum seekers from Indonesia in Japan.

The literature on Indonesian migrants in Japan does not seem to explore this problem either. There have been several studies on Indonesians in Japan, most of which have focussed on Indonesian migrant labourers. Indonesians who have visited Japan to participate in the country's Industrial Training and Technical Internship Programme have been the subject of some preliminary research (Nawawi, 2010). It is important to categorise the types of Indonesian immigrants who are currently working in Japan and to look into the well-being and legal rights of such migrants (Romdiati, 2003). However, according to existing research, the studies on Indonesian asylum seekers in Japan are still limited. Therefore, it is essential to gain a deeper understanding of the movements and routes of Indonesian asylum seekers in Japan from the perspectives of the two nations, and to explore the reasons why people decide to use asylum seeking as a strategy. The next section looks at the narratives of Indonesian migrant workers regarding seeking asylum in Japan.

Various Migration Channels into Japan

The trend of asylum seeking in Japan among Indonesians, particularly among former technical trainees, began in the early 2000s. In the context of the mid-2000s until the end of the 2010s, the asylum seeing visa was popular among Indonesians. At that time, it was difficult for former trainees to re-enter Japan. If they wished to live in Japan longer, they often used the strategy of marrying a Japanese national. At that time, the high skills-based professional visa, for engineers or specialists in the humanities and international development for example, was not that popular, and the specified skilled workers (SSW) visa had not yet been created. For people from the early batch of technical trainees in the 2000s, the asylum-seeking status became one of the ways to return to Japan.

The asylum-seeking status is widely known among these people as "*visa nanmin*". In that period, the number of Indonesian trainees under Japan's TITP increased significantly (Yoshida, 2017). The TITP left trainees with no option but to leave Japan and return to their home countries after three years of training and working in Japan. However, some of them managed to secure a legal residence permit by marrying Japanese nationals and remained in the country. Some of them eventually became permanent residents, and a small number became brokers for fellow Indonesians who wanted to work in Japan. The Indonesian community in Japan established strong social networks, including not only current trainees but also the former trainees, where they shared information related to work and life in Japan.

It is therefore not surprising that former Indonesian trainees receive information from fellow Indonesians in Japan about working opportunities in the country, including information on asylum-seeking status. Information about working in Japan with an asylum-seeking status is commonly circulated among Indonesian work seekers, via friends' recommendations, and through private groups on social media. They choose who to consult carefully and avoid sharing any plans regarding attaining asylum-seeking status with any formal organisations, because they do not want the authorities to know what they are doing.

It is also not uncommon for former technical trainees to become brokers and to help with fellow former trainees' returns to Japan, to work either with asylum-seeking status or as an undocumented migrant. Indonesian asylum seekers usually receive information about working with an asylum seeing visa from friends or via word of mouth on social media. Such narratives as "He can bring you to Japan", or "You can contact this person and he will take care of everything. You can make a deal with him directly", are common in closed online communities among Indonesian former trainees. The brokers usually post the information about work opportunities in Japan through their private network, on social media such as Facebook and LINE messenger.

Furthermore, such advertisements as: "There is this so-called *visa nanmin*. Want to come to work in Japan? I can help you with visa *nanmin*", were not uncommon among the Indonesian former migrant workers' group in 2017 and circulated through social media. Indonesian asylum seekers usually received information about working with an asylum seeing visa from friends, brokers, or via word of mouth on social media. Brokers were usually someone they know, sometimes referred to as "a friend". We found that the brokers shared certain characteristics, for example, being an Indonesian married to a Japanese national and currently living in Japan. The brokers make job offers to the candidates, referred to as "*shoukai*" (introductions), an important point in the recruitment process.

Our study found that brokers involved in the recruitment process came from various backgrounds, including Japanese, Indonesians, and people of other nationalities. However, one pattern emerged from the brokering practice, namely that the brokers do not work alone and that they create a transnational network between Indonesia and Japan. We found that Indonesian brokers have typically lived in Japan for up to twenty years. They had developed a sufficient network among Japanese people and had connections with Indonesian brokers in Japan, and people of other nationalities. In addition, they also had a tight connection with their fellow countrymen in Indonesia, who would serve as local brokers and as the first contact point for aspiring Indonesian job seekers who wanted to work in Japan.

One interviewee, Wahyu, told us the story of Adi, an Indonesian broker in Japan, whose business was to help former trainees who wished to re-enter Japan, even as illegal workers. Adi had long run his business as a broker. He came to Japan as a technical trainee in early 2000s. As one of the early generations of Japan's technical trainees, he was quite well known among the technical trainee communities in Japan. Upon completion of his training period in Japan, he married a Japanese national and eventually obtained a permanent residency that allowed him to live and work in Japan freely. The residence permit and the network he created during his work life in Japan granted him access to wider Indonesian technical trainee communities and allowed him to practice his brokering business until the end of 2017, when the Japanese authorities found out his about illegal business. He was interrogated and, as consequence, he was told to stop his business and to report to the local immigration office once a year, despite his permanent residence status. At that time, in 2017, the number of asylum seeker applications had increased significantly. Only 1% of the applications came from Middle Eastern and African crisis zones, according to a breakdown of the applications by nationality, with more than 80% coming from the Asia–Pacific region. 4895 applications were submitted by Filipino nationals, which was three and a half times more than in 2016 with 3116 applications. Vietnam came next, closely followed by Sri Lanka (2226) and Indonesia (2038) (Siripala, 2018). The sudden increase in asylum seeker applications in 2017 has been confirmed by our interviewees.

Brokers in our sample did not work alone. They worked in teams, solely based on trust. When a broker successfully facilitates and grants someone's wish to work in Japan, the broker will gain trust. This makes it much easier for brokers to find more prospective candidates to work in Japan. In some cases, brokers manage to develop their network by gaining the trust of former candidates, who then help the broker by finding more potential candidates and introducing them to the broker.

Brokers play a significant role in equipping job seekers with all documents necessary for living in Japan. One of the most basic documents for foreign nationals is the residence card. For undocumented migrant workers, brokers offer a service to create a fake residence card. All the procedures to make a residence card, such as sending the ID photo, as well as the name and address verification, are all carried out online. The payment is made in cash on delivery. Foreign communities in Japan who provide services to create fake residence cards are not limited to Indonesian brokers but also, according to our interviewees, brokers of other nationalities. Job seekers have to pay a certain amount of money for one residence card. One of our interviewees said that he had to pay about one *man yen* (about US$100) for one ID.

Job seekers who wish to go to Japan for work as undocumented migrants have to pay a recruitment fee. The fee varies, starting from 30 million Indonesian rupiah (about US$2,500) which includes the airfare, referral or introduction (*shoukai*) fee, the accommodation fee, or what they referred to as the "address fee", etc. All the costs are borne by job seekers before their departure to Japan. After their arrival, the brokers will ask for an additional monthly fee, deducted from their monthly wages. This mechanism is commonly found in the recruitment process for Indonesian work seekers who aspire to go to Japan (e.g., Azis et al., 2020).

An asylum seeing visa is appealing for Indonesian work seekers because they can apply for it, for free, at the local immigration office, while they have to pay several amounts of money to the sending organisations in Indonesia if they wish to come to Japan on a trainee visa. In most cases, one person has to pay a price which starts from 30 million rupiah (about US$2,500) so that they can join a local sending organisation and have their Japanese language training in order to become eligible to work in Japan as trainee under the TITP. Asylum-seeking status also allows the applicants to work even when their application is still under review. In addition to such reasons, there are other factors that make asylum-seeking status one of the options for work seekers, and why Indonesians keep coming to Japan to seek work, even as undocumented workers or as asylum-seeking workers.

The biggest factor is the demand from companies. Japanese companies prefer to recruit former technical trainees as they have adequate skills, such as language skills and cultural skills, to work in Japan. The companies do not want to take the risk of recruiting new people with no skills. Some of them prefer to recruit experienced workers even if they are staying illegally in Japan. It means that the employers desperately need foreign workers, regardless of their legal status. One of our informants said that he was asked by his employer, "Do you have another friend who can work here? I need people". The employer asked if he had friends who could work in Japan regardless of their legal status.

Both brokers and *shacho* (employers) ensure that the migrant workers stay at their work. Dimas shares his experience, "My broker said, 'Just don't resign, you continue working and later the *shacho* will handle everything—your job, and all administrative procedures in the company. Just focus on your work. If you work well, I will increase your wage'". The company should not hire foreigners without a legal visa; however, our data indicates that such companies, employing foreigners without an appropriate visa, exist because of the high demand for labour. In their search for employees, many Japanese companies are desperate enough to accept illegal foreign workers.

Moreover, in Japan, there can be problems with informal renting and fake address registration, since one address can be used for several people. Our data shows that the brokers take advantages of these conditions. As our data indicates, one of our informants lives in a shelter provided by the broker. It turned out that the broker had two houses. One house was for him and the other was for applicants with asylum-seeking status, and undocumented people. Surya recalled, "I live in the same *apato* (*apartment, flat*). The *apato* is like a shelter for undocumented Indonesians, either they came on a visa waiver or were runaways from their employer. One *apato* can shelter like ten people. It's an *apato* with a kitchen, one living room, and one bedroom. It's in the countryside". All these factors create a perfect environment for undocumented migrants to work and live in Japan. They provide a support system and a niche for these people to make living in the country.

However, since the Japanese government introduced the specified skill workers (SSW) visa, the number of undocumented foreign workers decreased, as well as the demand for the asylum-seeking visa. The SSW visa has been implemented since April 2019 to facilitate the entrance of semi-skilled foreign workers to Japan and to help ease the domestic labour force. There is no limit to the age of applicants, and this allows former trainees to come back to Japan again as workers, not trainees. Even though the SSW visa could be one of the solutions for former trainees to re-enter Japan and work, there are many issues regarding the SSW visa. One of the biggest issues of the SSW is the limited number of places that organise language and competency tests, as well as the limited knowledge on the jobs under the SSW visa programme.

Narratives of Indonesian Asylum Seekers

We found at least two categories of Indonesians who applied for asylum seeing visas in Japan. They share different characteristics depending on whether they have working experience in Japan or not. The first category is those who have prior working experience in Japan, mostly as technical internship trainees. The work experience provides these people with an understanding of what it is like to work in Japan. However, due to the TITP rules, they have to return to Indonesia once their internship contract ends. In most cases, upon returning to Indonesia, these people cannot secure a decent job and see working back in Japan as appealing. Some of them choose to look for opportunities so that they can return to work in Japan, even when it requires them to go down illegal paths. They are aware that the procedures are illegal.

The second category is those who have no prior working experience in Japan. People in this category are job seekers who aspire to work in Japan. They know a little about working in Japan and tend to have a low awareness of the legal pathways to work in Japan. This could be due to recklessness or simply due to a lack of Japanese language skills. In this section, we selected two narratives of Indonesian asylum seekers in Japan, one to represent each of the above categories. In their narratives, we use the context of the past few years, from 2017 to 2023.

Becoming Undocumented: The Story of Dimas

Dimas was a technical internship trainee, working in Japan in 2012–2015. As stated in the opening of this chapter, Dimas was one of those Indonesian returnees who could not find a decent job in Indonesia after his first return from Japan. He decided to work in Japan for economic motives. Dimas shared with us his aspirations and motivations for working in Japan.

> For me, I wish to work in Japan as long as possible. First, I like the country. I love Japan. In Indonesia, I can do nothing. There is not much to do in Indonesia. It is quite difficult for me, even as a university graduate, to find a job in Indonesia with decent pay, especially when you do not have great skills. People my age, I will soon turn 34 ... I think it would be difficult to find work in Indonesian private companies. That's why I would prefer to work in Japan, even if it is only a less skilled job. But I think the salary is worth the effort.

Upon returning to Indonesia, Dimas decided to continue his education at university. However, he later found that his university credentials did not help him to find a decent job in his home country. He was struggling in Indonesia until, in 2018, he first heard about working opportunities in Japan from his former technical intern community, using a visa waiver and an asylum-seeking visa. He became interested after he heard about this opportunity.

In 2017–2018, the asylum-seeking visa was very popular among Indonesian former trainees. "It was 2018 when I first heard about the asylum-seeking visa. Many of my friends were applying for that visa, so I was thinking, 'I think I should apply for that visa too!' But unfortunately, the Japanese immigration in Nagoya stopped accepting applications for such visas, so I followed my friends, becoming an illegal resident".

Dimas came to Japan for the second time in 2018, using a visa waiver intended for foreign nationals of a few selected countries to visit Japan on a short-term basis—Indonesia being among the countries that granted visa waivers limited to short stay purposes. Workers and brokers take advantage of this visa waiver and make use of it to enter Japan. In Dimas's case, brokers shared information with him about coming to Japan using a visa waiver, but they did not share any information about work in Japan. Work-related information was only given after his arrival in Japan. Dimas shared his experience entering Japan.

> We entered Japan individually, without being accompanied by anyone we knew. Once we successfully entered Japan, we got in touch with the broker in Japan through Facebook. He said, 'Where are you now? You should contact this person, chat, and go meet him. He will provide you with shelter'. After I arrived in Japan, the broker told me everything.

Initially, Dimas planned to go to Japan as a visitor first, and then to apply for an asylum-seeking visa later when he was already in Japan. However, Dimas did not know anything about the kind of work that would be available in Japan. All his decisions were based solely on mutual trust with the brokers. Dimas described this as follows, "We enter Japan like blind people. We did not know where to go. On the initial days, we stayed at hotels, while communicating with other Indonesian job seekers and the broker". Upon his arrival in Japan, Dimas managed to keep in touch with the broker and to find a place to stay. Initially, Dimas wanted to apply for an asylum-seeking visa but, in the end, he could not do that because the local immigration office no longer accepted such applications.

After failing to apply for such a visa, he became undocumented. He expressed his thoughts on being an undocumented worker and, particularly, on the potential benefits of working illegally. He compared working illegally to his situation when he was a technical internship trainee. "Speaking of the economic benefits, I think being an illegal worker is not that bad. The wage was higher than technical trainee. But when we talk about the quality of living, I think being legal is way better".

One of the most important factors why some people choose to be undocumented workers is the higher wages. When compared to the technical trainee, the wage of undocumented workers can be higher because the employers do not have to pay tax and so the workers receive the full amount of wage. This is why some of technical trainees choose to run away and end up becoming undocumented, while some of them apply for an asylum-seeking visa. "Even today, there are still many of my friends remaining in Japan illegally as undocumented migrants". Those undocumented people who remain in Japan are genuinely in a very vulnerable and uncertain situation.

From Work Seekers to Asylum Seekers: The Story of Surya

Surya came to Japan in 2018. Back in his village, he was unemployed and was struggling to find decent work. Back in 2016–2017, he was enrolled in a skill training centre (LPK) preparing himself to learn the Japanese language with the aim of working in Japan as a technical trainee upon completion of the language training programme. Unfortunately, after more than one year of training, he was stuck at the training centre. The centre did not give him an exact date when he could depart for Japan. He eventually gave up and quit the training centre. In 2022, one of his friends from the training centre told him that there was an opportunity to go to Japan with a help of a broker. Surya recalled,

> Initially, I wanted to join the internship programme as a technical internship trainee. But the sending organisation in Indonesia kind of gave me a false hope. I waited like years and they did not process my departure even though I had paid the processing fee, about 15 million rupiah. Then, at some point, I heard from my friend, who I then found out was already in Japan. I contacted him, and asked how he could already be in Japan? I asked, and he showed me his way. He said: 'You can apply for visa waiver and contact this person'.

His friend came from the same province and had been at the same training centre preparing for the technical trainee programme. Despite having paid the training centre, he and his friend had both given up on the language training and on the idea of going to Japan. However, as mentioned, Surya then found out that his friend was already employed in Japan. After that, Surya got in touch with him to ask for advice on how to get to Japan. He advised Surya to speak with a broker and to enter Japan with a visa waiver.

The broker promised him some job opportunities with a high salary. Some brokers would say that the job seekers could even choose the job they prefer. Surya recalled his experience, "He promised me a job in the manufacturing industry, but he lied. He said that I would be paid up to 2000 yen per hour. But that was all lies. The reality was far from that. After I came to Japan, he did not even give me any job. I was jobless for about four months. I had nothing to do".

Surya had to pay 160,000 yen after arriving in Japan. The broker promised Surya, when he was still in Indonesia, that he could go to Japan and work. The broker also promised that the work visa could be extended over and over. The broker claimed to have contacts with a dispatch company (*hakkengaisha*) and promised Surya a job. He even said that Surya could change job if he wanted. But the reality was that during the initial four months after his arrival in Japan, he did not have any job. The broker broke his promise.

> I felt disappointed. Disappointed because of a scam. Actually, I did not know anything about the work visa they promised me. I found out later after I came to Japan. If only I had known that they scammed me by promising me some jobs illegally, I would rather have waited and gone through the legal procedures to get my technical trainee visa. I would have preferred to use trainee visa because, I think, the asylum-seeking visa is more for when you need protection. It sounds like something big is happening in Indonesia when it isn't. If there were any other choices, I would not choose the asylum-seeking visa.

Surya not only felt disappointed but also found himself the victim of a job scam. He expressed his disappointment towards the broker who scammed him. He also felt embarrassed when people found out he was on an asylum-seeking visa. He told us, "People only know me as *kenshuusei* (*trainee*). I keep silent and tell no one. Because I feel ashamed if they find out that I am using an asylum-seeking visa. I don't want to work on an asylum-seeking visa. If only I had known this from the beginning. I feel like I am trapped, and I have no choice". Surya ended up living in Japan on a special activities visa (*tokutei katsudou* visa) and had to renew his visa four times, every six months during 2018–2020. At the time of writing, he lives in Japan undocumented and told us about his willingness to return to Indonesia soon.

From the two stories above, we can clearly see how this precarious circle works. A network that connects former trainee workers and prospective job seekers to Japan gets them caught up in the offers of brokers who fill the void and provide opportunities. They sell dreams, offering hopes of finding a better life in Japan.

Asylum Seeking in Japan: Opportunities and Survival Strategies

We have discussed the various channels that shape the phenomenon of asylum seeking by Indonesian nationals in Japan and have elaborated the narratives of Indonesian asylum seekers. Two major patterns have emerged from their narratives. The first pattern involves people who consciously aspire towards and apply for asylum-seeking status on their own. These are usually former technical trainees. For these people, asylum seeking becomes one of the alternative doors to work and live in Japan.

Our interviewees understand that asylum-seeking status is intended for people from countries with conflicts or problems. They are aware that they do not have cause to apply for asylum-seeking status, considering their situation back in Indonesia. They also are aware that many people misuse the visa for other purposes. Despite being aware of the asylum-seeking status, these people still apply for the visa, something which has drawn the attention of both the Indonesian and Japanese governments. From the Indonesian government's point of view, this situation is seen to be quite problematic. On the one hand, the government considers that Indonesian people who apply for asylum status in Japan have already abandoned their citizenship (Agustina, 2017) and, therefore, are already not under the Indonesian government's responsibilities anymore. On the other hand, the Indonesian government cannot neglect their own people when something happens to them in Japan.

While people were aware of their decision to go with the asylum status, they were in fact also victims of the migration industry. The fact that they were working while undocumented meant that they were technically breaking the law, but they should not be viewed as criminals. We found that structural factors in Japan, such as the demand for workers, and Japan's housing regulations, play a role in creating such a niche for undocumented migrants in Japan who want to make living. Legal pathways to work in Japan, such as technical trainees, specified skilled workers, and professional workers, mostly require foreign nationals to have a particular credentials and sufficient technical skills, as well as Japanese language skills. A lack of these requirements may hinder their mobility to Japan. Therefore, some of these people, with insufficient skills, choose to work in Japan illegally with all the risks, such as being deported and put on a blacklist, and being barred from entering the country for a specified time. Some of them end up applying for asylum-seeking status to avoid these risks, even when they have to abandon their citizenship.

The second narrative pattern involves work seekers who have no choice but to apply for an asylum-seeking visa so that they can survive in Japan. They initially received information about working in Japan from agents and brokers in Indonesia, and for them, asylum-seeking status became primarily a survival strategy. Our data shows that most Indonesian job seekers in this category whom we interviewed are victims of the migration industry and are in a vulnerable position. Their decision to seek asylum status was a part of their survival strategy. Furthermore, since they also had to make a living in Japan, asylum-seeking status granted them a temporary legal residence status that allowed them to find a job. Our interviewees shared their experience of having to stay in a small apartment with ten other undocumented people from Indonesia. It is not uncommon for undocumented migrants in Japan to create a community to provide a certain level of security despite their illegal status. They tend to choose to live in rural areas which are harder to reach by Japanese authorities. The broker helps them to rent an apartment, buy a car, and live their life just like Japanese people do, so they are not suspicious. Our data shows that the Indonesian work seekers we interviewed initially entered Japan legally but ended up undocumented. They made the decision to migrate to Japan on their own, wanting to take advantages of job opportunities provided by Japan's changing labour market. However, many actors in the migration industry, including the brokers, contribute towards shaping such opportunities.

Conclusion

Our study reveals that both Japan and Indonesia play an important role in opening the loophole for the surge in demand for asylum-seeking status, which is driven by economic migration. Japan's immigration laws were never designed to formally accept unskilled immigrants to aid with the nation's severe labour shortage. The decision to accept and open up Japan to the immigration of unskilled migrant labourers is still being debated. There is a conflict between the idea of Japan as a homogenous nation-state and the urgent need for trans-border labour importation. This, ultimately, requires the acceptance of these workers as temporary migrants, which Japan continues to resist today. As a result, Japan does not openly promote a policy of accepting a large, systematic influx of foreign workers. However, these circumstances contrast with the needs of Japanese industry, particularly for small and medium-sized business owners who rely heavily on the availability of low-paid and productive labour from abroad. Furthermore, the existence of brokers also contributes to the entrance of foreign workers.

In the meantime, structural poverty and inequality in Indonesia are seen as driving forces for the surge in Indonesian labour migrants. In Indonesia, employment opportunities, particularly in rural areas, are still very scarce, social inequality between the rich and the poor is very pronounced, and minimum wage conditions are very harsh. These circumstances can pose a threat due to rising crime, unemployment, inequality, and human trafficking. Also, the pre-departure procedural process for migrant workers, which is known to be arduous and complex, has led to some Indonesian migrant workers seeking work abroad by alternate routes. Hence, this situation creates a space for which the migration industry can exploit. The migration industry's presence involves the recruitment of people, institutions, and other intermediaries, to facilitate the flow of labour to destinations abroad. This migration industry is interrelated, including both the sending countries and the receiving countries, and involves many actors both in Indonesia and Japan. The situations both in Japan and Indonesia contribute towards creating a gap which more and more migrant workers fill by coming to Japan in search of work, regardless of the type of visa, be it documented, overstayed, undocumented, or asylum seeker.

From the point of view of asylum seekers, their involvement in the industrial migratory cycle is a very complex issue, which cannot simply be reduced to a matter of hurt national pride. There are many factors behind this situation, such as individual factors, community factors, and also structural factors consisting of political systems, migration policies, and governance. From the stories above, we can see that the experiences of Dimas and Surya may represent stories of many others. They are clearly victims whose vulnerabilities are exploited by many actors for money, even more so in an increasingly unequal world amid policies that are too state-centred or elitist.

As we have discussed throughout this chapter, this study argues that asylum seeking becomes a survival strategy for job seekers who aspire to find work in Japan. We found that several factors, such as the work seekers' personal motivations and external conditions both in Japan and Indonesia—including the existence of brokers and structural factors such as inequalities in the socio and political economy—all contribute towards shaping the conditions that pave the way to the emergence of asylum seeking as a survival strategy.

References

Azis, A., Wahyudi, R., Prasetyo, Y., Awigra, D., & Hayashi, M. (2020). *Shifting the Paradigm of Indonesia–Japan Labour Migration Cooperation*. Human Rights Working Group.

Agustina, D. (2017, November 18). *Terungkap Alasan Sejumlah WNI Minta Visa Suaka ke Jepang* [Reasons Revealed for a Number of Indonesian Citizens Asking for Asylum Visas to Japan]. Tribunnews.com. https://www.tribunnews.com/internasional/2017/11/19/terungkap-alasan-sejumlah-wni-minta-visa-suaka-ke-jepang?

Avci, Y. (2020). *An ethnographic inquiry into being an asylum seeker in Japan.* PhD thesis. University of Sheffield.

Bachtiar, P. P. (2011). Migration outflow and remittance patterns in Indonesia: National as well as subnational perspectives. *Philippine Journal of Development, 38*(1), 27–55.

Budianto, F. (2023). Welcoming the opportunities: Deciphering contemporary mobility of Indonesian professionals to Japan. *Intermestic: Journal of International Studies, 7*(2), 656–676.

BP2MI. (2022). *Indonesian migrant worker placement 2022.* https://www.bp2mi.go.id/statistik-detail/data-penempatan-dan-pelindungan-pmi-periode-tahun-2022

Faisal, M. (2022, July 26). *Efficient cross-border payment system can be boon to migrant workers, recovery.* The Jakarta Post. https://www.thejakartapost.com/opinion/2022/07/26/efficient-cross-border-payment-system-can-be-boon-to-migrant-workers-recovery.html

Goodman, R., Peach, C., Takenaka, A., & White, P. (2003). The experience of Japan's new migrants and overseas communities in anthropological, geographical, historical and sociological perspective. In *Global Japan* (pp. 13–32). Routledge.

Ichikawa, M., Nakahara, S., & Wakai, S. (2006). Effect of post-migration detention on mental health among Afghan asylum seekers in Japan. *Australian and New Zealand Journal 254 of Psychiatry,* (40), 341–346.

JITCO. (2017). *What is the Technical Intern Trainee Program?* https://www.jitco.or.jp/en/regulation/

Kalicki, K. (2019). Japan's liberal-democratic paradox of refugee admission. *The Journal of Asian Studies, 78*(2), 355–378.

Kimiko, T., & Wattles, M. (2019). A call to end human rights abuses at Japanese immigrant detention centers: Twenty-five years of grassroots advocacy at Ushiku Detention Center. *The Asia Pacific Journal; Japan Focus, 17*(5), 1–25.

Kondo, A. (2015). Migration and law in Japan. *Asia and the Pacific Policy Studies, 2*(1), 155–168.

Koizumi, K. (2015). Coping as an asylum seeker in Japan: Burmese in Shinjuku, Tokyo. In K. Koizumi & G. Hoffstaedter (Eds.), *Urban Refugees: Challenges in protection, services and policy* (pp. 241–268). Routledge.

Kuroda, K. (2003). Japan-based non-governmental organizations in pursuit of human security. *Japan Forum, 15*(2), 227–250.

Miyauchi, H. (2015). Immigration detention in Japan: Standing on a crossroad. *Migration Policy Review,* (7), 211–225. http://iminseisaku.org/top/pdf/journal/007/007_211.pdf

MHLW. (2023). *Zairyū gaikoku hito tōkei (kyū tōroku gaikoku hito tōkei)* [Statistics of Foreign Residents (Formerly Registered Foreign Residents Statistics)]. https://www.e-stat.go.jp/stat-search/files?page=1&layout=datalist&toukei=00250012&tstat=000001018034&cycle=1&year=20220&month=12040606&tclass1=000001060399&result_back=1&cycle_facet=tclass1%3Acycle&tclass2val=0

Nawawi. (2010). Working in Japan as a trainee: The reality of Indonesian trainees under Japan's industrial Training and Technical Internship Program. *Jurnal Kependudukan Indonesia, 5*(2), 29–52.

Niitsu, K. (2012, January). Perspectives on the immigration detention centers' visiting committee: consideration from the viewpoint of securing transparency. *CDR Quarterly,* (4), 39–53.

Onuki, H. (2015). A dilemma in modern Japan? Migrant workers and the (self) illusion of homogeneity. *ProtoSociology: An International Journal of Interdisciplinary Research,* 32, 59–82.

Oh, T. (2017). Shūyō to karihōmen ga utsushidasu nyūkan seisaku mondai Ushiku shūyōsho o jirei ni [Immigration policy issues reflected by detention and provisional release: A case study of Ushiku detention facility]. *Ajiataiheiyo Kennkyū Sentaa Nenpō, 14,* 32–39.

Ohashi, T., & Kodama, K. (2009) Zenken shūyō shugi wa ayamari de aru [The Japanese government policy on mandatory detention and its contradictions]. *Imin seisaku kenkyū,* (1), 85–103. http://iminseisaku.org/top/pdf/journal/001/001_085.pdf

Palmer, A., Missback, A. (2022, August 30). *Indonesia: A country grappling with migrant protection at home and abroad.* migrationpolicy.org. https://www.migrationpolicy.org/article/indonesia-country-grappling-migrant-protection-home-and-abroad

Palmer, W. (2016). Indonesia's Overseas Labour Migration Programme, 1969–2010. *Brill.* https://doi.org/10.1163/9789004325487

Romdiati, H. (2003). *Indonesian migrant workers in Japan: Typology and human rights.* http://kyotoreview.cseas.kyoto-u.ac.jp/issue/issue3/article_293.html

Siripala, T. (2018, February 16). *Japan's refugee applications exceed 10,000 for the second year running.* The Diplomat. https://thediplomat.com/2018/02/japans-refugee-applications-exceed-10000-for-the-second-year-running/

Statistics Indonesia. (2021). *National survey on socio-economics.* https://www.bps.go.id/subject/5/konsumsi-dan-pengeluaran.html#subjekViewTab3

Suzuki, M. (2003). Nanmin keiken to sedaikan kankei: zainichi Kanbojia kazoku no jirei o chūshin ni [Refugee experience of intergenerational relations: the case of Cambodian families in Japan]. *Nenpō shakaigaku ronshū,*

(16), 52–64. https://www.jstage.jst.go.jp/article/kantoh1988/2003/16/2003_16_52/_article/-char/ja

Takeda, I. (1998). Japan's responses to refugees and political asylum seekers. In M. Weiner & T. Hanami (Eds.), *Temporary workers or future citizens?* (pp. 431–451). Palgrave Macmillan. https://doi.org/10.1007/978-1-349-14418-1_14

Takizawa, S. (2018) *Japan's refugee policy: Issues and outlook.* Japan's Contribution to International Peace and Security Series: Japan Digital Library. http://www2.jiia.or.jp/en/pdf/digital_library/peace/Saburo_Takizawa-Japan_s_Refugee_Policy_Issues_and_Outlook.pdf

Takizawa, S. (n.d.). *Japan's refugee policy: Issues and outlook.* http://id.nii.ac.jp/1658/00001057/

The World Bank. (2017). *Indonesia's global workers: Juggling opportunities and risks.* https://thedocs.worldbank.org/en/doc/357131511778676366-0070022017/original/IndonesiasGlobalWorkersJugglingOpportunitiesRisks.pdf

Uemura, S. (2023, January 19). *Discussions underway on problems with technical intern program.* The Japan News. https://japannews.yomiuri.co.jp/society/general-news/20230119-84637/

Widarahesty, Y. (2022). "No Time to Be Sick:" Precarious Cycle of the Indonesian Technical Internship Trainee Program/TITP from Pre-Departure to Destination Country in Japan, *Ritsumeikan Journal of International Relations and Area Studies*, (54), 41–62.

Yamanaka, K. (2004). Citizenship, immigration and ethnic hegemony in Japan. In E. P. Kaufman (Ed.), *Rethinking ethnicity: Majority groups and dominant minorities* (pp. 159–178). Routledge.

Yoshida, R. (2017, February 20). Record 10,901 refugee applicants face abysmal odds of acceptance in Japan. *The Japan Times.* https://www.japantimes.co.jp/news/2017/02/10/national/record-10910-refugee-applicants-face-abysmal-odds-acceptance-japan/

CHAPTER 15

Conclusion

Polina Ivanova and Lara Momesso

Refugees and Asylum Seekers in East Asia

This project set out to examine refugee policies and experiences in two East Asian nations, Japan and Taiwan, which have received relatively little scholarly attention compared to Europe and other refugee-hosting countries and regions of the world. In the introduction, we emphasised the interconnection between human security and refugee policies and experiences, and we shed light on the similarities in the way human security is approached by Japan and Taiwan, despite the substantial differences between the two countries. This book explored this linkage from the standpoints of legal and policy frameworks, media studies, and the ethnography or phenomenology of individual experiences. As this book has shown, none of these aspects should be looked at in isolation, as they

P. Ivanova (✉)
Ritsumeikan University, Kyoto, Japan
e-mail: 21v00202@gst.ritsumei.ac.jp

L. Momesso
University of Central Lancashire, Preston, UK
e-mail: lmomesso@uclan.ac.uk

L. Momesso and P. Ivanova (eds.), *Refugees and Asylum Seekers in East Asia*, Palgrave Macmillan Studies on Human Rights in Asia,
https://doi.org/10.1007/978-981-97-2867-1_15

intersect and shape each other, and, together, they feed into national and international human security agendas.

First, Part I showed that the legal framework of refugee acceptance and recognition plays a direct role in shaping refugees' experiences, as the legal rules concerning their entry, stay, freedom of movement, employment, and social security might aim to foster newcomers' integration or not. Those rules will determine what kind of bureaucracy they will encounter on their asylum-seeking journey, what rights and freedoms they can enjoy or can lack, and to what extent they will be able to satisfy their needs and participate in the life of the host society. All those aspects, in turn, will have positive or adverse effects on their subjective experiences of safety, care, protection, belonging or, in contrast, on their feelings of loneliness, insecurity, and unappreciation. The global refugee regime with its "rules, norms" entrenched in the 1951 Convention Relating to the Status of Refugees and "decision-making procedures that govern states' responses to refugees" (Betts, 2015) does not apply to Taiwan, as a non-signatory to the Convention, and does not seem sufficient to ensure refugee protection in Japan. Developing effective legal frameworks at the national and possibly regional levels therefore seems crucial for refugee human security and positive integration experiences in both countries.

Next, Part II, which looks at media representation and public opinion, views human security not as a monolithic and fixed project but as a dynamic creative process. The chapters of Part II examine social construction and the perception of images of refugees and asylum seekers in traditional and new media. On the one hand, media representations reflect existing images of different groups of foreigners in a host society, while, on the other hand, mass media willingly or unwillingly reshapes and further consolidates those images, sometimes projecting on newcomers unwanted or unacceptable aspects of the host culture. These projections tend to affect the ways the populations in question are perceived and the types of responses they get from host nations, directly influencing their experiences in real life.

The average Facebook user may sometimes get the impression that society as a whole is intolerant of refugees, based on numerous aggressive posts. This is where a scholarly perspective on public opinion becomes especially valuable. Using carefully designed large-scale survey instruments, researchers obtain a much more nuanced and balanced view of the actual opinion of the wider public on refugee acceptance and integration. Results of such surveys should form the basis of the evidence informing policymakers' decisions to start accepting and accommodating more and diverse asylum seekers, and gradually liberalise immigration policies.

Finally, this volume also problematised the idea of human security by considering the experiences of specific groups that are marginalised or systematically discriminated against both in Taiwan and in Japan. Part III, on refugees' and asylum seekers' lived experiences, allows the reader to go even deeper, engaging their imagination and empathy as they grasp the affected people's situations beyond mere cognitive understanding. The editors believe that engaging the feelings and empathy of the wider public is an essential condition for making a positive change possible. One of the main strengths of human security as a conceptual framework for this book is that it offers a broader and more human-centred understanding of refugee and asylum seeker categories. For instance, Indonesian technical trainees applying for asylum in Japan could be labelled as "bogus refugees" or "fake refugees" if viewed through the lens of a narrow interpretation of the Refugee Convention. However, if we consider the circumstances of abuse and exploitation in their workplace, their lack of social support and of access to reliable information in the host country, along with the severe scarcity of employment opportunities in their country of origin, we can see how filing an asylum claim could become an act of despair and of last resort, to stay alive and to continue providing for their families. Viewing similar cases in the light of human security, Lester (2010) refers to them as "survival migrants", seeking to avoid populist and damaging distinctions between "good"/"genuine" refugees and "bogus" asylum seekers.

The Main Findings and Their Implications

By examining the three distinct yet interconnected areas, namely legal and policy frameworks, media representation and public opinion, and lived experiences of refugees and asylum seekers in Taiwan and Japan, this volume collectively contributed to the existing debates on human security. The book showed how both Taiwan and Japan, two East Asian democracies that aspire to integrate a human security agenda in different policy areas, fail when it comes to the acceptance, protection, and integration of refugees and asylum seekers in their own territories. The presence of non-citizens seems to challenge accepted notions of citizenship and perceptions of national security and sovereignty. As a result, national interests and state security end up being prioritised. This means that refugee regimes and asylum systems in Taiwan and Japan are often shaped by concerns linked to traditional security rather than human security.

As part of the major objective of this work, to raise awareness of the plight of asylum seekers in two East Asian island nations, we hope that the book will help to debunk certain myths and common stereotypes about migration in East Asia, for example, related to the alleged homogeneity of the Japanese society or the presumed absence of refugee populations in Japan or Taiwan.

The wide array of case studies and the considerable variety of approaches make a direct comparison between the chapters impossible. However, some tendencies and parallels do emerge from the cases investigated throughout the book. First, although asylum policies in Japan and Taiwan are slowly showing signs of improvement, they are overall still insufficient compared to international standards and inadequate to meet the needs of existing refugees and asylum seekers, let alone future displaced populations such as climate migrants. With only a few notable exceptions due to special political considerations, both countries seem to be largely closed to the mass immigration of refugees and asylum seekers. In Noll's (2003) terms, they are practising passive insulation, that is, they are remaining passive vis-à-vis protection seekers, relying on "natural impediments" such as geographical distance or seas, as well as active insulation in the form of visa systems, border control, carrier sanctions, both of which he qualified as the "outright rejection of protective obligations" (Noll, 2003, p. 279).

In response to the overall unwillingness of both countries to provide asylum, people in refugee-like situations adopt different strategies for getting into the country and staying there. While some may come as students, others attempt to establish themselves as ethnic entrepreneurs or file an asylum claim to gain precious time. One of the major differences between Japan's and Taiwan's immigration policies consists in their approaches to importing blue-collar workers. Taiwan has an official guest worker programme (Tierney, 2007) while Japan runs a similar programme covertly, disguised as "technical training" (Widarahesty, 2022). However, both programmes are characterised by the precariousness of workers and a lack of long-term integration opportunities, which undermines their human security and pushes some of them to search for asylum.

Despite the book's focus on refugees in two East Asian countries—Japan and Taiwan—some of its ideas may be applicable beyond this geopolitical scope. Migration researchers into other areas may easily discover parallels with their case studies as refugees in many parts of the world are experiencing similar uncertainty and ambiguity due to the inadequate policy responses and legal mechanisms in host countries. For instance, recent studies on Syrian refugees in Turkey also show how the host country government's reliance on temporary legislation and policies, ad hoc solutions, and discretionary power contributes to a prolonged liminality, or in-betweenness, for Syrian refugees (Şahin-Mencütek et al., 2023). In the context of African refugees living in camps for years, Abuya (2010) critically examines situations when "refugees remain in host countries for a prolonged, often unspecified duration of time, with no durable solution in sight" (Abuya, 2010, p. 127) and concludes that these situations "threaten the human security of refugees as well as the security of host states, the country of origin and the international community" (p. 125). These "protracted" situations and the uncertainty they bring tend to cause a breakdown in social structures leading in turn to "family breakdown, violence, socio-economic deprivation and health problems" (Abuya, 2010, p. 125). Uncertainty and the lack of durable solutions for refugees and asylum seekers, often imposed in the name of the security of the host nationals, generate insecurities in migrant populations.

Unlike the African continent, characterised by a series of "complex emergencies" (OCHA, 2003), or Turkey, which is hosting the greatest number of refugees in the world as of 2023 (UNHCR, n.d.) and is close to several zones of ongoing military conflicts, Japan and Taiwan have been enjoying a relative political stability and peacefulness for decades. There are no refugee camps, and any asylum seekers are spread throughout the population. Both countries also have relatively high living standards, and both are dealing with a demographic crisis of ageing and shrinking populations and related labour shortages. In this context, among the three durable solutions for refugees—voluntary repatriation, local integration, and resettlement in a third country (UNHCR-USA, n.d.)—the second option would seem the most logical and beneficial for both refugees and the host societies.

Local integration comprises legal, economic, and sociocultural dimensions (UNHCR, 2003, pp. 23–24). The legal dimension involves progressively granting refugees with a range of rights and entitlements; ideally, this process should lead to permanent residence and the acquisition of citizenship in the host country (UNHCR, 2003, p. 25). Article 34 of the 1951 Convention calls on states to "as far as possible facilitate assimilation and naturalization of refugees" in the host countries (UNHCR,

2010, p. 30). According to the UNHCR's estimates, 1.1 million refugees around the world have acquired citizenship of their country of asylum (UNHCR-USA, n.d.), and both Taiwan and Japan could contribute to these numbers more actively by offering legal pathways to citizenship to those refugees who have stayed in their territories for years and have established close links with the host country.

The economic dimension signifies that refugees can become self-reliant and can contribute to the economy of the host country, instead of being reliant on state aid or humanitarian assistance. High living standards such as in Taiwan and Japan also imply a high cost of living and a predominance of knowledge-intensive jobs. Therefore, refugees who wish to integrate in such societies typically require better education and greater efforts to become economically independent. Therefore, they need sustained support from the state and non-state actors to ensure their inclusion into the education system and labour market.

Finally, the sociocultural dimension of refugees' local integration means living without discrimination or exploitation and the ability to actively contribute to the social life of their new community in the host country. The contributing chapters have unanimously agreed that both Taiwan and Japan could do better in these three domains. Our findings show that both Taiwan and Japan fail to provide adequate support for the refugees' local integration and in cases of defining them as "evacuees", "students", or "migrant workers", they also deny them access to a third-country settlement. This lack of recognition and access to durable solutions jeopardises their human security both in the short term and in the long run.

Limitations of this Project and Recommendations for Further Research

Since the scope of the volume is limited to Japan and Taiwan, generalisations to the rest of East Asia should be made with caution, apart from inevitable parallels between refugee situations characterised by high degrees of uncertainty and a lack of durable solutions as discussed above.

This book has attempted to provide a broad coverage of different ethnic groups comprising asylum-seeking populations in Japan and Taiwan. As such, it has included entire chapters on Hong Kongers, Tibetans, Vietnamese, Indonesians, Kurds, and chapter sections on Afghans, Syrians, and Ukrainians. Nevertheless, the analysis has not been comprehensive and information on many important refugee groups is missing. Adapting to inadequate asylum systems, some groups of asylum seekers display distinct coping strategies. For example, some Indonesians choose to apply for asylum, whereas Syrians, Afghans, and certain Hong Kongers enrol as international students, while others may open ethnic businesses or choose marriage migration routes. Future studies may uncover more survival strategies among different refugee groups, evaluating their rationale and successfulness and informing policies to be able to support their integration more effectively.

Being aware that gender is an important dimension shaping migration and related processes, we believe that future research should explore how gender relations, roles, and hierarchies influence legal and policy frameworks, media representation, and public opinion, as well as the lived experiences of male and female refugees and asylum seekers. In line with this point, and reflecting a growing concern within the literature, it would be also important to explore the experiences of non-binary and queer individuals.

Recommendations for Policy and Practice

Since the findings show that the current asylum system is often incapable of protecting the human rights and dignity of asylum seekers, there is a pressing need/priority to build an efficient, robust, and up-to-date refugee reception and recognition system in both Japan and Taiwan. Another repeated recommendation from the chapter authors and human rights activists is to abolish detention for visa overstayers, and this proposal is being supported by some policymakers (Kawarada, 2021).

At the same time, sustainable solutions for refugees and asylum seekers cannot be achieved without a comprehensive reform of the entire immigration system. Many forced migrants come to the host country under different visa regimes, for example, students, trainees, workers, tourists, and marriage migrants. These people may either never seek asylum or choose to seek it later becoming refugees "sur place" (UNHRC, 2019, p. 26). Improving the human security of vulnerable foreigners in Japan and Taiwan would therefore require a structural reform of the immigration law and practice, making legal pathways for many migrant categories more transparent. This would include, for instance, facilitating mechanisms for migrants overstaying their visa to legalise their status and get access to social security and the official labour market. Additionally, the system for immigrant workers needs to be strengthened. Those who wish to work in understaffed industries should be allowed to come on a long-term basis, bring their families, be ensured of fair and equal treatment on a par with the local labour force, and be offered opportunities to naturalise if they desire.

Due to the lack of international recognition, Taiwan cannot join the Convention and the Protocol, and judging from the experience of Japan, adoption of the international mechanisms does not guarantee the effectiveness of the domestic asylum system. However, this should not stop Taiwan from creating effective systems of refugee reception, protection, and integration. As Chapter 3 advocates, Taiwan could learn useful lessons from other non-UN member states and territories. In addition, it may be time to think of alternative mechanisms of refugee protection, based on a regional framework. Several parts of the world have created regional instruments relating to refugees. A number of regional treaties regulate the issues of diplomatic and territorial asylum in Latin America, and the Organisation of African Unity adopted its own convention on refugees in Africa in 1969, with a refugee definition different from that of the Protocol and the Convention (UNHCR, 2019, p. 15). As consolidated liberal democracies, Japan and Taiwan could become leaders in creating an up-to-date and effective regional refugee regime in Asia based on ideas of human rights and human security. Building on the idea of "sovereignty as responsibility" (Bellamy & McDonald, 2002, p. 376), this volume calls on the Taiwanese and Japanese governments to take responsibility for the security of the non-citizens residing in their territory, to identify factors that generate insecurity among these populations, and to develop specific national strategies to address these issues.

Concluding Remarks

We believe in the continued relevance of the topics of refugee protection and inclusion. At the end of 2022, 108.4 million people worldwide were forcibly displaced (UNHCR, 2023b) which included over 14 million in Asia (UNHCR, 2023a). These trends are expected to continue and displaced populations will require long-term solutions. For instance, over 2.4 million refugees will be in need of resettlement in 2024, a 20% increase compared to 2023 (UNHCR, 2023c). Since the root causes of forced displacement are military conflicts, persecution, and human rights violations, along with the loss of livelihood due to environmental degradation and climate change, it seems important to connect national and regional refugee regimes with a broader agenda of human security and sustainable development. The practical implementation of human security principles may be realised through reliance on existing international frameworks, such as sustainable development goals (SDGs), particularly SDG 16 on peace, justice, and strong institutions, and SDGs 13, 14, and 15, related to the environment, as well as the Global Compact on Refugees with its Roadmap to 2030, which aims to ease the burden on host communities and to enhance refugee self-reliance (UN, 2018).

References

Abuya, E. O. (2010). From here to where? Refugees living in protracted situations in Africa. In A. Edwards & C. Ferstman (Eds.), *Human security and non-citizens: Law, policy and international affairs* (pp. 125–165). Cambridge University Press.

Bellamy, A. J. & McDonald, M. (2002). "The utility of human security:" Which humans? What security? A reply to Thomas and Tow. *Security Dialogue*, *33*(3), 373–377. https://www.jstor.org/stable/26298086

Betts, A. (2015). The normative terrain of the global refugee regime. *Ethics & International Affairs, 29*(4), 363–375. https://doi.org/10.1017/S0892679415000350

Kawarada, S. (2021, June 16). *Immigration chief vows to stop detaining all visa overstayers*. The Asahi Shimbun. Retrieved August 22, 2023, from https://www.asahi.com/ajw/articles/14374124

Lester, E. (2010). Socio-economic rights, human security and survival migrants: Whose rights? Whose security? In A. Edwards & C. Ferstman (Eds.), *Human security and non-citizens: Law, policy and international affairs* (pp. 314–356). Cambridge University Press.

Noll, G. (2003). Securitising sovereignty? States, refugees, and the regionalisation of international law. In E. Newman & J. van Selm (Eds.), *Refugees and forced displacement: International security, human vulnerability, and the state* (pp. 277–305). United Nations University Press. https://collections.unu.edu/eserv/UNU:2434/nLib9280810863.pdf

Office for the Coordination of Humanitarian Affairs (OCHA). (2003). *Glossary of humanitarian terms in relation to the protection of civilians in armed conflict*. United Nations publication. https://inee.org/resources/ocha-glossary-humanitarian-terms-relation-protection-civilians-armed-conflict

Şahin-Mencütek, Z., Gökalp-Aras, N. E., Kaya, A., & Rottmann, S. B. (2023). Conclusion. In *Syrian refugees in Turkey: Between reception and integration*.

IMISCOE Research Series. Springer. https://doi.org/10.1007/978-3-031-27366-7_6

The United Nations High Commissioner for Refugees (UNHCR) Nicosia. (2014). *The integration of refugees*. https://www.unhcr.org/cy/wp-content/uploads/sites/41/2018/02/integration_discussion_paper_July_2014_EN.pdf

The United Nations High Commissioner for Refugees (UNHCR). (2003). *Framework for durable solutions for refugees and persons of concern*. https://www.unhcr.org/media/framework-durable-solutions-refugees-and-persons-concern-0

The United Nations High Commissioner for Refugees (UNHCR). (2010). *Convention and Protocol relating to the status of refugees*. https://www.unhcr.org/media/convention-and-protocol-relating-status-refugees

The United Nations High Commissioner for Refugees (UNHCR). (2019). *Handbook on procedures and criteria for determining refugee status and guidelines on international protection under the 1951 Convention and the 1967 Protocol relating to the status of refugees*. https://www.unhcr.org/sites/default/files/legacy-pdf/5ddfcdc47.pdf

The United Nations High Commissioner for Refugees (UNHCR). (2023a). *Asia and the Pacific regional trends: Forced displacement and statelessness 2022*. https://data.unhcr.org/en/documents/details/101659

The United Nations High Commissioner for Refugees (UNHCR). (2023b). *Global trends: Forced displacement in 2022*. https://www.unhcr.org/global-trends-report-2022

The United Nations High Commissioner for Refugees (UNHCR). (2023c). *UNHCR projected global resettlement needs*. https://reporting.unhcr.org/unhcr-projected-global-resettlement-needs-2024

The United Nations High Commissioner for Refugees (UNHCR). (n.d.). *Refugee data finder*. Retrieved September 11, 2023, from https://www.unhcr.org/refugee-statistics/#:~:text=T%C3%BCrkiye%20hosts%20the%20largest%20number,in%20need%20of%20international%20protection.

The United Nations High Commissioner for Refugees, the United States of America (UNHCR-USA). (n.d.). *Solutions*. https://www.unhcr.org/us/what-we-do/build-better-futures/solutions

The United Nations. (2018). *Global Compact on Refugees*. https://www.unhcr.org/media/global-compact-refugees-booklet

Tierney, R. (2007). The guest labor system in Taiwan: Labor market considerations, wage injustices, and the politics of foreign labor brokerage. *Critical Asian Studies, 39*(2), 205–228. https://doi.org/10.1080/14672710701339410

Widarahesty, Y. (March 2022). "No time to be sick:" Precarious cycle of the Indonesian Technical Internship Trainee Program (TITP) from pre-departure to destination country in Japan. *Ritsumeikan kokusai chiiki kenkyū*, 54, 41–62. https://doi.org/10.34382/00016041

SPRINGER NATURE

GPSR Compliance

The European Union's (EU) General Product Safety Regulation (GPSR) is a set of rules that requires consumer products to be safe and our obligations to ensure this.

If you have any concerns about our products, you can contact us on ProductSafety@springernature.com

In case Publisher is established outside the EU, the EU authorized representative is:

Springer Nature Customer Service Center GmbH
Europaplatz 3
69115 Heidelberg, Germany

The manufacturer's authorised representative in the EU is Springer Nature Customer Service Centre GmbH, Europaplatz 3, 69115 Heidelberg, Germany. If you have any concerns regarding our products, please contact ProductSafety@springernature.com

Printed and bound by CPI Group (UK) Ltd, Croydon, CR0 4YY
01/10/2026
02225854-0015